MY EXPERIENCES
IN THE
WORLD WAR
VOLUME I

MY EXPERIENCES IN THE WORLD WAR

VOLUME I

JOHN J. PERSHING

MILITARY CLASSICS SERIES

FIRST TAB EDITION
FIRST TAB PRINTING

My Experiences in the World War, Volume I, by John J. Pershing.
Published by arrangement with Harper & Row Publishers, Inc.
All rights reserved.

Library of Congress Cataloging in Publication Data

Pershing, John J. (John Joseph), 1860-1948.
    My experiences in the World War / by John J. Pershing.
      p. cm.
    Reprint.
    Includes index.
    ISBN 0-8306-4006-1 (v. 1)
    1. Pershing, John J. (John Joseph) 1860-1948. 2. World
War, 1914-1918—Personal narratives, American.   3. World War,
1914-1918--United   States. 4. Generals—United   States—
Biography. 5. United
    States. Army—Biography. I. Title.
    D640.P454   1989
940.4′81′73—dc19   89-4261
                                                CIP

TAB BOOKS Inc. offers software for sale. For information and
a catalog, please contact TAB Software Department, Blue Ridge
Summit, PA 17294-0850.

Questions regarding the content of this book
should be addressed to:

    Reader Inquiry Branch
    TAB BOOKS Inc.
    Blue Ridge Summit, PA 17294-0214

Cover photograph courtesy of U.S. Army

Military Classics Series

The U.S. military today is enjoying a renewed popularity with the American public. To help serve this burgeoning interest, TAB is proud to present the *Military Classics Series.*

This series will bring back into print quality, hardcover editions of many of the most famous books by or about key figures in U.S. military history. Whenever possible these will be firsthand accounts—the autobiographies of noted military figures or the memoirs of journalists who were at the front. Some will be biographies written by knowledgeable friends and associates of the subject. All will provide the closest possible insight into the events that have shaped our military history.

The series will span the length of American military history—from the Revolution to Vietnam. Although the series will be limited to the wars and conflicts in which the United States participated, it occasionally will include an outside perspective through the autobiographies of allies and enemies alike.

These books have long been unavailable in hardcover for both readers and collectors. The *Military Classics Series* will present them in an affordable personal-library format for military enthusiasts.

To

THE UNKNOWN SOLDIER

CONTENTS

CHAPTER X

CHAPTER XI

CHAPTER XII

CHAPTER XIII

CHAPTER XIV

CHAPTER XV

CHAPTER XVI

CHAPTER XVII

CHAPTER XVIII

CHAPTER XIX

CHAPTER XX

CONTENTS

CHAPTER XXV

CHAPTER XXVI

FOREWORD

It was predictable that if General John Joseph Pershing would write an autobiography, it would be awarded a Pulitzer Prize. He wrote *My Memoirs of the Great War* in 1931, and it won for him the coveted literary award. It also could be surmised that when Cadet Pershing graduated from West Point as president of his class and captain of the cadets, he would one day become the Chief of Staff of the U.S. Army. He did in 1921.

When Pershing was 17 years old, he taught in a rural school for black children. It could be forecast that he would go on to become personnally involved in humanitarian causes, particularly with black people. Therein lies the story of how he acquired his nickname, "Black Jack Pershing." As a young lieutenant he volunteered to train a black cavalry unit, and he eventually charged up San Juan Hill with them in the Spanish-American War under the leadership of Colonel Theodore Roosevelt. He was the only white man in the outfit, and they called him "Lieutenant Black Jack." Cavalrymen in those days called their most respected officers by their rank and first name.

It was logical that in 1903 when Pershing was sent to the Philippines, he became a "diplomat" in pacifying the fanatical Moros in Mindanao, and in Japan in 1905 when he was the military attaché, he would request permission and go with the Japanese to Manchuria as an observer during the Russo-Japanese War. Therefore, it could be foretold that in 1906 President Theodore Roosevelt would promote him from captain to brigadier general, passing him over 862 senior officers. The president, in answer to an urgent national need, then sent Pershing back to the Philippines to be commander of the military department of Mindanao and the governor of the Moro Province.

There is one sad commentary about Pershing's life. In 1913 when he returned from the Philippines, he was assigned to the Presideo in San Francisco and soon after was dispatched to command the expedition into Mexico against Pancho Villa and his renegade forces. While in Mexico Pershing received the tragic news that a fire swept through his family quarters at the Presideo, killing his wife and three daughters.

A six-year old son survived. His wife was the daughter of Senator Francis E. Warren of Wyoming.

Greater things were in store for Pershing. When the United States entered the war against Germany in 1917, President Woodrow Wilson named Pershing to command the American Expeditionary Force being sent to Europe. The Allies, particularly the French, wanted the American troops to be used as replacements for losses in the British and French armies. But Pershing negotiated with them for the integrity of the American units. He said, "Let's not put new wine in old bottles," an old adage the French understood. Pershing and the American troops defeated the Germans at St. Mihiel in September of 1918.

In October of 1918, the Americans fought a bitter battle against the Germans in the Meuse-Argonne offensive at the Hindenburg Line. The German lines were penetrated, and the Allies marched across the front to victory. The armistice was signed on November 11, 1918.

A grateful nation asserted its appreciation, through the Congress, by honoring Pershing with the rank of General of the Armies. That rank established him as the greatest American general since George Washington.

General Pershing was born in 1860 and died in 1948. He is buried at Arlington National Cemetery. Buried next to him is his grandson, Richard W. Pershing, killed in Vietnam in 1968.

Gene Gurney
Editor-in-Chief
Military Classics Series

INTRODUCTION

My primary purpose in writing this story of the American Expeditionary Forces in France is to render what I conceive to be an important service to my country. In that adventure there were many lessons useful to the American people, should they ever again be called to arms, and I felt it a duty to record them as I saw them.

The World War found us absorbed in the pursuits of peace and quite unconscious of probable threat to our security. We would listen to no warnings of danger. We had made small preparation for defense and none for aggression. So when war actually came upon us we had to change the very habits of our lives and minds to meet its realities. The slow processes by which we achieved these changes and applied our latent power to the problems of combat in Europe, despite our will, our numbers and our wealth, I endeavor to describe. Therein lie the lessons of which I write.

Once realizing their obligations, the American people willingly sent their sons to battle; with unstinted generosity, they gave of their substance; and with fortitude bore the sacrifices that fell to their lot. They, too, served, and in their service inspired the armies to victory.

I am grateful to President Wilson and Secretary Baker for having selected me to command our armies and for the whole-hearted and unfailing support they accorded me.

To my comrades of the Allied armies I would say that I am not attempting to write a history of the World War, or of the epic part they took in it. I write of our own army and for our own people, without consciously magnifying or minimizing the effort of any army or any people. There is credit for all of us in the final triumph of our united arms. The struggle of the Allies was much longer, their sacrifices much greater than ours.

The men of all ranks who served with me in France added a brilliant page to the record of the American soldier's devotion to country. This modest work can only outline the stirring narrative of their achievements. No commander was ever privileged to lead a finer force; no commander ever derived greater inspiration from the performance of his troops.

J. J. P.

MY EXPERIENCES IN THE WORLD WAR

CHAPTER I

Telegram Indicating My Selection to Go to France—Confirmation by
Message from Chief of Staff—Review of Impressions—Germany's
Preparation—Our Government's Inaction and Lack of Foresight
—Training of Command in Mexico—Loyalty of People in the South-
west—Draft Law

ON May 3, 1917, four weeks after the United States had
declared war on Germany, I received the following
telegram from my father-in-law, the late Senator F. E.
Warren, in Washington:

"Wire me to-day whether and how much you speak, read and write
French."

At this time I was in command of the Southern Department,
and was stationed at Fort Sam Houston, which adjoins the city
of San Antonio, Texas. Naturally, Senator Warren's telegram
suggested that I was to be assigned to some duty in France, but
as no intimation had been given out regarding the extent of our
active participation in the war, the message was somewhat
puzzling. However, I telegraphed the following reply:

"Spent several months in France nineteen eight studying language.
Spoke quite fluently; could read and write very well at that time.
Can easily reacquire satisfactory working knowledge."

My reply, to be sure, was rather optimistic, yet it was comparatively accurate and perhaps justified by the possibilities to
be implied from Senator Warren's telegram. A few days later
I received from him the following letter:

"Dear Jack:

"This is what happened: Last night, about ten o'clock, the Secretary of War rang me up and wanted to know if I would call in and see him this morning, and I responded that I would if I could reach him at nine o'clock. This is the first time he has ever asked me to call for a consultation.

"When I reached him, he said, in the most distant and careless way: 'Oh, by the way, before I discuss the matter about which I asked you to call—do you happen to know whether Pershing speaks French?' (This is the first time your name was ever mentioned between the Secretary of War and me, direct.) I said I was not certain about that; that I knew he was a linguist along the lines of Spanish and, to some extent, Japanese, and all of the Philippine dialects (a pardonable exaggeration by one's father-in-law)—that perhaps my wife might know, as she speaks French a little and reads it readily. He said, 'Well, it is *of no special consequence,* only I happened to think of it at this moment.' I replied, 'Well, I'll ask my wife about it to-day and see whether she knows, and will let you know.' He then said, 'If you don't mind, do so.' And then he proceeded to discuss quite fully some appropriation matters on which I intended to go to work upon my arrival at the Capitol.

"Of course you will know what this means, the same as I do. It may mean nothing at all. But perhaps you have already written to the Department upon the subject or, rather, the one to which it pertains.

"I hope you will wire me promptly upon receipt of my telegram, so that I may tell the Secretary 'what my wife said about it(?).'

"Affectionately,

"F. E. Warren."

Shortly after the receipt of the private wire and before the above letter reached me, a telegram, dated May 2d, came from Major General Hugh L. Scott, the Chief of Staff, containing the opening words, "For your eye alone," followed by a message in code:

"Under plans under consideration is one which will require among other troops, four infantry regiments and one artillery regiment from your department for service in France. If plans are carried out, you will be in command of the entire force. Wire me at once the designation of the regiments selected by you and their present stations. * * * "

I construed this message to mean that these troops were to form a division, which, together with such others as might be sent over at once, would be under my command.

Within a day or so after the receipt of Scott's telegram, I intimated to Colonel M. H. Barnum, my Chief of Staff, that we might be called upon for a recommendation, and after consultation with him I selected the 16th, 18th, 26th and 28th Regiments of Infantry and the 6th Field Artillery. These, together with two other artillery regiments and the necessary auxiliary units, were later organized as our 1st Division.

I had scarcely given a thought to the possibility of my being chosen as commander-in-chief of our forces abroad, as afterwards developed, although my old friend, Major General J. Franklin Bell, had written me that he thought my selection almost certain. After I left the Philippines, in 1913, where he was in command, he and I had kept up an intermittent correspondence in which we freely exchanged confidences on army matters. In one of his letters written early in April, 1917, he spoke of the possibility of our sending an army to France and gave a list of the general officers who might be considered for the supreme command. Discussing the chances for and against each one, he predicted, much to my surprise, that all the others, including himself, would be passed over and that I would be selected. I was the junior on the list of major generals, hence could not fully accept General Bell's view, but he was so strongly convinced that he was right that he requested an assignment under my command. The major generals senior to me at the time were, in order of rank, Leonard Wood, J. Franklin Bell, Thomas H. Barry, Hugh L. Scott and Tasker H. Bliss.

From the day of my entrance into West Point up to middle age I had hoped the time would come when I could return to civil life while still young enough to take up law or go into business. But successive assignments that offered chances for active field duty and adventure had held me in the Army. Now that there had come an opportunity for service to the country such as had fallen to the lot of but few men, I considered myself especially fortunate to have remained. Throughout my career I have never ceased to wonder whether, after all, we are not largely the creatures of destiny.

When the incident occurred at Sarajevo that caused the smoldering embers of hatred and jealousy in Europe to burst into flame, my command, the 8th Infantry Brigade, was stationed along the Mexican Border and I was on leave, spending a few weeks with my family in Cheyenne, Wyoming. My wife and I had been in France in 1908 and witnessed the excitement of the French people during the crisis that followed the seizure by Austria of the provinces of Bosnia and Herzegovina. It was suspected even then that Austria had similar designs against Serbia, and the animosity that had grown up between them, added to the fears and ambitions of the nations likely to be aligned on either side, furnished plenty of inflammable material to start a war. But the thought of a world war, impending, perhaps imminent, actually stunned one's senses.

And yet, in reviewing the previous ten years it could be seen that events had distinctly and unmistakably pointed that way. Without entering into a discussion of the more remote causes of the war, perhaps all European nations that were involved must share a certain responsibility. But it is an outstanding fact that during the history of the preceding fifty years, with its background of age-old racial and religious prejudices, its maze of shifting alignments, diplomatic entanglements and conflicting national ambitions, the attitude of United Germany had become more and more aggressive and dominating.

After the Franco-Prussian War Germany had emerged as the strongest military power of Europe and was the leader in the development of military science and tactics. During the decade prior to the World War the improvement and increase of her heavier artillery and the organization of machine gun units had gone forward rapidly. The very extensive expansion and use of these arms by the Japanese in Manchuria had not escaped the notice of German observers, and her experts were quick to take advantage of the lessons of that war. While these facts were commonly known in military circles, neither the extent of the growth of her land forces that had recently taken place nor the forecast that she would complete her military program about the year 1914 [1] had made sufficient impression on her possible adversaries to cause serious alarm.

Then came the action of the German Government following the Sarajevo incident that suddenly forced the conclusion upon other peoples that the leaders of Germany intended to avail themselves of the opportunity to establish their country, if possible, as the dominant power of Europe. If there had been any doubt of this purpose, it was removed by the outcome of the many conferences with Austria, covering a period of nearly a month, which culminated in German support of the very arbitrary and humiliating demands on Serbia, even in the face of the latter's conciliatory reply.

Although observing statesmen and military men, some vividly, others only vaguely, had sensed the situation as a menace of war, yet few seemed to appreciate that a resort to arms under the circumstances would involve practically the whole civilized world. Apparently none of the powers visualized what it would mean in its appalling destruction of human life, its devastation of countries, and in the suffering of populations. Even the men in the armies who lived through those terrible years got only a limited conception of it all. Looking backward, however, it now seems strange that the results of such a conflict could not have been generally foreseen.

As we now know, the German militarists held up to their people the fear of the Slav as one reason for going to war, and frightened the financial interests by pointing out the danger of losing national prestige and commercial advantage unless Slav ambitions were checked. The German people were led to believe

[1] The French Yellow Book 1914, quoting from a secret German report of March 19, 1913, on the Agadir crisis, says: "At that time the progress made by the French Army, the moral recovery of the Nation, the technical advance in the realm of aviation and of machine guns rendered an attack on France less easy than in the previous period. Further, an attack on the English fleet had to be considered. This difficulty opened our (Germany's) eyes to the necessity for an increase in the army."

that the army was invincible, and were no doubt flattered by the thought of the glory and the grandeur that success would bring to their country.

The German military machine itself was without doubt more nearly perfect and powerful than any that had ever before existed. Their Great General Staff had fully considered every condition necessary to military success, and even solemn treaty obligations were not to stand in the way. The hour for Germany to seize her opportunity had arrived. The details of what happened in the beginning are well known and the world has long since fixed the blame where it properly belongs—on the shoulders of the German Government of 1914.

The violation of Belgian neutrality afforded Germany the advantage of invading France from the most favorable quarter, yet it was no justification for her to claim that strategical considerations impelled her to take this action. In disregarding the Treaty of London of 1839 Germany presented the strongest kind of evidence of her war guilt. Moreover, this overt act served to give notice to all nations that Germany intended to brook no opposition in her purpose to conquer her ancient enemy once and for all. I cannot escape the conviction that in view of this defiance of neutral rights the United States made a grievous error in not immediately entering a vigorous protest.

The argument might be made that as our Government was not a signatory to the treaty its violation was none of our business. But one of the stronger members of the family of civilized nations, to which, broadly speaking, we all belong, had committed an outrage against a peaceful neutral neighbor simply because she stood in the way. The plea was advanced by the Germans that Belgium could have avoided trouble if she had not opposed the passage of their forces through her territory, but if she had failed to resist she would have forfeited the respect of the world, whereas by opposing she gained universal admiration.

The invasion of Belgium was in fact an open declaration of Germany's attitude toward all neutral rights. If our people had grasped its meaning they would have at least insisted upon preparation to meet more effectively the later cumulative offenses of Germany against the law of nations, one of the most inhumane of which was the sinking of the *Lusitania*. Here was provocation enough for very positive action by any government alive to its obligations to protect its citizens. The fact is that the world knew only too well that we had for years neglected to make adequate preparations for defense, and Germany therefore dared to go considerably further than she would have gone if we had been even partially ready to support our demands by force.

It will be recalled that after some diplomatic correspondence the question of the use of submarines as it affected us rested until the sinking, without warning, of the *Sussex,* a Channel steamer carrying American passengers, on March 24, 1916. Germany was then notified that unless she should immediately declare and effect an abandonment of such methods of submarine warfare against passenger and freight-carrying vessels there would be no choice for us but to sever diplomatic relations with her. In reply, Germany made a definite promise to sink no more vessels without warning, although she made reservations as to the future.

Germany was informed that her reply was unsatisfactory, and there the question was again dropped, apparently without our seriously considering the action that we necessarily would be forced to take in the event of her resumption of ruthless methods. Little more than a gesture was made to get ready for eventualities; in fact, practically nothing was done in the way of increasing our military strength or of providing equipment.

As to our navy, however, Congress did appropriate more than $300,000,000 in August, 1916, for expansion, and some progress was made in beginning the construction of small craft and the establishment of a better administrative organization. This same Congress also passed an act [1] providing for the reorganization of our military forces, but scarcely a move was made to carry it out prior to our actual entrance into the war. Thus we presented the spectacle of the most powerful nation in the world sitting on the sidelines, almost idly watching the enactment of the greatest

[1] See Act of Congress June 3, 1916.

tragedy of all time, in which it might be compelled at any minute to take an important part.

It is almost inconceivable that there could have been such an apparent lack of foresight in administration circles regarding the probable necessity for an increase of our military forces and so little appreciation of the time and effort which would be required to prepare them for effective service. The inaction played into the hands of Germany, for she knew how long it would take us to put an army in the field, and governed her action accordingly. In other words, the date of resuming indiscriminate submarine warfare, February 1, 1917, was timed with the idea that the greater part of neutral and British shipping could be destroyed before we could be ready, should we by any chance enter the war.

Let us suppose that, instead of adhering to the erroneous theory that neutrality forbade any move toward preparation, we had taken the precaution in the spring of 1916 to organize and equip an army of half a million combatant troops, together with the requisite number of supply troops for such a force. This could have been done merely by increasing the Regular Army and National Guard to war strength. Such action would have given us the equivalent of forty average Allied divisions, ready to sail at once for France upon the declaration of war. Preparation to this extent could have been carried out by taking advantage of the concentration of the Regular Army and National Guard on the Mexican Border in 1916.

The actual situation on the Western Front when we entered the war was more favorable for the Allies than at any previous time. The strength of the German forces there had been greatly reduced because of the necessity for supporting the Russian front. Although reports were filtering in regarding the beginning of the revolution, there was little to indicate that Russia was not still a factor to be reckoned with. Actually the Allies had an advantage of something over 20 per cent in numbers, French morale was high, owing to their successful defense of Verdun, and the British armies had reached their maximum power.

Under these conditions, it is not extravagant to assert that the addition of 500,000 American combat troops in early spring would have given the Allies such a preponderance of force that the war could have been brought to a victorious conclusion before the end of that year. Even without such aid, the confidence of the Allies led them to undertake a general offensive in April. Although it ended in defeat, especially for the French, the failure can be attributed to a large extent to lack of secrecy of the plans. A well-planned campaign with the assistance of half a million Americans would have told quite another story.

Thus, through a false notion of neutrality, which had prevented practically all previous preparation, a favorable opportunity to assist the Allies was lost, the war was prolonged another year and the cost in human life tremendously increased. But, from another viewpoint, it is not improbable that if we had been thus prepared, our rights would have been respected and we would not have been forced into the war. We shall see as we proceed how great were the difficulties to be overcome because of our inexcusable failure to do what common reason long before our entry into the war plainly indicated should have been done.

My service on the southwestern frontier had extended from early in April, 1914, to March 15, 1916, when the Punitive Expedition under my command entered Mexico in pursuit of the Mexican bandit, Pancho Villa, and his followers, who had made a night raid on Columbus, New Mexico, and the camp of Regular Army troops stationed there. The expedition, which eventually numbered over 15,000 men, was under the shadow of the World War and the danger of our becoming involved in a war with Mexico was necessarily a handicap to the operations.

The temper of the people on both sides of the line and the tense feeling between Mexican regular troops and our own were such that had we continued our activities there is little doubt that serious complications would have arisen which might have brought on a war between the two countries. After we had penetrated about 400 miles into Mexican territory and overtaken Villa's band and others, and scattered them, wounding Villa himself, the increasing disapproval of the Mexican Government doubtless caused the administration to conclude that it would be better to rest content that the outlaw bands had been severely punished and generally dispersed, and that the people of northern Mexico had been taught a salutary lesson.

Activities in Mexico were discontinued in June, the more advanced elements were withdrawn and the expedition thereafter held a line of communications reaching only about 150 miles south of the border. As there was then little work to do except to protect this line, a systematic scheme of training was inaugurated throughout the command. Thorough courses in musketry and battle tactics for all units, beginning with platoons and leading up to the brigade, were prepared, and the principles of attack and defense were applied through practical exercises. In following out this progressive program, the liveliest interest was aroused in both officers and men, with the result that when the command left Mexico it was probably more highly trained than any similar force of our army had ever been before.

The contingents of the Regular Army and about 156,000 National Guard troops that served on the border during this period learned much that was beneficial to them in the World War. Most commands were given some tactical training and the officers had the chance to learn something of camp life and to develop practical leadership in handling units up to the regiment. The training and experience the National Guard received during this service raised their relative efficiency considerably above that attained under ordinary circumstances. Thus the only training, except ordinary routine, any of our forces received during the year prior to 1917, was given to the troops then in Mexico and to those stationed along the border.

It was said that a greater number of men were not sent to the border for want of equipment and supplies. This fact should have prompted immediate corrective action, which, if taken, might have prevented the delay that occurred later for the same reason when the large numbers of men were called out to prepare for service in the World War.

The officers and men along the border and in my command followed closely the press reports from abroad and kept themselves informed as far as possible on the progress of the war. I recall that the German attempt to take Verdun excited deep interest, and the determination of the French to defend that fortress at all hazards was highly praised. The battle of the Somme, fought during the summer by the British and French mainly to relieve the pressure on Verdun, furnished fresh examples of the so-called warfare of position.

Many Allied writers had proclaimed that trench warfare was a development of the World War which had made open combat a thing of the past. But trenches were not new to Americans, as both the Union and Confederate armies in the Civil War had used them extensively. While my command in Mexico was taught the technique of trench fighting, it was more particularly trained in the war of movement. Without the application of open warfare methods, there could have been only a stalemate on the Western Front.

In each succeeding war there is a tendency to proclaim as something new the principles under which it is conducted. Not only those who have never studied or experienced the realities of war, but also professional soldiers frequently fall into the error. But the principles of warfare as I learned them at West Point remain unchanged. They were verified by my experience in our Indian Wars, and also during the campaign against the Spaniards in Cuba. I applied them in the Philippines and observed their application in Manchuria during the Russo-Japanese War.

It is true that the tactics of the battlefield change with improvement in weapons. Machine guns, quick-firing small-bore guns and rapid-fire artillery make the use of cover more necessary. They must be considered as aids to the infantryman, expert in the use of the rifle and familiar with the employment of hasty entrenchments. It is he who constitutes our main reliance in battle.

When the opposing armies in the World War took to the trenches and established themselves in parallel lines hundreds of miles long, neither was strong enough to dislodge the other. Their elements of attack and defense, the first line, the supports and the troops in immediate reserve simply dug in. It then became siege warfare and the continuance of this situation, with indecisive attacks from time to time, diverted the attention of some observers from the fact that the real objective was the enemy's army.

To bring about a decision, that army must be driven from the trenches and the fighting carried into the open. It is here that the infantryman with his rifle, supported by the machine guns, the tanks, the artillery, the airplanes and all auxiliary arms, determines the issue. Through adherence to this principle, the American soldier, taught how to shoot, how to take advantage of the terrain, and how to rely upon hasty entrenchment, shall retain the ability to drive the enemy from his trenches and, by the same tactics, defeat him in the open.

The Punitive Expedition was withdrawn early in February, 1917, and I returned to El Paso to resume command of that portion of the border. A few days after the death of Major General Frederick Funston on February 19th, I was assigned to the command of the Southern Department as his successor, with headquarters at Fort Sam Houston, Texas.

In the passing of General Funston the Army suffered a severe loss. With little military knowledge previous to the Spanish War, but with rare native ability, he had taken advantage of his opportunities and, through experience in Cuba and in the Philippine Islands had become a most efficient commander. He was daring and resourceful in the field and all his campaigns were successful. Funston was a first-class fighting man who served his country loyally and ably.

With the declaration of war against Germany there was much excitement in the Southwest and many were the demands for protection against sabotage. Our first concern was to guard Government property and railways. Military detachments were sent to the most critical points. Orders had already been given to military commanders directing them to take measures to protect

military forts, important railroad bridges, tunnels, docks, munition plants, Government buildings and property, and to assert
vigorously the Federal power should any acts of violence occur.
With very few exceptions the sentiment of the people in the
states of Louisiana, Texas, Oklahoma, New Mexico and Arizona,
then included in the Southern Department, was strongly behind
the Government. Men and women of all classes in that area were
eager to aid and sought advice as to how they might do so to advantage. Their fine attitude gave every promise of the energy
and patriotism with which our people throughout the country
supported the war.

President Wilson recommended the draft as the best method of
raising an army. In the discussions in Congress on the subject,
many members spoke in favor of the volunteer system. Even the
Speaker of the House, the Honorable Champ Clark, of Missouri,
in a speech on the floor opposing the Draft Act, compared the
conscript to the convict. With such strong opposition it looked
as though the conscription law would fail to pass. Its opponents
forgot that during the Civil War the volunteer system had given
Mr. Lincoln and his commanders no end of trouble and that in
order to provide manpower the North was finally forced to
adopt conscription. Large numbers of shirkers were thus compelled to serve; hence the opprobrium that clung to the word
"conscript." It was very important that a repetition of the experience in the Civil War should be avoided. The advocates of a
volunteer army also ignored the experience of the British in the
World War, who, after a year and a half of effort to recruit their
armies under that system, had been obliged to resort to the draft.
In my opinion, it was so vital to our success that while in San
Antonio, contrary to my lifelong rule against meddling with legis-
lation, I persuaded the Governor of Texas that conscription was
sound in principle and got him to exert his influence with the
Texas delegation in Congress in favor of it. In writing at the
time to a friend of mine with reference to this subject, I said:

"We must avoid creating the impression that we are sending a
political army to Europe—the day of political armies is past. It would

be a whole lot wiser for us to stay at home until we are thoroughly prepared. Universal service is the only principle to follow that will lead to success in this war, and that should be well understood. We are in this thing for keeps and it is going to demand the utmost exertion and the best of preparation to win. We shall have to select the flower of the young manhood of this country and give them thorough training before we start. The only way we can hope to succeed is by dogged determination and perseverance. * * * No half-way measures are going to solve this problem. I am with the President in this matter, heart and soul. I am sincerely and deeply impressed with the necessity of clinging to rational lines in carrying out his policies. The President feels the importance of this situation and every honest American should stand right behind him and help to the utmost."

On the afternoon of April 29th, while busy at my desk at Fort Sam Houston, word came through the Associated Press that both houses of Congress had passed the Draft Act, although, as it turned out, amendments adopted by the two houses necessitated a conference, which delayed the passage of the Act in its final form until nearly three weeks later.

A number of local newspaper reporters called at once and wanted to know what I thought about it. I said that of course everybody had realized for some time that our actual participation with armed forces could hardly be avoided; that the responsibility that now rested upon the country was tremendous, and added: "The echo of that vote for conscription will be heard around the globe. It is a triumph of democratic government; a willing step taken by a free people under wise leadership. * * * It means that every man will have his rôle to play. To have a hand in affairs and know that he is a part of the system will make a better citizen of every man. * * * To witness the thing that has just happened is truly inspiring. I would rather live now and have my share to perform in the events of to-day than to have lived in any past period in the world's history. * * * This is the beginning of a wonderful era."

CHAPTER II

Arrival in Washington—Calls on Chief of Staff and Secretary of War—
Appointed Commander-in-Chief—Lack of Preparation Appalling—
Selection of Staff—Secretary Disapproves Roosevelt's Application to
Raise Volunteer Division—Many Requests to Accompany Me Abroad

I ARRIVED in Washington on the morning of May 10th, pursuant to orders, and called at once at the office of the Chief of Staff, Major General Hugh L. Scott. He informed me that, upon his recommendation, I had been selected to command a division to be sent to France. This confirmed the impression received from his message of May 2d. He spoke of the other general officers who were then senior to me, whose names were mentioned in the preceding chapter, and gave reasons why each one had been passed over. I greatly appreciated the opinion and action of the Chief of Staff, whom I have always held in high esteem.

We discussed the military situation and he outlined the general plans in so far as anything definite had been determined. The War College Division of the General Staff during the previous three months had presented a number of recommendations for action in the event of war. One of these provided for the enactment of a draft law, the study of which General Scott himself had initiated. Others were concerned with the size of the army to be organized and the necessity for the procurement of equipment and supplies. Some of the heads of supply departments had previously asked Congress for funds for the purchase of supplies, and others had made estimates, but nothing definite had been accomplished. On March 15th, acting under instructions of the Chief of Staff, the War College Division had submitted a rather general scheme which contemplated an army of 500,000 men. These were all eleventh-hour recommendations and definite action was not taken until May 18th, when Congress passed the law authorizing the increase of the military establishment through the application of the draft.

I was really more chagrined than astonished to realize that so little had been done in the way of preparation when there were so many things that might have been done long before. It had been apparent to everybody for months that we were likely to be forced into the war, and a state of war had actually existed for several weeks, yet scarcely a start had been made to prepare for our participation. The War Department seemed to be suffering from a kind of inertia, for which perhaps it was not altogether responsible.

The war plans functions of the War Department were in the hands of the General Staff, which had been established just after the Spanish-American War, on the recommendation of Mr. Elihu Root, then Secretary of War. Specifically the General Staff was charged with the study of possible theaters of operations, and with the preparation of plans for the mobilization, organization, supply, transportation and strategic employment of the necessary forces to meet all possible contingencies. But until a few weeks before the declaration of war neither the General Staff nor the War College had received any hint or direction to be ready with recommendations, except as indicated above. The General Staff had apparently done little more, even after war was declared, than to consider the immediate question of organizing and sending abroad one combat division and 50,000 special troops, as requested by the Allies.

In view of the serious possibility of war that had confronted the nation since the sinking of the *Lusitania,* there was no apparent reason why the General Staff should not have developed definite basic plans for the organization and employment of our armies in anticipation of the rapidly approaching emergency and without waiting for instructions from the Administration. To find such a lack of foresight on the part of the General Staff was not calculated to inspire confidence in its ability to do its part efficiently in the crisis that confronted us.

The truth is that the General Staff had not yet been properly organized. It was too much the inarticulate instrument of the Chief of Staff, who often erroneously assumed the rôle of Commanding General of the Army. There were many senior officers on the General Staff who understood little or nothing of its duties. The prominent bureau chiefs who possessed the advantage of disbursing Government funds continuously opposed the development of this planning and coördinating agency superior to them. Furthermore, Congress had recently reduced the number of officers allowed on the War Department General Staff. In these facts we no doubt find the basis of many of the difficulties that arose later in connection with the preparation of our army at home and its shipment and supply abroad.

My next call was upon the Secretary of War, Mr. Newton D. Baker. I was surprised to find him much younger and considerably smaller than I had expected. He looked actually diminutive as he sat behind his desk, doubled up in a rather large office chair, but when he spoke my impression changed immediately. We talked of my recent experience in Mexico and of conditions on the border, which, fortunately, were quieter than they had been for several years. He referred to my appointment and said that he had given the subject very careful thought and had made the choice solely upon my record. I expressed my appreciation of the honor, mentioned the responsibility of the position, and said that I hoped he would have no reason to regret his action.

At this time it was my understanding that I was to go over in command of a division, and as no such unit then existed in our Army it was urgent that it be organized as soon as practicable. As directed, I had already designated the infantry and artillery regiments to form the division, but details of interior organization, including the size of smaller units, their armament, the kind of auxiliary troops, and many such matters had not been determined.

I left Mr. Baker's office with a distinctly favorable impression of the man upon whom, as head of the War Department, would rest the burden of preparing for a great war to which the wholly unready nation was now committed. He was courteous and pleasant and impressed me as being frank, fair, and business-like. His conception of the problems seemed broad and comprehensive. From the start he did not hesitate to make definite decisions on the momentous questions involved. Yet, naturally, he did not then fully appreciate the enormous difficulties that confronted his department.

Still proceeding under the assumption that I was to command only a division in France, my feelings may well be imagined when, a day or so later, the Secretary of War called me in to say that it had been decided by the President to send me abroad as Commander-in-Chief, and that I should select my staff accordingly and prepare to sail as soon as possible.

In our conversation the Secretary indicated that several divisions and other troops would be sent overseas as soon as they could be prepared. The numbers could not then be fixed, of course, as the plans of the War Department were not fully developed until later. Moreover, there was always the determining factor in any calculation that might be made, and that was the amount of tonnage available for the transportation and supply of an army.

The thought of the responsibilities that this high position carried depressed me for the moment. Here in the face of a great war I had been placed in command of a theoretical army which had yet to be constituted, equipped, trained, and sent abroad. Still, there was no doubt in my mind then, or at any other time, of my ability to do my part, provided the Government would furnish men, equipment and supplies.

The new decision materially broadened the scope of my duties, and it became necessary at once to discuss with the War Department the outlines of the organization of our forces. Naturally the consideration of personnel and the assembly of a field general staff was of first importance, and the foundation of the supply system as an integral part of the organization was to be next in order. The efficiency of the staff and supply departments would depend largely upon the ability and experience of their chiefs, so that the selection of capable officers for these positions was of the greatest moment. This was a difficult task because there was only a limited number of available officers who had received even theoretical training in the duties of the staff in war.

Obviously it was advisable to choose my chief of staff as soon as practicable. After studying the records of several officers of my acquaintance, and of others who were recommended for the position, I chose Major James G. Harbord. His efficiency in every grade from the day of his enlistment as a private in the Army, in January, 1889, was not only of record but was well known to those with whom he had served. The first time I had ever heard of him was shortly before he was promoted to the grade of first lieutenant in the 10th Cavalry. An officer who had known him as a sergeant said that he was a most promising youngster and that the regiment would be fortunate to get him. I had met him later during his service in the cavalry and in the Philippine Constabulary.

Apart from sheer ability, a chief of staff, to be highly efficient, should have tact, and he must have the confidence of his commander. He would be of small value without the courage to give his own views on any question that might arise, and he must have the loyalty to abide by the decisions of his chief.

Throughout the war Harbord never hesitated a moment to express his opinion with the utmost frankness, no matter how radically it might differ from my own, nor did he ever fail to carry out instructions faithfully even when they were not in accord with his views. Entirely unselfish, he labored incessantly for what he believed to be the best interests of our armies. His ability, his resourcefulness, his faculty for organization, and, above all, his loyalty, were outstanding qualities, and these together with a compelling personality made him invaluable to the nation in this important position.

After consultation with the permanent heads of staff and supply departments, and with no little insistence on my part in more than one instance, the corresponding representatives to accompany me were designated, and they in turn chose their assistants. Although the list did not include all whom I would have selected, as some were not available, yet all rose to important places in the final organization, except one or two who failed in health. Fifty-nine officers and 128 clerks, civilian employees and enlisted men accompanied me abroad.[1]

The Selective Service Act (Draft Act) as submitted to Congress was prepared by the Judge Advocate General's Office under instructions from the Secretary of War. The draft was strongly

[1] The Personal Staff (Aides-de-Camp) consisted of: *Capt. Nelson E. Margetts,* F.A., later Colonel, Field Artillery; *Capt. James L. Collins,* Cav., later Colonel, Field Artillery; *1st Lt. Martin C. Shallenberger,* Inf., later Colonel, General Staff.

The original members of the General Staff were: *Maj. James G. Harbord,* Cav., Chief of Staff, later Major General; *Maj. John McA. Palmer,* G.S.C., later Colonel, Infantry; *Maj. Dennis E. Nolan,* G.S.C., later Brigadier General and Chief of Intelligence, A.E.F.; *Maj. Fox Conner,* Asst. Inspector General (attached), later Brigadier General and Chief of Operations, A.E.F.; *Capt. Arthur L. Conger,* Inf. (attached), later Colonel, General Staff, and regimental commander; *Capt. Hugh A. Drum,* Inf. (attached), later Brigadier General and Chief of Staff, First Army.

The Administrative and Supply Staff was: *Col. Benjamin Alvord,* Adjutant General, later Brigadier General and Adjutant General, A.E.F. (invalided home); *Col. André W. Brewster,* Inspector General, later Major General and Inspector General, A.E.F.; *Lt. Col. Walter A. Bethel,* Judge Advocate, later Brigadier General and Judge Advocate General, A.E.F.; *Col. Daniel E. McCarthy,* Q.M.C. (invalided home); *Col. Alfred E. Bradley,* M.C., later Brigadier General and Chief Surgeon, A.E.F. (joined in London; invalided home); *Lt. Col. Merritte W. Ireland,* M. C., later Brigadier General and Chief Surgeon, A.E.F., relieving General Bradley; *Col. Harry Taylor,* C. of E., later Brigadier General and Chief of Engineers, A.E.F.; *Lt. Col. Clarence C. Williams,* Ord., later Brigadier General and Chief of Ordnance, A.E.F.; *Col. Edgar Russel,* S.C., later Brigadier General and Chief Signal Officer, A.E.F.; *Maj. Townsend F. Dodd,* Aviation Sec., later Colonel and Chief of Air Service, A.E.F., until Sept. 3, 1917.

The total number in my party that sailed on the S.S. *Baltic* was as follows:

Regular Army Officers	40
Marine Corps Officers	2
O.R.C. Officers in active service	17
Enlisted Men	67
Field Clerks	36
Civilian Clerks	20
Civilian Interpreters	5
Civilians (Correspondents)	3
Total on *Baltic*	190

urged by the Chief of Staff, the Secretary of War, and the President, who had recommended it to Congress on April 2d. But it did not become a law until May 18th, thus deferring its application for forty-two days after the declaration of war. The question had been discussed in the press of the country for some time, with the result in the end that the principle of conscription was advocated by the majority of the leading newspapers. In doing so they rendered distinguished service to the nation by creating favorable public opinion to sustain the President and Congress in the enactment of this important law.

The administration of the draft was placed under the direction of Brigadier General E. H. Crowder, who was appointed to the position of Provost Marshal General for that purpose. The system of using polling places throughout the country and of having the registration under the supervision of local boards proved to be both simple and effective. The people of every community became directly interested in the creation of our armies, and were generally enthusiastic in their support of the war. The system of selecting men for service as worked out by the Judge Advocate General's Office was admirable and should stand as a model for the future.

The Act contained a provision authorizing the President to raise not to exceed four infantry divisions by voluntary enlistment. When Mr. Baker asked my view as to whether action should be taken under this provision I expressed myself against the principle except as to special or technical troops. While volunteer fighting units would naturally be composed of fine men, who would give a good account of themselves, there was no reason to suppose that they would be any better than those selected under the draft, similarly officered by their quota from the Regular Army. Moreover, the volunteers, as they had done in the past, would regard themselves as belonging to a special class and would expect priority both as to supplies and assignments. Any difference in the status of the various units such as would thus exist between volunteers and those who should come in through the draft would arouse jealousies almost certain to be subversive of discipline.

When one recalled the evils of the volunteer system in the Civil War, with the appointment of politicians to high command and the conferring of Medals of Honor upon whole regiments for a few days of extra service; and later, in the Spanish-American War, the insistent demands of the volunteers, politically and otherwise, that they should have preferential consideration, it was not difficult to foresee what would have happened in the World War.

The appeal of Colonel Roosevelt for permission to raise a volunteer division aroused popular sentiment in his favor throughout the country, but approval would have opened the door for many similar requests, and the policy would have interfered materially with the orderly and businesslike enforcement of the Draft Law. Moreover, the regular establishment would have suffered from the loss of an undue proportion of the best officers, who inevitably would have been selected for important positions in these special units at a time when their services were urgently needed in building more largely.

Another important reason for disapproving Colonel Roosevelt's application was that in such a war it was necessary that officers, especially those in high command, should be thoroughly trained and disciplined. Furthermore, he was not in the best of health and could not have withstood the hard work and exposure of the training camps and trenches. The Secretary of War, much to the disappointment of Colonel Roosevelt, wisely made an adverse decision in his case, which was confirmed by the President. It was evident that both Mr. Wilson and Secretary Baker were looking for trained leaders and were determined to avoid the embarrassment Mr. Lincoln experienced in the Civil War, when he was more or less driven to fill many high positions with political appointees who, in the end, had to be replaced by men trained in the military profession.

The following letter from Colonel Roosevelt will show his own fine attitude:

"May 20th, 1917.

"MY DEAR GENERAL PERSHING:

"I very heartily congratulate you, and especially the people of the United States, upon your selection to lead the expeditionary force to the front. When I was endeavoring to persuade the Secretary of War to permit me to raise a division or two of volunteers I stated that if you or some man like you were to command the expeditionary force I could raise the divisions without trouble.

"I write you now to request that my two sons, Theodore Roosevelt, Jr., aged 27, and Archibald B. Roosevelt, aged 23, both of Harvard, be allowed to enlist as privates under you, to go over with the first troops. The former is a Major and the latter a Captain in the Officers' Reserve Corps. They are at Plattsburg for their third summer. My own belief is that competent men of their standing and rank can gain very little from a third summer at Plattsburg, and that they should be utilized as officers, even if only as second lieutenants. But they are keenly desirous to see service; and if they serve under you at the front, and are not killed, they will be far better able to instruct the draft army next fall, or next winter, or whenever they are sent home, than they will be after spending the summer at Plattsburg. The President has announced that only regular officers are to go with you; and if this is to be the invariable rule then I apply on behalf of my two sons that they may serve under you as enlisted men, to go to the front with the first troops sent over.

"Trusting to hear that this request has been granted, I am, with great respect,

"Very sincerely yours,

"THEODORE ROOSEVELT.

"P. S. If I were physically fit, instead of old and heavy and stiff, I should myself ask to go under you in any capacity down to and including a sergeant; but at my age, and condition, I suppose that I could not do work you would consider worth while in the fighting line (my only line) in a lower grade than brigade commander."

Although it was not generally known that I was to go abroad, there was a flood of applications to accompany me. One of them was a personal appeal for service in any capacity by my old friend, Robert Bacon, who had been Ambassador to France. He had already given valuable aid to the Allied cause and because of his intimate knowledge of the French people and his tact and discretion I was glad to have him. Major Bacon became garrison commander at Chaumont and later, as colonel and aide-de-camp on my staff, rendered exceptional service at British G.H.Q., where he was chief of our mission. There is no doubt that his very strenuous activity in these various positions of trust and responsibility during the war shortened his life.

Another friend who was most anxious to join my headquarters was Willard D. Straight, whom I had known in Manchuria during the Russo-Japanese War. Although his request could not be granted, he came to France within a few months and served efficiently in the Army and with the Peace Commission, being on duty with the latter at the time of his death. Lloyd C. Griscom, with whom I had been pleasantly associated when he was our Minister and I was Military Attaché at Tokyo, asked to go with me, but it was impossible to arrange it. When he came over later as adjutant of the 77th Division, I at once detailed him as my representative at the War Office in London.

A few days before my departure, while at lunch at the Metropolitan Club with Charles E. Magoon, ex-Governor of Cuba, Charles G. Dawes joined us. The three of us had been friends in the days when we were together at Lincoln, Nebraska, Magoon and Dawes as young lawyers, the latter with a decided talent for business, and I as military instructor at the State University. Dawes was an applicant for a commission in one of the engineer regiments then being organized, under the direction of Mr. Samuel M. Felton, from volunteers with experience in railroading, and wanted me to help him get the appointment. I asked him whether he knew anything about engineering, and he said that when a youth he had carried a chain a month or so for a surveyor out in Ohio. I was not much impressed with his pretensions as an engineer or as a prospective military possibility, but I did have knowledge of his business ability and experience and knew that he would be valuable in some position requiring his qualifications, so I spoke to the Secretary of War in his behalf.

Requests from National Guard officers and from Governors for the early acceptance of their State units poured into the War

Department.   The clamor became so general and so insistent that the Secretary of War happily conceived the idea of forming a composite division to include troops from every State in the Union.   I thought the suggestion a good one and gave it my hearty endorsement.   This was the origin of the 42d (Rainbow) Division, which was later to distinguish itself in many important engagements.

CHAPTER III

Conference on Munitions—Shortage of Guns, Ammunition and Airplanes —Training Camps for Officers—Cantonments—French and British Missions Want American Replacements—Attend Red Cross Conference—Call on President Wilson—Letters of Instruction

OUR deplorable situation as to munitions was fully discussed at a conference called by the Secretary of War in his office on the afternoon of May 10th.[1] A general survey of our requirements for the immediate future was made as to rifles, machine guns, light and heavy artillery, ammunition and airplanes. It was brought out that we had for issue, not in the hands of troops, only about 285,000 Springfield rifles, 400 light field guns, and 150 heavy field guns.[2]

As it was impossible, because of manufacturing difficulties, for our factories to turn out enough Springfield rifles within a reasonable time, the Secretary, after hearing the facts, decided to adopt the Enfield rifle for our infantry. It was then being manufactured for the British in large quantities at private factories in our country and a slight modification of the chamber only was necessary to make it fit our ammunition. More than 2,000,000 of these rifles were manufactured during the war.

Although Congress had appropriated $12,000,000 for the procurement of machine guns in 1916, it was reported to the conference that we had less than 1,500 guns and that these were of four different types. This condition existed because the War Department had not decided definitely which type to adopt for

[1] Those present were the Secretary of War; Major General Hugh L. Scott, Chief of Staff; Major General Tasker H. Bliss, Assistant Chief of Staff; Major General William Crozier, Chief of Ordnance; Major General Erasmus M. Weaver, Chief of Artillery; Brigadier General Joseph E. Kuhn, President of the War College; and myself.
[2] We eventually had with the armies in France: 1,761,000 rifles; 2,106 75-mm. field guns, and 1,485 heavy guns; besides about half as many of each at home.

our Army, although an order had been placed late in 1916 for a quantity of the heavy Vickers-Maxims. Tests of machine guns were held in May, 1917, and an entirely new type was pronounced acceptable and adopted by the Ordnance Department. Until these could be manufactured we had to purchase machine guns of the Hotchkiss type from the French.

Our capacity to manufacture small arms ammunition in large quantities was assured through the operations of private factories. As in the case of Enfield rifles, this was due to increased production for sale to the Allies prior to our entry into the war and not to any preparatory action by the War Department. Except for our 3-inch artillery ammunition, we did not have enough to provide for more than nine hours' supply, even for the limited number of guns on hand, firing at the rate ordinarily used in laying down a barrage for an infantry attack.

The situation at that time as to aviation was such that every American ought to feel mortified to hear it mentioned. Out of 65 officers and about 1,000 men in the Air Service Section of the Signal Corps, there were 35 officers who could fly. With the exception of five or six officers, none of them could have met the requirements of modern battle conditions and none had any technical experience with aircraft guns, bombs or bombing devices.

We could boast some 55 training planes in various conditions of usefulness, all entirely without war equipment and valueless for service at the front. Of these 55 planes, it is amusing now to recall that the National Advisory Committee for Aeronautics, which was then conducting a scientific study of the problem of flight, advised that 51 were obsolete and the other 4 obsolescent. We could not have put a single squadron in the field, although it was estimated later that we should eventually need at least 300 squadrons, each to be composed on the average of some 24 officers, 180 men and 18 airplanes, besides a large reserve of planes for replacements.

The expectations of the Allies concerning our assistance in the air are shown by the following cable from the French Prime

Minister, received about May 24, 1917, which formed the basis of War Department effort:

"It is desired that in order to coöperate with the French Aeronautics, the American Government should adopt the following program: The formation of a flying corps of 4,500 airplanes—personnel and matériel included—to be sent to the French front during the campaign of 1918. The total number of pilots, including reserve, should be 5,000 and 50,000 mechanics.

"2,000 airplanes should be constructed each month as well as 4,000 engines, by the American factories. That is to say, that during the first six months of 1918, 16,500 planes (of the latest type) and 30,000 engines will have to be built.

"The French Government is anxious to know if the American Government accepts this proposition, which would allow the Allies to win the supremacy of the air.

"RIBOT."

This message, in its appeal for such a large number of aviation personnel and airplanes, was really a most convincing confession of the plight of the Allied armies. But more than that, it strikingly brought home to us a full realization of our pitiful deficiencies, not only in aviation but in all equipment. The appropriation in July, 1917, of $640,000,000 for aviation indicated that Congress understood the predicament that confronted us, but what a commentary it was on the lack of that wisdom which should have prompted both the people and their representatives to earlier action.

Thus the deeper we went into the situation the more overwhelming the work ahead of us seemed to be. As the degree of its accomplishment within a reasonable time would be the measure of our aid to the Allies, extreme haste in our preparation was urgent. We were called upon to make up in a few months for the neglect of years during which self-satisfied provincialism and smug complacency had prevented the most elementary efforts toward a reasonable precaution to meet such an emergency.

In an attempt to provide the thousands of additional officers needed for the first 500,000 troops tentatively considered necessary under the War College plan, the Secretary of War about the middle of April directed the establishment of training camps, one for each of the proposed sixteen infantry divisions that were to form such a force. Noncommissioned officers from the Regular Army and the National Guard, augmented by graduates of schools and colleges where military instruction was given, were put through a three months' course of instruction in these camps.

Early in April, before the declaration of war, I had sent the following telegram from Fort Sam Houston to The Adjutant General of the Army:

> "Have inaugurated intensive training along lines of European war experience, with a view to prompt preparation regular regiments for foreign service if needed. Suggest early announcement that all cavalry and infantry regiments this department are to be increased to war strength. Many regiments have already received recruits considerably beyond peace strength. If new increments are to be added to Regular Army in near future recommend corresponding number recruits in addition to above be attached as rapidly as enlisted so that advantage may be taken of training now in progress."

On May 12th, after waiting more than a month, orders were issued directing the recruitment of all line organizations to war strength.

Among other subjects considered with the Secretary was the assembly for training of the National Guard and the men to come in under the draft. The organization of our Army had never been based upon the tactical requirements of battle, but we still maintained our troops at small posts, as in the days of Indian warfare. Some of these posts, although they lacked sufficient barracks and training areas for units as large as a division, could have been advantageously used in the earlier stages of training up to the limits of their accommodations.

In lieu of any previous plans, the Secretary contemplated the construction of cantonments in different parts of the country, and on May 7th the Commanding Generals of the several departments were directed to select sites for that purpose. Under the circumstances, the proposed plan seemed to be the only alternative for training the larger units, provided this building program could be carried out without delay; but it should have been possible to obtain enough tentage for the Regular Army and the National Guard at once so that training for the necessary additional drafts to fill them could have been started in their respective localities. Time was the most important factor to be considered.

The actual construction of cantonments was not begun until nearly three months after we had entered the war, and even though the task of erecting them was accomplished in record time, some ninety days more had elapsed before they were ready to receive troops. Thus, it was, with some exceptions, practically six months before the training of our new army was under way. Even then several of these camps were not favorably located and training was seriously handicapped on this account during the fall and winter months.

About this time the Allies brought up the question of utilizing our men to build up their armies. As we shall see, the subject arose from time to time in one form or another and we had to fight against it until the end of the war.

Both the French and British Missions, under M. Viviani and Mr. Balfour respectively, then in our country, were very keen to have American recruits to fill up the ranks of their armies. The French really wanted us to send small, untrained units for incorporation in their divisions. Their views were clearly set forth in a memorandum by the French General Staff which was presented by their Military Attaché. Marshal Joffre, of the French Mission, however, evidently learned that such a proposal would not appeal to us, so he suggested that we also organize our own divisions, and urged that one division be sent over immediately to stimulate French morale, which he frankly confessed was then at low ebb. In addition, he asked for 50,000 trained men for service on their railways, in the shops, and with their medical units.

The following is quoted from the French memorandum:

"We cannot expect to see American armies, entirely organized with staffs and artillery, which are indispensable to the service of large forces, before the expiration of a period of preparation the duration of which it is impossible to estimate.

"On the other hand it seems possible to obtain from America within a brief period of time a portion of the great resources of that nation in combatant and noncombatant personnel which is available."

Speaking of maintaining the strength of existing French formations, they proposed:

"Voluntary enlistment in French armies, using French depots, centers of instruction and instruction units. With this system of intensive training we could utilize men with the least delay. This is a solution which divides American effort, but which has the advantage of furnishing us immediate aid and of hastening the victory.

"It could be understood that these volunteers could be withdrawn from the French Army and placed at the disposal of the American Commandant when the regularly organized forces arrive."

Another proposal, known as the "General Nivelle Scheme," requested that we send 80,000 men to perform various kinds of work. The following quotations will indicate the French attitude as to command, as well as their view regarding the urgency of their requirements:

"In order that there may not be any officers of higher rank than the French officers with whom these auxiliary troops will be called upon to work it is preferable that in the different units there should not be for the present any officer above the rank of captain. When the units will become sufficiently numerous to require superior officers these can be chosen from the captains of existing units.

"The important thing is to act quickly and to send groups or units of the character asked for as rapidly as possible. However small the first expeditions may be it is of capital importance that there should be no hesitation in sending them at once, even half units will be welcome."

A definite proposal that our men should be drafted into the British Army was also pressed by the military representative with the British Mission, Major General G. T. M. Bridges. His suggestions were set forth in the following letter to Major General Scott and also mentioned in conversation with me:

"Dear General:

"You asked me to write you my views as to the coöperation of your military forces in Europe. They are as follows:

"1. If you ask me how your force could most quickly make itself felt in Europe, I would say by sending 500,000 untrained men at once to our depots in England to be trained there, and drafted into our armies in France. This is the view alike of our Commander-in-Chief in France and the Chief of the Imperial General Staff (Sir Douglas Haig and Sir W. Robertson), their reasons being that we are short of men, the war is at a critical stage, when we may yet be able to turn the scale and force a decision during the summer, and *every day* counts. Our recruits are put into the field after 9 weeks' training in England, and 9 days in France, and give a good account of themselves. With your intelligent men under our system and instruction this would be found ample. In no other way could those 500,000 men make their presence felt before what we call the fighting season is over for the year. Both Sir Douglas Haig and Sir William Robertson, however, recognize the difficulties attending such a course in view of the fact that you are engaged in raising a national army. However, I put it forward for your consideration whether in view of your enormous manpower you cannot do both, in which case the drafts sent to us could eventually be drafted back into the U. S. Army and would be a good leavening of seasoned men. * * *

" * * * In view of the large armies now engaged, a few divisions would have to come under command of either the British or French Commander-in-Chief. * * * "

Speaking then of armament, he advocated the adoption of the British Enfield and their 18-pounder in preference to the French Lebel rifle and 75-millimeter field gun. Going on, he said:

"9. It appears to me that the above considerations may have some weight in the decision of your Government as to whether your initial forces are directed to the care of our army or to the French. The French may be able to promise a separate line of supply for a small force. I understand they are extremely anxious to have your army with them, and they are probably willing to sacrifice a good deal to this end. I feel certain that Sir D. Haig could not promise this, but would stipulate that your divisions would have to come into line with ours as regards ammunition supply. If with the French you would probably want your own food supply also.

"A few other points occur to me in this connection. You will have the language difficulty to contend with if your divisions go to the French. The French have very few English-speaking officers; not so many as they think. A good instructor can indeed seldom speak English, and men will soon get tired of being instructed through interpreters.

"We have been told that the sentiment in this country is in favor of fighting with and for the French. We understand this sentiment. * * * I think I have made it clear there are serious military disadvantages, and you will be sacrificing some of your efficiency for this sentiment, and making, in my opinion, the task of your commanders and staff more difficult in the field. Once you had a sufficient force in France, however, it would be quite feasible to place your army between the French and ourselves, where it could, if so desired, be under French direction, and supplied by us. * * *

"10. We would be glad if you would consider the question of allowing recruiting of American citizens for the British, Canadian and French Armies, from the surplus you will have over your requirements. We are all going to suffer from a shortage after this summer's fighting. * * * "

General Bridges requested that, in the event we could not see our way clear to draft men as individuals, then minor units, such as battalions and regiments, should be incorporated in British divisions.

I was decidedly against our becoming a recruiting agency for either the French or British and at that time this was the attitude of the War Department also. While fully realizing the difficulties, it was definitely understood between the Secretary of War and myself that we should proceed to organize our own units from top to bottom and build a distinctive army of our own as rapidly as possible.

The evident rivalry between the British and French for control and use of our forces, even before we had an army in the field, bore out my impression that those two Governments were not working entirely in harmony. It had been apparent for some time that there was a lack of coöperation between their armies. Their efforts were often separate and distinct. First one and then the other would attack, each apparently without reference to the other. Generally speaking, such methods could not seriously affect the enemy, who would thus be at liberty to utilize his reserves against them in turn. I had often remarked that the Allies would never win the war until they secured unity of action under some form of coördinated control.

History is replete with the failures of coalitions and seemed to be repeating itself in the World War. Marlborough, in the War of the Spanish Succession, complained of the lack of coöperation among the armies. His plans were impeded by the jealousies of the allied commanders and it required all his gifts of diplomacy to secure concerted action. Napoleon said that it was not difficult to beat a coalition. The lack of unity in military operations conducted jointly by allied armies often results from divergence of war aims. In the pursuit of these aims, governments may seek to place part of their forces in a position that would be advantageous after the war is over and lose sight of the fact that complete victory can only be achieved by beating the enemy's army. The success of such operations depends upon complete military coöperation. The absence of entire united effort between the Allied armies on the Western Front during the earlier years of the war was probably due merely to lack of understanding between the commanders, but its continuance would have undoubtedly led to their defeat.

My first meeting with Marshal Joffre was during his farewell call on the Secretary of War late in May. I entered just as he and his party were leaving. He spoke of the serious situation in France and expressed the hope of seeing American troops on the Western Front very soon. Here was a Marshal of France who, as Commander-in-Chief of the French Army for nearly three years, had made his name immortal, apparently appealing for military assistance from a man recently designated to be commander-in-chief of an army not yet in existence. I have often wondered what must have been his thoughts under the circumstances, but whatever he may have felt as to the new commander himself, the totally unready situation that he found in America could not have been very encouraging. It is a pleasure to say that this great soldier became my loyal and consistent personal friend.

While I was in Washington the American Red Cross had assembled some hundreds of business and professional men and women from all parts of the country to consider plans and devise ways and means of raising funds. The Red Cross had already been active in France, but now that we were in the war the time had come for extraordinary effort.

One day during the conference Mr. Henry P. Davison, President of the Red Cross, Mr. Eliot Wadsworth and Mr. John J. O'Connell burst into my office and insisted that I should go before the meeting and speak. I protested vigorously, but it was of no use, as they literally dragged me off then and there. When we reached the hall, Mr. Herbert Hoover had the floor and was describing his experience in Belgium as director of relief provided by America for the needy inhabitants. Mr. Hoover was speaking in a low voice as if quite embarrassed and this gave me some courage, although when the chairman, the late ex-President Taft, introduced me he very vividly expressed my feelings by saying he was sure that I would rather face a battery of artillery than face that gathering. Among other things, I said in substance:

> "Now that we are in the war, the Red Cross has new obligations. Its great work is to help the Allies. The people of France especially are in sore straits. The losses they have suffered have reduced their power to fight and to produce. We must supply their needs. It is our duty to assist them to rehabilitate themselves so that they can continue in the war. We must help their widows and orphans. We must help the French people in every way possible. The Red Cross will not fail."

The announcement was made by Mr. Davison that $100,000,000 would be needed to carry on the work with our own and the Allied armies. I did not think it would be possible to raise such an enormous sum through subscription and could hardly believe that so much money would be necessary. But the men handling the affairs of the society had large vision, as the contribution in that first drive was more than $114,000,000, and between June, 1917, and February, 1919, the total amount subscribed was over $400,000,000. This response to Red Cross needs was a striking example of the generous spirit of our people. How happy it would have made Clara Barton, whom I knew in Cuba during the Spanish-American War, if she could have been similarly supported, but the Red Cross was not then considered of such importance. I recall that after the surrender of Santiago, when she was helping to feed the more needy Cubans, I gave her a lot of surplus rations that had been accumulated by my regiment, the 10th Cavalry, for which she was very grateful.

About the middle of May arrangements were made for me and my staff to sail, but on account of prowling German submarines sailings were uncertain and our departure was postponed from time to time until May 28th. While important that we should get off, yet the extra time was well employed, especially by the members of the staff, in studying conditions and requirements and in placing advance requisitions for supplies in so far as our needs could be foreseen. The details of organization for the 1st Division were worked out under my direction and orders for its concentration and embarkation prepared before we left.

The last few days included several formal calls on diplomatic representatives, with a semi-official luncheon or dinner thrown in here and there. The French Ambassador and Madame Jusserand gave a luncheon at the Embassy that was memorable for its cordiality and charm. She was American by birth and was most enthusiastic over our entry into the war. With tears in her eyes, she said, "I always thought you would come in, and now I can be proud of my native country, for with America and France again fighting side by side I know we shall win." Another similar occasion was an informal luncheon with Mr. Balfour, the cultured head of the British Mission, where, instead of books and politics, the conversation turned to the more practical phases of Allied coöperation. The Secretary of State and Mrs. Lansing also entertained at dinner several members of the special missions then in Washington, among whom was the Prince of Udine, the Chief of the Italian Mission. In meeting the members of these various missions one could not help being impressed by their extreme anxiety for the future.

On the afternoon of May 24th, the Secretary of War and I called on President Wilson for my first and only meeting with him until he came to France after the Armistice. After engaging in conversation with Mr. Baker for a few minutes on the subject of shipping, he turned to me and said, "General, we are giving you some very difficult tasks these days," to which I replied, "Perhaps so, Mr. President, but that is what we are trained to expect." Mr. Wilson spoke of my recent expedition into Mexico and inquired about my acquaintance with France. I had naturally thought that he would say something about the part our Army should play in the war in coöperation with the Allied armies, but he said nothing.

Upon leaving, I said, "Mr. President, I appreciate the honor you have conferred upon me by the assignment you have given me and realize the responsibilities it entails, but you can count upon the best that is in me." His reply was, "General, you were chosen entirely upon your record and I have every confidence that you will succeed; you shall have my full support." The President then asked me to convey to His Majesty the King of Great Britain and to the President of France his greetings and best wishes. His manner was cordial and simple and I was impressed with his poise and his air of determination. His assurance of confidence in me was gratifying, but in the difficult situation that arose later regarding the manner of giving military aid to the Allies he was inclined to yield to the persistent importunities of the Allied representatives in Washington. In the actual conduct of operations I was given entire freedom and in this respect was to enjoy an experience unique in our history.

On May 27th, the day before I was to sail, the Secretary of War sent me a letter of instructions concerning my command, authority and duties in Europe, which is quoted here in full:

"WAR DEPARTMENT
"Washington

"May 26, 1917.

"SECRET

"FROM: The Secretary of War.

"To: Major General J. J. Pershing, U. S. Army.

"SUBJECT: Command, Authority and Duties in Europe.

"The President directs me to communicate to you the following:

"1. The President designates you to command all the land forces of the United States operating in Continental Europe and in the United Kingdom of Great Britain and Ireland, including any part of the Marine Corps which may be detached for service there with the Army. From your command are excepted the Military Attachés and others of the Army who may be on duty directly with our several embassies.

"2. You will proceed with your staff to Europe. Upon arrival in Great Britain, France or any other of the countries at war with the Imperial German Government, you will at once place yourself in communication with the American Embassy and through its agency with the authorities of any country to which the forces of the United States may be sent.

"3. You are invested with the authority and duties devolved by the laws, regulations, orders and customs of the United States upon the commander of an army in the field in time of war and with the authority and duties in like manner devolved upon department commanders in peace and war, including the special authorities and duties assigned to the commander of the Philippine Department in so far as the same are applicable to the particular circumstances of your command.

"4. You will establish, after consultation with the French War Office, all necessary bases, lines of communication, depots, etc., and make all the incidental arrangements essential to active participation at the front.

"5. In military operations against the Imperial German Government, you are directed to coöperate with the forces of the other countries employed against that enemy; but in so doing the underlying idea must be kept in view that the forces of the United States are a separate and distinct component of the combined forces, the identity of which must be preserved. This fundamental rule is subject to such minor exceptions in particular circumstances as your judgment may approve. The decision as to when your command, or any of its parts, is ready for action is confided to you, and you will exercise full discretion in determining the manner of coöperation. But,

until the forces of the United States are in your judgment sufficiently
strong to warrant operations as an independent command, it is understood that you will coöperate as a component of whatever army you
may be assigned to by the French Government.

"6. You will keep the Department fully advised of all that concerns your command, and will communicate your recommendations
freely and directly to the Department. And in general you are vested
with all necessary authority to carry on the war vigorously in harmony
with the spirit of these instructions and towards a victorious conclusion.

"Newton D. Baker."

At the same time, the Chief of Staff handed me a letter, which
is also quoted in full:

"War Department
"Office of the Chief of Staff
"Washington, D. C.,
"May 26, 1917.

"Secret

"Major General John J. Pershing, U. S. A.,

"Washington, D. C.,

"Dear General Pershing:

"In compliance with the orders of the President assigning you to
the command of the United States forces in France, the Secretary
of War directs that you proceed, with the necessary staff, to Paris,
France, via England.

"The Secretary of War further directs that, upon your arrival in
France, you establish such relations with the French Government and
the military representatives of the British Government now serving
in France as will enable you effectively to plan and conduct active
operations in conjunction and in coöperation with the French armies
operating in France against Germany and her allies.

"As a preliminary step, the Secretary of War deems it desirable
that you have a thorough study made of the available bases, lines of
communication and camps of instruction, so that you may direct
preparations for the arrival of successive contingents of our troops in
France. The equipment and training for active service of the troops
under your command in the trenches or on the firing line should
be carried on as rapidly as possible. While the entrance of our forces
into the theater of active operations will be left entirely to your judgment, it should not be unduly hastened. Yet it is believed that the
purpose of your presence in France will be materially advanced by the
appearance of our troops upon the firing line.

"The Secretary of War desires that you keep the department fully advised of all questions of importance concerning the operations of your troops and that you submit your views from time to time upon such questions, as well as upon matters pertaining to the general situation in Europe. He also expects that, as the superior military representative of the United States in France, you will exercise such general authority as will best contribute to the fulfillment of your mission in France.

"Very sincerely,
"Tasker H. Bliss,
"Major General,
"Acting Chief of Staff."

I have never understood why there should have been two letters of instructions emanating from the same authority. However, they are both admirable examples of the powers that should be vested in a commander in the field and were never changed or amplified in any essential. The insertion of the directions contained in paragraph five of the Secretary's letter regarding the identity of our forces was prompted by the efforts which had been made by both the British and French Missions to have the United States utilize her manpower as replacements for the Allies. But the policy of building up eventually an independent American army had been discussed and was fully understood by the Secretary of War and myself.

As to coöperation, the instructions contained in the two letters are apparently in conflict. According to the Secretary's letter it might be that our armies would actually serve in conjunction with any of the Allied armies. According to the letter of the Chief of Staff it would be limited to service in coöperation with the French Army. However, the general character of our mission was such as to indicate clearly that our forces should operate in combination with any of the Allied armies in France, according to circumstances.

CHAPTER IV

Voyage to Europe—Arrival in Liverpool and London—Reception by the King—Divine Service at Westminster Abbey—Trip to Cliveden—Luncheon at Buckingham Palace—Call on General Robertson—Visit to Parliament House—Dinner by Ambassador Page—Visit to Training Center—Luncheon with Lord Derby, Minister of War—State Dinner at Lancaster House—Resolute Air of People—Departure for Paris

MY party assembled at Governors Island on the date of sailing and we left from there to go aboard the British steamship *Baltic*. Upon my arrival at his headquarters, Major General J. Franklin Bell, then in command of the Eastern Department, most warmly extended his greetings and congratulations and presented the officers of his staff. After a brief conversation, he drove with me to the pier and reminded me of his letter in which he had asked for an active command. Knowing his physical condition, I was forced to remain noncommittal to this very dear friend. Though several years senior to me in rank and service, he would have served loyally, and I should have been fortunate to have had him, as his experience would have made him invaluable.

Despite persistent and powerful opposition in and out of the Army, General Bell, while Chief of Staff, had succeeded in developing through our service schools an effective system of training a limited number of officers for command and staff duty, and for this contribution to our success he deserves high praise. It was a source of keenest regret to me later that his failing health made it impossible to permit him to undertake arduous service in the field. His last days were filled with sadness and disappointment at not being allowed again to lead American soldiers in battle. It can be said of Franklin Bell that our army has never produced a finer type of officer and gentleman.

41

All of my party had been directed to proceed with the utmost secrecy, even to the extent of wearing civilian clothes until we reached the ship. Although we stole silently aboard the tender that carried us out through the fog and down the bay, the large number of quartermaster and other officers stationed near New York dashing about in uniform rather ostentatiously that day really gave notice that something out of the ordinary was happening. As if this were not sufficient notice the large number of boxes and crates piled up on the dock, addressed to various chiefs of supply departments, A.E.F., in my care, and the artillery salute fired from the batteries on Governors Island made the announcement of our departure complete. It can be said to the credit of the representatives of the press, however, that they were most discreet, as the newspapers in general published nothing about us until after we had landed in Europe.

It was the purpose of the British Admiralty, from which all their ships received sailing orders, to transfer my party to another vessel at Halifax, but after lying off that port in thick weather for about forty-eight hours the *Baltic* was directed to steer her course to a designated rendezvous.

Among the passengers were several British and Canadian officers with distinguished service at the front to their credit. They kindly consented to answer questions on the subjects of organization, training, and fighting. The conferences thus held and a study of confidential reports from the British and French helped to put us more closely in touch with many details which could not have been learned otherwise except through experience. The study of the French language was also taken up by many of the officers and refresher classes were in session at all hours under direction of those who had sufficient knowledge to become teachers.

One evening was given over to the customary entertainment for the benefit of British seamen's families, in which several of us took part as speakers, including one of the British officers; Mr. Frederick Palmer, the war correspondent; Mr. Charles H. Grasty, of the *New York Times;* and myself. The national anthems of the Allies and our own *Star Spangled Banner* were sung with enthusiasm, and on the whole the evening was given a pronounced inter-allied flavor.

During the voyage most of my time was spent in discussion with the heads of staff departments regarding their respective duties and plans. Major Harbord and I considered an organization for the General Staff, and the skeleton outline of principles then approved became the basis of the larger organization later adopted after a study of French and British general staff systems. Arrangements were made and officers designated to initiate immediately upon arrival in England and later to carry on in France the necessary investigations concerning ports, railways, and possible lines of communications. It was on board the *Baltic* that I tentatively decided that as a beginning we should plan for an army of at least 1,000,000 men to reach France as early as possible. Preliminary consideration was also given to such important subjects as the composition and organization of our forces; where they could best operate for decisive action; their relation to the Allied armies; and the availability of shipping for the transportation and supply of our troops.

The commander of the *Baltic,* Captain Finch, was a typical British sea-dog, who inspired every one with confidence in his efficiency. He very properly insisted that all should attend boat drills and each one become familiar with his assignment in case it should be necessary to abandon ship. In passing through the danger zone we all wore civilian clothing as it was certain that in the event of a successful attack by a German submarine its crew would fire upon any small boat carrying men in uniform.

On June 5th the *Baltic* began to zigzag on her course and we then realized that we were actually in the danger zone. The next morning the sight of an escort of two American destroyers, the *Tucker* and the *Rowan,* steaming well out on our flanks gave all on board somewhat of a thrill and fully restored confidence. Although there were many rumors and occasional alarms, no submarines were observed. The weather was perfect throughout the voyage except for the fog about Halifax, and if we had been going over for pleasure it would have been a delightful trip. But we were all very busy and kept at work without interference except by our medical officers, who, not to be remiss in their immediate obligations, vaccinated us every day or so against all the diseases that might be prevented by such measures.

(Diary) London, Sunday, June 10, 1917. Arrived at Liverpool on Friday morning and London that afternoon. Attended dinner given by the officials of the British War Office.

On Saturday paid a visit to Buckingham Palace, accompanied by my staff, and went from there to our Embassy. Called on the Duke of Connaught.

Attended divine services to-day at Westminster Abbey with several members of my staff. I accompanied Ambassador and Mrs. Walter Hines Page to the country for luncheon with Major and Lady Astor, and returned after dining with General Sir Arthur and Lady Paget.

We reached our anchorage in the Mersey River on the evening of June 7th and steamed into Liverpool the next morning under a clear sky. I had been in Europe twice before, my first visit being in September, 1899, en route to the Philippine Islands, as a bachelor, and the next in the autumn of 1908, on leave of absence, en route home from a second tour in the Islands, accompanied by my wife and two small children. The sojourn in France with my family had been filled with delightful visits to friends and with motor trips to historic places. The recollection of those happy days often came back to me very vividly in striking contrast with the troublous days of the war.

The *Baltic* reached the dock at 9:30 A.M., and a cordial reception awaited us. Rear Admiral Stileman, of the British Navy, and Sir Pitcairne Campbell, K.C.B., commanding the Western District of Home Defense, with the Lord Mayor and Lady Mayoress, came on board at once. After formal introductions, I went ashore with our hosts, accompanied by the principal members of my staff, to return the salute and walk through the ranks of the guard of honor. As we stepped off the gangplank onto British soil, the band struck up the *Star Spangled Banner* to welcome us, this being the first time in history that an American Army contingent was ever officially received in England.

The very smart-looking guard of honor was from the 3d Battalion, Royal Welch Fusiliers, and most of the men in ranks had seen service in France, many of them proudly wearing wound chevrons. Not the least picturesque member of the detachment was the thoroughly groomed, ribbon-bedecked goat, the regimental mascot, which strode up and down with an air of considerable importance.

The selection of the Royal Welch Fusiliers as guard of honor had a sentimental significance in that the regiment not only fought against us at Bunker Hill but it fought beside us during the Boxer Rebellion in China. An interesting feature of the uniform of the Royal Welch was a black patch on the neck and upper part of the back of the tunic. During our Revolutionary War they wore the periwig with its queue, and while serving in Nova Scotia after having fought in the British Army from Bunker Hill to Yorktown they learned that it had been discontinued. As the last regiment to wear the queue, they took the ribbons with which it had been tied and sewed them on their tunics. This "flash" was later recognized officially as a distinctive mark of their uniform. The preservation of this badge of former service struck all of us as a characteristic example of the conservatism of the British that served so well during the World War to hold the people to their traditional obligations.

Following the reception on the wharf, we returned on board and stood along the rail at the salute while the band played *God Save the King*. The formalities being over, about fifty British and American newspaper men assembled in the lounging room for an interview. My natural aversion to that sort of thing was strongly reënforced by the conviction that this was not the time to do much talking. After evading several questions, I finally yielded to their insistence and said:

> "Speaking for myself personally, the officers of my staff, and the members of my command, we are very glad indeed to be the standard bearers of our country in this great war for civilization. To land on British soil and to receive the welcome accorded us seems very significant and is deeply appreciated. We expect in course of time

to be playing our part, and we hope it will be a very large part, on the Western Front."

The royal coach was attached to a special train for our use and after leave-taking we pulled out for London. En route Captain Charles de Marenches, of the French Army, who had been sent by General Pétain, reported for duty as a member of my personal staff, in which position he rendered invaluable service throughout the war.

Within a few hours our train reached Euston Station, where we were heartily welcomed by Lord Derby, Secretary of State for War; Field Marshal Sir John French; Lieutenant General Sir Francis Lloyd; Brigadier General Lord Brooke; Mr. Walter H. Page, the American Ambassador; Admiral William S. Sims, U.S.N., and many others. We were escorted to the Savoy Hotel and became guests of the British Government. There was nothing unusual to mark our arrival except the cordial reception at the station and a few complimentary notices in the press. Our appearance on the streets attracted little attention, as many of our military men had passed through England on one mission or another and the American uniform had become a common sight in London.

That evening the senior members of my party were tendered a dinner at the Savoy by members of the British War Office and we had an excellent opportunity to meet and get acquainted with many officials who were later on to be of material assistance to us. Brigadier General Lord Brooke was assigned as my aide while in England and Major Maitland Kersey kindly acted as guide about London. It was on one of my visits with the latter to a tailor shop that I first met Field Marshal, then General, Lord Allenby, who later achieved fame in the campaign in Palestine. Several officers were detailed to look out for members of the staff and arrange for them to meet the heads of the British staff departments whom they wished to consult.

Together with my senior staff officers, I was invited to visit the King at Buckingham Palace on the morning of June 9th. His Majesty, smartly dressed in the uniform of a Field Marshal, received me in democratic fashion for a few minutes before the others were presented. I gave him the President's message, to which he replied with high praise of Mr. Wilson, commenting upon the very large war powers of our Chief Executive. His Majesty was pleased that America had come into the war and dwelt upon the fact that Anglo-Saxon peoples were at last united in a common cause. He mentioned the great cost of the war, the large numbers of men Great Britain had already furnished the Army and Navy, and the tremendous losses they had suffered. He severely condemned the German submarine atrocities and told of the recent sinking of several vessels with the loss of practically all on board. He was not optimistic over the outlook and expressed the hope that we "would send over a large number of destroyers." As to aviation, he had heard through the dispatches the extravagant claims of certain boastful Americans and he asked me whether we really expected soon to have 50,000 airplanes in the field. I had to acknowledge that such reports were extremely exaggerated and that we should not be sending over any planes for some time to come.

He inquired particularly regarding the organization of our Army and the prospects of our bringing a large force to France. I explained the Draft Act and what I thought would be the plans of the War Department, but it turned out that my views were rather optimistic, at least as to the immediate future. He mentioned with satisfaction the successful explosion on June 7th of extensive mines under an important German position on Messines Ridge, which was subsequently captured by the British. Incidentally, I visited this spot after the close of the war and found that the craters had become large lakes, one of which was being used at the moment as a bathing pool by hundreds of German prisoners employed in clearing the débris from the battlefields. His Majesty was exceedingly well informed, interesting and earnest, and his informal manner made one feel quite at ease.

When I presented my staff he spoke a few words of welcome, and among other things said:

"It has always been my dream that the two English-speaking nations should some day be united in a great cause, and to-day my dream is realized. Together we are fighting for the greatest cause for which peoples could fight. The Anglo-Saxon race must save civilization."

Leaving the palace, we went to our Embassy and the members of my staff were presented to the Ambassador by my old friend, Irwin Laughlin, the Counselor, with whom I had served at our Legation in Tokyo when I was there as Military Attaché. During the conversation which followed, Mr. Page remarked how happy he was that America was at last in the war, and added, "Now I am able to hold up my head and look people squarely in the eye." He said he had always believed it our duty to help the Allies and that many times in trying to maintain cordial relations between the two Governments he had been tremendously handicapped, but now his task would be less difficult. He was very modest and unassuming, but his courage, his broad knowledge of affairs and his practical common sense enabled him to render distinguished service to our country during a distressing period. Throughout his career as ambassador he was beloved and honored by the British people, who admired his virile personality. Many Americans, however, did not approve of his rather apologetic attitude toward his own country prior to our entry into the war.

I had a talk with Admiral Sims, who was not in personal command of our fleet serving with the British Navy, but remained in London with an office at our Embassy and directed the movements of our naval vessels, especially destroyers, from there. He was not satisfied with the support given him from home and complained that the Navy Department had not sent all the destroyers asked for. He said the Department seemed to fear attacks along our coast and did not realize the danger to the cause in the enormous destruction of merchant shipping going on in European waters. His report of these losses was nothing short of startling, but he thought they might be checked if he could have a sufficient number of destroyers. Without more of this class of vessels, Sims was not sanguine over the prospects of protecting our transports. However, he made it clear that every possible effort would be made to that end. This conversation increased my anxiety about getting the American forces to France in time to beat the German armies before they could gain a decision over the Allies.

Our objective was well defined and we could not delay for the possible destruction of the German submarine fleet. The war could not be ended until the German land forces were beaten. Troop movements overseas had been conducted in previous wars while hostile fleets were intact. I was with the Shafter Expedition in 1898, and sailed from Tampa, Florida, for Santiago, Cuba, while the Spanish fleet was still in being, and had seen Japanese transports cross the China Sea en route for Manchuria while Russian fleets were in existence. Irrespective of the outcome of the warfare being waged against submarines, we had to assume the risks and put our armies into the battle at the earliest moment if the Allies were to have the superiority which was necessary to defeat the Germans.

After the usual visits of courtesy to the houses of the other members of the royal family, I called by appointment on Field Marshal the Duke of Connaught. His intimate knowledge of American affairs in general, acquired, no doubt, while he was Governor General of Canada, and of our military history in particular, made the call most interesting. As a soldier of experience, the Field Marshal, more than any other official in England with whom I talked, seemed to realize the difficulties that lay before us and the time it would take to overcome them.

Nothing that occurred while we were in London left me with a deeper impression of British stamina than the religious services at Westminster. The Archbishop of Canterbury spoke feelingly of the nation's sacrifices and, referring to our presence, expressed confidence in the successful issue of the war. I had visited the Abbey before, but this joint meeting there with the British, high and low, amidst the old things, the traditions, the history, seemed to symbolize the unity of aims and purposes of our two peoples, through which, fighting shoulder to shoulder, we should one day achieve the victory.

The drive with the Pages from London to Cliveden through the well-kept countryside was delightful. The Ambassador told me that Lady Astor and her husband had been very helpful to him since he had been in England and he wanted us to meet them. When we arrived, they greeted us cordially, introduced their four children and made us feel entirely at home. Lady Astor, a native of Virginia, whom everybody called Nancy, was quite as informal as she ever could have been as Miss Langhorne back where she was born. We soon found ourselves seated with some twenty people at the luncheon table, over which she presided with simple dignity.

In the afternoon we strolled through the estate and presently came to the Canadian hospital nearby, where Lady Astor was hailed with affection. As we went through the wards she seemed to know every man by name and had a cheerful word for each one. My visit to this hospital was my first contact with the tragic side of the war. At her request, I was glad to speak to a group of convalescent soldiers assembled on the lawn, who accepted my remarks, no doubt, as coming from a neighbor who spoke their dialect. It was altogether an interesting afternoon, made so particularly by our charming hostess who had adapted herself to British surroundings without sacrifice of the dominant American traits so evident in her character.

In the evening several of us, including Harbord, Alvord and Brewster of my staff, had dinner with General Sir Arthur and Lady Paget, in company with Ambassador and Mrs. Page, Lady Drogheda and Mrs. Leeds. Lady Paget, formerly Miss Stevens, of New York, was very happy at the news that one of her sons had been promoted to the grade of Brigadier General. Sir Arthur had passed the age for active service and at the moment was in command of Home Defense Forces.

(Diary) London, Monday, June 11, 1917. In company with the Pages had luncheon with the King and Queen and Princess Mary.

In the afternoon called on General Robertson and visited Parliament House. Attended dinner given by the American Ambassador.

There was an air of charm and simplicity at Buckingham Palace that permitted a freedom in the conversation more or less intimate. The plain fare was quite in keeping with the food situation throughout England. All were enthusiastic over our entry into the war and hopeful that we might soon participate actively. After leaving the luncheon table, the King, the Ambassador and I stood near a window overlooking the garden, which, as his Majesty explained, instead of growing flowers as usual was producing a crop of potatoes. He told of the visit of the Kaiser to London a few years before and how he had brought his Chief of Secret Service along and put him up at one of the hotels to learn all he could, while the Kaiser himself was, of course, a guest at the Palace.

His Majesty spoke bitterly of the inhumanity of the Germans and dwelt especially on the night bombing of London. Pointing to the beautiful statue of Queen Victoria, just outside of the window, he said, with a solemn expression of profound indignation, "The Kaiser has even tried to destroy the statue of his own grandmother." If the resentment of King George at the air raids over London reflected the feelings of his people, then the German Government made a very serious blunder in carrying on this hideous form of warfare against the unarmed masses, of whom the greater part were women and children. There is no doubt that these attacks served to strengthen British determination to fight to the last man.

After leaving the Palace, I called on General Sir William Robertson, Chief of the Imperial General Staff. He was a rugged, heavy-set, blunt soldier, of Scottish descent, whose record in the army had been exceptional in that he had risen from the grade of private to his high position. As he sipped his tea, I explained our plan for the organization of our armies by raising the small Regular force and the National Guard to war strength and training additional units besides. As the British themselves had gone through the same experience about two years before, I stressed the fact that the latter process would take considerable time. Like all the British officials, he was much in favor of having our army serve with or near their forces. He pointed out that we were both Anglo-Saxons, spoke the same language, and gave other reasons to support his views. It seemed necessary to explain in detail that as the American Navy was working in conjunction with the British Navy we should probably plan to place our land forces beside the French if there were to be any preference. It appeared logical that we should do this as we were to operate on French soil and use French ports, railways and matériel. The main thing, I went on to say, was to form our own army as soon as possible and use it to the best advantage in beating the Germans.

I emphasized our lack of tonnage and told him that we must have additional shipping if we were to bring over an army worth while, but his reaction to this was not encouraging. He said he thought that it was entirely out of the question for the British to provide us with any shipping since they were already in sore straits to find vessels for their own national necessities.

At Parliament House I met several of the members and had tea on the terrace overlooking the Thames with Mr. Winston Churchill, then Minister of Munitions. Unusually well informed on American affairs, he showed the keenest interest in our plans and prospects. The equipment of our armies was naturally one of mutual concern and I found him ready to provide British artillery if necessary. We had, however, already practically decided to adopt the French types of artillery.

In the evening a few of us were entertained at dinner [1] by the American Ambassador. I had suggested to him that I much preferred not to have a formal dinner, as we had come on a

[1] Among those present were Mr. Lloyd George, Prime Minister; Mr. Arthur Balfour, Minister of Foreign Affairs; M. Paul Cambon, French Ambassador; Lord Derby, Minister for War; Lord Robert Cecil; Admiral Jellicoe; Admiral W. R. Hall; General Sir William Robertson; General Macdonogh; General Sir John Cowans, Quartermaster General; General Sir Francis Lloyd; Field Marshal Viscount French; Mr. W. H. Page, American Ambassador; Admiral Sims; General Smuts, of Boer War fame; Mr. Irwin Laughlin, Counselor of the Embassy; Col. Wm. Lassiter, Military Attaché; and Mr. Edward Bell, First Secretary.

serious mission, but he was so elated that our country was in the war that he insisted on our meeting some of his British friends in this way. It was a notable company of men in official life, civil, military and naval. Our activity as participants in the war was to bring us into contact with every one of them during the succeeding two years.

(Diary) London, Tuesday, June 12, 1917. Spent a most interesting forenoon visiting the training center of General Paget's command, where recruits are given a nine weeks' course before going to the front. Returned to the city for luncheon with Lord and Lady Derby and later called on Mr. Lloyd George. Attended State dinner.

At the training camp we witnessed an interesting demonstration of British methods of making an attack, including the tactical formations of successive thin lines, the employment of special weapons incident to trench fighting, and defense against gas. With the use of trench mortars and hand grenades the exercise was more realistic than anything we had so far seen in our own service. Most of the men engaged were unfit for active duty at the front, many of them having been wounded or sent home ill and only sufficiently convalescent to be useful for home defense or for training new drafts. Many British officers realized that the period of nine weeks' training for recruits was insufficient, but such preparation was for trench warfare only. Much to my surprise they gave little thought to the possibilities of open warfare in the near future, if at all.

On our return to London a few of us were guests at an informal luncheon given by the Secretary of State for War and Lady Derby. Their hospitality was only equalled by Lord Derby's very earnest desire in his official capacity to be of service to us. He was more than courteous and during my short stay we formed a friendship that later made coöperation easy wherever his authority was concerned. According to arrangements which he kindly made, his assistants took a personal interest in giving the members of my staff every facility for the study of British combat formations, tactical training, supply and replacement systems, and for consultation with their experienced staff officers on all subjects that would aid us in completing our staff and line organizations.

Mr. Lloyd George, the Prime Minister, when I met him, went right to the point and inquired as to when our troops would be organized and trained and the numbers we expected to send over. He was affable and expressed a desire to help us in every possible manner, but when I stressed our need of assistance to transport our troops he did not seem to be particularly interested and gave little hope that the British would be able to furnish us any shipping whatever.

In the evening a State dinner [1] was given at Lancaster House to the senior members of my party. It was official without being either stiff or formal and was intended not only as a social welcome tendered us by about twenty of the leading officials of the Government but as a gathering for friendly discussion. The British, of course, wanted to show their satisfaction that we were in the war, although I feared that they were building too high their hopes of early American aid.

Much to my gratification, the speeches were limited to toasts to the King and the President. Mr. Lloyd George, who presided, was in excellent humor and frequently joked with his confrères at his own and other tables. Lord Curzon was late in arriving, which the Prime Minister said was no doubt due to the fact that he had lately taken a young American wife. And he added that the delay reminded him of French officials, who were proverbially late. The various social functions which we attended in England and France occupied considerable time, but they were the means of establishing good feeling and understanding, so important for a beginning.

Underneath the surface of the seeming cheerfulness there was

---

[1] Attended by Mr. G. N. Barnes, M.P.; General Lord Brooke; Sir Edward Carson; Lord Robert Cecil; Major Spender Clay; Mr. H. J. Creedy; Earl Curzon; Lt. Gen. Sir F. Davies; Sir M. de Bunsen; The Earl of Derby; The Hon. Sir Eric Drummond; Mr. H. W. Forster; General Furse; Lord Hardinge of Penhurst; Gen. Sir D. Henderson; Col. James; Major Maitland Kersey; Sir Guy Laking; Col. Lassiter, U.S.A.; Gen. Macdonogh; Capt. MacDougall; Mr. J. I. MacPherson; Viscount Milner; Mr. W. H. Page, the United States Ambassador; Admiral Sims, U. S. Navy; Mr. R. F. Synge; Mr. Andrew Weir.

more than a suggestion of serious apprehension. U-boat activities were spoken of almost in whispers. At the dinner, we were again told of the total losses, which, including April, had reached 3,000,000 tons, and during April and May amounted to 1,500,000 tons. It was an appalling increase. The figures could not be given out, of course, for fear the knowledge would hearten the enemy and frighten the Allied peoples, and the public did not know until long afterward just how grave the situation was. From a rough calculation, it was easy to conclude that if the destruction of British shipping continued at that rate there would soon be none left either to help transport an American army to Europe or to supply it after arrival.

Under the circumstances, the apparent unconcern of the British as to our need of shipping is not difficult to understand. They were seriously alarmed regarding their own food situation. It seemed to me, however, that they had allowed their pessimism to carry them too far, but at the moment they could see no relief for the future and hence no prospect of aiding us in tonnage.

In the bearing and attitude of the people in general there was little to indicate the uneasiness which they felt regarding the outcome of the war, although one frequently caught a troubled expression among the faces of people in the streets. There was, naturally, considerable military activity to be seen, but the people went about their business apparently in the usual fashion. The shortage of food and the continuous air raids at night had a depressing effect. From nearly every family some member was numbered among the dead, but there were few women in mourning. In the seacoast towns there was said to be considerable fear of invasion, much the same, no doubt, as existed along our Atlantic seaboard during the Spanish-American War, so that probably larger forces than necessary were held for home defenses to satisfy coast residents. The burden of three years of war, with no end in sight, bore heavily upon the people and hidden forebodings filled many a heart. Still underneath all this there was an unflinching courage and dogged determination that held the man at the front up to his task and the people at home solidly behind him. London was the objective for men on leave for a few days and individuals or groups of the various units were easily identified, from the "Tommy," smart in his plain uniform of dark khaki, and the bare-kneed Highlander in checkered kilts, to the Canadian and Australian in campaign hats much like our own. They were over from France for a change and rest, newcomers constantly taking the places of others as the brief period of vacation expired. Under the surface these soldiers perhaps saw more of depression than the casual observer and most of them were glad to get back to the front, where "things were different," they said.

Early on the morning of June 13th we were off for France, and after taking leave of our hosts or their representatives we boarded a special train for Folkestone, where we took the Channel boat to Boulogne. We left with the feeling that our stay in London had been pleasant, in spite of war conditions, and above all, that it had been profitable. Much detailed information was obtained while in England that was to be of the greatest value to us later on.

CHAPTER V

Landing at Boulogne—Enthusisastic Welcome in Paris—Visit Tomb of
Napoleon—Call on President Poincaré—Luncheon at Élysée Palace—
Visit General Pétain's Headquarters—Résumé of General Situation
—Failure of Nivelle Offensive—Resulting Depression

AFTER an exceptionally smooth passage our cross-Channel
boat reached Boulogne about 10 A.M., and there, lined up
at present arms under the covered dock, stood a guard
of honor of French Territorials in field uniform, while the band
played the American and French national anthems. Then both
civil and military representatives came on board with enthusiastic
greetings. As we stepped on shore with our new hosts, we were
made doubly welcome in words that expressed both gratitude
and hope. It was a significant and solemn moment and I am
sure that each one of us silently wished that our Army might have
been more nearly ready to fulfill the mission that loomed so
large before us. The French troops, together with the assembled
men, women, and children from the town in the background,
presented a colorful picture, and as we walked along the ranks
of the guard of honor it was observed that their stripes and
decorations indicated that every man had seen service at the
front.

Among those who came to greet us were the Under-Secretary
of War, M. Besnard; Colonel Jacques Aldebert de Chambrun,
who later became one of my aides; Brigadier General Peltier, a
one-armed veteran, who was to be liaison officer at my headquarters; Brigadier General Duport, representing Major General
Pétain; Major Thouzellier, representing Marshal Joffre; Admiral
Ronarc'h, representing the Navy; Major General Dumas, commanding troops in the North; the Prefect and other local French

officials; and Lieutenant General Fowke, Adjutant General of the British Expeditionary Force.[1]

There was some delay in our departure for Paris, and to pass the time we were taken to see the old sixteenth century fort overlooking the harbor, which it formerly protected. Although the railway to Paris runs through an attractive part of France, our five days in London had been so strenuous that I retired to my compartment for a rest and did not see much of the country. The journey, as I afterwards learned, was regulated so that we should arrive about the close of business hours in the evening in order that the French people might take part in an impromptu welcome, the idea being to give them visual evidence that Americans were actually coming.

The officials who met us at the station included M. Painlevé, Minister of War;[2] Marshal Joffre; M. Viviani; Major General Foch, then Chief of Staff; Ambassador William G. Sharp, and many others. There was nothing formal about our reception, in fact it was cordially informal, simple and brief, with no speech-making, and consisted merely of introductions all around. The station was packed with people and the atmosphere seemed electrical with pent-up enthusiasm. In the assignment to automobiles, M. Painlevé and I were placed together and took the lead, followed by the members of my staff, each with a distinguished French companion.

The acclaim that greeted us as we drove through the streets en route to the hotel was to me a complete surprise. Dense masses of people lined the boulevards and filled the squares. It was said that never before in the history of Paris had there been such an outpouring of people. Men, women, and children absolutely packed every foot of space, even to the windows and

---

[1] In the French armies there are two grades of general officer: Brigadier General and Major General, the next and highest rank being Marshal. In the British armies the grades are Brigadier General, Major General, Lieutenant General, and General, then Field Marshal. In our service we follow the British except that General is the highest rank.

[2] M. Painlevé became Prime Minister in September, 1917, but continued to hold the portfolio of Minister of War.

housetops. Cheers and tears were mingled together and shouts of enthusiasm fairly rent the air. Women climbed into our automobiles screaming, "Vive l'Amérique," and threw flowers until we were literally buried. Everybody waved flags and banners. At several points the masses surged into the streets, entirely beyond control of the police.

In every possible manner the French gave full sway to their emotions. It is not easy to imagine that any people could be so wildly demonstrative. It was most touching and in a sense most pathetic. It brought home to us as nothing else could have done a full appreciation of the war-weary state of the nation and stirred within us a deep sense of the responsibility resting upon America. After our arrival at the Crillon Hotel I was again and again forced to appear on the portico of my apartment to greet the dense crowds that lingered in the Place de la Concorde. The acclaim by the people of Paris was in no sense a personal tribute to me like that given to Marshal Joffre in America. It was simply a spontaneous outburst of joy over the evidence of support from a nation whose traditional friendship was sincere and unselfish. I was to see its parallel when the Armistice was signed and on two other occasions, once when President Wilson arrived, and later when the Victory Parade took place on July 14, 1919.

A group of press representatives, largely French, called later for an interview and my knowledge of their language was immediately put to the test. After a sentence or two I concluded in my mother tongue and for some time thereafter limited further attempts to an occasional familiar phrase. Former Ambassador, "Uncle Bob" Bacon, as he was informally known at my headquarters, used to tell how Mr. Roosevelt "murdered" the language in his speech before the French Institute, and this gave me courage to try again in an address here and there.

On the evening of our arrival Ambassador and Mrs. Sharp gave a dinner for me and the principal officers of my staff, which was attended by many distinguished French civil and military officials and several members of the American colony. No one could have been more elated than the Ambassador, who no doubt expressed the sentiments of all Americans in France when, with trembling voice, he said: "You cannot realize the satisfaction I feel that we are in the war and that you are here to prepare for our participation. It is a great day for America and for France. The civilian now gives way to the soldier," and he added, "I hope you have not arrived too late." That same thought was in everybody's mind, so low was the morale of Allied peoples and their armies.

(Diary) Paris, Thursday, June 14, 1917. There never could have been another welcome such as that given us yesterday by the populace of Paris. Difficult to see how we are to meet the expectations of the French. To-day I visited Les Invalides, including Napoleon's tomb. Called on President Poincaré and had luncheon with him and Madame Poincaré at the Palace. Afterwards went to the Chamber of Deputies, thence to Le Bourget aviation field. Later called on the Minister of Marine. Dined with the Minister of War.

Although I was very anxious to get to work, it was necessary for me to make certain official calls and attend a few entertainments that had been planned for us. The French suggested that we should first go to visit Napoleon's tomb in Les Invalides. Founded in the reign of Louis XIV as a hospital for disabled veterans, the building has become the great French war museum and now contains, as every one knows, many beautiful works of art, together with relics that cover the history of French wars for generations.

We were taken to the tomb of Napoleon and down to the crypt, where I was handed the great key and was asked to unlock the heavy wrought iron entrance door. We were shown the uniforms and the baton that belonged to Napoleon and then his sword. Our veteran escort reverently removed the sword from the case and offered it to me as if to transmit some of the genius of the great captain. So much of French sentiment and tradition are associated with this tomb and its treasures that every one who visits there with Frenchmen must share their feelings of profound emotion. This incident, more than any other connected with my reception, impressed me with the martial spirit of the French people.

I called next to pay my respects to President Poincaré and to present greetings from President Wilson. "The French people are very happy," he said, "that America is in the war. Your coming is a great satisfaction to us." He inquired generally about our plans, seeking, as they all did, some assurance that we should soon be in the trenches. His attitude was rather formal and reserved, but he at once impressed me as a man of ability and force.

The President and Madame Poincaré invited me and several members of the staff to the Élysée Palace to luncheon, which was delightful in every particular. Nowhere are such things done so well as in Paris at the palace of the President. The plate, the silver, the linen are models of taste, while the menu and service find no parallel elsewhere. M. and Mme. Poincaré both understand English thoroughly and she speaks it perfectly. From her account, and that of many others, of the deplorable conditions and the sorrow throughout France, I seriously wondered whether the morale of the people could be restored. She felt certain that it could be and cheerfully added that our presence had already heartened them.

In the afternoon I visited the Chamber of Deputies in company with our Ambassador and heard a speech by M. Viviani in which he referred with much feeling to his reception in the United States and mentioned his having been privileged to deliver an address before Congress. His eloquence over America's entrance into the war and what it meant to France caused prolonged cheering and an enthusiastic recognition of our presence by the Deputies.

Later on several of us went to the aviation field at Le Bourget, where we saw numbers of airplanes always held in readiness to take the air against raids by enemy aircraft. The defense system also included the latest developments in anti-aircraft guns, both at Le Bourget and in the suburbs. The exhibition of attack and pursuit formations and of other expert flying left us with the painful thought that our aviation had a long way to go to attain similar efficiency.

Incidentally, I must mention our wild automobile ride to Le Bourget. Not to be outdone by aviators, the Prefect of Police directed our car through the crowded streets of Paris at not less than sixty miles an hour, all the while yelling and swinging his arms and scattering traffic right and left as though we were going to a fire. Every block furnished a new sensation, each hair-breadth escape from a crash being more narrow than the one before. This was far too dangerous for me, so, yielding to my protests, the Prefect on the return trip broke no more records for speed.

I next called on the Minister of Marine, M. Lacaze, who dwelt on the gravity of the losses by submarines and the consequent menace of food shortage. France was actually dependent for her food supply upon some 1,200,000 tons of British shipping that had been allotted to her use. Although the Minister claimed that the food situation was becoming serious, the British held that the French Government failed to limit the consumption of food by the people to the same extent they did.

In the evening the Minister of War gave us a dinner, where we met several members of the Cabinet and made some new and important acquaintances. The dinner was held at the Ministry in a room fitted up for the occasion with rich tapestries and other decorations. It was a sort of get-together party that marked the real starting point of our association with the various French bureaus and their chiefs.

(Diary) Paris, Saturday, June 16, 1917. Lunched yesterday with Marshal and Madame Joffre at the Military Club. He and I were called to the veranda several times to greet the crowds. Visited the Senate and met its President, M. Dubost, and other Senators. In company with the Marquis de Chambrun and his brother, Colonel de Chambrun, descendants of Lafayette, drove to Picpus Cemetery and placed a wreath on Lafayette's tomb.

Harbord and I visited the French General Headquarters at Compiègne to-day and had luncheon with Major General Pétain. Went

to front lines near Saint Quentin with Major General d'Espérey and got our first glimpse of enemy positions.
Attended special performance at the Opéra Comique this evening in my honor.

The visit to French General Headquarters was primarily to meet General Pétain and the officers of his staff. Pétain is above medium height and weight, he wore a full mustache, slightly gray, and was then about sixty. He has a kindly expression, is most agreeable, but not especially talkative. His keen sense of humor became apparent from the jokes he told at the expense of some of his staff. Our conversation after luncheon was almost entirely on military affairs, including America's probable part in the war, which, as matters stood, gave little promise of becoming effective until the following spring.

My impression of Pétain was favorable and it remained unchanged throughout the war. Our friendship, which I highly treasure, had its beginning at this meeting. Complete coöperation is difficult even under the most favorable conditions and is rarely attained between men or peoples of different nationalities, but it seemed probable that Pétain's breadth of vision, his common sense and his sound judgment would make for understanding, and this proved to be the case.

At the luncheon there were several general officers, among whom was Major General Franchet d'Espérey, then in command of a group of armies under Pétain. He was considered one of the ablest and most aggressive officers in the French Army and was very popular with his men. He was short and stout, of ruddy complexion, and somewhat quick tempered, but a most agreeable companion. As we wished to get a glimpse of the actual front, he took us by motor as near as possible without drawing the fire of the enemy's artillery, although at the time there was little activity on that part of the front. The point of observation that we reached was opposite Saint Quentin, which was then within the enemy's lines, and which was later near the center of the great German drive of 1918 against the British. On the return trip the chauffeur, after being cautioned several times, continued to drive at a somewhat dangerous speed, which so exasperated the General that he finally threatened the chauffeur with violence, whereupon the speed was greatly reduced.

(Diary) Paris, Monday, June 18, 1917. Our headquarters are temporarily at 27 and 31 rue Constantine. We have scanty accommodations but sufficient for our probable brief stay in Paris.

Harjes, of Morgan, Harjes Bank, called to-day. I spent the afternoon in conference with the staff.

Basically the Allied situation appears to be worse than reported.

As we were now ready to begin the foundations of our great military structure, it seems pertinent to give a brief summary of what had happened in Europe during the war up to that time.

1914. Although the Germans in 1914 had failed in their immediate purpose, their armies were in almost complete possession of Belgium and occupied rich industrial regions of northern France, embracing one-fourteenth of her population and about three-fourths of her coal and iron. They held a strongly fortified line 468 miles in length, stretching from the Swiss border to Nieuport on the North Sea. They were within forty-eight miles of Paris and the initiative remained in their hands. The close of 1914 found the Russian armies ejected from East Prussia and driven back on Warsaw.

The entry of Turkey into the war, because of the moral effect upon the Moslem world and the immediate and constant threat created against Allied communications with the Far East, led to an effort by the Allies in the direction of the Dardanelles.

1915. Italy joined the Allies in May, 1915, and gave their cause new strength, but the effect was more or less offset when Bulgaria entered on the side of the Central Powers.

The threatening situation on the Russian front and in the Balkans was still such that Germany was compelled to exert an immediate offensive effort in those directions and to maintain only a defensive attitude on the Western Front. German arms achieved a striking series of successes in the vicinity of the Mazurian Lakes and in Galicia, capturing Warsaw, Brest-Litovsk and Vilna. The Central Powers overran Serbia and Montenegro.

Meanwhile, the Italian armies forced Austria to use approximately one-half of her strength against them.

In the west the French and British launched offensives but the objectives were limited and the results unimportant.

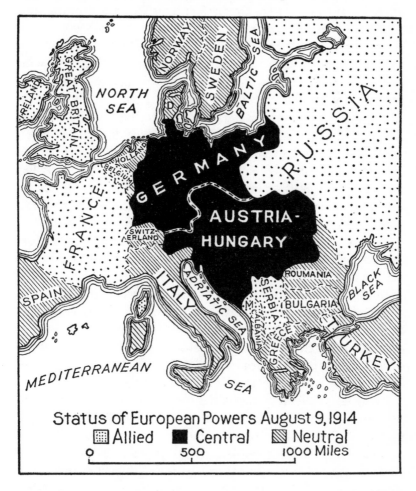

Status of European Powers August 9, 1914
▦ Allied   ■ Central   ▧ Neutral
0   500   1000 Miles

The Dardanelles expedition, having failed in its mission, was withdrawn in January, 1916. In Mesopotamia the Allied operations had not been wholly successful. Although the British fleet had established its superiority on the sea, the German submarine blockade had developed into a serious menace to Allied shipping.

1916. Germany no doubt believed that her advantage on the Eastern Front again warranted an offensive in the West and her attack against Verdun was accordingly launched in the spring of 1916. Every preparation by the Germans was made in the most thorough manner. Although unprepared for the attack, the French met it with great courage. There followed probably the most severe battle of the war, which was only ended the following summer by the successful offensive of the British and French armies along the Somme, which forced Germany to return to the defensive in the West. Russia was not yet beaten and early in June, aided at the same time by the threat of the Italians in the West, she began a great drive in Galicia that proved disastrous to Austria. Roumania, having entered on the side of the Allies, undertook a promising offensive against Austria. In September, Germany initiated a campaign in the East which, before the close of the year, was calamitous for Russia as well as Roumania.

1917. Germany, retaining on the Eastern Front the forces considered sufficient for the final conquest of Russia, was prepared to aid Austria in an offensive against Italy. The relatively low strength of the German forces in the West and the successful defense of Verdun by the French, however, led them, with much confidence, to attempt a decision on this front in April, known as the Nivelle Offensive. Their casualties were very heavy and the effort signally failed. Meanwhile, the revolution in Russia forecast the final collapse of the Czarist régime.

Financial problems of the Allies were becoming more difficult, supplies were being exhausted, all of which added to their tremendous losses caused discouragement, not only among the civil populations but throughout the armies as well. Allied resources in manpower were low and there was little prospect of materially increasing their armed strength, even in the face of the probability of having practically the entire military force of the Central Powers against them in the spring of 1918.

Thus, during three years Germany had seen practically all her offensives excepting that at Verdun crowned with success. Her battle lines were held on foreign soil and she had withstood every Allied attack since the Marne. The German General Staff could now foresee the complete elimination of Russia, the possibility of defeating Italy before the end of the year, and, finally, the campaign of 1918 against the French and British on the Western Front which might terminate the war. With the results of the submarine campaign in her favor, it cannot be said that German hopes of final victory were extravagant, either as viewed at that time or as seen in the light of history.

The Nivelle defeat, previously referred to, well-nigh blasted Allied hopes. Naturally enough, the successful defense of Verdun in 1916 and the British gains along the Somme seemed to revive the spirit of determination and confidence of the Allies, especially the French, who were encouraged to undertake this offensive in the following spring. The superiority of the Allies over the Germans on the Western Front at the time was more than 20 per cent, or, as measured in divisions, it was 190 to 154.

Under the circumstances, it was decided in November, 1916, while Marshal Joffre was still Commander-in-Chief, that the Allies should attempt to break through the German lines on a broad front between Soissons and Reims. In December, General Nivelle, of Verdun fame, succeeded to the high command, and a change in the ministry in March brought in M. Painlevé as Minister of War. Although some opposition had developed to the plan, the new French commander determined to carry it out with some modifications.[1]

By agreement between the two Allies, the British were to assist by making a subsidiary attack on the Arras front, and preliminary attacks were to be made on other portions of the French and British front to draw German divisions to those fronts. After this the French were to assault the weakened German lines on the Aisne and overwhelm them. In order to insure the coöperation

[1] See Painlevé's "How I Appointed Foch and Pétain," in which he states: "In January, 1917, three months before opening his offensive movement, General Nivelle declared, 'We shall break the German front at will, provided we do not attack it at its strongest point, and provided we carry out our operations by means of surprise and sudden attack, in from twenty-four to forty-eight hours.' "

of the two armies, it was understood between the British War
Cabinet and Government and the French Government that except in so far as he might consider that this would endanger the
safety of his army, Marshal Haig should conform his preparations to the views of the Commander-in-Chief of the French
Army (General Nivelle). It was further agreed that during the
operations Marshal Haig should carry out the orders of General

Nivelle.[1]   Marshal Haig was not pleased with the arrangement
and insisted on such modification as would insure his retaining
control of his own forces.

The French had assembled a strong mobile force close in rear
of their assaulting divisions, ready to pass through the gap they
expected to make in the enemy's lines, believing that they could
thus carry the battle into the open and by pressing strongly compel a retirement along the whole front.   Unfortunately, the Germans had obtained from captured documents complete details

[1] See Charteris' "Field Marshal Earl Haig."

of the French plan of attack and had made complete preparations accordingly. In fact there seems to have been so little secrecy observed regarding the intentions of the French that it was a matter of common gossip.

The British, on April 9th, began operations by an advance in the region of Arras, and this was followed, on April 16th, by the French attack between Soissons and Reims. The initial assault of the French was made with great dash and the fighting continued violently for two days. Suddenly on the third day, according to the Minister of War, the attack was thrown into such confusion that it was halted without important gains.[1] However, the responsibility for the abrupt termination of the action was charged to political interference to stop excessive losses on the one hand and military failure on the other.

The unexpected withdrawal of the enemy in March from the line of the Somme contributed to his advantage as it shortened the line and left him a number of extra divisions available for defense against the threatened point. It also caused delay in Allied plans that gave the enemy further time for preparation.

[1] See Painlevé's "How I Appointed Foch and Pétain," in which he says: "After preliminary attacks by the British along the Scarpe, huge masses of French and French Colonial troops, in the early morning of April 16, 1917, poured over the top and surged toward the line of German trenches stretching from Soissons to Reims. The Nivelle offensive was on; the Verdun school of warfare was pitted against the Somme school. It was one of the most brilliant military onslaughts in the whole history of the war.

"Less than one hour elapsed. Then—

"On the plateau of Craonne, on that of Vauclerc, our infantry whirled backward and forward, caught by the cross fire of innumerable machine guns hidden in hollows or concrete shelters. At the end of the day we had advanced 500 meters instead of the 10 kilometers demanded by the schedule of the attack. Before Brimont in the east, before the Laffaux Mill in the west, our attack had been stopped with a like brutal completeness; and even though, in the region of Juvincourt, we smashed the enemy's first position, his massed counterattacks, launched with powerful artillery support, annihilated our shock troops. The plain of Juvincourt became a cemetery for our tanks.

"On the whole vast battlefield there was one point upon which passionately eager attention had been fixed—the historic Hurtebise Farm, at the junction of the Craonne and Vauclerc plateaus. There, it was said, the black troops of Mangin would crush all enemy resistance and begin their overwhelming march on Laon. Yet that was one of the places where fighting was most furious, where our attack was most promptly stopped."

The result was a disastrous defeat for the French, in which they suffered the tremendous loss of over 100,000 men.

Having heard a great deal about what was to be accomplished by this offensive, and having such high hopes of its success, the disappointment of the people was bitter. The reaction in the army itself became grave indeed and disaffection in the ranks was widespread, amounting in places to open mutiny. An officer who served at French G.H.Q. says that "the revolt broke out in most perfect order, as if rigorous orders were applied. There was no spilling of blood, however. The officers, although disobeyed, were respected except on very rare occasions. 'You are abused in the same manner as we. We will not harm you but we have had enough.' Thus they spoke to the officers. 'The war must come to an end.' These scenes sprang up in sixteen army corps all at one time or at very short intervals." [1] This was the situation in the French armies when General Nivelle was replaced by General Pétain.

The morale of the British armies held up well, notwithstanding the French defeat. The British continued their attacks intermittently for several weeks with local successes here and there. But their losses were altogether out of proportion to the results, amounting to nearly 177,000 from April 9th to June 6th.

The collapse of the French offensive indefinitely suspended further attempts to carry out combined operations. This adverse situation after three years of struggle was so depressing that the prospects of Allied victory probably never before looked less hopeful. This was the situation that confronted us upon our arrival in France in June, 1917.

[1] Jean de Pierrefeu's "Three Years at the Great General Headquarters." Chapter 3, Vol. II.

CHAPTER VI

Joffre Heads Liaison Group—Red Cross Relief for French—Allied Morale Low—Pétain's Clear Statement of Why the War Should Continue— My Comment—Non-Existence of Plans—Study of Port and Rail Facilities—Logical Front for American Effort—Agreement with Pétain

(Diary) Paris, Tuesday, June 19, 1917. Held conference on Sunday with Major Grayson M. P. Murphy, head of the Red Cross in France, and his assistant, Mr. James H. Perkins, on coöperation with the Army.

Marshal Joffre and aide came for conference this morning. Thirty-four French officers requested as instructors by War Department reported ready to sail. Have prescribed Sam Browne belt for our officers.

AS soon as the formalities incident to our arrival were over, and I made them as brief as possible, we got down to work, as it was urgent that we should begin at once to lay the foundation for the development and employment of the American Army. The size of the army, its organization, its place on the front, and the selection of lines of communication all had to be determined as far as practicable before our troops in any numbers should arrive. In connection with our supply system, preliminary consideration had to be given to improvements in facilities at ports, the erection of storehouses and shelter, arrangements for logging and sawing lumber in French forests, the procurement of animals, the purchase of guns and munitions, shipment from home of raw material for their manufacture, agreements for the early supply of airplanes, increases in trackage and rolling stock for French railways, and numerous other matters which came along in the natural course of events. Under the title "Line of Communications," the great business organiza-

71

tion for receiving, transporting and supplying our forces was to be built up.

In order to expedite handling the many questions that must arise, especially in our relations with the French War Office, which controlled practically all industrial facilities and transportation, it was M. Painlevé's idea that there should be a group of French officers placed at our disposal. He thought that an agency familiar with the French organization, authorized to communicate directly with the bureaus involved and through which we could make our wants known, would aid us in matters of procurement.

Marshal Joffre was designated as the head of this liaison group and his first visit was to explain how the proposed system was to work. The instructions received by him from the Minister of War were transmitted to me in a polite note which set forth his conception of the duties of the mission. Naturally, it was pleasing to think of being associated with Marshal Joffre, but I thought that the adoption of the plan at this time would only add an extra channel through which requests must pass and that this would complicate rather than simplify matters. The scheme indicated that a sort of tutelage was contemplated, which also made it objectionable.

In my opinion it would be more expeditious to utilize the French officers then on duty at my headquarters and to develop a workable system through experience. I explained my views to M. Painlevé and readily arranged for the officers of our supply departments to confer directly with the chiefs of the corresponding bureaus of the French organization. In the beginning it looked as though we should have easy sailing but we soon found that we had much to learn in dealing with French bureaus, either directly or indirectly.

During the three years preceding our entry into the war several charitable organizations from home, each independent of the others, had become engaged in aiding the Allied armies and peoples, and now that we were in France these societies began to appeal for some kind of official recognition. While most of them were doing excellent and necessary service, there was considerable overlapping, and it was desirable that their efforts should be coördinated. As the Red Cross was our principal agency for such work, I requested this organization to undertake the general direction of American charitable endeavor. We decided also that it could best handle the task if given a semi-official status. Therefore, Major Murphy, the head of the Red Cross in France, was attached to my headquarters. My cable a few days later informed the Secretary of War of the plan, as follows:

"June 23, 1917.
"Have had several conferences with Red Cross management in order to coördinate work with American Army, French Army and civilian population. Aid for latter two classes especially important. Assistance now and during coming winter will have great influence upon morale of French Army. Major G. M. P. Murphy, head of Red Cross in Europe, has complete confidence of Davison. * * * He will control and direct all Red Cross activities among Allies. * * * "

The French situation gave me the gravest concern. Pacifist sentiment was prevalent in France and in many quarters there was talk of a peace parley. Old political feuds were revived and the influence of defeatism was openly charged against the ministry. This pessimistic and despondent mood of the people further depressed the morale of their armies as men at the front contemplated another winter of suffering and distress for their families. To help meet these conditions, I suggested to Major Murphy that the first duty of the Red Cross should be to aid needy French people. As a result, he and his assistant, Mr. Perkins, proposed that funds be distributed to soldiers' families wherever necessary.

When the idea was presented to General Pétain he expressed the keenest appreciation and at once undertook through his military organization to obtain the necessary data. The Red Cross arranged to make 5,000,000 francs (nearly $1,000,000) available to be distributed by local charitable agencies as rapidly as the information could be furnished as to where funds should be sent. This gift, to which a like amount was added later, proved to be most valuable during the ensuing months in building up French morale. Our Red Cross did not stop there, but extended help to the British by contributing £200,000 (approximately $1,000,000) to the British Red Cross. These appropriations for immediate use were merely the beginning of extensive and generous aid given in many ways to the peoples and the armies of the French, British, Belgian, Italian, and other Allied nations.

(Diary) Paris, Friday, June 22, 1917. Purchase of horses and mules in France taken up with War Department. Prices high but payment justified by tonnage saved.

Dorothy Canfield, the novelist, took breakfast with me yesterday. We talked of earlier days in Lincoln, Nebraska, where her father was Chancellor of the University and she my star pupil in mathematics.[1] Dr. John Finley called and was surprised to find that we had met before, when he spoke on "Slang" at Wellesley College, where I was present, with my wife and 500 other alumnæ.

Dined with the Harjes' last night to meet General Pétain, who gave a disquieting report on French morale.

Lunched to-day with Prime Minister and Madame Ribot. Having been American before her marriage, she was very frank in speaking of the depression among the people.

The opinions of Pétain and the Ribots made conditions look more gloomy than ever. There was no question that, underneath the great enthusiasm shown by the people on the afternoon of our arrival, there existed serious despondency among all classes. The terrible strain of the previous years of continuous fighting, with heavy losses, was telling against both the French and the British. Temporary successes in different theaters of war had brought small comfort, followed as they had been all too frequently by disastrous reverses.

With the actual conditions in mind, one could fully understand why the Allies had been so insistent that a contingent of American troops be immediately sent to France to bolster Allied morale. While not yet prepared to do any fighting, we could

[1] I was Commandant of Cadets at the University of Nebraska from 1891 to 1895, and during the first two years I was also instructor in mathematics.

and did furnish men for service behind the lines. We also provided raw material and certain manufactured supplies as rapidly as possible and gave financial aid without stint.

The following significant statement made by Mr. Lloyd George at a meeting of the Allies at the Quai d'Orsay on May 4, 1917, showed that the Allies expected little real military aid from us and doubted whether the shortage in tonnage would enable us to maintain large American forces:

> "It is upon the shoulders of France and Great Britain that the whole burden of the war rests. * * * America is still an unknown. We must not count upon her aid in a military way for a long time to come. Five hundred thousand Americans brought to this side of the water would be useful to us, if the war lasts so long, but we must live while awaiting them, and we do not know whether we will have next year the tonnage necessary to maintain such considerable forces transported from the other side of the Atlantic."

The possibility of our being able to send a completely trained and equipped army within a reasonable time, even though there had been sufficient shipping, was remote because of our woeful state of unpreparedness. We had no such army and could not have one for several months to come. Allied hopes were still centered on our sending individual recruits or companies to maintain the strength of their armies, and if a military crisis had arisen at this time our condition would have compelled us to comply with their wishes. It was most fortunate that the Central Powers did not then have the necessary forces on the Western Front to assume a vigorous offensive.

In our after-dinner conversation at the Harjes', speaking confidentially, General Pétain confirmed the reports of the very low morale of the French, both in and out of the army, and suggested the possibility of having President Wilson use his influence to strengthen the resolution of those in control of the French Government. He also spoke of a statement he intended to give out and asked if I would write something for publication to support it. What he said so clearly set forth the facts as we saw them at the time that I must quote some extracts from it, as published under the title of "Why We Are Fighting":

"We are fighting in order to drive the enemy from our territory and, by a firm and complete peace, to prevent such an unprovoked assault from ever being repeated.

"We are fighting because by a cowardly withdrawal we would criminally betray both our dead and our posterity.

"We are fighting so that peace may restore to our country a freedom of action and inspire a responsibility which, were the war to have a bad ending, would be much worse than what our people suffer to-day. * * *

"As early as July 29 Nicholas had, by a personal dispatch to William, offered to submit the problem to the Hague tribunal. William rejected the offer, but, doubtless being conscious of the crime he had committed, suppressed this very important dispatch in the German White Book.

"That is confession. When Vienna was, perhaps, on the point of negotiating, William hastened to force the conflict by declaring war on Russia before Austria could even act and to the despair of the entire world.

"It is, indeed, true that for many years Germany had wished to make war on Russia and France. For a long time she had been preparing to the smallest detail for a simultaneous invasion of both countries by the organization of a spy service, entirely unprecedented, and by the most complete military preparation. * * *

"Germany had the hope to crush us in a few months. Traitorously attacking through Belgium, and with formidable forces, she believed she could certainly be in Paris long before England could send anything but a 'miserable little army.'

"What Germany desired, the Pan-Germanists demonstrated. In particular she desired, besides our departments of Nord and Est, Flanders, Artois, Lorraine, our most valuable mineral, industrial, and agricultural resources, and to extract from us ten times the gold that she got in 1871.

"Beaten on the Marne and Yser, stopped at Verdun, obliged by many defeats to yield ground, besieged by almost all Europe, has Germany renounced this odious dream?

"Not in the least. The more we have inflicted severe losses upon her, the more does she desire compensations.

"Doubtless humiliated by her defeats, starved by the blockade, bleeding ever in her battles, does she desire peace?

"But she wants it full of honor, as they say; that is to say, full of profits. It is such a peace she has pretended to offer us—a peace of prey.

"Proof of Germany's bad faith is in her reply to President Wilson when she refused to set forth her aims in the war—proof that they could not be revealed.

"That is to say, because Germany does not dare to lay them before the world to-day. She maintains all her pretensions. She desired war in order to realize them. The only one in Europe prepared for it, she alone desired it, brought it about, precipitated it, decreed it, and rendered it inexplicable by her procedure, atrocious by her methods.

"By keeping secret and having no honest desire to declare her pretensions for domination, she stands as the sole obstacle to peace."

My press comment on General Pétain's article, published the next day, was as follows:

"I have read General Pétain's article with the deepest interest. His answer to the question is complete and logical. The facts set forth should convince the world of the justice of our great cause.

"I cannot think it possible that any one should hold a different view of why we are in the war. It is quite beyond reason that any one, knowing the truth, should fail to condemn the course pursued by the German Government, and the truth has been clearly pointed out by the distinguished Commander-in-Chief of the French Army.

"There must be no peace except a lasting peace. The ideals for which the Allies are contending must be held sacred. France will continue her splendid fight for human rights and human liberties, and fresh examples of heroism by her valiant armies will still further inspire those fighting by her side."

The more serious the situation in France, the more deplorable the loss of time by our inaction at home appeared. It is true that a committee at the War College in February had presented a brief outline report on the organization of a limited force, yet no comprehensive general plan had been considered for the formation or employment of such a force, much less for a larger one. In an indorsement on a War College memorandum dated May 28, 1917, which referred to a recommendation by the French that administrative, engineer, quartermaster, sanitary, and dock personnel be sent first, to be followed by combatant troops, the Acting Chief of Staff, Major General Tasker H. Bliss, said:

" * * * General Pershing's expedition is being sent abroad on the urgent insistence of Marshal Joffre and the French Mission that a force, however small, be sent to produce a *moral effect.* We have yielded to this view and a force is being sent *solely to produce a moral effect.* If all necessary arrangements are not made on the other side, it is the fault of the French General Staff and not of ourselves, since their officers were and are fully cognizant of our unprepared state for sending a *serious* expedition for *serious* business. Our General Staff had made no plan (so far as known to the Secretary of War) for prompt dispatch of reënforcements to General Pershing, nor the prompt dispatch of considerable forces to France. * * * But it seems evident that what the French General Staff is now concerned about is the establishment of the important base and line of communications for a much larger force than General Pershing will have. They evidently think that having yielded to the demand for a small force for *moral* effect, it is quite soon to be followed by a large force for *physical* effect. Thus far we have no plans for this. * * * "

Figuratively speaking, then, when the Acting Chief of Staff went to look in the secret files where the plans to meet the situation that confronted us should have been found, the pigeon-hole was empty. In other words, the War Department was face to face with the question of sending an army to Europe and found that the General Staff had never considered such a thing. No one in authority had any definite idea how many men might be needed, how they should be organized and equipped, or where the tonnage to transport and supply them was to come from.

As already noted, both the Joffre and Balfour Missions did not hesitate to make proposals regarding the employment of Americans, and each had expressed the hope that our men, either as individuals or in small units, might be assigned for training and service with their respective forces. Their suggestions were no doubt prompted to some extent by the belief that we would be unable within a reasonable time to build up a separate army capable of operating independently, although it was suspected that this was not the only reason and that the Allies were not keen for us to have an independent combat army. There was certainly a sentiment among them in some quarters that while our entry into the war was necessary to bring victory, we had come in late and therefore could not expect much credit for what we should do. The thought found some basis in the attitude of the leading Allies regarding one or two other nations, whose entry into the war was often openly attributed in Allied circles to the selfish desire of being found on the winning side at the end of the war. Of course it was never even hinted that our action was prompted by such motives, but there is little doubt that the formation of an American army was not looked upon with favor. Our belief in the existence of such an attitude on the part of the Allies naturally stirred in our minds a feeling of distrust, which was emphasized by their later efforts to dominate, and which, therefore, continued to be a factor in all our relations up to the end.

In the midst of the various opposing opinions and schemes of the Allies, the idea remained fixed in my mind that the morale of our troops, their proper training, and their best strategical use all demanded their concentration into an American army instead of being allotted beyond our control as replacements in the ranks of the Allied armies. In fact, every consideration dictated that our army should in no sense be in a subordinate relation to the others, but that we should plan from the start to build up our own independent organization.

(Diary) Paris, Tuesday, June 26, 1917. The question of quarters in Paris for myself and my personal staff most satisfactorily settled through the kindness of Mr. Ogden Mills, who has placed his residence at 73 rue de Varenne, with its beautiful garden, at my disposal.[1]

Went to Compiègne to-day, accompanied by Major James A. Logan and Captain de Marenches, to confer with General Pétain. We tentatively agreed on the American front and the use of certain ports and lines of communication and the sector for our first offensive.

[1] The building and the magnificent garden, with century old trees, date from the early part of the reign of Louis XV. The house was greatly improved during the reign of the first Napoleon. It was once owned by the widow of Marshal Lannes. Mr. Mills restored the grounds to their former beauty and fitted up the mansion with all modern conveniences.

Although we were generally committed to operate with or near the French when our army should be ready, it was necessary to consider the different possibilities of the problem as a whole before making the final decision. We realized that the selection of the actual front must be strategically sound to permit the American Army to strike at a point where a successful offensive would operate to defeat decisively the German Army.

After our forces were organized, equipped and trained at home, they must be sent from different parts of the United States for distances varying from 3,000 to 6,000 miles to reach the battle front. Our merchant marine had never recovered from the great loss in ships during the Civil War, and we were now confronted with the question of transporting our armies across the sea in the face of the serious menace of submarines.

Granting that shipping would be found, we must select terminal ports in France available for our use and reasonably free from submarine dangers, and consider the construction of additional berths. Railway lines must be designated and repaired, new lines must be built and increased rolling stock provided in order that the system should be ready to transport our troops to the front upon their arrival and debarkation. Then came the question of handling the enormous quantities of munitions and supplies that would have to be furnished in order to maintain our forces once they should engage in active operations.

These were some of the problems that confronted us. Their solution demanded prompt action in making plans and persistence in carrying them out. Much of the necessary material for docks, railways, and storehouses must come from home, together with labor to utilize it. Without the utmost effort it would have been impossible to have the army and its supply system ready when the time came for decisive achievement.

Soon after our arrival in London several members of my staff[1] were sent to study the availability of the various ports of France

---

[1] Col. D. E. McCarthy, Q.M. Corps; Col. H. Taylor, Corps of Engineers; Lt. Col. M. W. Ireland, Medical Corps; Maj. H. A. Drum, Gen. Staff; Capt. H. B. Moore, Q.M. Corps.

and to examine the rail facilities leading to the Western Front. In doing so, we had to consider the unprecedented quantities of munitions, railroad rolling stock and other means of transportation incident to the conduct of trench warfare required by the Allied armies, which then numbered more than 5,000,000 men.

The British wanted our army to operate with or near their forces and presented the argument that instead of undertaking the improvement of French ports and railways elsewhere we could use those behind their lines. But we could not be dependent upon facilities already heavily taxed to serve another army. The imposition of the additional burden upon Channel ports and upon railroads leading to the British front would have created a complicated situation with the risk of a breakdown under great stress. The American Army could not occupy a portion of the line between the British and the French without restricting its sphere of activity. Moreover we would have largely displaced the French armies, whose location was based on the defense of Paris, to which above all things they were committed. Also, we might have found ourselves in a position that would have made it difficult to avoid amalgamation and service under a foreign flag, and that possibility alone was sufficient to preclude consideration of the Channel ports.

As to the French systems, all lines running from the base at Paris to the front were bearing their maximum burden. If we were to have independent and flexible lines of communication, our army could not be tied down to the railways they were using. Our rail communications must be carefully chosen to avoid any increase in the load that had to be carried by the systems already in use by the two great Allied armies. But an additional reason for not accepting any of these suggestions was that we could not take the chance of the disastrous effect that German success against the Allies would have upon us if our lines of supply were coextensive with theirs.

The only ports on the west coast of France that would accommodate vessels of more than moderate draft, and that were otherwise free, were St. Nazaire, Bassens and La Pallice, while

Nantes, Bordeaux and Pauillac were capable of taking light draft shipping. These ports had the advantage also of being

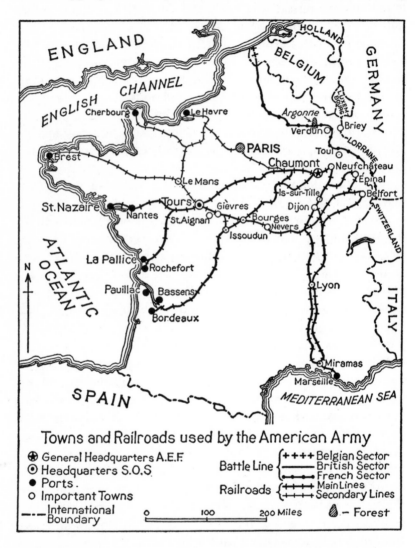

Towns and Railroads used by the American Army

⊕ General Headquarters A.E.F.
⊙ Headquarters S.O.S.
● Ports.
○ Important Towns
—··— International Boundary

Battle Line { ++++ Belgian Sector / ———— British Sector / ●·●·● French Sector }

Railroads { +++++ Main Lines / +++++ Secondary Lines }

0   100   200 Miles   🌢 — Forest

somewhat beyond the patrolling area of German submarines trying to blockade the British Isles. In 1914, after the Germans had overrun northern France and were almost at the gates of

Paris, the British temporarily occupied St. Nazaire as a base for their then relatively small force.

The main railroad routes from these ports toward northeastern France were not included in the service of the rear for either of the Allied armies, and hence, as compared with routes farther north, they were more available for handling material and supplies for our armies. The double-track railways from St. Nazaire and Bordeaux united at Bourges, running thence to Nevers, Dijon and Neufchâteau, with radiating lines extending from the latter point toward the Lorraine sector. It was estimated that these lines, with the collateral routes available, could be improved to meet all our needs, but in case another port and auxiliary line should be necessary we had in reserve the port of Marseille and the railroad leading north.

After all, the principal thing was to determine the sector of the front where our forces, fighting as a unit, would be most effective. Without doubt our mission would eventually lead to large aggressive operations instead of the limited offensive attitude of the French and British. In other words, it was essential that we should prepare to strike the enemy where a definite military decision could be forced.

The sphere of activities of each of the armies in the West had been necessarily restricted, because, as we have seen, the British were committed to operations covering the channel ports, and the French had to consider the safety of Paris. Each of these Governments was very sensitive to the national obligations involved and neither army had sufficient strength to extend operations to other fronts. Therefore, on the active front anywhere west of the Argonne Forest there would have been little space or opportunity for the strategical employment of our army.

On the battlefront from the Argonne Forest to the Vosges Mountains a chance for the decisive use of our army was clearly presented. The enemy's positions covered not only the coal fields of the Saar but also the important Longwy-Briey iron-ore region. Moreover, behind this front lay the vital portion of his rail communications connecting the garrison at Metz with the armies of the West. A deep Allied advance on this front and the seizure of the Longwy-Briey section would deprive the enemy of an indispensable supply of ore for the manufacture of munitions. It might also lead to the invasion of enemy territory in the Moselle valley and endanger the supply of coal in the

STRATEGICAL FEATURES
which influenced selection of
LORRAINE SECTOR
by
AMERICAN ARMY

Saar basin. Allied success here would also cut his line of communications between the east and west and compel his withdrawal from northern France or force his surrender.

Under the circumstances, the enemy could but regard the Verdun salient as threatening this sensitive area in the event that the Allies should find themselves capable of taking the offensive on that front. It was the desire to improve his position and also his prestige that prompted his violent and persistent attacks in the attempt in 1916 to capture Verdun.

Another point was that northeastern France afforded accommodations for billeting and training troops not found elsewhere within striking distance of the front. Few troops had been located in that section and certain classes of supplies not yet exhausted could be obtained locally.

As to our main depots, it was important that they should be easily accessible and also be at a safe distance from the front, because we were to engage a determined enemy who would possibly soon be capable of conducting successful offensives in more than one direction. The area through which the lines under consideration passed embraced Tours, Orléans, Montargis, Nevers and Châteauroux, which were available for the relatively safe location of depots, hospitals and training centers and at the same time were centrally situated with regard to practically all points on the Western Front.

The low morale and the worn condition of the Allied armies suggested that they might be unable to protect their communications and, therefore, it was essential that we should have our own independent system, even though the greater distance from the western ports to the northeast would somewhat increase transportation difficulties. Moreover, this line possessed advantages that would permit us to operate with our bases and depots of supply reasonably secure in case the burden of defense should eventually fall upon us.

In view of the availability of these western ports and the railway lines leading to northeastern France, it was logical to conclude that, from the purely military standpoint, the employment of the American armies on the Lorraine front would prove the most beneficial to the Allies. Accordingly in conference with Pétain, the tentative understanding was reached as to the region for our activities and the location of the line of communications indicated. However, instead of an indefinite front in Lorraine, it was necessary to have a particular sector in mind in order to plan and construct the requisite rail and distributing facilities. From a glance at the map it will be seen that before any decisive operation could be carried out, either on the Verdun or the Nancy fronts, the reduction of the St. Mihiel Salient would be necessary because of its flank position with regard to either, and also because it controlled the railroad, through Commercy, essential to the supply of an army operating in the vicinity of Verdun or Nancy.

Looking forward to the active employment of our armies, it was virtually understood between Pétain and myself that the American sector should include St. Mihiel. I suggested that our first offensive would naturally be the elimination of the salient, with which he fully agreed. The strategical advantages and the moral effect of an initial American success there were so evident that even then we entered into a more or less detailed discussion of the proposal. A few weeks later I formally approved a provisional plan for our activities in Lorraine, which, at that time, we calculated could be carried out in the following spring or summer, with an operation against the St. Mihiel salient as a preliminary move.

CHAPTER VII

Arrival 1st Division—Censorship—Inspection of Ports—American Troops in Paris—Enthusiastic Reception—Fourth of July—Urgency for Haste —Cable for 1,000,000 Men—Problem of Their Supply—Letter to Secretary of War

(Diary) St. Nazaire, Thursday, June 28, 1917. A group of Alsatians, regarding me of Alsatian ancestry, called yesterday to express the hope that the American armies might restore their province to France.

Arrived at St. Nazaire to-day to meet the advance elements of the 1st Division and to inspect the port. Had lunch with Admiral Gleaves on flagship *Seattle*.

THE first section of the 1st Division convoy had brought to St. Nazaire the division headquarters, the 16th Infantry, two battalions of the 28th Infantry, one battalion of the 5th Marines, some motor transport troops, and some stevedores. To see the naval vessels and transports flying the American flag in the harbor gave us all a thrill of pride. It was a pleasure to meet the naval commander, Rear Admiral Albert Gleaves, who was to have general charge of the convoy system. The Admiral very kindly invited me and the senior officers of the division to take luncheon with him on board his flagship, the *Seattle,* where he explained some of the problems that lay ahead of him. The convoy, which totaled fourteen vessels,[1] was divided into four sections, each being escorted by one cruiser and four or five destroyers. The number of troops in this convoy, including one regiment of marines, was about 14,500. The regiments of the 1st Division had all served under my command at one time or another. They were now, however,

[1] Admiral Gleaves in his "History of the Transport Service," (p. 33) says: "Looking back to the first expedition of June, 1917, it seems indeed that the hand of Providence must have been held over those arks or the task never could have been accomplished."

87

composed of a large percentage of recruits and would have to go through a long period of training. After a few days spent in the cantonment at St. Nazaire, the infantry of the division was sent to the training area of Gondrecourt, north of Neufchâteau, and the artillery to Valdahon, near Belfort.

Major General William L. Sibert, who had won distinction as an engineer in the construction of the Panama Canal, was in command of the 1st Division. The two infantry brigades were commanded by Brigadier Generals R. L. Bullard and Omar Bundy, both of whom had many years of line service behind them. I had known all three of these officers for many years, as we had been cadets together at West Point, although all belonged to classes ahead of mine.

The general officers and the regimental and battalion commanders who had arrived were assembled and I gave them a brief outline of the Allied situation and explained the tentative plans for the training and employment of our troops. I also cautioned them regarding the observance of censorship rules and directed that, except officially, under no circumstances should the discussion of military affairs with people either in or out of the service be permitted.

The importance of strict censorship was emphasized by the unauthorized publicity given the next day to the arrival of these first troops. It had been understood that the regulations restricting reference to the Allied armies by the press should apply to the American forces. But to my utter surprise the French and British papers, in their eagerness to let their people know that the elements of the American Army had really reached France, carried full accounts of the arrival of this convoy, giving the port of debarkation, the designation of units and the number of men. The publication of this piece of news was in open contravention of the censorship rules and called for immediate steps to prevent further infractions. I directed Major Frederick Palmer, who was in charge of the press correspondents with our army, to take up the question with the French at once. He entered a vigorous protest to the authorities, and arranged to place in the French Press Bureau an American representative to whom all matters regarding our army was to be submitted for approval.

The special purpose of censorship and other precautions to prevent the publication of military information was to keep the enemy from learning of our plans and movements. Secrecy gives a commander the possibility of surprising his opponent and the surest road to defeat would be to let the enemy know all about one's plans and preparations. The operations of an army cannot be successfully conducted under any such open methods. It was impressed upon our forces and upon the correspondents that every person who, either willfully or inadvertently, disclosed facts of military value thus gave the enemy an advantage, and that such person, if in the army, might actually be responsible for the unnecessary sacrifice of his own comrades.

The rules of censorship were prescribed in considerable detail, but they were not always wisely applied, as no two censors ever construed them alike. In order to be on the safe side, the censor oftentimes eliminated from press dispatches and personal correspondence information that was harmless, but in the main few errors were made. In the enforcement of the regulations it was a question of deciding between giving our anxious people at home facts which they had every right to know and the necessity of keeping the enemy in the dark regarding our numbers, plans and movements. There is no doubt, however, that the suppression of news prevented our people from obtaining a clear and contemporaneous conception of the great and oftentimes brilliant achievements of our armies and left such knowledge to be gleaned from meager accounts by participants or from the later writings of historians. It was unfortunate that such rules had to be enforced, as otherwise much that might have been published at the time may never be known; however, there was nothing else to be done without serious risk.

During my stay at St. Nazaire I further investigated the conditions of the port. It is a typical seaport town. The descendants of its ancient Celtic population, though now of a decided mixture, still retain the old customs and peculiarities. It was one of the principal shipbuilding ports of France, with two deep-water channels leading to the sea. There was a locked, double basin capable of taking ships drawing twenty-eight feet. In this basin were a limited number of berths, of which at first we were assigned five. The shore arrangements for handling cargo were almost archaic and the storage space was practically confined to the dock sheds. Railway cars in order to be spotted had to be shunted one at a time by means of a turn-table worked by hand. The rail connections with the main lines and the dock yard accommodations were entirely inadequate. Although the facilities were then above the average of French ports, it was evident that radical changes in the system of handling cargo would be necessary to obtain the maximum of efficiency that would eventually be required.

Neither the local official personnel nor the port employees at St. Nazaire appeared fully to realize that their country was in the throes of a great war. They seemed to accept our arrival as a routine matter, and longshoremen continued to handle the supplies of rations and other stores in their customary deliberate and easy-going fashion. The people of the town showed some curiosity and French Army officials began to offer assistance to the troops once they were ashore. Our officers related some of the difficulties already encountered in attempting to expedite the handling of cargo, but all of us were destined to experience many discouragements before the end of the war in our efforts to improve conditions, both here and elsewhere.

I also visited Nantes, a city of 200,000 inhabitants, some thirty miles inland from the mouth of the Loire. The city boasts a fine modern cathedral, an excellent museum of art, an ancient château, then used as a prison, and many fine old buildings occupied by factories and shops. The people of this city have always been loyal to the principles of liberty and the officials were very gracious in their desire to aid us. As a port, however, only vessels of light draft could be accommodated and the facilities were very much out of date.

(Diary) Paris, Wednesday, July 4, 1917. Dined the 1st with Marshal and Madame Joffre. She told an amusing story of their courtship and how he was in love with her when she was a girl. She did not want to marry a fat major then, she said, but accepted him later when she became a widow. It is a charming household.

Two of the Roosevelt boys, Theodore, Jr., and Archie, reported yesterday. Unable himself to participate, their father's fine spirit is represented by his sons.

The Garde Républicaine Band serenaded me early this morning and I had to appear on the balcony, partially dressed. In an impressive ceremony this forenoon at Les Invalides, a battalion of our 16th and one of French troops were paraded together. The American battalion then marched to Lafayette's tomb and was loudly cheered by crowds of people along the route.

Lunched at Chamber of Commerce, visited our Embassy in the afternoon, and attended banquet in the evening given by General Foch, the Chief of Staff.

The French wished to honor our Independence Day, and suggested that some of our troops should participate with theirs in its appropriate observance. The people of Paris had not yet seen any American troops and the authorities felt also that their actual appearance on the streets would have a good effect on French morale. A battalion of the 16th Infantry was brought from St. Nazaire for the occasion. Although these troops were from a Regular regiment, we were not prepared to make much of an impression from the military point of view as the unit had recently been raised to war strength and about two-thirds of the men were recruits. The untrained, awkward appearance of this unit, which was regarded by French officers as representing our Regular Army, could not have escaped their critical observation. However, if they could have foreseen the triumph of this same battalion and of others that took part in the second battle of the Marne, we might have been spared many delays and difficulties in carrying out our plans.

The ceremony held in the Court of Honor at Les Invalides was a fine gesture in recognition of our entry into the war. The President of the Republic, M. Poincaré, presided and was accom-

Note: Total strength of the A.E.F. on June 30th, 523 officers, 13,836 enlisted men.

panied by Marshal Joffre and other high officers and a group of French veterans of former wars. The impressive formalities were carried out with studied precision. A stand of our national colors was presented by the President to our battalion and a pair of guidons to me. There in this national shrine, sacred to the memory of the glorious past of the French people, where Napoleon assembled his cabinet to do honor to the immortal Washington when he died, and where Napoleon himself lies buried, an official welcome was extended on Independence Day to America's first contingent of troops. No other occasion that I recall was more significant or more clearly indicated the depth of French sentiment and affection for their old ally.

This first appearance of American combat troops in Paris brought forth joyful acclaim from the people. On the march to Lafayette's tomb at Picpus Cemetery the battalion was joined by a great crowd, many women forcing their way into the ranks and swinging along arm in arm with the men. With wreaths about their necks and bouquets in their hats and rifles, the column looked like a moving flower garden. With only a semblance of military formation, the animated throng pushed its way through avenues of people to the martial strains of the French band and the still more thrilling music of cheering voices. By taking parallel streets, I was able to gain several successive vantage points from which to watch this unique procession pass. The humbler folk of Paris seemed to look upon these few hundred of our stalwart fighting men as their real deliverance. Many people dropped on their knees in reverence as the column went by. These stirring scenes conveyed vividly the emotions of a people to whom the outcome of the war had seemed all but hopeless.

The exercises at the cemetery consisted of a few speeches, the principal speaker being Mr. Brand Whitlock, our Ambassador to Belgium. I had been previously asked to deliver an address but had designated Colonel C. E. Stanton, of my staff, an old army friend of mine and somewhat of an orator, to speak in my place.

M. Painlevé, Ambassador Sharp and I were standing together listening to the various speeches and as the exercises were drawing to a close Painlevé said to me, "Aren't you going to speak?" I said, "No, Colonel Stanton is speaking for me." "But," he said, "you must speak," and Sharp backed him up, so I was ushered to the stand and spoke entirely extemporaneously. As the day was filled with inspiring incidents, I found no difficulty in saying a few words regarding their significance.

It was on this occasion and upon this spot that utterance was given to an expression that could have been born only of inspiration, one that will live long in history—*"Lafayette, we are here!"* Many have attributed this striking utterance to me and I have often wished that it could have been mine. But I have no recollection of saying anything so splendid. I am sure that those words were spoken by Colonel Stanton and to him must go the credit for coining so happy and felicitous a phrase.

The annual luncheon of the American Chamber of Commerce, which I attended, really took the form of a celebration of our entry into the war. All the speakers naturally adopted our participation as their theme. Many high French and American officials were present, including Marshal Joffre and M. Viviani, who were given an ovation by the Americans.

In the afternoon the usual Fourth of July reception at the Embassy became almost a gala occasion. It gave me an opportunity to meet nearly all of our countrymen then in Paris, and I was overwhelmed with the warmth of their greetings.

This eventful day was brought to a fitting close with a dinner given by General Foch, where we fraternized with representative officers of the French Army, both from the front and from the War Office. The evening was enlivened by the presence of several opera singers, whose appropriate patriotic selections appealed to the sentiments of both the French and ourselves.

(Diary) Paris, Monday, July 9, 1917. Had conference on Thursday with Colonel Thornton, British Army, regarding transportation problems.

Cabled Washington Friday asking for 1,000,000 men by May.
Wrote Secretary of War to-day giving résumé of situation.

The parade of our troops through Paris doubtless fortified the
morale of the people to a certain extent, but we all knew that
eventually something very much more effective would have
to be done. While it was important to consider the temporary
state of mind of the Allies, yet after all, the outcome of the war
would depend upon the size of the force we could bring to their
aid. In order to get at the real situation before advising the War
Department of what we should undertake to do, a thorough
study was made of the actual and potential strength on both
sides. The low state of Allied morale was already well understood. While the full extent of defection in the Russian armies
was not realized at this time, enough was known to lead to the
conclusion that they could not be counted on to give much further
assistance to the Allies.

In that event, of course, Germany would be relatively stronger
than before and would probably be capable of transferring a
large proportion of her eastern armies to France. Although the
Allies were at the moment superior on the Western Front, the
advantage in general, both as to manpower and morale, was
decidedly in favor of the Central Powers. The real question, then,
was whether the Allies could hold out until we were ready.
It was clear that no half-way measures on our part would answer
and that Allied hopes lay in American military assistance on a
vast scale at the earliest moment.

The Allies thought an American force of 500,000 men the
maximum that we could have in France in 1918, but it was my
opinion that this number would not be enough to meet the
situation. Although this would aid, we could not be content
merely to lend a helping hand but we must prepare to strike a
decisive blow. While the appearance on the front of any American force was still months away, there was little doubt that if we
could induce Allied coöperation we should be able to give much
greater assistance than they believed possible. Our study having

confirmed the correctness of my tentative estimate made on the *Baltic*, I therefore cabled Washington on July 6th, as follows:

"Plans should contemplate sending over at least 1,000,000 men by next May. * * * This estimate would give practically half million men for trenches. Inasmuch as question affects all Allies whose common interests demand that we exert maximum military power consistent with transport problem, suggest early agreement be reached among Allies which would provide requisite transportation * * * and limit sea transportation to food and military supplies and the exclusion of every kind of luxury as well as other supplies in excess of immediate needs of countries dependent upon oversea supplies."

The question, in its finality, was, therefore, one of sea transportation, but so far all efforts to get the Allies, especially the British, to consider giving help to bring over men and supplies had been futile. They did not seem to realize that America would be practically negligible from a military standpoint unless the Allies could provide some shipping. Nor did they seem to appreciate that time was a vital factor. But the spirit of full cooperation among the Allies did not then exist. They seemed to regard the transportation of an American army overseas as entirely our affair. This apparent indifference also gave further color to the suspicion that perhaps an American army as such was not wanted. The situation from our standpoint was grave and embarrassing, for it looked as though it might not be possible for us to save either the Allies or ourselves.

A careful calculation, with a minimum factor of safety, showed that to maintain an army of 1,000,000 men with all kinds of supplies, including munitions (guns, ammunition and aviation), would call for the daily delivery in France of at least 25,000 tons of freight and continuous berthing capacity for 20 or 25 vessels. As a matter of course we expected that the use of certain facilities such as ports, railways and storehouses would be granted us by the French Government, but even with the most generous attitude on their part an extensive program of new construction would be necessary in order to accommodate the large amount of tonnage required. Many new berths would have to be built outright, the railway rolling stock and personnel would have to be greatly expanded, and considerable additional trackage laid. The estimated area on which storehouses would have to be erected for the shelter and care of supplies amounted to many square miles. As we expected eventually to expand our forces to at least 2,000,-000 men in France, the great task that lay before us can well be imagined. To achieve these results in time to be of any real assistance to the Allies was to test our resourcefulness and energy to the limit.

I recall an after-dinner discussion of this problem with Admiral Sims, during which I stated that according to our plans we should eventually need ships, port and rail facilities, and personnel to handle 50,000 tons of freight per day from home for the 2,000,000 men we expected to have. It was somewhat of a surprise to find that Sims apparently regarded this as very much of an exaggeration or else as just an army joke. Although I insisted that it was a positive and serious statement based upon our preliminary study, I doubt whether he was convinced until the time came in 1918 when we had that number of men in France and were actually discharging daily and sending to the front over 45,000 tons of munitions and other supplies.

The following letter to the Secretary of War gives a résumé of the situation as to morale as viewed at that time:

"July 9, 1917.
"Dear Mr. Secretary:

"I feel it important that I should write you confidentially something of the general situation in France as it appears from certain facts that have come to me since my arrival in Paris. Sometime before our arrival, as you know, the French Army had been badly hammered, so much so that its morale dropped to a very low ebb. As a consequence also the people themselves became very much disheartened and gave voice to rather severe criticism of the army management in general. The result of all this was that Nivelle was replaced by Pétain as commander-in-chief.

"Dissatisfaction in the army has rather continued to grow and has probably been encouraged by the French civil socialistic element, no doubt influenced by German socialists. It is generally known that several instances of mutiny have occurred among the troops, and that it became necessary recently to execute some of the ringleaders, variously reported to number from thirty to one hundred and twenty.[1] The socialistic element of the Chamber of Deputies itself has subjected the army to criticism that still further served to unsettle the minds of the people, and add to the discontent of the army.

"The fact is that France is very tired of this war. The common people openly complain of the heavy taxes, and protest that they are being ground down to enrich government contractors, and possibly officials well up in government service. Prices of food are high, so that the general cost of living weighs heavily upon the civil population. Coal costs from $80.00 to $90.00 per ton and the supply is very limited. Complaints from families have their effect on the men in the ranks, so that the fighting ability of the troops may be seriously impaired by their discontent. The army authorities seem to be gravely concerned, as is indicated by the fact that General Pétain, last week, asked me to meet him at the home of a mutual friend for conference.

"At this meeting, he told me frankly that affairs were not going well in France, and that unless the Government and the people would stand by the army and assist at home, instead of undermining its morale by criticism and fault-finding, he felt that something bordering on revolution might result. Such an outcome, he said, would permit the Germans to dictate the terms of peace instead of the Allies. He, of course, feels that our entering the war has brought courage to the nation, but, realizing as he does that we shall not be in a position to render any material assistance before next spring, he thinks that, in addition to that, some outside pressure might be brought that would check political intrigue among government officials and prevent a further loss of confidence among the people at large.

"As you know, of course, politics ordinarily play a very important part in every act of the average French public official who is very much inclined to over-play the game. Of course anything like a revolution in France at this time might not be easy to stop, and the final burden of the war might thus fall upon our shoulders. Realizing the low spirits of the people, I have taken advantage of an occasional opportunity, without appearing to meddle and without talking too much, to speak encouragingly of the splendid stamina of the French people and of the army, and have endeavored to inspire confidence among them in their military organization and its commander.

"With this same idea of bolstering up French morale, General Pétain has issued a public statement setting forth the reasons why

[1] It is now known that only twelve of the ringleaders were executed.

the French are fighting. Before giving it out, he asked me if I
would do something to back it up after it was published. I am enclosing a translation of General Pétain's article, and my brief comment published the following day.[1]

"General Pétain believes that perhaps there may come a time when
President Wilson, for whom the whole French nation have a sublime
admiration, might take some action through the French Ambassador
at Washington, or otherwise, that would stiffen the French Government into a full realization of the seriousness of these matters and
of their responsibility in the premises. By this I mean the civil end
of the Government in whose hands rests so much obligation to support their army commanders.

"On the other side of this general view of the subject, our Ambassador here holds the opinion, which I have gained from general
conversation with him, that all factions in France are working together harmoniously. I should add also that many others hold this
same view. Of course they all know of the general complaints and
all that, but they do not regard them as indicating anything serious.
I have the very highest regard for Mr. Sharp, and for what he says,
and what I say is in no way a criticism of him. He is in every
sense a high-minded and, I believe, efficient and conscientious official.
But I am writing in order that you may also have the viewpoint of
the French Commander-in-Chief, whose views I could not safely
mention to any one else.

"It must be stated that our Fourth of July celebration with troops
participating has stirred all France; also that yesterday the Government
and the Chamber of Deputies seem to have had a very satisfactory
understanding, and the French people are in much better spirits than
when General Pétain made the above comments on the situation.
General Pétain himself now says that the morale of the army has improved lately. So for the present things look better.

"My own opinion is that the army, as it stands to-day, can hold
on until spring against any probable effort of the enemy, but that
poverty and discontent, magnified by the socialistic press, especially
should the Government fail to continue to back up the army, may
so dishearten the people and the army that the latter will lose its
morale and disaster follow.

"I shall do everything consistent with my position to encourage
and hearten both people and soldiery. With the Red Cross now
under an organization that is working practically under my very
general control, much can be done to cheer up the soldier in the

[1] These enclosures have already been set forth in Chapter VI.

trenches and to help his family at home during the coming winter. The Y.M.C.A. is also working with us in its own field toward the same end.

"I should very much prefer that all this be held as entirely confidential in so far as my conference with General Pétain and my remarks about the Ambassador are concerned. For General Pétain's sake, as well as my own, no suggestion or recommendation should be made connecting him or me in any way with whatever course that may be considered advisable, should future events seem to suggest action along the lines indicated.

"I trust, Mr. Secretary, that you will understand that I am writing you only because I feel that in no other way could I place before you a view of the situation and its possibilities. In conclusion, I would add that I have the utmost confidence in General Pétain, and believe that he is a loyal patriot, whose sole aim is to serve and save France.

"With high personal esteem and respect, I remain,

"Yours very sincerely,

"JOHN J. PERSHING."

CHAPTER VIII

Organization for First Million Men—Expansion of Supply Service—
General Headquarters Staff—Shortage General Staff Officers—Experts
in Business, Industry and Transportation Required—Timber and
Lumber Procurement—Forestry Service—Troops Requested for Italy
—Artillery Procurement Arranged—Welfare Organizations—Organi-
zation of Line of Communications

(Diary) Paris, Wednesday, July 11, 1917. Called last night on
Ambassador Sharp, who thinks French morale is rather better.
Neither of us believes that anything can come of peace talk.

Completed conference to-day on organization of combat units. Indications are that railway situation is worse than early reports show.
Immediate shipment engineers and material for dock construction,
also men and equipment for Forestry Service, urged on Department.
1500 locomotives reported allocated to Russia by Council of National
Defense. Have cabled for priority on 600. Took up question of
winter clothing with War Department. James Gordon Bennett, who
called, has complete faith in Allies.

AS plans for the manufacture of many of our supplies at
home, especially munitions and equipment, were largely
dependent upon early decisions by me as to the tactical
organization, armament and equipment of troops, all of which
should have been settled months before by the War Department
itself, it was very essential that the outline of organization for
the first million men should be determined without delay. After
my departure for France a board of officers [1] was sent over by the
War Department to look into these questions, and this group,
acting upon my suggestion, very wisely concluded to work in
conjunction with the Operations Section [2] of my staff, already

[1] This board consisted of Col. Chauncey B. Baker, Col. W. S. Graves, Col. C. P.
Summerall, Col. D. E. Aultman, Col. M. L. Hersey, Lt. Col. H. E. Ely, Lt. Col. E. D.
Anderson, Lt. Col. K. Walker, Lt. Col. S. A. Cheney, Maj. M. E. Locke, Maj. G. S.
Simonds, Maj. F. A. Ellison and Capt. J. G. Quekemeyer.
[2] The principal members of the Operations Section at this time were: Lt. Cols. John
McA. Palmer and Fox Conner and Majors A. B. Barber and H. A. Drum.

engaged in similar studies. To evolve and perfect a complete scheme of organization and armament for all combat units from the platoon and company on up through the battalion, regiment, division, and army corps, and for the necessary special troops, was an enormous task, particularly in view of the urgency for prompt action, and the realization that the recommendations would have a far-reaching effect upon the operations of our army.[1] As these studies approached completion, the War Department board and my staff were called together at my quarters in joint session, over which I presided, and after deciding certain points of difference the plan which became known as the General Organization Project was adopted and forwarded to Washington on July 11th, with the following statement:

"It is evident that a force of about 1,000,000 is the smallest unit which in modern war will be a complete, well-balanced, and independent fighting organization. However, it must be equally clear that the adoption of this size force as a basis of study should not be construed as representing the maximum force which will be needed in France. It is taken as the force which may be expected to reach France in time for an offensive in 1918, and as a unit and basis of organization. Plans for the future should be based, especially in reference to the manufacture, etc., of artillery, aviation, and other material, on three times this force—*i.e.,* at least 3,000,000 men."

The fact that when we entered the war our Government had done little or nothing toward the organization or equipment

[1] The infantry units of the A.E.F. were organized and commanded generally as follows:

Platoon, 58 men, commanded by 2d or 1st lieutenant.

Company, 6 officers and 250 men, by a captain.

Battalion, 4 companies, by a major.

Regiment, 3 battalions and a machine gun company, 112 officers and 3,720 men, by a colonel.

Brigade, 2 regiments and a machine gun battalion, 258 officers and 8,211 men, by a brigadier general.

The organization of the field artillery, engineers, signal corps, air service, and other arms and services was along lines similar to the infantry.

Division, 2 infantry and 1 field artillery brigades, 1 engineer regiment, 1 machine gun battalion, 1 signal battalion, and trains; 72 guns, 260 machine guns, 17,666 rifles; 979 officers, 27,082 men; by a major general.

Corps, 2 to 6 divisions, by a major general.

Army, 3 to 5 corps, by a lieutenant general or major general.

Group of Armies, 2 or 3 armies, by a general, lieutenant general or major general.

of an army, not to mention its transportation beyond the sea, was a tremendous handicap which few of our people realized then and which is not generally understood even as this is written, thirteen years later.

As a necessary preliminary step in building up the supply service, early consideration was given to plans for the expansion of railroads, the building of docks, and the erection of storehouses, for which the procurement of the necessary material was the first essential. Washington had been advised of the requirements in rolling stock to increase the efficiency of French railroads, but to indicate the urgency of early action the following cable was sent:

> "July 11, 1917.
>
> "The further our investigations proceed as to general conditions and the state of the French resources, the greater appear their deficiencies and the smaller their abilities to aid us in material and labor. Therefore deem it of the utmost importance that this be realized at home. Dock facilities available for our use will be very cramped when we begin to send over continuous convoys of troops and supplies. Therefore construction of additional dock accommodations should be pushed. The railroads we are to use are also deficient in equipment and need repair. Material and rolling stock should be shipped without delay. The French have practically no material available so that both material and labor must come from the United States. * * * "

Coincident with other immediate questions, the development of a satisfactory general staff system to meet the demands of modern warfare required my special attention. The history of our Army offered no guide to the organization and duties of the general staff under conditions involving the handling of millions of men in a great war. After Congress had created the General Staff in 1903, considerable hostility grew up against it in both Houses. Moreover, there existed no little opposition to it within the Army itself, especially in the entrenched supply departments and bureaus at Washington. A certain limited class of line officers who regarded their commissions as sufficient evidence of superior qualifications and as carrying a vested right to live at the expense of the Government with a minimum of exertion, also decried it. But the main thing that retarded its evolution was the lack by the successive Chiefs of Staff, of a clear conception of its proper functions and the consequent centralization of details in their hands.

It required no genius to see that the coördination and direction of the combat branches and the numerous services of large forces could be secured only through the medium of a well-constituted general staff, and I determined to construct it on the sound basis of actual experience in war of our own and other armies.

Our most highly trained officers as a rule came from the Staff College at Fort Leavenworth and from the Army War College, but the majority of the relatively small number of graduates from these schools were scattered throughout the United States and our overseas possessions. During the first two months in France the work imposed upon the few staff officers who had accompanied me was very heavy. However, after urgent and repeated requests, I was fortunate in having at my disposal later in the summer a small group of men which included some of the most efficient and highly educated officers in our Army.[1] After selecting the best features of the French and British staff systems, a general staff organization was created with this nucleus of officers, which effectively met every demand made upon it throughout the war and which remains to-day as a model for present and future guidance.

Not only did G.H.Q. need an efficient general staff to work

---

[1] In addition to those already with me, the officers included in the following cable I regarded as especially fitted for the duties for which they were desired:

"Request Robert C. Davis, Adjutant General, be sent these hdqrs. earliest date. Request Frank Moorman or J. O. Mauborgne be sent these hdqrs. earliest date for duty as code expert. Request Samuel T. Hubbard, Jr., Signal Corps, now here, be called to active service and ordered report to me. Request ten of following named officers be sent to report to me by second convoy for General Staff duty: Frank R. McCoy, George Van Horn Moseley, Malin Craig, Alfred W. Bjornstad, H. B. Fiske, Allen J. Greer, Paul B. Malone, Edgar T. Collins, Samuel R. Gleaves, Laurence Halstead, Nicholas W. Campanole, Aristides Moreno, Preston Brown, LeRoy Eltinge, W. B. Burtt, Frank T. Hines, Edward L. King, J. P. McAdams, W. C. Sweeney, J. B. Barnes, Kerr T. Riggs, W. H. Winters, Wait C. Johnson, Stuart Heintzelman, Upton Birnie, Jr., Kirby Walker, Berkeley Enochs. * * * "

out plans and exercise direction in their execution under the Commander-in-Chief, but combat units and the various services also required qualified staff officers. In order to provide some training without awaiting the establishment of our own schools of instruction, the French and British kindly offered to admit our officers to their schools or attach them to their units until we could get our own courses started. The urgency of sending officers to France for instruction and experience in staff duty was presented to the War Department in July in a cable recommending that 200 graduates of the School of the Line or the Staff School be sent over, or if such number could not at once be spared that selected officers of the National Guard and Reserves be substituted, but the Department only partially complied with the request.

As the details of our mission abroad developed, it soon became evident that in all that pertained to the maintenance and supply of our armies as distinguished from the purely military task, men with expert knowledge and broad experience in business, industry and transportation would be necessary. In the technical branches of the Army were many officers with theoretical training in special lines, but, with some notable exceptions, they generally lacked broad constructive or administrative training. The more important activities requiring special knowledge included the management of railways, the handling of shipping, the direction of forestry and lumbering, the use of radio and wire communications, and the development of aviation and chemical warfare. From the start I decided to obtain the best talent available and was fortunate in practically every field to find able men who were anxious to do their part.

The earliest application of the principle came in connection with timber and lumber procurement. We naturally expected to obtain in France much of the enormous quantity of lumber for barracks and timber for piles, telegraph poles, and fuel, especially as it would be impossible with our limited tonnage to bring a great amount across the Atlantic. The British were being allowed to cut in certain French forests and had installed sawmills here and there, and we sought similar permission, realizing that the French did not have the men to turn out timber and lumber for us and that we must do the work ourselves. Both the French and British Missions to Washington had obtained promises of American forestry engineers, but our needs took precedence and theirs had to be deferred. The French somewhat reluctantly granted us the privilege of cutting timber, but we encountered considerable delay in the allotment of forests.

A cable to the War Department early in July recommended the immediate organization of a forestry service consisting of sawmill units to be composed of experienced lumbermen, and eight to ten thousand unskilled laborers to build roads and to handle lumber. Special request was made for the appointment of Professor Henry Graves, Chief of the United States Forestry Service, then on the ground, as the man to take charge of lumber operations. A number of other specially qualified men were asked for as lumber operators, logging engineers, forest examiners, and organization experts. This being the first intimation given the War Department that such a force would be needed, naturally some time elapsed before it could be organized, brought over and put to work.

(Diary) Paris, Tuesday, July 17, 1917. Dined on Friday with Thomas Nelson Page, our Ambassador to Italy, who praised Italian armies and wants us to send them troops.

On the morning of the 14th, as guest of President Poincaré, witnessed near the Bastile the presentation of Legion of Honor insignia. The review of 11,000 veterans, including squads bearing colors of all regiments from the First Empire down, was an inspiring sight. Attended a Franco-American manifestation in the afternoon at the Trocadéro, where national anthems were sung and the famous composer, Saint-Saens, played selections from his own compositions.

Visited Red Cross building and Y.M.C.A. headquarters to-day with Colonel Bradley. Both associations are progressing in organization and extending their activities.

Sent cable urging manufacture of artillery. Have requested that passports to visit France be refused to officers' families.[1]

[1] This recommendation was approved by the Secretary of War with the concurrence of the Secretary of State. It was construed to apply to wives and sisters.

The suggestion from Ambassador Page that we send a few divisions to aid the Italians indicated that they were about to enter the lists with the other Allies to contend for an allotment of American reënforcements. The Ambassador seemed disappointed to find me strongly opposed to the use of our troops anywhere except on the Western Front and as components of our own army.

The question of artillery procurement caused me much concern. The almost negligible amount on hand when we went to war consisted mostly of field guns of the 3-inch type, then largely in the hands of troops, in the Philippine Islands or elsewhere, and unavailable for issue. Moreover, for calibers heavier than the 3-inch type our Ordnance Department had adopted nothing which was really up to date.

When George Washington was once asked which arm of the combat service he would increase if he could have the choice, he replied that it would be the artillery. Since his day its ratio to infantry in all armies has gradually grown. The most striking change in our time developed in the Russo-Japanese War, when the proportionate increase, especially by the Japanese, became greater than ever before. Our American observers in Manchuria fully reported to the War Department the increased employment of artillery, but in those days it was idle for any military man to talk of more guns for our Army, and the Government made no attempt to keep pace with this tendency in modern armies. On the other hand, Germany quickly realized the growing importance of artillery and so effectively did she develop this arm that during the first years of the World War the Central Powers had a decided superiority over the Allies. It is hardly believable that the Allies should have failed to appreciate their disadvantage in the face of the significant demonstration by the Germans in Belgium in 1914, of the value of heavy artillery, yet apparently not until its further prodigious use against the Russians did the Allies fully appreciate its necessity.

A board of officers[1] from my staff, appointed while on the

---

[1] The members of this board were Col. C. C. Williams, Lt. Col. Fox Conner and Capt. J. B. Taylor.

Baltic to study this subject, made a preliminary calculation, based upon the immediate organization on a war footing of an army of 500,000 men. It was estimated that we should have, as an initial requirement, 2,524 guns with a possibility of obtaining only 80 in September and 40 in October from our own foundries, and with no prospect of further deliveries until June, 1918. The enormous proportion of both light and heavy guns used by both sides, the knowledge of our deficiency and the realization of the length of time that must elapse before we could manufacture and deliver them made it imperative that we seek other sources than our own to help equip our armies.

Following up an intimation, it was learned definitely that, although not fully supplied themselves, the French could increase the output of their factories provided they could get steel from the United States. As it seemed probable that we should operate in proximity to their armies, we adopted the French types for the usual calibers and sought their assistance in obtaining the guns needed, at least for the first two years. We secured an agreement that our troops, as they came along, would be provided with French guns and ammunition, including not only the 75's and 155's but 37-millimeter guns and 58-millimeter trench mortars as well. In advising the War Department by cable of the arrangement, late in June, it was insisted that nothing should diminish our efforts at home, not only to produce these types, but also those of the 4.7-inch and 6-inch mobile types. In my cable of July 14th, the expedition of the 8-inch and 9.5-inch howitzers then under manufacture was also urged. It was most fortunate that we were able to get these guns from the French, as up to the end of the war no guns manufactured at home for our army, of the types used, except 24 8-inch mortars and 6 14-inch naval guns, were fired in battle. Trench guns of the 3-inch and 6-inch mortar types, with ammunition, were purchased from the British.

The Red Cross reported excellent progress, especially in its first efforts to assist the French, as agreed upon with General Pétain. Its organization by Major Grayson M. P. Murphy for war work with our own armies was now about completed. The establishment of canteens and huts at the ports and other important points had already begun and the numbers increased as fast as needed. These centers of service later maintained dispensaries and provided beds and bathing facilities for men traveling under orders or on leave. When the necessity arose the Red Cros° actively coöperated with the Medical Corps in the field, contributing large quantities of supplies and oftentimes additional nurses. The work of the society, directed from a central office in Paris, eventually embraced practically every endeavor touching the health of the armies.

The Y.M.C.A., with Mr. E. C. Carter in charge, was equally earnest, its principal field of activities being that of recreation and entertainment. Through bureaus of information it also undertook to provide personal services for officers and men, both in France and England. It supplied athletic equipment and encouraged sports; conducted clubs and hotels, furnishing reading matter and writing material; cared for the women of the Y.W.C.A., and made a beginning at educational work wherever possible. Later on, at my request, the Y.M.C.A. also undertook to conduct our regimental and regional canteens in which they carried certain supplies for sale to troops. Although handicapped at all times by lack of tonnage, land transportation and efficient personnel, this enormous task was creditably performed.

In addition to these two societies, the Knights of Columbus engaged in welfare work without material interference with the organizations above mentioned. It also grew to be a most helpful agency. The Salvation Army came, and filled a place all its own, leaving on the armies a distinct impression of sincere and unselfish service. Later came the Jewish Welfare Board, which gave especial attention to Jewish soldiers. All these organizations rendered valuable service to our troops.

(Diary) Paris, Thursday, July 19, 1917. Held conference yesterday with General Staff on details of organization of Line of Communications and location of sections pertaining to the rear.

To-day, accompanied by de Chambrun, called on M. Jules Cambon, of the Foreign Office. Visited American Hospital for French army patients at Neuilly.

The Line of Communications, under one chief, with headquarters first at Paris and later at Tours, included all supply activities and installations up to the Zone of Operations. For convenience in administration, it was subdivided territorially into sections, each being a unit in itself bearing a certain relation to others, and all subject to the same directing authority. It required efficient organization in order to function as a whole in maintaining a constant flow of supplies to our forces. Each base section embraced at least one important port for the discharge of munitions, equipment and other supplies from home. A certain percentage of subsistence elements was stored [1] near the ports and the balance sent forward to plants in the Intermediate Section for storage and assortment by classes or components. Munitions and equipment went to special depots toward the front. The Advance Section embraced stations from which the distribution of supplies was made direct to the troops as needed. Along the Line of Communications the Medical Department located its principal hospitals for the care of the sick and wounded. Many of its units were installed in buildings borrowed from the French and others in hospitals we ourselves constructed. The Line of Communications, through which the enormous demands of our armies were handled successfully, became known later as the Services of Supply.

As to ports, St. Nazaire, La Pallice and Bassens were designated for permanent use, while Nantes, Bordeaux and Pauillac were tentatively chosen for emergencies. We arranged that Le Havre and Cherbourg could also be used if necessary, while

---

[1] Our largest storage plants were:
Base
St. Sulpice, with eventually 2,627,000 sq. ft. of covered storage.
Montoir-de-Bretagne, with 3,447,000 sq. ft.
Intermediate
Gièvres, with 3,839,000 sq. ft.
Montierchaume, with 1,214,000 sq. ft.
Advance
Is-sur-Tille, with 1,355,000 sq. ft.

several smaller ports became available, chiefly for the discharge of coal from England. When our tonnage increased, Marseille and Toulon were used to relieve the pressure on other ports and Brest became a port of debarkation for troops.

To all intents and purposes our forces were based on the American continent. With enemy submarines menacing our shipping and the quantity of available tonnage yet unknown, and with a line of communications by land stretching from three to four hundred miles from the French ports to our probable front, the organization had to overcome many difficulties which the Allies could hardly understand or appreciate, least of all many of the higher commanders upon whose coöperation success depended. It was a large military undertaking, quite distinct in character from the conduct of armies on the battlefields, but which, to be successful, required coördinating direction by the same authority.

In order that the estimates and plans regarding our participation should be realized, this organization behind the lines would have to become a great army in itself. But it would be one organized simply as a great business enterprise to receive and transport not only the combatant troops but every conceivable requirement shipped from home or obtained abroad for their maintenance. Concisely stated, the establishment behind the Zone of Operations would practically require the organization in France on an unprecedented scale of another War Department, and this is precisely what it became.

CHAPTER IX

Visit Field Marshal Haig—Study British Organization—Meeting of Allied Leaders—Conference of Commanders—War Department Program of Troop Shipments—Tonnage Inadequate—Need of Replacements— Allies Adopt Defensive Rôle—Submarine Losses Decreasing—Loose Handling of Secret Information at Home—Suggested Importation of Farmers for France—Request Prompt Action Forest Allotments

(Diary) Paris, Tuesday, July 24, 1917. Have just concluded four-day visit to British G.H.Q. Made detailed inspection of systems and methods in offices of the Adjutant General, Chief of Artillery and the General Staff.

Called Saturday at headquarters of the British Second Army, commanded by General Plumer. Visited flying fields and shops on Sunday with General Trenchard, who is most enthusiastic over aviation. German planes attacked British G.H.Q. Sunday night but did no damage.

On Monday visited the British Fifth Army, General Gough. Saw troops there studying miniature enemy trenches preparatory to attack. Had an instructive forenoon to-day at Railway Transportation Offices, returning to Paris this evening.

I T had been my intention to pay an earlier visit to Field Marshal Sir Douglas Haig, the British Commander-in-Chief, in response to his cordial invitation, but the many important questions to be considered had made it necessary to defer that pleasure longer than I had wished.

Accompanied by Colonel Harbord, Colonel Alvord and Captain Geo. S. Patton, Jr., I left Paris on July 20th and motored northward over a well-kept highway through Beauvais and Montreuil. It was harvest time, and as we sped along the beautiful avenues of tall shade trees, the succession of cultivated fields, farm houses, woods and small villages which unfolded before our eyes in sunlight and shadow, presented a wonderful panorama. Our reverie was soon interrupted, as the presence of British troops here and there indicated that we had reached their zone of operations.

Our first stop was to call on Lieutenant General Fowke, the Adjutant General of the British armies, at Montreuil. Here a very smart-looking guard of honor, from the Ancient and Honorable Company of Artillery, was drawn up in the courtyard and gave a military touch to the hearty personal welcome extended by the General himself. After a few minutes' survey of the offices, we drove with General Fowke to his quarters, where we had luncheon. It was a pleasure to be with him again, as I had not seen him, except for a moment at Boulogne, since we were together in Manchuria twelve years before, when, as observers with the Japanese forces, both of us had been attached to Kuroki's army. Naturally, we rather monopolized the luncheon conversation recalling old times.

Going through the various branches of his department in the afternoon, we found some one at each office ready to give us information. We delved into the organization, the system of recruitment, and the routine method of handling correspondence and records in the British Army. Although our military system had been practically copied from the British a century and a half earlier, it was surprising to find so few points of difference after this lapse of time.

It was almost dusk when we arrived at an old château, halfhidden in a magnificent grove of chestnut trees at Blendecques, which was occupied by the Field Marshal. His cordial greeting and that of the members of his household at once made us feel very much at home. There was nothing to disturb the quiet of the place save the sound of distant guns wafted in from the front by the evening breeze.

At dinner the conversation naturally turned to the situation in the various armies. All were keen to know about our organization and the prospect of our putting troops in the field; but as our active participation depended on many factors, such as training, equipment, and shipping, my replies were necessarily indefinite and no doubt disappointing. In turn, we asked many questions, and it was especially interesting to hear the importance of artillery emphasized by its Chief, Major General Birch, who spoke of the difficulties they had experienced in supplying themselves with guns that matched the enemy's. Referring to the British lack of artillery at the beginning of the war, he said there was reason to believe that they had finally attained a superiority over the Germans. A glance at the chart, seen later at his office, showed that the British then had 3,712 field guns and howitzers and 2,258 guns of other calibers, which gave them a sufficient number of guns of all calibers to average one to every twenty-five yards of their more than eighty miles of front. These figures were transmitted to the War Department to support my cable urging the haste in gun construction at home.

Sir Douglas told me some of the details of Nivelle's attack in the spring, how it was known far and wide beforehand, and spoke particularly of the serious discontent among the French troops which had resulted from their defeat. Although he had placed himself under Nivelle's command for these operations, he had felt, he said, little confidence in the outcome from the start. He also commented on the failure of the French to coöperate fully on various occasions. His remarks entirely confirmed the belief that I had long since held that real teamwork between the two armies was almost totally absent.

During my visit General Robertson happened to be there and we had a detailed discussion of the question of manpower. The British casualties in the Arras Offensive [1] during April and May had amounted to nearly 175,000 officers and men, and preparations were under way at that moment for another attack soon to be made on Passchendaele Ridge. This was the beginning of the operations that lasted until late in the autumn, with casualties which increased the total for the year to about 500,000 officers and men. The British High Command, however, claimed that they had inflicted heavy losses on the enemy, and it was obvious that the serious aspect of the general situation had not noticeably dampened their aggressive spirit or weakened the purpose of the British War Office to continue.

[1] The British losses up to the middle of June were almost twice as great as Nivelle's in April, although they did advance their lines somewhat.

There was considerable criticism by certain officials of the British Government regarding the excessive loss of men in these offensives, which, it was alleged, could not materially affect the final outcome. The superiority of the Allies during the first half of 1917 would, no doubt, have produced greater results if there had been unity in the conduct of operations, but the Allies did not appear to realize that without it there could be little prospect of gaining more than a local advantage. The theory of winning by attrition, with isolated attacks on limited fronts, which was evidently the idea of the British General Staff, did not appeal to me in principle. Moreover, their army could not afford the losses in view of the shortage of men which they, themselves, admitted.

Sir Douglas discussed the difficulties that he had encountered in handling rail transportation. He said that at first he had army engineers in control and later specially selected officers, but that in neither case were the results satisfactory. Finally, Sir Eric Geddes, an experienced general manager of railways, consented to take charge, and he in turn selected expert railroad men as assistants, with almost immediate improvement. I visited the headquarters of the Transportation Corps at Nashville, humorously named for General Nash, who had succeeded Major General Geddes, after whom the place had previously been called Geddesburg. The organization was patterned after the railway systems in England, but in addition to rail construction, transportation and management, it also had control of docks, debarkation, and the handling of supplies. This general plan of organization and of selecting experts for the task was later adopted for our armies.

Probably the most important thing we did on this visit was to study the organization of the Headquarters General Staff, in which we were graciously aided by Major General Butler, Assistant Chief of Staff. He and his subordinates were most patient in explaining the details of the several staff sections and the relations of each one to the others. We also examined the organization of the general staff of a field army, visiting the Second Army for this purpose. Unfortunately, General Plumer, the Army Commander, was absent—although I met him later—but every courtesy was shown by his Chief of Staff, Major General Harington. At the headquarters of Lieutenant General Morland's Corps, we had a talk on corps organization, after which the usual five o'clock tea was served.

Scarcely anything during this visit more strikingly impressed upon me our unpreparedness than what I saw during a few hours spent with Major General Trenchard at the flying field. Here we witnessed expert fliers doing every imaginable stunt, saw planes of all classes, and inspected the thoroughly equipped repair shops. The incomparable spirit of the young officers and the enlisted personnel especially impressed me, as it did later in our own aviation service. Every man seemed to be disappointed when a flight of planes departed for the front without him. Trenchard himself was an expert flier and one of the most progressive officers of aviation in any army. He was a very strong advocate of bombing and the British were doing a great deal of it at that time. It is interesting to note that a year later General Trenchard brought the British Independent Bombing Corps to our front, where it served with our air forces for the St. Mihiel operation.

Our visit to the Fifth Army Headquarters brought us more closely in touch with the active part of the front. After a general inspection, during which we saw immense quantities of engineering material and equipment accumulated in preparation for the coming offensive, we went to a small area nearby, where the plan of the German front to be attacked had been reproduced in miniature. All the details of the terrain had been worked out from air photographs and were shown in relief. The plan was large enough so that the men could actually study the approaches and walk through the various trenches of the successive lines.

We returned to have luncheon with General Gough, the Army Commander, whom we found in good spirits and, true to his Irish blood, most hospitable, jolly, and friendly. He gave us the rare treat of seeing and hearing his band of Irish bagpipes, which played many lively and familiar airs. The effect was such that I think any of us, with small encouragement, would have tried a jig or a clog dance. Their playing on the march was unique, in fact they played best while marching and the drum major seemed then to be happier.

Our visit to the British General Headquarters was most instructive as every opportunity was given us to study intimately the details of the British wartime organization. After similar studies of the French system, we selected from each those features best suited to perfect a well-balanced staff for our own army. The cordial relations and good understanding established between Sir Douglas Haig and myself and between the members of our staffs later proved very advantageous to us. In London, long after the Armistice, Sir Douglas, in an after-dinner speech, referred to this visit, which happened during a period of depression, and said that our timely appearance at his headquarters had aroused in them a strong feeling of hopefulness for the future.

(Diary) Paris, Thursday, July 26, 1917. Had breakfast yesterday at the Crillon with Mr. Lloyd George. He is alert and energetic and has a clear conception of Allied problems. Took lunch with Mr. Balfour, who thinks we have reason to feel easier regarding submarines. Representatives of the various Allies met for conference on general situation. In the evening, M. Ribot, Prime Minister, gave a State dinner to officials attending conference.

To-day attended luncheon to Allied representatives given by the President and Madame Poincaré at the Elysée Palace. In conference this afternoon with Pétain, Cadorna, Robertson, and Foch at latter's office. Discussed military plans, talked about tonnage possibilities and shortage of personnel. All pessimistic and reserved. Had dinner with Minister of War.

Mr. James Stillman, just returned from a tour of France, confirms reports of serious depression.

The conference referred to in the diary was one of those periodical meetings held to discuss the situation, both political and military, and to decide upon policies and programs. The French were anxious that we should participate, and M. Ribot had requested Washington to designate our Ambassador and me to attend. M. Jules Cambon, of the Foreign Office, whom I had known many years before when he was Ambassador at Washington, asked me also to urge that we should be represented. Speaking for the French Government, he felt that we should begin to take part in Allied councils and have a voice in directing policies.

It seemed to me, after full consideration and consultation with Ambassador Sharp, that if we participated in the conference our discussions should be limited to military questions in which we were immediately interested and that it would be wiser not to discuss any other subjects at the time. But as our participation, even in this limited way, might be misunderstood by the Allies, a possibility which the President wished to avoid, arrangements were made for a separate meeting of the military leaders.

During breakfast with Mr. Lloyd George, he pointed out the grave consequences of continued German success against Russia, his conclusions concerning the outlook being, like those of almost every one else, that Russia could no longer be relied upon for much help in a military way. He said the existing situation made it especially important that America should assume part of the responsibility of deciding the course to be followed by the Allies. In reply to this I explained the reasons why the President felt that for the present we should join only in the consideration of the military aspects of the general situation.

This meeting with the Allied military leaders, which was my first, brought out little that was hopeful. The political relations of the Allies were touched upon in a general way, but only so far as they might affect the military situation. The most significant recent event, of course, had been the crisis in Russia. Kerensky had succeeded in reviving the spirits of the Russian armies in Galicia and for a short time they were able to make considerable gains against the Austro-Germans. In the end, however, they had been badly beaten and reports indicated that great demoralization existed throughout the nation. Although lacking in complete information, the opinion prevailed in the conference that Russia was practically eliminated as a military factor. The general idea seemed to be that the Germans, with the men they could take from the Russian front, would be able to renew offensive activities on the Western Front in the spring at the latest.

With reference to American assistance, I gave in detail the situation as to the strength, immediate and prospective, of our army, especially in the light of the latest plans of the War Department, and laid special emphasis on the necessity for additional shipping. A cablegram had just been received in response to mine of July 6th, in which I had requested that at least a million men reach France by the following spring. This message, indicating that the War Department foresaw small chance of securing the necessary tonnage, was read to the conference:

"By using all shipping which is now in sight for the purpose and which will be available after month of November, the plan proposes to transport to France by June 15, 1918, 21 divisions, comprising about 420,000 men, together with auxiliary troops and replacement troops, line of communication troops, and others, amounting to 214,975 men, making a total of 634,975 men. These will be in addition to the second half of General Sibert's division now preparing to go. The plan proposes the following number of troops to be sent on or about the given dates: August 15th, 5,500 auxiliary and replacement troops; September 1st, 13,000 auxiliary and replacement troops; October 1st, two divisions or 41,750 men; November 1st, two divisions or 39,250 men; November 15th, one division or 20,500 men; December 1st, 13,000 auxiliary and replacement troops; January 1st, three divisions or 59,750 men; January 15th, one division or 28,000 men and 8,000 auxiliary troops; February 1st, two divisions or 39,250 men; February 15th, one division or 20,500 men; March 1st, 13,000 auxiliary and replacement troops; April 1st, three divisions or 59,750 men; May 1st, two divisions or 39,250 men; May 15th, one division or 20,500 men; June 1st, 13,000 auxiliary and replacement troops; June 15th, two divisions or 54,250 men and 14,250 auxiliary and replacement troops."

Although short of my recommendations, even this schedule could be carried out only by a very large increase in tonnage. The other members of the conference were of the opinion that if new adjustments could be made there might be shipping for nine or ten of our divisions before spring. So, for the moment, there did not seem to be the slightest chance of transporting a million men to France by the following June.

As to the state of their respective armies, Robertson pointed out that the British casualties had been heavy during the year and their manpower greatly reduced. Pétain mentioned their severe losses and said that the French could only slightly augment their strength. Cadorna said that the Italian Army was little, if any, better off. The depletion of their resources in men caused considerable anxiety among the Allies in the face of the probability of having to meet the full force of the Central Powers in the spring.

After canvassing the whole situation, the conference expressed the unanimous opinion that a defensive rôle should be adopted on all secondary fronts. The British and French representatives hoped that the surplus troops resulting from this course might be available to strengthen their armies in France, and General Cadorna, of course, thought the Italian armies should have their share. The following cable conveyed to Washington the conclusions of the conference:

"Informal conference Commanders-in-Chief Allied armies held Paris July twenty-sixth, present Generals Robertson, Pétain, Foch, Cadorna, Pershing. Steps to be taken in case Russia should be forced out of war considered. Various movements troops to and from different fronts to meet possible contingencies discussed. Conference also weighed political, economic and moral effect both upon Central and Allied Powers under most unfavorable aspect from Allied point of view. General conclusions reached were necessity for adoption of purely defensive attitude on all secondary fronts and withdrawal surplus troops for duty on Western Front. By thus strengthening Western Front believed Allies could hold until American forces in sufficient numbers arrive to gain ascendancy. To accelerate participation American forces and provide necessary transport for American army and movement of armies from secondary fronts conference recommends that question of shipping be immediately taken up by Inter-Allied Commission. However, consensus of opinion was that steps should be taken by Allies to determine part to be played by America, Great Britain, France and possibly Japan to support Russia with a view to avoiding extreme eventualities."

About this time further disturbing reports were submitted to me confidentially by one of our naval officers sent by Admiral Sims. They were based upon tonnage losses for May, June and July, and seemed to confirm the conclusions of a month previous that there would soon be insufficient Allied shipping left to bring over an American army of the strength required, and that the Allies would find it difficult to keep up their supply of food from overseas and provide matériel necessary to carry on the war. The data presented appeared to prove that if the rate of destruction of shipping could not be reduced, the war would be lost before we could fire a shot.

This report was certainly most pessimistic, but it did not dispel my confidence in the success of the plan which had been tested and was about to be inaugurated of sending ships over in convoys under the protection of naval vessels. Additional destroyers requested by Admiral Sims had by this time increased such craft in European waters and as a result the activities of submarines had been somewhat diminished for July as compared with April. Submarines could not afford to take great risk in the presence of cruisers and they were especially fearful of destroyers. They had learned of the disastrous effect of depth bombs used by destroyers and trawlers and also that detection would be almost certain in operating against a convoy. Yet for the time being, ship construction in British yards continued below losses and our Shipping Board at home had scarcely stopped wrangling over materials and types. All these facts caused everybody to realize the extreme urgency of speed, and that in turn gave some hope that the prospects might soon become brighter.

It was my belief, even in the face of the heavy losses, that with complete coöperation under expert management and distribution the shipping would be ample for all purposes. This would require, of course, that it be placed under some central authority, but the governments, especially the British, that controlled most of it, while apparently desirous of helping, did not seem inclined to think they could make any concessions. They had entered into arrangements to assist each other with shipping for foodstuffs, but there was no such thing as the pooling of Allied tonnage for general purposes.

Although the Allied authorities at this stage were concerned over the question of tonnage, on which the success of Allied military effort really hinged, their doubt of the possibility of any considerable numbers of our troops being ready at an early date to operate as a distinct American force probably made them less active in trying to find shipping for our purpose. At the same time, one could not help thinking that with our consent to feed men into the various armies, the governments concerned would find it possible to send over vessels to bring their respective allotments across.

However, the discouraging reports on the situation did make such an impression on the military leaders that, as reported in my cable, they suggested the possibility of pooling all available shipping and accordingly recommended a commission to consider the question, with special reference to the transportation of the American Army. In order to reach a solution, it was necessary, in the first place, to ascertain as nearly as possible what the requirements in shipping would be and then investigate the various sources from which ships might be obtained. In any such survey it was essential that we should be represented by men with expert knowledge to present our case before this commission.

The success of submarine warfare had been largely dependent upon advance knowledge concerning movements of vessels. As there was no doubt that the sailing dates of much of our shipping reached Germany through spies, one way to reduce the danger would be to close their sources of information. In the beginning the practice of our War Department in transmitting secret intelligence was extremely loose. The data regarding sailings were, of course, sent to my headquarters, but at the same time, or often before, they were given to both French and British Military and Naval Attachés and Missions in Washington. These officials immediately transmitted the news by cable to their respective Governments, with the result that it usually became almost common knowledge. Frequently, in the early days of troop movements, word regarding sailings reached us first through civilian channels in Paris. Finally, after consultation with Admiral Sims, through his representative, I recommended that all data regarding movements of transports be given only to our naval authorities, to be transmitted by their secret code. This precaution largely, if not entirely, checked the leakage through the channels named. Yet persistent protests had to be made before the War Department could be induced to discontinue its careless methods.

But there were other means possessed by the enemy of finding out about our movements. One message, intercepted by the French, sent from some wireless station in Spain to the German General Staff, announced the arrival of several American vessels at Nantes and of 10,000 American soldiers at St. Nazaire, and also gave the routes taken by our transports. Another, evidently intended for submarines, reported the departure of a convoy from New York. These and similar facts that came to my knowledge were cabled at once to Admiral Sims and to Washington.

The War Department was also advised of the probability that certain favorably located Portuguese and Spanish ports were being used by German submarines. Wireless messages intercepted in France indicated that enemy agents located at such ports had established a regular system for obtaining valuable information regarding Allied movements at sea. While it was said that Spain sympathized with the Allies, still some anxiety was manifest on account of the reports of the activities there of German interests. It being important that Spain should remain neutral, the whole situation was cabled to Washington and presumably diplomatic representations of protest were made to the Spanish Government.

At the time of this gloomy outlook regarding tonnage losses, the question of supplies appeared precarious enough for Washington to send to me for comment a suggestion that had been received regarding the possibility of augmenting the food supply for our armies through increased cultivation of the soil in France and northern Spain by American farmers. Armies in the past in that part of the world had often subsisted themselves and such a possibility had already been discussed at my headquarters. But in my opinion, as cabled to the War Department, it would be wiser to increase our military forces more rapidly and then, if necessary, relieve the older classes of French soldiers from the front to enable them to return to their farms.

(Diary) Paris, Saturday, July 28, 1917. Had luncheon with James Gordon Bennett and found him more aggressive than ever. Called on M. Painlevé, with Major Graves of the Forestry Service, to urge immediate permission to cut timber.

Notwithstanding previous promises of forest concessions, granted, it is true, with some hesitation, the French officials were slow to designate areas for our use. As a regiment of forestry engineers stood ready to go to work and the necessity for large quantities of lumber had become urgent, I called at the War Office and laid the matter before M. Painlevé, who never failed to do all he could do to expedite our business. He was surprised to find that nothing had been done, and at once gave positive instructions that action should be taken immediately. Eventually, at my suggestion, the requisition system of obtaining forest concessions was adopted and we had no further trouble.

This was only one of numerous instances in which delay compelled me to go direct to the supreme authority to get decisions on matters of recognized importance. It should not be inferred from this instance, however, that there existed any inherent disinclination on the part of the French to aid us, but it often required considerable personal effort to overcome the inertia in the various bureaus. In this instance and in others the question of authority between officials also entered as a factor.

CHAPTER X

Leadership for Higher Units—Visit 1st Division Billeting Area—Relations between Troops and Peasants—G.H.Q. Located at Chaumont—Order to Troops on Attitude Toward People and Property—Calling of National Army Delayed by Lack of Equipment—French Furnish Machine Guns and Automatic Rifles—Organization of Military Police—Railway Problem

P ROBABLY the most important factor in building up an aggressive army is the selection of leaders. Without efficient leadership the finest of troops may suffer defeat by inferior forces skillfully led. During my experience, covering a considerable period of years, many otherwise able and conscientious officers had been seen to fail for want of initiative, one of the important requisites of a successful leader. The lack of leadership by a number of officers of high rank in the French and British Armies in the early days of the war afforded an immediate object lesson for us on the necessity of selecting capable officers for important positions.

In our Regular Army in time of peace, the system of promotion by seniority, instead of by selection, deprives many capable and energetic officers of the opportunity to command the larger units, which would help to prepare them for higher places in time of war. The same comment applies with equal or greater force to our National Guard, in which politics adds another factor often adverse to efficiency in the higher grades.

Inasmuch as our success would depend upon the offensive spirit among combat troops, it was essential that vigorous and intelligent leadership should, if possible, be assured at the outset. I therefore urged the choice of relatively young and alert officers for the active command of higher units. It was especially desirable that this be done early in order that they might gain experience and also have the chance to prove themselves worthy. The following were my recommendations on the subject to the Secretary of War:

> "My observation of British and French Armies and most exacting arduous service conditions at the front fully convinces me that only officers in full mental and physical vigor should be sent here. Contrary course means certain inefficiency in our service and possible later humiliation of officers concerned. General officers must undergo extreme effort in personal supervision of operations in trenches. Very few British or French division commanders over forty-five or brigadiers over forty. We have too much at stake to risk inefficiency through mental or physical defects. Strongly recommend conditions be fully considered in making high appointments and suggest that no officer of whatever rank be sent here for active service who is not strong and robust in every particular. Officers selected for appointment general officer of line should be those with experience in actively commanding troops. Officers not fulfilling above conditions can be usefully employed at home training troops."

These recommendations were not altogether followed at home, in fact very little effort seems to have been made at selection, so that some officers without ambition or initiative, whose inefficiency should have been well known, and others whose age and physical condition were such as to disqualify them for strenuous service, were given important assignments. Generally speaking the policy of the War Department from the beginning to the end of the war seemed to be to appoint officers to the higher grades according to seniority with the intention of weeding out the inefficient later on. It was not a sound policy and it caused no end of trouble in France, because after the appointment of such officers it was a slow process to eliminate them. Presumably the method of appointing according to rank was suggested by the successive Chiefs of Staff.

Of course there were difficulties in applying the principle of selection, which I thoroughly understood. But a process of elimination of officers known to be inactive could have been applied easily enough. The records of all officers were kept in the Adjutant General's office and a careful study of these would have enabled the Chief of Staff and his assistants to cross off those in the grade of colonel or lieutenant colonel whose records showed them lacking in enterprise and activity. Selection could then have been invoked and a list of relatively young and vigorous general officers would probably have been the result. Most of the general officers appointed were known to me and not a few, who under the rule of seniority had been commanders of regiments and departments, had lacked the energy even to train their commands or themselves in battle exercises where favorable opportunity had been afforded. However, those appointees who were unprepared professionally for the duties of modern war eventually fell by the wayside as victims of a system that had failed to stimulate activity of mind or body in times of peace.

(Diary) Paris, Friday, August 3, 1917. Left Tuesday for St. Dizier and Ligny-en-Barrois, accompanied by Harbord, Colonel de Chambrun and Captain Patton, mainly to examine possible locations for headquarters.

Went to Menaucourt and Naix on Wednesday, saw Marines under Colonel C. A. Doyen; then to the 28th Infantry, Colonel B. B. Buck, at Saint Amand and Tréveray; the 26th, Colonel G. B. Duncan, at Saint Joire; thence to the 16th Infantry, Colonel W. H. Allaire, at Abainville; and the 18th Infantry, Colonel U. G. McAlexander, at Houdelaincourt. All troops well turned out, billets reasonably comfortable. The French 47th Infantry Division detailed to assist in training our 1st Division. The French troops made a fine appearance.

At Neufchâteau in the afternoon saw sixteen American newspaper correspondents under charge of Major Frederick Palmer. Regret we cannot permit them to tell what we are doing. At Mirecourt later met Major General de Castelnau, commanding the Eastern Group of French Armies. He is of the old school, very courteous, about seventy, short and sturdy. Spent the night at Vittel. Accommodations ample, surroundings beautiful, but rail communications inconvenient and social attractions objectionable.

Inspected Chaumont yesterday, where French commander, Major General Wirbel, pointed out disadvantages while the Mayor, M. Lévy-Alphandéry, favored its selection as our headquarters. Afterwards continued on to Paris.

Held conference with Ambassador this evening.

In driving through those areas nearest the front, one could not help being depressed by their deserted appearance. As the limited crops of grain had been mostly harvested, little work of any kind was going on in the fields. Few people were seen even in the villages, except old men and women, with now and then some small children. We noticed but few animals, either along the roads or in the pastures. It was almost as though the population had disappeared with their flocks and herds. Many families had moved away, and, of course, most of the able-bodied men were in the armies. There were no ruins, for the reason that no fighting had taken place in that section. The country simply had an abandoned look.

It would have been out of the question to supply barracks or tentage for all our troops in France and we had adopted the billeting system, whereby the troops of a division as they arrived in their training area were spread around by regiments, battalions or companies in the various towns and villages. Regardless of accommodations the billets were usually preferable in winter to either barracks or tents.

The smaller French villages, which consist merely of groups of farmhouses, were not generally sanitary from our point of view, as the residue from the stables, regarded as invaluable fertilizer, was usually stored in the streets, where the unsightly heaps, with their pungent odors, reminded one of a country barnyard. At the expense of considerable labor on the part of troops, with such help from the French as could be impressed, most of these dumps had to be removed before our men were content to settle down to work. Where there was not enough spare room in the dwelling houses of the inhabitants, which was usually the case, the barn or stable lofts were quickly converted into fairly comfortable quarters, with hay or fodder in lieu of barrack beds or cots. On account of the danger, no fires were allowed in these billets and even smoking had to be prohibited.

My inspection of the 1st Division showed that it was well settled in its training area in the region of Gondrecourt, south of Bar-le-

Note: Total strength of the A.E.F. on July 31st, 726 officers, 16,022 enlisted men.

Duc. The troops of the division had already established friendly relations with the French peasantry and had quickly adapted themselves to their new mode of life. The training of the division was proceeding and the officers and men were eager for the day when they could test their strength against the enemy.

As the natural consequence of the financial condition of the frugal French provincial, he was wont to profit unduly by the presence of the British and ourselves, and the open-handed pay-day habits of the Americans served to give some encouragement to this inclination. As a result, some coolness grew up later between our men and their early friends. While one can appreciate the temptation to take advantage of such an opportunity, yet the average American soldier, quite overlooking the great inconvenience our troops caused the people and their kindness in general, could not quite bring himself to understand this attitude. As a matter of truth, the liberal spending indulged in by our men was a source of difficulty to the French themselves, as the resulting higher levels of prices for commodities imposed hardships on those who did not enjoy the profits flowing from sales to the Americans.

At the conclusion of my inspection of various places, Chaumont was selected as the best site for my General Headquarters. It was on our line of communications to the front and centrally placed as to probable sectors of our operations. The fine regimental barracks there furnished office space for our headquarters and we were able to obtain ample billeting accommodations in private houses for all except the enlisted men, who were provided with temporary barracks.

This old town of some 15,000 inhabitants is situated near the upper Marne, on a plateau that dominates the wooded hills and cultivated valleys of the surrounding country. Of historical interest is the fact that in 1814 Chaumont was the scene of the conference between the sovereigns of Great Britain, Austria, Russia and Prussia to decide the fate of Napoleon. The house in which this meeting of emperors and kings occurred became in our day a club where the younger French and American officers no doubt frequently discussed the form of punishment that the Allies should eventually impose upon the Kaiser. The people of the town were very hospitable and soon became our warm friends. When the end arrived, we were loath to leave behind us a community so generous and open-hearted and for whom we felt such affection and esteem. Americans who had the good fortune to live in Chaumont will always cherish their association with its charming people.

The extreme patience and fortitude of the French, their industry and their frugality, made all the more necessary through the hardships of war, demanded that we should not by any avoidable act render their situation more onerous or reduce their capacity to produce by any disregard of their interests. That all our forces might understand these obligations, an order was published, from which the following is quoted:

"For the first time in history the American Army finds itself in European territory. The good name of the United States and the maintenance of cordial relations require perfect deportment of each member of this command. It is of the greatest importance that the soldiers of the American Army shall at all times treat the people of France, especially the women, with the greatest courtesy and consideration. The valiant deeds of the French Armies and those of their Allies by which they have together successfully maintained their common cause for three years, and the sacrifices of the civil population of France in support of their armies command our profound respect. This can best be expressed on the part of our forces by uniform courtesy to all the French people and by faithful consideration of their laws and customs. * * *

"The intense cultivation of the soil in France and the conditions caused by the war make it necessary that extreme care be taken to do no damage to private property. The entire French manhood capable of bearing arms is in the field fighting the enemy. Only old men, women and children remain to cultivate the soil. It should therefore be a point of honor with each member of the American Army to avoid doing the least damage to any property in France."

It was hardly necessary to issue such a proclamation as it was noticeable from the beginning that the attitude of the men toward the inhabitants and their property was most commendable. I do not believe that in all history there has ever been an army on foreign soil so considerate and observant of the rights and interests of the people. The peasant class made a strong appeal to every man in the army. Their simplicity, their love of the soil, and the long hours of work in the fields by the old men and women and the young boys and girls remained the constant admiration of our soldiers. I am inclined to think, however, that the excellent behavior of our soldiers, the rather unmilitary appearance of the earlier contingents in ill-fitting uniforms, and their apparent lack of formal discipline created at first the impression in the minds of the French officials that such men were not likely to become aggressive fighting troops.

(Diary) Paris, Monday, August 6, 1917. Had conference on Saturday with M. Albert Claveille, head of Bureau of Transportation, regarding railway matters. Washington says lack of equipment will delay call for National Army.

Colonel Williams reports French behind in delivery machine guns and automatic rifles. Conferred with Harjes today about services of Norton-Harjes Volunteer Ambulance Unit.[1] Had an interesting evening with Pétain as dinner guest. He spoke confidentially of plans for an offensive; wants me present.

In the organization of our armies for the World War it was evident that if any considerable numbers were to be sent abroad, an additional force would be needed over and above the Regular Army and the National Guard. The War Department therefore established what was called the National Army, to be composed principally of men who were to come into the service through the draft. Most of the divisions of the National Army were organized in August and September and some men were then assigned to them. As the time approached to begin the training of the smaller units, it was found that after equipping the special troops urgently needed in France there was little equipment left even for the additional men required to fill up the National

[1] Harjes had established and was supporting a volunteer ambulance unit for service with the French.

Guard. Unfortunately, this made it necessary to delay calling out more drafts for the units of the National Army. However, considerable numbers were called into service and proceeded with preliminary instruction, but the lack of equipment seriously delayed their progress.

The development of the machine gun as an infantry weapon, following the experience of the Russo-Japanese War, had been carried to a high degree of perfection, especially in the German Army, where its value was more fully appreciated than among the Allies. In this, as in every other line of preparation, we were far behind all others. The question of adopting new types of machine guns and automatic rifles for our army had been discussed at home for years and test after test had been made, but the nearest approach to a decision was an acrimonious discussion in and out of the press between the Ordnance Department and certain inventors. The result was that when we entered the war no conclusion regarding the best make of gun had been reached that, in the opinion of the War Department, would warrant its manufacture in quantity. Not only were we without sufficient machine guns, but our organization tables did not anticipate their use in anything like the numbers employed by the enemy.

To equip our advance divisions, especially in view of the possibility of an emergency requiring prompt entry into the line, arrangements were made to purchase Hotchkiss machine guns and Chauchat automatics from the French. But, on account of delay in deliveries, instruction of our troops in the handling of these weapons was slowed down considerably. Notwithstanding these handicaps, the most modern conception of the use of machine guns was taught in our schools, and our machine gunners eventually reached a high degree of proficiency.

At this time the production of the Vickers machine gun was proceeding slowly. Soon after the adoption of the Browning automatic weapons, following the tests in May, the manufacture of both the heavy gun for ground work and the light gun as an automatic rifle was begun, although none of these became available for use in battle until September, 1918. The Lewis machine gun, about which there had been so much controversy involving the Ordnance Department, was not considered suitable as an automatic rifle but was recommended for airplanes.

Our earlier divisions were seriously handicapped in their preparation at home by lack of machine guns for training, many units not receiving this arm until after their arrival in France. When it is recalled that each division at the beginning of the war was allowed only 92 machine guns and no automatic rifles, and that under our war organization 260 machine guns and 768 automatic rifles were required, the result of delay in providing these guns needs no further comment.

> (Diary) Paris, Tuesday, August 14, 1917. Had M. Painlevé, M. Viviani and M. Claveille to luncheon on Thursday, hoping to make coöperation easier. Took dinner with General Nash and Colonel Thornton, British Army, Manager and Assistant, respectively, for their rail transportation in France.
>
> General Hornwood, British Provost Marshal General, called to-day with Colonel Ely to discuss military police. Visited Mrs. Whitelaw Reid's hospital, which she wishes us to take for officers.
>
> Department recommends Mr. Atterbury for railway chief; have requested that he be sent over.

The maintenance of good order among our troops under the peculiar conditions of service in France was most important and for this purpose a military police was essential. Such a force, under the control of the Provost Marshal General, corresponded to the police department in a well-organized city, except that its jurisdiction included only those in the military service. The British, whose situation was similar to our own, gave us helpful information regarding their system, which, with slight modification, was adopted for our armies. In our previous wars, the Provost Guard, so called, usually consisted of troops of the line detailed for the purpose but without any special training for such duty.

Colonel Hanson E. Ely was selected to organize the police corps and made a good beginning in laying the foundation, but, at his own request, he was shortly relieved and sent to regimental duty. His successor, Colonel W. H. Allaire, became Provost Marshal General until the following July, when he was relieved by Colonel J. C. Groome. In September, 1918, Brigadier General H. H. Bandholtz, on account of his special fitness for such work from his experience as Chief of Constabulary in the Philippine Islands, became the permanent head of the corps. Due credit must be given to each of these officers but particularly to Bandholtz for the smart appearance and the high efficiency of the military police. Its services were indispensable in directing and handling traffic during combat activities, in preventing straggling and in maintaining order among scattered groups of our armies both before and after the Armistice. The organization on November 1, 1918, numbered 463 officers and 15,912 men, spread practically over the whole of France.

The use of railways for the movement of troops and supplies had never before attained any such proportions as in the World War and there was no service, except sea transportation, upon which we placed greater dependence for our success. The long haul from our ports to the front made it highly important that the rail system be organized according to the most modern methods and managed by experienced personnel.

The first study of railway conditions in France was made by a Board of Engineers chosen by the War Department headed by Major Wm. Barclay Parsons, afterward Colonel 11th Engineers. This board submitted an exhaustive report of its investigations and conclusions, which fully agreed with the opinion of Colonel Taylor, my Chief of Engineers, and his assistants. These independent investigations showed that the French railways, especially those that we planned to use, were sadly in need of physical rehabilitation and that the additional burden to be placed on them would require on our part an immense program of construction of new yards, terminals, multiple tracks, cut-offs, regulating stations and other additions. Both groups of engineers felt also that the methods of the French would have to be greatly improved to meet the extraordinary demands that would arise in handling our traffic. It was apparent that we could not depend entirely on the French without great risk of failure at a critical moment, and it was evident that if we expected the maximum efficiency in this service we must provide our own personnel as well as additional locomotives and cars, all to be as far as practicable under American management. Differences in language, customs and methods combined to make this one of our most delicate and trying problems, as any one who has traveled on French railroads can readily imagine.

A separate transportation corps had never been provided in our army; in fact, no department had been specifically charged with the management of railroads. In the Quartermaster Corps a bureau issued transportation requests, routed personnel and freight and settled the accounts, and it was the understanding that in time of war the army engineers would step in and take charge when railway operation should become necessary. With this plan in view, commendable progress had been made toward both procurement and organization by Colonel Taylor. Complete estimates for rolling stock and construction at ports, terminals and yards, including an accurate survey of building and equipment requirements, had been made under his direction by Major W. J. Wilgus, formerly Vice President of the New York Central, afterwards Colonel, a clever and brilliant man of vision who had been a member of the Parsons Board. These estimates without change served as a permanent guide for railway construction plans and material.

Coördinate with the procurement and maintenance of railway material and equipment, we were confronted with the vital question of organization for operation and management. We had no officers in the Regular service of sufficient experience in railway administration to insure success. Therefore, the evident course to pursue, to which the precedent of both the British and French pointed the way, was to create a transportation corps, immediately under the direction of some man of outstanding reputation in the railroad world. In accordance with the principle of obtaining the most competent men for important positions, the following cable was sent on July 29th:

"Have made thorough study of railroad situation and am convinced that operation of railroads must be under man with large experience in managing commercial railroads at home. Successful handling our railroad lines so important that ablest man in country should be selected. After almost disastrous results with inexperienced military men running railroads British selected ablest man could find to have charge transportation. Question here mainly one of physical operation and management in intimate relation with French who retain general control which is necessary to handle ordinary commercial traffic. Question of railroad transportation of course involves equipment maintenance and new construction at front as army advances and should be practically independent department although nominally under engineers. Railroad man chosen should be sent here without delay together with three or four able assistants of his own selection. Later on it is believed these men should be given appropriate military rank."

This elicited the reply mentioned in the diary recommending Mr. W. W. Atterbury, General Manager of the Pennsylvania Railroad, for the place.

CHAPTER XI

Visit French and American Troops with Pétain—Inspection French Regulating Station—Witness Successful French Attack—Recommend Production Powder and Explosives at Home—Difficulties of Coördination with Allies and War Department Bureaus—Purchasing Agency Established

(Diary) Paris, Tuesday, August 21, 1917. Visited billeting areas of French 47th Division and our 1st Division with General Pétain on Sunday.

Inspected St. Dizier Regulating Station and witnessed French attack near Verdun yesterday. Visited French hospital at Souilly.

Returned this morning with M. Painlevé, Minister of War, on his train.

AS I had accepted General Pétain's invitation to see the French offensive that was to take place on the 20th, I motored to French G.H.Q. on Saturday afternoon, the 18th, accompanied by Colonel Palmer and Captain Carl Boyd, and after dinner left with General Pétain and two or three members of his staff on his train for an inspection of French and American troops. We reached Gondrecourt the next morning and began with a review of the French 47th Infantry Division, which was paraded on a prominent plateau near Houdelaincourt. Before the march past, several officers and men, drawn up in front of the center of the lines, were decorated by Pétain for gallantry. It was a proud moment for each one to have his badge of courage pinned on his breast by the distinguished Commander-in-Chief of the French Army. Indeed, while awards were bestowed upon but a few outstanding individuals, the whole division shared in this recognition of its splendid services. The ceremony could hardly have been more impressive. With not a soul in sight save those in uniform, the stillness was like that which follows a battle, leaving the distinct feeling that these brave men were being decorated on the field of honor.

To the stirring strains of the famous *Sambre et Meuse,* the division swung past in review in almost perfect lines and with the élan characteristic of French troops. General Pétain then had the officers assembled by Major General de Pouydraguin, the division commander, and in a brief talk praised their appearance and especially their record. He encouraged them to promote the morale and efficiency of their men in preparation for arduous work yet to come. This division had been in every serious engagement of the war and its losses had been very heavy, as could be easily surmised from the youthful appearance of the officers, most of whom had risen from the ranks to replace casualties among their seniors. General Pétain told them that because of its fine record the division had been given the special honor of assisting in the instruction of the American 1st Division.

Accompanied by Brigadier General Bundy, Colonel William M. Cruikshank, and others, I took Pétain to see some of our troops being trained in throwing grenades, and in the use of the French automatic rifle. An amusing story was told us in connection with the grenade instruction. It seems that one of the men insisted on throwing his grenade immediately after setting the fuse instead of waiting till he slowly counted seven, which was necessary so that the explosion would occur as the grenade reached its destination. After being cautioned several times by his officer, the man said, "Captain, I just can't hold these grenades any longer because I can feel them swelling in my hand."

We visited several villages occupied by French and American troops. As we passed through our billets and inspected the kitchens, Pétain inquired particularly about the components of our ration and the manner of cooking and serving meals. The French soldiers were furnished wine in place of coffee provided for our men, and the allowances differed in other respects, ours containing a larger meat component. But when it came to cooking, the French were ahead of us, although our men preferred our own to either the French or British ration.

In going around with General Pétain it was significant that every honor which the scant population could show was paid to him. All the villages were decorated and the people appeared in gala dress. At each place some young girl especially selected for her good looks presented the General with flowers, for which she expected and proudly received the customary acknowledgment of a chaste kiss on each cheek.

In many places we had to climb ladders to reach the American billets in the hay mows. In one loft I happened to stand apart near a neatly made bunk and in the dim light Pétain mistook me for the sergeant in charge. He asked me how we liked our billets and a number of other questions about our life in France, which I answered respectfully, playing the part the best I could. He did not know the difference until he was told by some of the amused members of his staff after we had descended.

Motoring to Souilly, the headquarters of the French Second Army, we met Major General Fayolle, commanding the Group of Armies of the Center, and Major General Guillaumat, Commander of the Second Army, whose Chief of Staff explained in detail the plan of the battle that was to take place the next day. We had luncheon with Fayolle, whom later I came to regard as one of the ablest of the French generals. In appearance he was rather frail, no longer young, but active and alert.

On our visit to the military hospital at Souilly, Pétain presented Mlle. de Baye, a nurse, with the Croix de Guerre, as she lay on a cot suffering from a severe wound inflicted by a piece of shell two days before. When he told her who I was, she said, "I am glad you are here, General, to see how a French woman can suffer for her country." She was so happy over her decoration, however, that I am sure that for the moment she had entirely forgotten her pain.

The following morning, at my suggestion, we went to St. Dizier, to inspect the regulating station. There we met M. Painlevé, the Minister of War, who had come to the front to witness the battle, in company with M. Albert Thomas, the Minister of Munitions. I spent a most instructive forenoon studying the method of distributing supplies to units at the front.

The regulating station was essentially a development of the World War. All rations, clothing, fuel, ammunition and other supplies came in bulk from depots in the rear to one of these stations, and from there the trains, one each day or so, for each division or corresponding group went forward as far as safety would permit, carrying everything needed for the period. The supplies were then sent by the light railway to the railhead, thence by divisional trucks or wagons to the proper organizations. The system seemed simple enough but to make it work successfully thorough organization and expert management were necessary. This was especially true when it had to serve large forces, as was the case during the St. Mihiel battle the following year, when we handled through this station the greater part of the supplies for the more than half a million Americans on that front.

In the afternoon I had a most agreeable surprise. Motoring to the command post of the XVI Corps, which conducted this offensive, I found an old friend of Russo-Japanese War days, Major General Corvisart, in command. As viewed from his post, with the sun at our backs, the battlefield lay before us like a panorama, and we could easily follow the advancing French lines, one particular unit under observation being the famous Foreign Legion, in which I had become interested many years before from reading Ouida's tale, "Under Two Flags."

Being entirely assured regarding the outcome of the battle, Corvisart and I dropped into reminiscence of our former service together in Manchuria. We had been military attachés in Japan at the same time, both of us being assigned to General Kuroki's army as observers. I inquired about Major Caviglia, the Italian attaché, and learned that he was then a lieutenant general commanding an army in northern Italy. We recalled that when we were with the Japanese Army, Caviglia used to wake us every morning singing Italian opera. Corvisart said that the Austrian attaché had been advanced to the same rank and position as Caviglia. Sir Ian Hamilton, of Gallipoli fame, already held the rank of major general when he was observer with the Japanese.

Colonel Fowke had become lieutenant general and adjutant general of the British forces. And so we ran through the list up to the German attachés. Colonel, then Captain, Hoffmann had but recently succeeded Ludendorff as chief of staff on the Russian front and later became a general. He was a jolly sort and was quite popular among the group attached to Kuroki's army. I then asked about Major von Etzel, the senior German attaché, and it was easy to anticipate the reply as Corvisart, with a smile of satisfaction, pointed to the battlefield and said, "I have just beaten him to-day. He is commanding a division opposite me."

This attack of the French Second Army, although made astride the Meuse River, was directed principally against Le Mort Homme hill and Hill 304, both famous in the struggle of 1916. In order to destroy the wire entanglement and other obstacles, as a precaution against heavy losses, the infantry assault was preceded by four days' continuous bombardment, and relatively the amount of artillery ammunition expended exceeded that of any previous engagement, its value being, as I was informed, $75,-000,000. The proportion of the artillery force as compared to the infantry in this battle was as eleven to ten. The firing attained such precision and volume that the German troops in the forward positions were submerged and the attacking infantry reached most of its objectives by nightfall the first day, making an advance of three miles and capturing 6,000 prisoners.

The sector where the French attack took place was to have a peculiar interest for me before the end of the war. My headquarters as commander of the First Army one year later occupied the building in Souilly, then used by Major General Guillaumat, and the line reached by Corvisart's troops in this battle became our jump-off line in the Meuse-Argonne battle. In fact, every foot of the ground covered in this inspection with General Pétain became associated with America's greatest effort in the war. After visiting the French installations and the manifold activities carried on behind this front, with the shifting masses of combat troops and the thousands engaged in the services of supply and transportation, it seemed quite improbable that we should be able to marshal a sufficient army in time to replace the French on this front until late in 1918.

I found it most agreeable as well as instructive to be with Pétain in this intimate way and have an opportunity to hear something of his experience. His discussion of the defense of Verdun, in which, as French commander, he served with such marked distinction, was especially entertaining. As we drove about, he spoke of the courage of his men and of the tremendous losses they had sustained. He pointed out the vast amount of road work, including the Voie Sacrée from Bar-le-Duc to Verdun, rebuilt under his directions for the constant movements of large bodies of troops and supplies necessary to maintain the defense.

In lighter vein, his comments on French politicians during this trip were amusing, if not always complimentary, and he congratulated me many times on being so far removed from political interference. One afternoon the conversation drifted to painting and he asked me how many times I had sat for my portrait. "Several times already," I said. "The last one, which I thought very good, was done by a distinguished artist by the name of Jonas (English, Jonah) for *l'Illustration*." Immediately he said, "Don't let them publish it! Don't do it! Every officer whose portrait by Jonas has appeared in that journal has been relieved from his command." Not that I am superstitious, quite the contrary, but I immediately forbade the publication of the portrait, and to this day it has never appeared.

From the time of Nivelle's failure in April, the depression in the French armies had been so great that Pétain, who succeeded him, had been content simply to hold the trenches, and no French offensive operation of consequence until this one had been attempted. From the moment of his assignment, Pétain began to build up the shattered morale of his armies, and probably no other officer in France could have performed the task so well. His immense success in the defense of Verdun had won for him the confidence of the army and the country, and yet he remained the same modest, unassuming character, consistent and conservative. He, perhaps better than any other, understood the temperament of the French soldier, whom he handled with infinite patience and tact. Without flourish of trumpets, he went among the disaffected regiments with counsel and advice. The recalcitrant element he severely disciplined, even to the execution of several leaders. In establishing a Department of Morale, he took steps to counteract defeatist propaganda among the men on leave. During his visits of inspection he mingled with the troops and listened to stories of abuses, which, as far as possible, he corrected on the spot.

Pétain had visited some ninety divisions and impressed them with his personality and prestige. As his efforts began to bear fruit, he concluded to try a limited operation, to be carried out by specially selected units. The plans for the attack, which we had just witnessed, were worked out in minute detail and with the utmost secrecy in order to insure success, its avowed purpose being to stimulate the morale of both the army and the people. Pétain himself and the Ministry were much pleased with the result.

It is my opinion that, under the circumstances, Painlevé's selection of Pétain to be Commander-in-Chief of the French armies had as important an effect on the outcome of the war as the later appointment of a supreme commander for the Allied armies.

(Diary) Paris, Thursday, August 23, 1917. Held conference yesterday with General Blatchford.[1] Continued lack of construction material emphasizes imperative need of shipping. Conferred with Major Murphy regarding coördination Red Cross work and shipments of supplies. Discussed airplane types with Colonel R. C. Bolling, who is efficiently working out details to send home. Ambassador and Mrs. Henry Morgenthau, Major and Mrs. Robert R. McCormick, and a few others dined with us last evening.

After careful consideration of the subject of powders and explosives, it is certain that we must undertake their manufacture ourselves.

[1] Brig. Gen. (later Maj. Gen.) Richard M. Blatchford was then Commanding General of the Line of Communications, which included the ports.

It was highly important that the gravity of our tonnage situation be brought forcibly to the attention of the Allies. Apropos of the approaching conference on shipping, I sent the following cable to Washington:

"August 23, 1917.
"Reference proposed meeting of shipping representatives Allied powers London, American representative will be confronted with question of shipping required by United States and should be strongly supported in demand upon Allies for sufficient commercial shipping to carry out army program * * * any consideration of less tonnage should be opposed by our representative. * * * The British, and especially the French, have reached absolute limit of manpower and any augmentation their military forces cannot be expected. Imperative hasten our organization and training so that we will have the troops contemplated your project in Europe for active service by May or June. Military activities of Allies on land should be strongly reënforced by combined navies and destruction U-boat bases accomplished if possible. High British army officers confidentially condemn waiting policy British Admiralty. * * * In view of gravity of shipping question recommend our Government insist upon aggressive policy by combined British and American Navies. * * * Our position in this war very strong. * * * Allies now fully recognize dependence upon our coöperation and we need not hesitate demand both aggressive naval policy and full share Allied commercial shipping. Recommend American representative shipping conference be instructed accordingly."

Numbers of officers of all Allied armies felt very strongly that in order to check the losses by submarines the two navies should take some risk and attempt to destroy the bases from which these boats operated. I do not know, however, whether any steps were ever taken to convey this suggestion to the combined navies.

A study by a joint French and American commission of the question of production of powders and explosives in France showed that the greater part of the raw materials for their manufacture must be imported, and that, due to the shipping situation, France in December would produce only about half of the current output. It was apparent, therefore, that to avoid calamity the United States must not only furnish powder and explosives for all of its own forces but must supply about half the French requirements, and the War Department was so advised. By this arrangement a large saving of tonnage would be effected, as the weight of raw materials was ten to twenty times that of the finished product. As nitrates for the manufacture of powder and explosives had to be imported mostly from Chile, the hazard to shipping would be reduced by avoiding the long haul to France. Millions of dollars were expended in the construction of plants at home in an attempt to produce nitrates, but none had been turned out before the end of the war. In view of these costly experiments, it would seem wise during peace to make some provision for the future.

Our efforts to arrange for the procurement in France of munitions, aviation, various classes of equipment and supply, and the use of facilities, brought our officers in close contact with bureaus of the French Government. In the beginning we were largely dependent upon these bureaus to make up deficiencies in many things necessary to complete our preparations. The failure of the French to realize the necessity of hearty coöperation became evident very early in our relations with them. The higher authorities apparently understood, and promises of assistance were readily given, but when we got down to actual details we encountered difficulties. This was true especially as to the granting of docking facilities, the allotment of rail transportation, and the assignment of forests for lumber procurement.

One confusing thing we encountered was the lack of a clear division of authority between bureaus and departments. Even after three years of war there remained considerable question between the Zone of Operations and the Service of the Rear as to the control of munitions and transportation. The Commander-in-Chief claimed to have the final voice in the allotment of artillery, aviation, and railroad rolling stock, but his authority behind the Zone of the Armies was not conceded by the bureaus of the War Office, and was especially contested as to rail transportation. In actual practice, he was not really vested with control of material except that in the possession of the armies, but his influence as commander-in-chief was such that his approval was usually necessary to insure definite action.

In our dealings with French bureaus we had to overcome many obstacles. The subordinate one might happen to encounter at the start was usually impressed with his own importance and would undertake to make a decision, which would lead one to think the matter practically settled, only to find that this official had little if any authority and that his action was not approved by the senior next above him. Then, having already lost much time, it would be learned that this was not the proper office after all. At last reaching the responsible bureau, one was likely to be told that the thing could not be done, no reason being apparent except that it never had been done. So, frequently throughout the war, it was necessary for me to make a personal appeal to the Minister concerned that orders be given for supplies or services already promised and which, therefore, we had every reason to expect should be furnished. Although our own departments at home were considered rather adept in the use of red tape, yet, to use an apt though inelegant comparison, the art of tying things up in official routine was in swaddling clothes in America as compared to its development in France.

After a few contacts with their system one marveled that the French had managed to get along so well in supplying their armies during three years of war. The French are very intelligent and they have a highly organized government, but from the practical viewpoint they often become deeply involved in nonessential details and lose sight of the main objective. I always likened the average French bureau official to a certain narrow type of quartermaster who held sway at an earlier period in our army and who regarded all government property under his charge as his own, and when he finally issued it always made the recipient feel that he was being especially favored.

However, such difficulties were not confined to dealings with the French. While not entirely disadvantageous to be 3,000 miles from base, it was often very much of a handicap. Our War Department officials could not always understand conditions as we did and some of them were often none too willing to accept our views. A few of the chiefs of supply departments seemed to have the notion that it was their duty to negotiate our purchases abroad. Without notice, they frequently placed orders with the French or British Governments that duplicated those already given by my staff, and they did so even after having full information that we had ordered the same things. So independent of control or suggestion had some bureaus of our War Department become that it was a long time before their chiefs would consent to leave such matters to their representatives at my headquarters acting under my authority.

Another source of confusion arose, especially in the beginning, through our War Department seeking the opinion of Allied representatives in Washington on my requests. After we had made an exhaustive study and sent specific recommendations to Washington it was not uncommon for the Chief of Staff or the head of a supply department to refer the matter to a foreign representative for his views or those of his Government. This official would naturally refer the matter back to his home office and eventually it would reach me through French channels with a request for my opinion. Such procedure discredited my recommendations and placed my entire staff in an embarrassing position in the eyes of the foreign Government concerned, to say nothing of the delay in complying with our requests, which, in many cases, were of immediate and almost vital importance. The following protest was cabled to Washington, but, as will be seen later, the practice of interference was not at once discontinued:

"The Chief of Staff, Washington.
"Inquiry comes from * * * through French War Office as to my views on this subject (organization of our units recommended three months before). Have replied that my views would always be sent my own superiors through proper channels. Seems unwise that our General Staff should permit such inquiries to be made, at least through a Civil Commissioner."

This sort of thing also suggested to the French the idea, at least temporarily, of handling our business directly with Washington.

An example is recalled in connection with procurement of horses. We had obtained from the French a definite promise to furnish us with 7,000 animals per month beginning September 1st. Some ten days after this arrangement was made, the French War Office cabled the French Commissioner at Washington, who in turn transmitted it as a sort of dictum to our War Department, that it would be impossible for the French to furnish us any horses or mules and that our Government should begin at once to supply them, although the French offered to lend us 4,000 animals with the understanding that they would be replaced by November 1st. This news was cabled to me and it was the first notice we had that the French did not expect to fulfill their promise.

(Diary) Paris, Wednesday, August 29, 1917. The correspondents called on Saturday and were given confidentially a general outline of plans.

Had dinner on Sunday with Mr. and Mrs. Edward Tuck, in company with Ambassador Sharp, Ridgeway Knight [1] and others.

Representative Medill McCormick has come to make a study of conditions. Have detailed Lieutenant Colonel Dawes as Chief of Purchasing Board. He tried to beg off, but when its importance was explained he gracefully accepted.

In view of the uncertainty of obtaining more than a limited amount of ocean tonnage, it was natural that we should procure abroad as large a proportion of supplies as possible, and our supply departments began at once to make inquiries to meet the demands for construction material, subsistence stores and engineering equipment. Many sources of general supply had been developed by the French and we soon found ourselves not only in competition with them, but also with the British; then, too, our own different departments had begun to bid against each other. The principal article that caused rivalry was lumber, the Corps of Engineers and the Quartermaster Corps having entered into a lively contest for advantage, with a consequent elevation of prices. This condition, involving immense quantities of lumber required at once for barracks, hospitals, docks and wharves, was not only

[1] Mr. Ridgeway Knight was one of the well-known American artists in France.

annoying to us but it gave the French much concern. They very soon, and naturally, imposed restrictions upon sales that made it difficult for us to meet even our most urgent requirements until the whole question was readjusted.

In our Army at home it had long been the custom for each department to make its own contracts without regard to the others, except that the quartermaster was supposed to purchase and distribute certain military stores and other things that were in common use by the entire Army. Our sources of supply at home during the years of peace had been so great and the needs of the Army relatively so small that it had not been necessary to consider the possibility of shortage. In France, however, it was imperative to regulate purchases in order to prevent a rise in prices that would add to the financial burdens, especially of the Allies, who were much less able to pay than we were. Besides that, quantities of all kinds of supplies were limited, which was the principal reason why it became necessary to arrive at some understanding for a just allotment.

In an effort to reach a solution, I appointed a board of officers to study the question of purchases, and suggested that some agency might be created that would supervise procurement in general, and by coördinating our own and Allied needs check the scramble for supplies. In a rather extended discussion, the board came to the conclusion that a centralized agency to control purchases would be illegal and unanimously recommended the continuance of existing methods. But an emergency confronted us and it was no time to discuss technicalities. Some business-like method had to be adopted to meet the situation. In other words, a remedy for an approaching chaotic condition resulting from the independent, uncontrolled action of the several services must be found. To my mind the solution seemed to be merely a matter of coördination. Therefore, I tore up the recommendation and established a Purchasing Board to consist of one or more representatives of each service making purchases of any sort, including the Red Cross and the Y.M.C.A. Lieutenant Colonel Dawes, 17th Engineers, well known as a man of large business experience, was appointed as the head of this Board, the members of which were to meet together and make known their respective needs and then agree among themselves as to where and by which department each purchase was to be made, thus mutually assisting instead of competing with each other. Under the arrangement, coöperation with the French was established and the agency became increasingly effective in handling our procurement activities.

CHAPTER XII

THE most important question that confronted us in the preparation of our forces of citizen soldiery for efficient service was training. Except for the Spanish-American War, nearly twenty years before, actual combat experience of the Regular Army had been limited to the independent action of minor commands in the Philippines and to two expeditions into Mexico, each with forces smaller than a modern American division. The World War involved the handling of masses where even a division was relatively a small unit. It was one thing to call one or two million men to the colors, and quite another thing to transform them into an organized, instructed army capable of meeting and holding its own in the battle against the best trained force in Europe with three years of actual war experience to its credit.

Few people can realize what a stupendous undertaking it was to teach these vast numbers their various duties when such a large percentage of them were ignorant of practically everything pertaining to the business of the soldier in war. First of all, most of the officer personnel available had little or no military experience, and had to be trained in the manifold duties of commanders. They had to learn the interior economy of their units— messing, housing, clothing, and, in general, caring for their men—as well as methods of instruction and the art of leading them in battle. This great task was, of course, under the direction of the War Department.

To supplement the instruction at home, a general scheme of schools for the A.E.F. was prepared by the Operations and Training Section of my General Staff, but in order that this instruction should be as complete and uniform as possible and at the same time be coördinated with other activities, I decided that training should be handled by officers who could devote their entire time to it. An additional section of the Headquarters General Staff was, therefore, established, called the Training Section, to function under my personal direction. As chief of this section Colonel Paul B. Malone was chosen, with Colonel H. B. Fiske as his assistant.

In the preparation of a course of training a special study had been made not only of the basic principles taught by the Allies but also of the methods employed to give these principles practical application. The British and French were not entirely in accord in their ideas of organization or of battle tactics and each sought to impress us with the superiority of their respective systems. Our officers engaged in this duty were directed to keep in view the development of the most efficient fighting machine as quickly as possible and as a means to this end to adopt only sound doctrines of training and make them essentially our own.

The British methods of teaching trench warfare appealed to me very strongly. They taught their men to be aggressive and undertook to perfect them in hand-to-hand fighting with bayonet, grenade and dagger. A certain amount of this kind of training was necessary to prepare the troops for trench warfare. Moreover it served to stimulate their morale by giving them confidence in their own personal prowess. Through the kindness of Sir Douglas Haig, we were fortunate early in our experience to have assigned to us Lieutenant General R. H. K. Butler and other officers of the British Army in addition to French officers to assist in this individual training. Later, several French and British officers also came to lecture at a number of our schools.

We found difficulty, however, in using these Allied instructors, in that the French and, to a large extent, the British, had practically settled down to the conviction that developments since 1914 had changed the principles of warfare. Both held that new conditions imposed by trench fighting had rendered previous conceptions of training more or less obsolete and that preparation for open warfare was no longer necessary. French publications and manuals were generally in accord with this theory. It was, perhaps, logical to expect that the French should take this view as, nationally, unlike the Germans, they had been on the defensive, at least in thought, during the previous half century. It is true that on occasions the French assumed the offensive, but the defensive idea was ever in mind.

In the situation that followed the first battle of the Marne, the great armies on the Western Front were entrenched against each other and neither had been able to make more than local gains. The long period during which this condition had prevailed, with its resultant psychological effect, together with the natural leaning of the French toward the defensive, to which should be added the adverse effect of their recent spring experience, had apparently combined to obscure the principles of open warfare.

If the French doctrine had prevailed our instruction would have been limited to a brief period of training for trench fighting. A new army brought up entirely on such principles would have been seriously handicapped without the protection of the trenches. It would probably have lacked the aggressiveness to break through the enemy's lines and the knowledge of how to carry on thereafter. It was my opinion that the victory could not be won by the costly process of attrition, but it must be won by driving the enemy out into the open and engaging him in a war of movement. Instruction in this kind of warfare was based upon individual and group initiative, resourcefulness and tactical judgment, which were also of great advantage in trench warfare. Therefore, we took decided issue with the Allies and, without neglecting thorough preparation for trench fighting, undertook to train mainly for open combat, with the object from the start of vigorously forcing the offensive.

Our units then in training were nearly all recruits and many of the officers and noncommissioned officers were easily influenced by the ideas of the French designated to assist us. In order to avoid the effect of the French teaching it became necessary gradually to take over and direct all instruction ourselves. For the purpose of impressing our own doctrine upon officers, a training program was issued which laid great stress on open warfare methods and offensive action. The following is a pertinent extract from my instructions on this point:

> "The above methods to be employed must remain and become distinctly our own. All instruction must contemplate the assumption of a vigorous offensive. This purpose will be emphasized in every phase of training until it becomes a settled habit of thought."

Intimately connected with the question of training for open warfare was the matter of rifle practice. The earliest of my cablegrams on this subject was in August, in which it was urged that thorough instruction in rifle practice should be carried on at home because of the difficulty of giving it in France:

> "Study here shows value and desirability of retaining our existing small arms target practice course. In view of great difficulty in securing ranges in France due to density of the population and cultivation recommend as far as practicable the complete course be given in the United States before troops embark. Special emphasis should be placed on rapid fire."

The armies on the Western Front in the recent battles that I had witnessed had all but given up the use of the rifle. Machine guns, grenades, Stokes mortars, and one-pounders had become the main reliance of the average Allied soldier. These were all valuable weapons for specific purposes but they could not replace the combination of an efficient soldier and his rifle. Numerous instances were reported in the Allied armies of men chasing an individual enemy throwing grenades at him instead of using the rifle. Such was the effect of association that continuous effort was necessary to counteract this tendency among our own officers and men and inspire them with confidence in the efficacy of rifle fire. Ultimately, we had the satisfaction of hearing the French admit that we were right, both in emphasizing training for open warfare and insisting upon proficiency in the use of the rifle.

My view was that the rifle and bayonet still remained the essential weapons of the infantry, and my cables, stressing the fact that the basic principles of warfare had not changed, were sent in an endeavor to influence the courses of training at home. Unfortunately, however, no fixed policy of instruction in the various arms, under a single authority, was ever carried out there. Unresponsive to my advice, the inclination was to accept the views of French specialists and to limit training to the narrow field of trench warfare. Therefore, in large measure, the fundamentals so thoroughly taught at West Point for a century were more or less neglected. The responsibility for the failure at home to take positive action on my recommendations in such matters must fall upon the War Department General Staff.

There were other causes, as we shall see later, that led to confusion and irregularity in training to such an extent that we were often compelled during the last stages of the war to send men into battle with little knowledge of warfare and sometimes with no rifle practice at all.

In the system of schools established in the A.E.F. there were centers of instruction for all units up to divisions, including the training centers for replacements; and corps schools for unit commanders and noncommissioned officers of all arms. Under the supervision of General Headquarters were the General Staff College; the schools to train instructors for corps schools; others for candidates for commissions; schools for recruits; and schools for specialists of every staff and supply department and every other branch of the service.

A school system would have been desirable in the best of armies, but it was indispensable in an army which had to be created almost wholly from raw material. The training of troops for combat was, of course, the primary objective, and schools for instructors were merely a means to that end. In order to give troops the advantage of the latest tactical and technical developments and to make up for the defects of training at home, the plans contemplated an additional period of training for divisions of about three months after reaching France. This gave us an opportunity to secure a certain uniformity in standards, and was especially valuable in affording the newly arrived troops the benefit of experience in the immediate atmosphere of war.

The very limited number of General Staff officers at my disposal had been able to outline basic plans, but as our forces grew increasing numbers were needed, especially to aid in the direction of troops in battle. My cables had failed to make much impression on the War Department as to the difference in functions between staff officers with an army in the field conducting operations and those on duty at the War Department, where they were charged mainly with preliminary organization and training and with directing the procurement and shipment of supplies and equipment. In our army abroad, staff experts were necessary in administration, intelligence, tactical training, and especially in operations, as well as in directing the supply and transportation of the active armies. The following cable expressed my views:

"Urgency training general staff officers for particular duty at army headquarters cannot be overestimated. Their services are needed now to study details in connection with operations and other duties. Our staff officers generally have little conception of problems involved in directing armies * * * or of strategic questions involved. * * * We are now planning for spring campaign and success not possible without thoroughly efficient General Staff. Limited number of officers brought in June much overworked and unable to handle and fully consider many subjects requiring immediate action. Impossible to make this appeal and recommendation too strong and urgently request matter be taken up with Secretary of War without delay."

To help meet this lack of experienced general staff officers with our armies, the General Staff College established at Langres, a few miles south of Chaumont, provided an intensive course of three months, which, though brief, covered instruction in the details of our own staff organization and administration, our system of supply, and the coördination and employment of our forces in combat. While the student officers were selected for their aptitude, it was not possible to graduate thoroughly trained staff officers in such a short time, but the urgency was so great that the course could not be made longer. Having been taught a common doctrine, with a loyal sense of coöperation well accentuated, they were fairly well grounded in theory and had to trust to the costly school of experience for the rest.

(Diary) Paris, Saturday, September 1, 1917. Held conference with Atterbury, who has just reported.

As French continue to urge trench warfare, went to Compiègne for conference with Pétain; made clear the necessity for basic elementary training of our troops. We also considered procurement within Zone of Armies. Headquarters transferred to Chaumont to-day.

As has been previously stated, in response to my request for an experienced railroad man, Mr. Atterbury, of the Pennsylvania Railroad, was selected and sent to report to me. In our first brief conversation we merely ran over the problem in a general way. Considerable headway in the organization of our railroad system had already been made by the Corps of Engineers. Much to my surprise, Atterbury seemed to be very familiar with the situation, and his personality, his force, his grasp of the difficulties of the task and his willingness to undertake it appealed to me at once. So, without hesitation, and with a feeling that undoubtedly the right man had been found, I told him that he would be placed in charge of railroad transportation. A few days later, in consultation with Colonels Taylor and Wilgus, we determined the details of readjustment required. An independent transportation department was created to operate and maintain the broad and narrow gauge railways and the canals in American use, and to construct roads and wharves, shops and other buildings for railway purposes. It was found necessary, however, to leave construction under the Corps of Engineers.

Upon Atterbury's suggestion, a cable was sent requesting certain men to fill important positions in the organization. The list included J. A. McCrea, General Manager of the Long Island Railroad, for general manager, with C. M. Bunting as business manager, H. C. Booz as engineer for construction, and J. G. Rogers as deputy, the last three of whom were then with the Pennsylvania

NOTE: Total strength of the A.E.F. on August 31st, 1,616 officers, 35,042 enlisted men.

Railroad. The railway problem was far from easy and many were the obstacles to be overcome, both in our own and in the French services. Successful management would have been very doubtful under a leader without Atterbury's patience, ability, and force of character.

(Diary) Paris, Monday, September 3, 1917. Called on General Foch, Chief of Staff, yesterday on routine of procurement, but his office has no control. Afterward talked with Minister of War on the same subject. De Chambrun, de Ferronay, and my own staff working for better liaison with French bureaus.

Conferred with Atterbury this morning, also with Colonel Bolling. Took Colonel Dawes this afternoon to call on Minister of War and explained purpose of our purchasing agency. Went with Brigadier General William L. Kenly to call on the Minister of Munitions, hoping to expedite manufacture of airplanes for our service.

Frequent conferences with heads of our various activities enable me to give direction and impetus and promote coördination.

It was foreseen that with the removal of my headquarters to Chaumont our supply officers would find it difficult to keep in close touch with the corresponding French bureaus in Paris, and that since we were to be within the Zone of the Armies, coöperation with French Army Headquarters would assume greater importance. Inasmuch as the line of authority separating this zone from the rear was not distinctly defined, it was evident that procurement in general, especially regarding the use of facilities, might become complicated. In my discussion with M. Painlevé he stated that he thought that with intelligent liaison officers there should be no difficulty, and promised to expedite our business with the bureaus.

Visits to our training areas by the French, official and otherwise, had become rather frequent. One of the visitors, M. Clemenceau, who was always a power, called at the headquarters of the 1st Division, accompanied by General de Castelnau, the commander of the Group of Armies with which this division was serving. In the course of the conversation with General Sibert, the division commander, M. Clemenceau, with considerable emphasis, urged that our troops be put into the line without delay. It was explained to him by General de Castelnau that as soon as they were sufficiently advanced the troops of the division were to be placed by brigades with the French in a quiet sector near Lunéville.

Although there was nothing threatening in the situation and no immediate probability of a serious German offensive, M. Clemenceau wished to know why they could not go in at once. General Sibert told him that the division had been in the area but a short time and had only recently begun training, and that the American Commander-in-Chief must determine when and where the division should be employed. M. Clemenceau went on to say that America had now been in the war several months and the French people were wondering when they expected to take an active part. He said that the French Army was exhausted by the war and that its morale was poor. He insisted then, as he did with even greater vehemence later in an official capacity, that it was not so much a question of troops being ready as it was of giving relief to the Allies.

Although the division was only partially trained, it could have been used in case of necessity, but no emergency existed at this time and no suggestion had been made that the division should go into the line for serious work. It was obviously quite out of place for M. Clemenceau to make any such demand, yet there is little doubt that he gave expression to a very general sentiment among the French people at that moment. They simply wanted to see American troops in the trenches.

I could well understand this attitude of the French Army and the people, and realized that their morale was none too high. However, the censorship of private letters of soldiers in their Army showed that it was gradually growing better, based largely upon the hope of considerable aid from America. Quite apart from sentiment, however, it was a question of having the Division in fair shape before placing it even in a quiet sector, as the Germans would certainly take advantage of our first appearance in the line to strike a blow at American prestige.

From another point of view, M. Clemenceau's visit left the

impression that the French were inclined to dictate what disposition we should make of our units. In many of their suggestions
it was easy to see the possibility of amalgamation lurking in the
background. Another circumstance that suggested the same
thought, the knowledge of which came to me about this time,
was that the French High Commissioner at Washington had
reported difficulty in persuading the Secretary of War to divert
tonnage to send over units other than those designated for our
army. It was difficult to construe his move in any other light than
as further evidence of the none too well concealed opposition of
the French to our building up an army. Such methods were, of
course, irregular, but nevertheless similar pressure to alter our
program was repeatedly used by both French and British before
the end of the war. There can be little doubt that the Allies,
especially the French, entertained the hope that we would provide
them not only with replacements, but with laborers and technical
troops as well.

In looking back over the period immediately prior to our entry
into the war, the very primitive state of our aviation still gives
me a feeling of humiliation. The Punitive Expedition of 1916
went into Mexico with eight of the thirteen antiquated tactical
planes which constituted our all in aviation. In a country almost
uninhabited, save for a few villages scattered here and there,
where the difficulties of obtaining information were almost in-
surmountable, a well-trained, up-to-date fleet of airplanes would
have been invaluable. These old planes were not in any sense
properly equipped as compared with those being used by other
nations even then, and with no adequate facilities for repair work
they were constantly in danger of going to pieces, yet the services
of our aviators in Mexico stood out strongly as an indication of
what American fliers were to accomplish in the World War.

The daring and the courage of men like Townsend Dodd,[1]

[1] Colonel Dodd served through the World War but was killed in an airplane
accident on October 5, 1919. The fliers who were with me in Mexico, with their rank
at that time, were: Captains B. D. Foulois and T. F. Dodd, and Lieutenants C. G.
Chapman, J. E. Carberry, H. A. Dargue, T. S. Bowen, R. H. Willis, W. G. Kilner,
E. S. Gorrell, A. R. Christie, and I. A. Rader.

Foulois, Dargue and others who were with that expedition aroused my most enthusiastic admiration. While there were many hairbreadth escapes in Mexico, fortunately all our fliers were spared to form the nucleus of our World War aviation corps, in which they all served with distinction. Although at the date of our entry into the war more than a year had elapsed since the beginning of the Mexican Campaign, there were still only thirty-five trained fliers and about one thousand men in aviation, with only a few training planes, none of which were suitable for anything else.

An extensive program following cabled recommendations from the French Premier after we entered the war [1] seems to have been adopted at home as the basis of our efforts. Upon the recommendation of the Chief Signal Officer, Brigadier General George O. Squier, Congress made an appropriation of $640,000,000 in July, 1917, in an effort to overcome past negligence. There followed many extravagant claims by prominent civil officials connected with aviation and by the press, that we would soon have large fleets of airplanes in operation and that we would end the war at once with a preponderance of aircraft. But Congressional action, even though generous, furnished no magical power to transform our Air Service from a mere skeleton into a real fighting force in an instant. Everybody who stopped a moment to think knew that time would be necessary and that it was idle to count upon airplanes from our own factories within a year, or perhaps longer.

The failure of our aviation bureau to keep abreast of airplane development in the contending armies cost us serious delay. With a lack of data in the beginning, little progress had been made at home on our aviation program at the end of five months. Fruitless efforts to describe mechanical construction, give definite information concerning production, and otherwise reach decisions, by cable, prompted Washington to send to France a special mission of which Major R. C. Bolling [2] was the head. Through

[1] Chapter III, page 28.
[2] Major Bolling, then Colonel, was killed during the German advance on Amiens in March, 1918, while on a special mission in that region.

his ability and expert knowledge he rendered exceptional service in coöperating with aviation officials of the Allies and in obtaining the necessary technical information upon which to base action at home. The investigations made by his mission confirmed the view that our manufacturers could not begin to furnish airplanes before the summer of 1918. At this time it looked as though we should not have even sufficient airplanes for training, and much less be able to furnish them for our troops as they went into the line. With my mind filled with these impressions, and realizing the vital importance of aviation, my efforts were unceasing to overcome the deficiency.

After inquiry as to French capacity to turn out airplanes, I made a contract with the Air Ministry late in August committing us to an expenditure of $60,000,000 for 5,000 planes and 8,500 engines to be delivered as rapidly as possible at intervals before the first of June, 1918, on condition that we should provide certain tools and raw materials. To make a contract to pay such an amount appeared somewhat bold, but under the circumstances some one had to take the initiative in providing planes needed at once for the development of our air force.

As aviation was in no sense a logical branch of the Signal Corps, the two were separated in the A.E.F. as soon as practicable and an air corps was organized and maintained as a distinct force. In order to coördinate our training with that at home, Brigadier General William L. Kenly was sent over the latter part of August and was appointed Chief of Aviation in the A.E.F. Colonel William Mitchell, who had succeeded Major Dodd, the first Chief of Aviation, was given jurisdiction in the Zone of the Advance. Colonel Bolling was placed in charge in the Zone of the Interior and soon succeeded in securing better coöperation through an Inter-Allied Aircraft Board.

The next essential step was the training of airplane pilots, and accordingly arrangements were made for our men to enter flying schools in England, France, and Italy, after they had passed their preliminary tests at home. Vacancies were held for us in the Allied schools but we were unable to take full advantage of this opportunity because of the delay in sending over fliers. However, we proceeded with the establishment of our own training centers, the first of which, located at Issoudun, was planned for a capacity of 900 pilots by spring. Other school facilities offered by the French were utilized later, such as those at Clermont-Ferrand and Tours.

Before we entered the war, a number of young American aviators enlisted in the French air service and later, after persistent efforts on the part of a few leading spirits, the French Minister of War granted them permission to form an organization to be known as the American squadron. This unit was placed under a French captain and later still became known as the Lafayette Escadrille. Fortunately, some ninety of these experienced American fliers who had thus volunteered in the French Army from 1914 to 1917 joined our aviation, and their services as instructors and in combat proved of inestimable value to us.

Our matériel was to come from both American and European sources. We established an acceptance park at Orly to receive and distribute matériel obtained abroad, and a production center at Romorantin where all airplanes and engines from home were handled. Other plans in progress contemplated the extension at the front of our air and ground organization, of which we shall see more later.

CHAPTER XIII

Established at Chaumont—Visit from M. Poincaré—Allied Missions at G.H.Q.—Gas Service Established—Tanks Recommended—Service of the Rear Project—Priority Schedule—Birthday—Robertson and Derby on Shipping—Pope's Peace Proposal—Visit to Le Valdahon—Signal Matériel Lacking—Hospitals Needed—Coal Supply Critical

(Diary) Chaumont, Thursday, September 6, 1917. Left Paris yesterday morning for Chaumont, stopping at Troyes for lunch. Headquarters offices duly installed here in regimental barracks. Surroundings give relief from depression of Paris. On my invitation, President Poincaré came this morning to inspect 1st Division. Colonel Wagstaff reported as head of British Mission.

DRIVING to Gondrecourt with my Chief of Staff and aides, we found General Pétain, his staff and an escort of French troops drawn up at the station, where President Poincaré and his party, including the Minister of War, were received with due formality. The President and I led the way by motor to Houdelaincourt, where the ceremony of inspecting the 1st Division was held.

It was a compliment to the Division to have a visit from the head of the French Republic and every man was on his mettle. The troops were already assembled when we arrived. As the President and I walked through the ranks he commented very favorably on the appearance of the men and was quite struck with their size and their youth and vigor. After the command had marched in review, the President asked to meet the officers and made them a very happy speech. Upon the conclusion of his talk they showed their appreciation by promptly giving him three rousing cheers, which pleased him very much.

From the purely military point of view, the impression gained by the President at this review could not have been particularly favorable, as at least two-thirds of the men were recruits and over one-half of the officers had been but recently commissioned. Moreover, the men had been hard at work on combat training and this, together with the uneven ground of the muddy hillside where the review was held, made military precision difficult. However, he was a very keen observer and no doubt drew great satisfaction from the thought that many other Americans were coming and that with a few more months of training this group of 25,000 Americans would make a fine addition to the forces of the war-worn Allies.

(Diary) Chaumont, Saturday, September 8, 1917. Have seen various officers of Missions [1] at my headquarters. General Ragueneau, as Chief of the French Mission, becomes General Pétain's representative.

Miss Elizabeth Hoyt, Secretary of the Red Cross, took luncheon with us and gave an interesting account of recent Red Cross activities. Governor Henry J. Allen, of Kansas, and William Allen White, also of the Red Cross, came to call.

Saw Malone and Fiske, of Training Section, and cabled urgent request for instructors for army schools and staff college. Brigadier General William Lassiter dined with me this evening.

In order to maintain closer relations among the Allied armies and to keep each Commander-in-Chief advised regarding the morale, proposed operations, and movements of troops of other armies, and in fact all matters that might affect the general situation, a system had grown up whereby the army of each nation was represented at the headquarters of the others by a group of officers called a mission. Consequently, when we definitely established headquarters at Chaumont we exchanged missions with the British, French, Italian, and Belgian armies. That of the French naturally became the largest and most important, as

[1] The Chiefs of Missions were:
French: Brig. Gen. C. M. Ragueneau until August, 1918, when Col. J. L. A. Linard succeeded him.
British: Lt. Col. C. M. Wagstaff (later Brig. Gen.) until late 1918, when he was succeeded by Lt. Col. F. K. Puckle.
Italian: Brig. Gen. Ippolito Perelli from June, 1918.
Belgian: Major J. Th. Tinant.

it was entrusted with handling most of the questions that arose in our relations with the French.

The missions with us, especially those of the French and British, did not always confine their activities to normal lines, but often took occasion to advance their ideas regarding the training and use of our army. The French continually argued that we would contribute more to the Allied cause by helping to strengthen French and British units than by building up an independent army of our own, and the British were not far behind in their efforts along this line. Knowing this attitude, it was necessary to be on the lookout to avoid commitments to suggestions that might eventually involve the question of amalgamation. Apart from this, however, and considering their services as a whole, it should be said that the fine spirit of helpfulness and coöperation shown always by the members of these missions appealed to us, and many close friendships grew out of our association with them.

(Diary) Chaumont, Tuesday, September 11, 1917. On Sunday, saw representative of Postal Department sent to organize service for the armies. Conferred with several staff officers. Dr. Woods Hutchinson called. Chemical Warfare department, known as "Gas Service," established in A.E.F. System of schools for our forces completed.

Conferred yesterday with Brigadier General Williams; prospect of obtaining tanks not hopeful unless they can be produced at home. Project for upbuilding services of rear adopted.

The use of poisonous gases in warfare had been discussed at the Hague Conference in 1899 with the result that several nations pledged themselves against the employment of projectiles whose only object was to give forth suffocating or poisonous gases. This action had created a feeling of security regarding such a possibility. Germany had subscribed to the agreement, and when her armies disregarded this pledge and became the first to use gas shells, the impression was that the Germans had now thrown every consideration of humanity to the winds. The first gas attack occurred on April 22, 1915, against the French in the northern part of the Ypres salient. It came as a complete surprise and caused great consternation among the troops. Its effect on the

French was vividly described later by Sir John French in his report to Lord Kitchener as follows:

"Following a heavy bombardment, the enemy attacked the French Division at about 5 P.M., using asphyxiating gases for the first time. Aircraft reported that at about 5 P.M. thick yellow smoke had been seen issuing from the German trenches between Langemarck and Bixschoote. The French reported that two simultaneous attacks had been made east of the Ypres-Staden Railway, in which these asphyxiating gases had been employed.

"What followed almost defies description. The effect of these poisonous gases was so virulent as to render the whole of the line held by the French Division mentioned above practically incapable of any action at all. It was at first impossible for any one to realize what had actually happened. The smoke and fumes hid everything from sight, and hundreds of men were thrown into a comatose or dying condition, and within an hour the whole position had to be abandoned, together with about 50 guns."

This action by the enemy forced the Allies to adopt the use of gas themselves as a matter of retaliation. From that time on its employment became common to all combatants.

On July 12-13, 1917, the Germans used a new gas against the British, called "mustard gas," the effect of which I reported to our War Department by cablegram:

"Following with regard to the new gas called 'Mustard Gas' used by the Germans sent for your information. Since July 18th the British have suffered 20,000 casualties from this gas alone. Five per cent have been fatal, 14 per cent have been serious, while the balance have been mild. This so-called gas is really a liquid carried in shells which scatter the liquid on the ground. There is a slight odor of mustard of which men nearby are sensible. One can remain in this odor for five minutes or so without suffering any harm. The action is not noticeable for four or five hours after exposure. Then the soldier feels a burning of the eyes and a dryness and parched condition of the skin. He then becomes blind and the respiratory passages develop a condition similar to that in diphtheria. There are usually exterior burns on the exposed parts of the skin, hands, back of neck, and tender parts, as gas attacks the skin regardless of clothing. In mild cases the subject is blind and incapacitated for duty for about three weeks. In serious cases for a considerably longer period. The only defense is prompt use of gas mask and even this only guarantees a reduction in losses."

The use of gas in warfare presented an entirely new problem to us and the organization of a service to handle it demanded immediate attention. The first plan of the War Department provided that the Engineers should devise and handle the mechanical features and the Medical Department the chemical, but this soon proved to be impractical and it became evident that, as we had maintained at the beginning, a separate service would be necessary. Meanwhile application was made for a complete chemical laboratory to be shipped to France for use mainly in investigation, supplementing similar work in the United States.

Considerable information concerning gases and the organization of gas service troops had been gathered by my staff. Lieutenant Colonel Amos A. Fries, who was designated as Chief of the Gas Service, made some further investigation in the British and French armies, and as a result an order issued on September 3d established a department known at that time as the Gas Service. It was charged with the organization of personnel, the supply of material, and the general direction of the service, offensive as well as defensive. Other branches of the army assisted in providing material and appliances.

Experiments were at once begun to discover new gases and devise improvements in gas masks. In order to save tonnage and avoid the dangers of explosion in transit, it was decided, after consultation with the Allied services, to request the shipment from the States of the basic elements and manufacture the chemical products in France. After making thorough tests of different types of masks, we adopted the box respirator used by the British, and a preliminary purchase of 100,000 was made to meet immediate demands for training.

With the development of trench weapons and special tactical methods of defense, never had the offensive been more costly in human life than in this war. The ingenuity of the Allies was put to the test to devise new engines of war that would make the attack possible without excessive losses.

While the tank, which was simply an armored caterpillar-traction motor car, was favored by many officers as an aid to infantry in the attack, this opinion was by no means unanimous. Our investigations, however, led to the conclusion that we should accept Allied experience and also adopt the tank as a weapon. As to types, both the French (light) Renault, weighing six tons, and the British (heavy) Mark VI, a tank of thirty tons, appeared to be useful according to circumstances, and it was estimated that we ought to have at least 1,200 of the former and 600 of the latter. They were to be variously armed with machine guns, 6-pounders and 3-inch guns, with a proportionate number especially built to carry twenty-five men each and others to carry supplies. Negotiations for their procurement were begun with the respective Governments and it was found that the French wanted us to manufacture 2,000 Renaults for them. As there was little or no prospect of our obtaining tanks abroad, their manufacture at home was recommended and full details of requirements were accordingly cabled to Washington.

The World War was a struggle involving all national resources, and that fact was particularly emphasized by a close-range study of the many requirements for preparation. Every industry and every art, beginning with the farms and mines, must contribute its full share, and every citizen must fulfill his obligation to serve. America's part in the contest could be successful only by the combined efforts of the armies and the people. The man with the rifle was merely the privileged representative of a thousand others who were as deeply concerned in the result as he was. Thus while the people at home were hurriedly trying to overcome the heavy handicap of past neglect in providing men and equipment, we in France were equally strenuous in doing our part to prepare units for battle and to perfect arrangements to insure the required flow of material and supplies of every nature toward the front.

To discharge cargo and handle it along the Line of Communications and to assist in the more pressing work of construction, we had already been compelled to use incoming combat troops. One regiment of marines, and other troops, had been detained in the rear several weeks for these purposes, but makeshifts of this sort could not solve the problem and would only increase the danger of a breakdown in the end.

In order to provide supply troops as they were needed to correspond with the growth of our combat armies in France, a general scheme was prepared and sent to Washington on September 18th as a guide for the War Department. This project embraced the great body of specialists and laborers that would be necessary to run railroads, construct wharves and storehouses, saw lumber, and receive, store, and transport systematically the immense volume of supplies and material that would be consumed by our armies. Thorough organization and training for such work were as essential as tactical training for the fighting man. It was desirable that the quotas for these purposes should arrive progressively along with corresponding increments of material and supplies so that a balanced development could be maintained.

This outline of personnel, known as the Service of the Rear Project and the Organization Project for combat troops, formed the basis of our personnel structure in France. From the combination of these projects, a statement was prepared prescribing the order in which the troops and services enumerated should arrive. This schedule of priority, forwarded to the War Department on October 7th, divided the initial force called for into six phases, each including a combatant army corps of six divisions, with the service of the rear troops to correspond. With this schedule, Washington was provided almost from the start with a clear-cut program.

But we went still further than that. The supply departments worked out an automatic system for the shipment of the various classes of supplies and equipment, corresponding to the phase schedule of combat and service troops. It was intended to obviate the necessity for frequent cables under the old peacetime monthly requisition method to which the War Department was wedded. This automatic schedule contemplated the accumulation and maintenance in France of a certain quantity of supplies in reserve storehouses, with an equal amount distributed at accessible points farther toward the front. When it became apparent that the submarine danger was growing less, the total amount was limited to forty-five days' supply.

These outlines of our requirements in men, equipment, supplies, and material gave Washington something definite to follow. But the lack of a central control in actual procurement, during the early months of our participation in the war, resulted in unlimited competition among our supply departments at home, and the situation became one of almost overwhelming confusion. Later on threatened military crises led to frightened importunities of the Allies for immediate aid, from manpower to steel ingots, and the combination of swiftly moving events wellnigh wrecked the whole supply scheme at several points before we were to see the end of the war.

(Diary) Chaumont, Thursday, September 13, 1917. Unusually busy to-day with details of administration. Many reminders of another birthday [1] have been received, including a surprise party by the staff this evening.

As this was exactly three months after I had reached France, the time seemed to be passing very rapidly with little apparent progress against the day when an American army should be on the front line. Winter was approaching, with the prospect of increasing hardships for the troops and the people. These thoughts were not particularly cheerful, but there was a lighter side. The wishes for good fortune that came from all parts of our country on my birthday showed a widespread solicitude in our behalf and revealed anew the sincerity of the patriotic sentiments that so strongly supported us. Although we could but look forward to the service ahead of us as being full of difficulties, yet, with the nation behind us, there was much of encouragement to be garnered from the messages received at this time.

(Diary) Chaumont, Saturday, September 15, 1917. Transportation Department created, with Atterbury as Director General.

Had luncheon to-day with General Wirbel, the local French commander, at which General de Castelnau and General Hellet, his

[1] The St. Mihiel victory came precisely one year later.

Chief of Staff, leading civil officials, Harbord, Bacon and others of
my staff were present. It was a sentimental occasion, showing that
the people really feel grateful to us.

Received letter from General Robertson on shipping. Conferred
with General Staff and approved priority schemes for shipment of
supplies.

The luncheon given by General Wirbel indicated an attitude
of good will in the community toward Americans. As Madame
Wirbel and her daughters received us, I was attracted by the
youngest, a beautiful child of six, and undertook to chat with her
in French. As she did not reply to my questions, I said, "Com-
prenez-vous?" With childish frankness, she replied, "Non,"
much to the amusement of several of the less respectful members
of my staff. This occasion was opportune, as it brought together
officers of the two armies who were to be closely allied in service.
In a brief speech, General Wirbel referred with much feeling
to the aid America was bringing to France and to the fraternal
relations among us. My response, I fear, was considerably below
the high plane that he reached. General de Castelnau was even
less oratorical than I, and merely said that he hoped we should
all soon have the chance to water our horses in the Rhine.

The importance of shipping for the American Army was beginning to receive attention in Allied circles as indicated by
personal discussions and correspondence. In a letter General
Robertson spoke of their increasing losses in men and of his
anxiety regarding the voyage of our troops across the Atlantic.
He said the tonnage question was entirely between Great Britain
and ourselves, as none of the other Allies could furnish any shipping to speak of. He suggested that Admiral Mayo and I should
go to London to consider with the Admiralty shipping arrangements needed for American troops the following year. His letter
showed the possibility of coöperation in the future when it should
have been immediate. On top of this, in conference a few days
later with Lord Derby, the British Minister of War, I was told
that his Government could not be counted on to furnish us ships
as transports.

The substance of General Robertson's letter was cabled to Washington suggesting the importance of taking advantage of the opportunity offered to obtain additional shipping. A few days later we were told that arrangements for trans-atlantic transports were being made by the Shipping Board. This information was contained in the following cable:

"President of the United States says question of shipping is being looked after from here and that arrangements now being made would be confused by such a conference as you suggest. Our shipping must necessarily be supplied by ourselves and Shipping Board here is in direct conference with British authorities controlling their shipping."

The question of greatest importance to the Allies and ourselves was to get American troops across at an early date. As no advice was received beyond the above cable, it was presumed that arrangements were being made by the Shipping Board for all necessary tonnage.

There was little in the general situation to give comfort to the Allies. Losses by the British through continued operations were still growing. There no longer remained any doubt as to Russia's fate, and it was consequently certain that German troops on that front would be released for service in the west. Under the circumstances, the tired Allied peoples were easily influenced by rumors. The Pope's proposal, issued in August, started some talk of peace, but because it failed to condemn Germany's violation of treaties and her inhumane submarine warfare the note did not make a favorable impression on the Allies. In fact, it was criticized in terms that were not at all moderate. The various replies from the different Governments did, however, arouse some hope, which was altogether unwarranted by the real attitude of the authorities of the belligerent powers on either side. The discussion of the proposal was unfortunate because the French people, not realizing that peace was improbable, lost some of their courage, and the depression from this and other factors caused uneasiness among both civil and military leaders.

From our sources of information, which included the Intelligence Bureaus of the Allied armies, we got the impression that

Austria, Bulgaria, and Turkey would make peace on any reasonable terms if they could do so. But the German Government dominated the policy of all the Central Powers and it was certain that any peace less favorable to them than the *status quo ante* would not be entertained. The German military leaders thought they would eventually win and did not believe that the blockade would produce serious discontent in their country. In fact, the German people themselves, as well as their Government, feeling that with Russia now practically out of the war they would have an enormous advantage which the Americans would not be able to overbalance, firmly believed in ultimate victory.

My cable to the Secretary of War will show our estimate of the situation at the moment, as far as the French were concerned:

"September 15, 1917.
"There is considerable talk of possibilities of peace this winter and discussion is heard among people of all classes, including those high in military rank. Failure to stop German armies and revolt among Russian troops have had depressing effect upon Allies. Present French Cabinet believed to be strongly in favor of continuation of war, but French people in state of mind to accept any favorable proposition. Believe that withdrawal of Germans from Belgium with concessions as to Alsace and Lorraine and return to antebellum status in Balkans would be hard for French to resist, especially with the prospect of giving Germany satisfaction from Russia. * * * Recent British attacks beginning with latter part of July have been very costly and British morale not as high as two months ago."

(Diary) Chaumont, Tuesday, September 18, 1917. Visited artillery school at Le Valdahon on Sunday with Harbord, de Chambrun, Boyd, and Collins. Progress of artillery and the instruction of 100 young officers very satisfactory.

Colonel Russel called yesterday to urge cabling for telegraph and telephone material ordered before leaving Washington.

Examined Medical Department's plans to-day with Colonel Bradley and find good progress. There will be no repetition of experience of '98.

The military post of Le Valdahon, near the Swiss border, used by us as a school for our field artillery, was one of several which had been kindly set apart for Americans in different parts of

France. The others were at Coëtquidan and Meucon, near St. Nazaire, and at Souge and Le Courneau, near Bordeaux, and also at Montmorillon, Saumur, and Angers, with a school for heavy artillery at Mailly, southeast of Reims. The extensive artillery ranges and the large aviation field at Le Valdahon afforded exceptional facilities for coöperation between the artillery and the air service and for the instruction of officers of both services as airplane observers. This school was then under the direction of Brigadier General P. C. March, an energetic and alert commander. At the time of my visit, the field artillery brigade of the 1st Division was there for training.

Concerning the Signal Corps and its progress, before leaving Washington Colonel Russel had ordered a large consignment of material for both telegraph and telephone lines, but so far none had been received, except what was sent with us on the *Baltic*. Finding it necessary to establish our own telephone system in Paris, where the city service was almost useless, we were fortunately able at once to obtain enough material for the purpose in England and France.

The lines throughout France were so inefficient and unreliable, as government-owned utilities usually are, that in order to provide unfailing connections it was necessary for us to put in much new construction along our channels of supply, from base ports to headquarters. In addition to rebuilding entirely some of the more important lines, we were able to utilize others by replacing the old wire. As a rule, efficient telegraph and telephone service in the zones of our activities was obtained only by superimposing our system on that of the French, and using our own officers, operators, and maintenance. We soon completed direct connections from Chaumont to our offices in Paris, and later to the Headquarters of the Services of Supply at Tours, and also to London.

The Signal Corps had, of course, to anticipate the communications necessary in battle. Therefore, definite decisions were required some time in advance as to spheres of operations. Tons of material, the most of which, except wire, was obtained in

France, and a great amount of labor were used in the actual installations. The main telephone and telegraph lines in proximity to the battle areas were, when practicable, laid underground to prevent destruction. Wire communication within smaller units was handled by their own personnel with Signal Corps matériel.

Besides a thorough network of wire connections, it was considered advisable also to have wireless apparatus available for use if necessary between important points. The employment of radio in airplanes also was essential to the successful coöperation of aviation with artillery.

The perfection of our communication system in the A.E.F. demanded the most modern terminal, station, and line equipment. In order to assist the efficient, though limited, personnel of the Regular Army Signal Corps, the ablest men available to help plan and build, as well as to operate, were called into service from civil life as emergency officers.

One of the crying needs, when we once began to use our own lines, was for experienced operators. Instead of trying to train men of the Signal Corps, I requested that a number of experienced telephone girls who could speak French be sent over, and eventually we had about 200 girls on this duty. Some doubt existed among the members of the staff as to the wisdom of this step, but it soon vanished as the increased efficiency of our telephone system became apparent. No civil telephone service that ever came under my observation excelled the perfection of ours after it was well established. The telephone girls in the A.E.F. took great pains and pride in their work and did it with satisfaction to all.

The Medical Department's plans constantly received my careful attention through frequent conferences with the Chief Surgeon, Colonel Bradley, and his assistant, Colonel Ireland. Most of the older officers remembered with something akin to horror the unsanitary condition of our camps at Chickamauga and elsewhere, and the resulting high death rate from disease during the Spanish-American War, and all concerned, especially the medical men, were resolved that nothing like that should be repeated in our armies in the World War.

Our problem of handling the sick and wounded was more difficult than that of any of the Allies because we had no civil hospitals of our own available. Full provision, therefore, had to be made for hospital accommodations in France, as only convalescents manifestly unfit for further service could be sent home. The early estimates submitted in August, based upon a small force of 300,000 men, called for 73,000 beds in permanent, semi-permanent, or temporary hospitals, and plans for expansion were on hand to keep pace with the expected requirements of our armies once they should become engaged. While this beginning appeared quite liberal, it was calculated to meet further demands of the immediate future.

All the facilities throughout France were available for the French, but they had so many sick and wounded that their hospital resources were pretty well exhausted. As there seemed to be only a few suitable buildings that could be assigned to us, we had to plan a great deal of new construction. This called for additional labor and material, both of which were scarce, and although there was some delay we managed by persistent effort to keep pace with requirements.

While the medical personnel must bear a certain ratio to the size of the army, yet as we did not expect to be actively engaged until spring, and the demands for men for every other purpose were pressing, the allowance of medical personnel had to be restricted temporarily.

The French used the ordinary railroad facilities for the transportation of their wounded, but the distances from our probable front to the zone of available hospital accommodations, and thence to our base ports made it advisable to have the most approved rail equipment. Negotiations were at once started in England to obtain hospital trains, which began to arrive early in February. The ward cars were of the Pullman passenger type, with double tiers of berths. Each train had, in addition, a kitchen and dispensary, with an operating car, a dining car, and sleeping cars for medical officers and nurses. Nineteen trains of fifteen cars each were in operation at the time of the Armistice.

One of the important duties of the Medical Department was the prevention and cure of venereal disease, which in all other wars had caused serious reductions in effectives. Its prevalence in the Allied armies presented no exception to previous experience. From the purely practical standpoint of difficulty in replacing men, the possibility of having large numbers of ineffectives from this cause could not be contemplated without making every effort to prevent it. Among the first measures taken to restrict the evil was the promulgation of very stringent regulations in which medical officers and all others were enjoined to impress continence upon our troops, not only as a military obligation but as a patriotic duty. Commanding officers were directed to encourage and promote high moral standards of living among the members of their commands. General orders placed the responsibility for good conduct directly upon the soldier himself and prescribed that where men became unfit for duty through misconduct summary punishment would follow. This question was destined to give us considerable concern because of the difference between the French attitude and our own regarding the suppression of the sources of infection, but our efforts on the whole were remarkably successful. The percentage of ineffectives in our army from this cause was much lower than that of the Allies and surpassed any previous record in the history of wars.

(Diary) Paris, Thursday, September 20, 1917. Arrived from Chaumont by motor on Tuesday and have spent two busy days here. Coal shortage so serious that we are borrowing for current needs. In conference with Lord Derby and Major General Sir Frederick Maurice yesterday found they can furnish some coal but no tonnage to carry it. Lord Derby offered any supplies England can spare.

Admiral Mayo, Atterbury, Dawes, and Commander Sayles, naval attaché, lunched with us to-day to discuss coal situation. Mayo agrees that Navy and Army interests should be considered together.

Orders issued to-day directing strictest economy in use of fuel and oil.

The capture or destruction by the German Army of many of the mines of northern France had forced the importation from

England of a large proportion of the coal needed for various purposes in both France and Italy. Lack of cross-Channel tonnage had produced a serious situation for the French and ourselves, and the danger of a coal shortage during the approaching winter gave us much concern. Italy was even worse off owing to her greater distance from the sources of supply. The continuous manufacture of munitions in France demanded a constant inflow of coal, the railroads needed an assured amount, while the troops and civil populations had to have their proportion. The French foresaw the gravest consequences unless increased quantities could be brought regularly from England, and our necessities were tied up with theirs. Although the French themselves were not working their remaining mines to the fullest extent, yet when it was proposed that American miners be sent to assist them, the suggestion was not favored because of internal labor conditions.

We needed some 40,000 tons of Channel shipping to keep us going at this time and we would require an even larger amount as our activities increased. In an endeavor to make independent provision for our Army on the same basis as the Navy, which was being supplied from British sources, Colonel Dawes was sent to confer with Admiral Sims, only to be told that our Navy in European waters could not furnish us any tonnage. A statement of the situation was cabled to Washington with the request that steamers, possibly from the Great Lakes, be sent.

As satisfactory arrangements could not be made through Admiral Sims, an appeal was made to Admiral Mayo, who was already fully alive to needs of the American Army. He suggested the possibility of shipping coal from America in naval colliers, or as ballast for our transports. The following cable was sent as a result of this conference:

"Situation in both Italy and France reference coal regarded * * * as very serious. England has plenty of coal but cannot furnish transportation, although possible obtain some British assistance to carry coal across Channel for ourselves. * * * Question of transportation should be considered as a whole and entire problem of coal for

American forces including both Army and Navy be coördinated and obtained from nearest sources. When not otherwise employed full use should be made of available navy colliers and army freight transports to supply coal for our army and help France."

The outcome of our efforts, with the very effective assistance of Admiral Mayo, was that some colliers, one of which was already at Brest, were ordered into service for immediate use and these were supplemented later by vessels from the Shipping Board. The organization of the cross-Channel service was completed under the control of our Quartermaster Corps and later transferred to the Transportation Department. Although the coal question became more or less critical at various times during the winter, in the main we were fairly well supplied.

CHAPTER XIV

French Mission to Aid in Procurement—Importance of Rifle Again Emphasized—More Ordnance Indecision—Inefficiency in Loading Transports—Urgent Need of Labor—Weekly Summary of Events—Over
1,000,000 Tons Shipping Needed—Letter to Secretary on Vigor of
Officers, Training, and Promotions—Visit to 1st Division—French
Appeal for Mechanics—Ladies of Chaumont Present Flag

(Diary) Chaumont, Monday, September 24, 1917. Held conference
Saturday with Atterbury, Wilgus, Harry L. Rogers and William D.
Connor on readjustment of staff relations in S.O.S. Pétain designates
Ragueneau, Chief of Mission, as representative of Minister of War
and French G.H.Q. in procurement.

To-day discussed Gas Service organization with Colonel Fries.
Sent positive cable to War Department on training.

Work at office very strenuous,[1] but riding every day keeps me fit.

IN negotiating with the French for supplies and material, the
understanding was that we should deal with the French Mission at my headquarters in regard to such as were controlled by
the Zone of the Armies, and directly with the bureaus of the War
Office as to those under control of the Services of the Rear. But
in practice this plan proved quite too complicated. So, after considerable discussion, it was agreed by the Minister of War, General Pétain, and myself that procurement in general should be
handled through the French Mission. While this plan held in
principle, yet our purchasing officers, in ordnance and aviation
especially, usually found it necessary to conduct negotiations
directly with the corresponding French ministers and bureaus in
the War Office, and in these matters my personal intervention
and assistance were frequently required.

Having learned that despite recommendations little or no

[1] My diary shows conferences of more or less importance with some twenty-five
different officials from the 21st to the 24th inclusive. This was about the average
of those early days of organization.

attention was being given at home to the importance of teaching our men the use of the rifle, it seemed necessary again to emphasize my views, especially after further knowledge of the neglect of rifle training in Allied armies. The infantry soldier, well-trained in stealthy approach and in the art of taking cover, makes a small target, and if he is an expert rifleman there is nothing that can take his place on the battlefield. The following quotation from one of my cables will suffice to show my attitude:

"Sept. 24, 1917.

" * * * Strongly renew my previous recommendation that all troops be given complete course in rifle practice. * * * Specialties of trench warfare instruction at home should not be allowed to interfere with rifle practice or with intensive preliminary training in our schools of soldier, company and battalion."

On this latter point the following, which was dwelt upon in the A.E.F. with all vigor, was added:

"I cannot too strongly impress upon the War Department the absolute necessity of rigid insistence that all men be thoroughly grounded in the school of soldier. Salutes should be rendered by both officers and men in most military manner. * * * The loyalty, readiness and alertness indicated by strictest adherence to this principle will immensely increase the pride and fighting spirit of our troops. The slovenly, unmilitary, careless habits that have grown up in times of peace in our Army are seriously detrimental to the aggressive attitude that must prevail from highest to lowest in our forces. Strict methods used at West Point in training new cadets in these elementary principles have given the Academy its superior excellence. These methods should be applied vigorously and completely in the forces we are now organizing."

(Diary) Chaumont, Wednesday, September 26, 1917. The French agree that we should retain exclusive jurisdiction over American soldiers in France. Find Captain R. B. Owens, the head of Electrics, University of Nebraska, when I was there, now Russel's assistant.

Chief of Ordnance at Washington delays storehouse construction by requesting views of French Commissioner regarding our necessities. Colonel Jefferson R. Kean, Medical Corps, just arrived, assigned to command medical units with British. Frederick Palmer spent last night with us.

Have again cabled relative to carelessness and delay in loading of transports.

The War Department had brought up the question of civil jurisdiction over the members of our forces in France and had inquired regarding the attitude of the French. A committee of the American Bar Association, being of the opinion that counsel and advice might be needed, had offered the free services of several of its members familiar with French laws and language. My Judge Advocate, Colonel W. A. Bethel, presented our opinion to the French authorities, which was that according to the principles of international law and in view of the conditions under which the American Army was serving in France its members should not be subject to criminal prosecution in French courts but should be answerable only to our own military tribunals. This view was readily accepted by the French and very properly the jurisdiction over our forces, both civil and military, remained in our hands.

With reference to storage for ordnance, a very careful calculation had been made of our requirements by my Chief of Ordnance, Colonel Williams, and sites for three large depots and shops were selected at Gièvres, Méhun and Foëcy, besides storage depots at the ports of St. Nazaire and Bordeaux, and in the forward area at Is-sur-Tille and Jonchery. There were also many smaller plants at various points in the S.O.S. With the exception of special repair shops it had been requested that the matter of construction be left in the hands of my Chief of Ordnance. Satisfactory types of buildings had been developed by the French and British and the organization of our Ordnance Department was such that the work could be done by men on the ground. However, the Chief of Ordnance in Washington was apparently unwilling to accept our calculation and asked the French Commission at Washington to obtain the views of the French on the subject. The Commissioner transmitted the request to his Government and the Government sent it to General Pétain, who, of course, referred the question to me. My reply, which went direct to Washington, naturally supported the original recommendation. At times it seemed that the last refinement was being invoked to cause delay. The following cable regarding the incident was sent to the Chief of Staff:

"* * * This endless chain should clearly indicate the necessity of handling such matters direct with my headquarters. Ordnance officers here capable of managing this construction work, thus leaving to Chief of Ordnance more important duties and decentralizing his office as to details that should be handled here. Request approval of my recommendation and reply by cable.

"* * * Again recommend that all requests for information required by our War Department be sent direct to these headquarters as invariably such matters are referred here by French either directly or indirectly."

It appeared to be difficult for some of the bureaus of the War Department to think in terms of a world war and they naturally hesitated to make decisions on questions involving the large requirements in supply, construction, and material. If they had only realized the pressing necessity for early preparation and had accepted the views of the men on the spot, it would have saved time and patience.

As a matter of fact, my cables were too often regarded merely as recommendations which the bureaus might approve or not, as they chose. This conception of their functions by the bureaus was entirely erroneous in that there had been no previous study of these questions made at home and they could not, from that distance, know what we needed as well as we ourselves knew. Moreover, in principle it was simply their duty to furnish the army overseas what it asked for, if possible, as otherwise we could not be held responsible for results.

As pertinent to this disregard of my requests in some quarters of the War Department, we received on a certain date confidential cable advice of sailings that were to take place from New York. This information had been furnished the French representative nine days earlier. After protesting once more against the dangerous practice of giving this sort of advance information to the French, the Chief of Staff at Washington finally stated that it would be discontinued entirely.

(Diary) Chaumont, Friday, September 28, 1917. Infantry Officers' Schools established at Valbonne and Valréas with General Bullard as Commandant of both.

Washington promises every effort to load vessels promptly and shorten round trip. Many complaints coming in of labor shortage.

General Kenly and Colonel Mitchell came to discuss aviation. Approved their recommendation for location air parks, depots, and receiving stations.

Approval of organization project for army in France, submitted early in July, just received from Washington nearly three months later.

Up to this time we were not getting the full use of even the limited shipping at our disposal, as the average time for a round trip of our transports, estimated to be forty days, was being exceeded considerably. The delay was partly due to our inability to discharge rapidly at French ports on account of meager dock facilities and shortage of labor, but that loss of time occurred at ports of departure was shown by the fact that the average time of the first twelve transports to make the round trip from St. Nazaire was over fifty-five days. These facts were cabled the War Department and the reply was as follows:

"Future estimates cannot be based on past performance of present transport fleet. In taking over and outfitting first transports, many necessary repairs and alterations were not originally made. Installation of additional ventilation and heating systems all require time, necessitating delays on this side. Installation of necessary armaments, modification of emplacements, all of which must necessarily be done here, are largely responsible for excessive turn-around up to date. Transports must be self-sustaining which requires large additional amount of coal. Some labor difficulties have been encountered to date. Greater fleet when turned over will be absolutely ready for service. Estimates this office that turn-around for fast vessels of fleet will not exceed three weeks, for slower vessels five weeks, for cargo transports six weeks. Time of dispatching troop transports abroad at present seems to this office excessive, especially with reference to last fleet. Every effort is being made to expedite sailing of vessels, bearing in mind necessity for every precaution being taken which entails some delay on account of convoys."

There was ample evidence of great confusion at home due to lack of efficient supervision, even in New York harbor, where experts should have been easy to find. Ships were seldom loaded to their full capacity; supplies greatly needed were often left behind; nonessentials were being sent over; many things were broken due to careless loading; and troops were often shipped to one port and their equipment to another. The Washington bureaus oftentimes followed blindly some out-of-date supply table perhaps drawn up under a former régime by an antiquated desk soldier long since retired and forgotten. As an illustration, I recall a bill of lading from one of our transports that was presented to me about this time as a curiosity. It listed a number of articles quite useless to an army in the field and provoked the following cable:

> "For all departments. Recommend no further shipments be made of following articles * * * bath bricks, book cases, bath tubs, cabinets for blanks, chairs except folding chairs, cuspidors, office desks, floor wax, hose except fire hose, step ladders, lawn mowers, refrigerators, safes except iron field safes, settees, sickles, stools, window shades. Further stop orders will follow soon."

I have often wondered what manner of man was responsible for shipping such things, whether on supply tables or not, thereby wasting tonnage, when winter clothing, building material, steel and any number of real necessities were being delayed.

All of these facts suggested a condition of affairs during those earlier months that must have paralleled the inefficiency displayed in the management of our transport system in the Spanish-American War, a comparison that was frankly stated in the following cable:

> "October 10, 1917.
> " * * * Assignment of Medical Department with troops heretofore arriving indicates lack of supervision. The field hospital ambulance company that came with 26th Division arrived without any except personnel equipment and without transportation of any kind. Regimental detachments came with combat equipment only. Medical officers report their equipment was loaded on ships on which they sailed but prior to sailing it was taken off and sent on other ships.

Manner in which these regiments came to France does not indicate much improvement over conditions Spanish-American War. * * * "

It was then six months after we had entered the war and little system at points of embarkation was apparent.

We were short-handed, both at depots and along the Line of Communications, in all classes of labor that should have been sent over long before. The Quartermaster Corps in France was seriously handicapped in handling, caring for, and issuing stores and supplies. The engineers had laid out many projects of construction and made a beginning on those most necessary, but it looked as though we should be unable to keep up with the demands for facilities and accommodations.

The need for stevedores had become most urgent. Combat troops were still being used to unload cargo and thus much time was lost by the employment of labor that was entirely unsuited for this sort of work. Moreover, it was important that the combat troops should be sent inland to receive their battle instruction. The French, although short of labor themselves, had lent us a few prisoners and also some women, to help out, but neither class was satisfactory. Under these conditions, there was danger that our ports would become hopelessly congested. About the middle of October, fifteen weeks after I made my initial request, which had been followed by further urgent appeals, the War Department promised to send stevedores at once.

From our point of view it was not understood why any number of laborers, both skilled and unskilled, should not have been sent to France promptly. It may be stated, however, that it was hinted that there remained in Administration circles a lingering hope that after all it might not be necessary to send a large army abroad. The slowness in beginning the preparation of cantonments at home and in organizing the ports of embarkation, the delay in sending over both labor and combat troops, and material for the construction of docks and railways, and the apparent failure to utilize available tonnage or to obtain an additional amount elsewhere, could all be explained on the above hypothesis. Otherwise, even granting our deplorable want of preparation, it must be conceded that there existed at home either a lack of comprehension of the importance, the urgency, and the immensity of the task, or of competent leadership in handling it.

The French now came forward with a strong plea for mechanics for airplane construction, claiming that we had promised to furnish them. Whatever the understanding may have been, it was manifest that we should not be likely to get many airplanes unless we made an effort to provide the French additional help. Accordingly the matter was fully explained to the War Department and a request made for 3,000 mechanics in November, a like number in December, and 6,000 in January. The French offered some of their slow ships to carry them across, but it was not regarded as safe at that time to employ transports of less than sixteen knots speed, as they could not be sent with the regular convoys. The War Department agreed to provide mechanics, but concluded that our shipping could transport them as fast as they were ready.

A weekly summary of events was started in order to keep Washington advised of the general situation as it appeared at my headquarters. These reports were based mainly upon information gathered by the Intelligence Section of the General Staff from every available source, and in addition to the résumé of facts, it is remarkable how accurate they were in drawing conclusions and in forecasting conditions. The following is an extract from the report for the week ending September 30th:

"German Army consists of 146 divisions on Western Front and 91 on Eastern Front. Western armies have suffered since July 31st by British and French attacks * * * but their fighting efficiency not seriously impaired. * * * The object is to keep Germany to the strategic defensive rôle and diminish her manpower and secure important local objectives in preparation for greater successes when U. S. is ready.

       *   *   *   *   *   *   *

"Politically the power of the War party in Germany and the morale of the German people have been considerably strengthened by the military success at Riga and by the disorganization in Russian Army and Government. * * * Germany's iron supply is adequate for the moment * * * but manufacturing problem one of increasing difficulty. * * *

"Conflicting war aims and interests among Germany's allies have brought increasing friction. * * * The abandonment of Bagdad to the British has caused the Turks to grumble, while the failure to send troops to attack Salonika has brought unrest to the Bulgarians. Austria's dissatisfaction over the abandonment of the Roumanian campaign for operations at Riga has been mentioned, yet those disaffections have not reached a magnitude where * * * a political detachment appears diplomatically feasible.

"Finally, the war still retains a character such that continuous hard blows offer the only path to success."

(Diary) Chaumont, Monday, October 1, 1917. Received authority to discharge officers for inefficiency, which will help to maintain high standards. British steel situation reported critical and they demand shipments as offset to coal. Lassiter recommends securing Austrian vessels interned in Spain.

It was natural to expect that our continuous demands on the Allies for munitions and supplies of all sorts, including such items as artillery, airplanes, ammunition, horses, coal, and lumber, should be met by requests that we furnish American skilled labor and raw material. The immense proportion of artillery ammunition required called for large quantities of steel and explosives, and the prospect of increased expenditure could be foreseen in the certainty of general activities the following year. The British were urgently demanding steel, and asked that we send over 50,000 tons in our own ships, suggesting this be considered as balancing our request for coal. The War Department thought our tonnage was not equal to any such burden and advised us that shipping for England was being handled through the British Shipping Board.

Estimates of tonnage necessary to carry out the War Department program [1] indicated that the amount of shipping then employed would have to be increased to over 1,000,000 tons and that

---

[1] See cablegram quoted on page 118, Chapter IX.

Note: Total strength of A.E.F. on September 30th, 4,406 officers, 57,125 enlisted men. Divisional units arriving in September included the first elements of the 26th Division (National Guard from New England), Major General C. R. Edwards.

to maintain the forces overseas thereafter would require the constant use of 800,000 tons. The possibility of acquiring the Austrian fleet, consisting of twenty-one vessels, was suggested to the War Department. The actual tonnage of vessels we had in service on October 1st was only 255,228 tons, and so far there was no indication as to when the "Greater Fleet" already mentioned would be ready.

One of my periodical letters to the Secretary of War gives a brief résumé of several matters of interest at the moment:

"France, October 4, 1917.

"*Personal and Confidential.*

"Dear Mr. Secretary:

"I wish to express my sincere appreciation of your note of August fifteenth regarding the handling of our affairs in France. Things have not always gone to my own satisfaction, but it has been, and will continue to be, my whole endeavor to carry out, with a broad view, the purpose for which we entered the war, and to do so in accordance with the wishes of the President and yourself.

"The details of a thorough staff organization, and the studies on construction, including railroads and docks, and the estimates for material therefor, have entailed a great amount of labor. The scarcity of trained officers to assist in working out these problems has been severely felt. Of course I realize the need for trained officers at home, and have not lost sight of the many knotty problems you have had to solve. In turn, I wish to congratulate you warmly upon the way you have handled them.

"Our relations with the French and British have been very cordial. Both Allies fully appreciate our difficulties and have given assistance accordingly. Our requests of the French, of course, have been many, and they have occasionally seemed a little restless that we have not moved faster in our preparations, but I have asked them to be patient and hold on until we could get our stride.

"A tentative system of instruction and training has been outlined, based upon the best information obtainable, and schools of instruction have been organized to provide instructors. The French have helped us train the First Division, while the British are taking as many young officers as they can accommodate in their schools. Our impression is that the French rather favor defensive tactics, while the British incline more to the offensive. I am making every effort to inculcate a strong, aggressive, fighting spirit among our forces, and to overcome a more or less perfunctory attitude engendered by years of peace.

"My earnest thought has been devoted to organization, and it is believed that the general system evolved will, in a short time, become more or less automatic, especially as to the services of the rear. The administrative staffs and my General Staff have been brought into thorough accord. The new railway transportation department, under Mr. Atterbury, as material and personnel arrive, will soon be able to meet our transportation requirements. But the delay in the arrival of forestry troops and dock material will postpone construction and may result in some congestion. The purchasing agency, under Colonel Dawes, is coördinating American purchases in Europe in conjunction with the French and British control, and will bring a great saving in the cost of supplies and economy in transportation.

"Training our troops for this new and exacting service is exceedingly important, and relatively difficult because of the large proportion of young officers who are generally able enough, but without experience. It may be added that there are older officers also who are not up to this work. Planning and directing individual training and instructing new officers in the tactical handling of our units require not only activity, but experience in such work as well, together with ability to grasp and apply the technical developments of the war.

"I hope you will permit me to speak very frankly and quite confidentially, but I fear that we have some general officers who have neither the experience, the energy, nor the aggressive spirit to prepare their units or to handle them under battle conditions as they exist to-day. I shall comment in an enclosure [1] on the individuals to whom I refer particularly. Both the British and French higher officers emphasize in the strongest terms the necessity of assigning younger and more active and more impressionable men to command brigades and divisions. We would commit a grave error if we fail to profit by their experience. A division commander must get down into the trenches with his men, and is at all times subject to severe hardships. I regret that I did not write you fully on this subject, but I only partially realized the difficulty you would have in making these assignments and contented myself with sending a cablegram relative to the activity required of brigade and division commanders.

"None of these classes of officers have the vigor and alertness to inspire our men with confidence, and our soldiers deserve the best

[1] Remarks in this paragraph refer to certain officers, listed confidentially, who were considered unfit physically and professionally.

leaders we can give them. The French Army was filled with dead timber at the beginning of the war, and many French failures are due to this fact. General officers must be fitted physically and mentally, must have experience and must have the go and initiative if they are to fill positions fraught with such momentous consequences to the nation and which involve the lives of thousands, perhaps hundreds of thousands of our men. All the officers referred to are friends of mine, but that should count for nothing. There are so many active, energetic, able men for selection that I strongly recommend that no general officers who are in any way physically inactive or unsound be sent here to command units. I deemed it my duty to you and to the President to give you my very best judgment in such matters, regardless of individuals.

"There is one thing more, if you will pardon me. An army is a better fighting unit if it is a contented army. All other things being equal, this can best be produced by giving the most efficient officers merited recognition. Always having high efficiency as a guide, I believe promotions could safely be made from various arms on a basis of length of service and experience.[1] The French Army has adopted this principle and efficient officers have been promoted and assigned without very much regard to the arm of the service. Any high class officer who has made good with troops in one arm very soon grasps the duties of another arm.

"Perhaps some declaration or expression announcing this principle for future selections might go far to allay some feeling of discontent found both here and at home among very capable officers who have been passed by juniors selected from another arm. Of course I realize that for special corps, like Railway Transportation and Aviation, the plan for selecting men with particular qualifications must be followed. Nor have I any doubt that all sides of this promotion question have been considered, but simply give you this as an observation.

*   *   *   *   *   *   *

"The Russian situation looks gloomy from our point of view, but appears to have had a stimulating effect upon German morale. As to complete Allied success next year, much depends upon what Russia may do, and Russia's failure may prolong the war through 1919. Germany seems confident that Russia is no longer much of a factor. However, six months of winter may make a change in the situation.

*   *   *   *   *   *   *

[1] This refers to a rule in making promotions to the grade of brigadier general by which vacancies were filled proportionately from the different (combat) arms.

"Again renewing my purpose to do everything within my power and ability for our success, I remain, Mr. Secretary, with highest esteem and warm personal regards,
"Yours faithfully,
"JOHN J. PERSHING."

(Diary) Chaumont, Thursday, October 4, 1917. General de Castelnau called on Tuesday to discuss entry of 1st Division into the line.

Witnessed attack maneuver of the division yesterday and conducted critique. Took luncheon with General Sibert and his staff.

Ambassador Sharp came to-day with M. Joseph Reinach for a visit and had lunch with us. Have cabled appeal for officers fitted for General Staff.

The French, always solicitous regarding the progress of our training, were anxious that our most advanced American unit take its place in a quiet sector for the experience. The main reason they advanced for suggesting front-line training at this time, with which I fully agreed, was that it would give new encouragement to their armies and through them to the people. The 1st Division itself was keen to take a more active part and was soon to have the opportunity.

This division had been billeted in the training area since July 15th and had begun to show the excellent effects of the system of training we had prescribed. At the maneuver which I attended the officers handled their units with considerable skill, particularly Major F. H. Burr, who directed an attack with his battalion of the 28th Infantry, and Major Theodore Roosevelt, Jr., who conducted a similar problem with a battalion of the 26th Infantry. At the division school the bayonet exercises, special rifle practice, firing with trench mortars, grenade throwing, and other trench training activities were well carried out. I returned much pleased with the evidences of efficiency in this organization, which was later to become famous among the armies on the Western Front.

When Ambassador Sharp and M. Reinach, a noted French journalist, lunched with us, the latter proved to be an entertaining guest, with his running comments on public men, their ages, peculiarities and shortcomings. Replying to some remark concerning his youthful outlook at the age of sixty, he said in English, with a pronounced French accent, "You know, when one is born young, one remains young always." Ambassador Sharp came just to pay a visit to "the boys," as did many other Americans in France in those days. Such visitors always left apparently in better spirits after contact with our men, and the Ambassador was especially buoyant. While we had only a handful of troops, their energy and enthusiasm were really an inspiration.

(Diary) Paris, Wednesday, October 10, 1917. Spent Sunday at Gondrecourt. Attended 1st Division Field Meet, with General Harbord, General Ragueneau and Representative Medill McCormick. We lunched with Bullard.

Yesterday evening the officers at G.H.Q. called to extend congratulations on confirmation of my appointment as General. All heads of permanent staff departments appointed to grade of Brigadier General.[1]

A group of Major Generals are over on tour of inspection.[2] Delivery of airplanes by French doubtful.

Division commanders from the States and their chiefs of staff were being sent over to visit the battlefields, armies, and schools in order to become acquainted with conditions and to experience the atmosphere of war. It was important that they should appreciate the realities and the urgency of thorough preparation of their commands. It was thought they would be impressed with the aggressive spirit that characterized our training in France by coming into close touch with our methods. These officers were sent to visit the Allied fronts and to see exercises at our own training fields and schools and were also escorted along the Line of Communications. I took occasion to give them personally my conception of the course of training that should

[1] The following were so appointed: J. G. Harbord, Chief of Staff; Benj. Alvord, Adjutant General; H. L. Rogers, Quartermaster General; W. A. Bethel, Judge Advocate General; Edgar Russel, Chief Signal Officer; C. C. Williams, Chief of Ordnance; and A. E. Bradley, Chief Surgeon.

[2] Major Generals F. J. *Kernan*, A. P. Blocksom, W. M. *Wright*, C. G. *Morton*, W. H. Sage, C. G. *Treat*, E. St. J. Greble, G. *Bell*, Jr., H. *Liggett*, J. F. Morrison, F. S. *Strong*, J. Parker, C. M. Clement, J. F. *O'Ryan*. Those whose names are in italics afterwards served in the A.E.F. Major General Morrison unfortunately became ill in France and much to my regret was unable to come over with his division.

be followed at home, making a special point of rigid discipline, rifle practice, and the instruction of junior officers in open warfare. Quite a number of the division commanders who came over as observers were either physically unfit or had reached the age when new ideas fail to make much of an impression and consequently I recommended that both classes be left at home for other duty or be retired.

All contending nations were finding themselves hard pressed to meet the demands for matériel, although according to reports the Allies were worse off than the Central Powers. The French had agreed to furnish us 5,000 airplanes but they were encountering difficulty in expanding their production, the alleged reason being the non-arrival of raw material and skilled labor from the United States, to which I have referred. My frequent appeals did not bring us the men and material and our contract for airplanes hung in the balance. The fact is that we never did catch up with our own or French requirements in labor, either skilled or unskilled, or in raw materials.

But there were also demands at home for mechanics, and as the supply was by no means unlimited, to provide them both at home and abroad was not an easy matter. Nevertheless our situation was growing more serious and it was important that we should furnish the French as many mechanics as we could without further delay. I therefore clearly presented the situation to Washington and recommended that these men be sent in civilian clothes, with brassards and overalls, if uniforms were not available.

(Diary) Chaumont, Sunday, October 14, 1917. Received approval of my suggestion that soldiers be permitted to subscribe to Second Liberty Loan.

Representatives of Aero Club, Mr. Harold E. Porter and Mr. Sidney Veit, called yesterday at Paris office to offer coöperation. Sent strong cable requesting motor transportation be expedited.

A touching ceremony took place to-day at the Hôtel de Ville, where I was presented with a beautiful American flag embroidered by the ladies of Chaumont. Took luncheon with Mayor.

The event which occurred in Chaumont on October 14th I shall ever recall with pleasant memories. I had been invited to appear at the Hôtel de Ville, and my party and I went there at the appointed hour. I was surprised to find a large crowd of townsfolk gathered in the main square, and the neighboring houses bedecked with flags. As we entered the hall, the Mayor, much to my surprise, pointed out a marble slab on which there was an inscription recording the establishment of our headquarters in Chaumont. Following introductions to the assembled guests the Mayor, in a moving speech, presented me with a flag in the name of the ladies of the city, as a souvenir of their appreciation of America's aid in the war. As usual, I had not anticipated that there was to be any speech-making and could hardly find words to express my feelings. Toasts were drunk, friendly sentiments expressed, and altogether the ceremony was very delightful. A number of us went to the Mayor's residence for luncheon and were delighted by the charm of the home and the cordiality of our host and hostess. I keep this flag as one of my most highly prized souvenirs, recalling, as it does, my sojourn among the hospitable people of that community.

I cannot resist commenting on their Mayor. He was one of those Frenchmen, of whom there are not a few, who, like the corresponding American species, can grow eloquent on almost any subject. They often rise to unwonted heights of oratory and make a profound impression whether one happens to understand the language or not. From this point of view the Mayor quite surpassed all his previous efforts. As Mayor he was most efficient and the people evidently so regarded him, which is proved by the fact that he had been the municipal head of that quiet little town on the upper Marne a number of times and was afterwards sent to the Assembly.

CHAPTER XV

Visit from Joffre—French Unrest—Pessimism Reported Among Our Officers—1st Division Enters Trenches—French Success on Aisne—Caporetto Disaster—Inspection of Ports

(Diary) Chaumont, Monday, October 15, 1917. Marshal Joffre came yesterday, upon my invitation, to visit our troops. He reviewed 1st Division to-day near Tréveray and spoke to the officers. We lunched at Neufchâteau, then inspected other troops and billets.

Am gratified that Major General Morrison, upon my recommendation, has been appointed Director of Training at home.

WHEN Marshal Joffre came to Chaumont, the French military officials were anxious to show their respect and it was arranged to have both an American and a French guard of honor drawn up to salute him upon his arrival at my residence. These two small guards vied with each other and both seemed to get a great thrill out of the ceremony. After an interesting evening with the Marshal and his staff as our guests, we left the next morning by motor car for Tréveray, accompanied by Generals Ragueneau and Alvord, Colonels de Chambrun and McCoy, and Captain Boyd. The troops of the 1st Division were drawn up in line ready to receive us and presented a much better appearance than at the review by President Poincaré. The men were especially keen to be inspected by a Marshal of France and their pride was clearly evident by their perfect lines as they swung by in the march past. The Marshal in turn was enthusiastic over their vigorous appearance and military bearing.

One incident occurred that was not on the program. On the way to the field for the ceremony a well-groomed mule that happened to be running loose, pricked up his ears, looked us over and decided to trot along with us. One of my staff wagered that this wise animal knew what was going on and would be present to witness the review. Sure enough, when we reached our position this Missouri product had preceded us. Cautiously approaching, he displayed the greatest curiosity in the guest of honor. As all efforts to drive him away were futile, he hovered near as an interested spectator of the proceedings, much to the amusement of Marshal Joffre.

I gave a luncheon at Neufchâteau for the Marshal's party and the senior officers of the 1st Division. After that we saw the training conducted by the First Corps School and visited the American and French billets at the village of St. Blin, where the 101st Infantry, 26th Division, and the French 69th Division passed in review in excellent form. As we started toward Chaumont, other American and French units were drawn up by the roadside in honor of the Marshal. It was rather late and darkness overtook us while passing on foot through the lines. The trumpets of each regiment sounded as we approached and with the lights from our automobiles close behind us illuminating the trees that bordered the highway and the faces that peered through the shadows to catch a glimpse of the Marshal, the scene suggested some legendary painting. Finally we halted, and the troops, including the French 151st Infantry, which had made a remarkable record at Verdun, marched past us. As the regiments came out of the darkness into the spotlight of our autos they made a moving picture never to be forgotten.

The political unrest in France at that time found expression in frequent criticism of the Government under M. Painlevé. It was whispered in some circles that there might be a *coup d'état* led by an outstanding military figure. The removal of the Marshal as Commander-in-Chief of the French armies had not dimmed his popularity as the idol of the people and he might easily have been selected as the leader of such a movement had it been seriously projected. In speaking of its possibility as we drove back, he said, confidentially, that it had been discussed and that it might occur under certain circumstances. But, much to his credit, he hastened emphatically, and I think very sincerely, to disclaim any ambition in that direction. If the idea was ever really considered among the opposition to the Government, it never got beyond a very small coterie. In fact, there existed no actual crisis that was likely to precipitate a change in the form of government. The Republic had stood firmly for three years under the extreme stress of war and there seemed little probability of its being overturned at this time by such a stroke.

On October 17th the following summary was sent to Washington showing the estimate of the situation in Europe:

" * * * The Germans on Western Front have been reënforced by four divisions from the Russian front, giving a present total of 150 divisions.

"Persistent reports from widely separated sources of an (early) offensive by Germany and Austria against Italy. * * *

"Manifest that Germany is making determined effort to use present economic difficulties of Switzerland to excite Swiss people against Allies * * * French report activity on part of Swiss in construction of fortifications on French border.

"Reports indicate that after the failure of the Peace Conference asked for in Pope's peace proposal the German Government began active efforts to stiffen the spirit of the country * * * in support of new Pan-Germanist party whose platform is a victorious peace. * * * "

(Diary) Paris, Saturday, October 20, 1917. General Charteris, Chief of British Intelligence, visited G.H.Q. on Thursday.

Arrived in Paris from Chaumont last night. Called this morning on Ambassador Sharp, who thinks Painlevé Ministry will not last much longer. Dined with M. Painlevé this evening but saw no indications of uneasiness on his part. Among the guests were Marshal Joffre and General Foch.

Just heard that dispatch from Berlin to *New York Times* represents me as saying that German lines are impregnable. Have cabled that our shortage of winter clothing is critical. Have again insisted by cable on special training with rifle and bayonet.

The reported statement attributed to me that the German lines were impregnable might have been idle gossip, but it was more probably circulated to create the impression that our armies were starting on a forlorn hope. While not in the habit of taking notice of statements that appeared in the press, this was so far from the truth that I cabled the Secretary of War that the report was absolutely false and without any foundation whatever. In every reference to our future operations I had strongly maintained that it was not only possible to break the German lines but that it would be done. The very system of training that we were persistently following was based on the determination to force the Germans out of their trenches and beat them in the open. On no other theory could they have been defeated.

Yet without question there were not a few among our Allies and probably some in our own army who thought the task impossible, supporting their view by citing the failures of the previous three years, especially that of the spring of 1917. It was none the less a surprise, however, when a report came directly to me that such views had actually been expressed in the presence of civilian visitors by officers of rank in our army. I was indignant to learn of that kind of talk and in commenting on it to the Americans who had heard such statements made, I said that "the German lines can be broken, they must be broken, and they will be broken," and those present will recall that it was said with considerable emphasis. Positive steps were taken at once to eradicate such notions, or at least to prevent them from being openly stated, and I was determined to relieve immediately any officer, without regard to rank, who should express any such opinion. The following letter, couched in no uncertain language, was sent to the several division and other commanders:

"1. Americans recently visiting our training areas and coming in contact with officers in high command have received a note of deep pessimism, including apprehension of undue hardships to be undergone, of the disadvantages of billeting as compared to field conditions that have prevailed in our own country, of the great numbers of the enemy, and a belief in the impregnability of his lines, mingled with some comment on the peculiarities of our Allies, and generally have come away with an impression that the war is already well along toward defeat for our arms. It is especially to be regretted that such an impression has been derived mainly from general officers who, if prompted by considerations of soldierly duty, of leadership, of patriotism, fortitude and ambition, should maintain quite an opposite attitude.

"2. While realizing that optimism cannot be created by order, it should be unnecessary to point out that such a state of mind on the part of officers in responsible positions is at once reflected among their troops, and it is not an overstatement to say no officer worthy of command would give expression to thoughts of depression, much less communicate to untutored civilians false ideas of the morale of our troops. A conservative firmness and faith in our cause is not inconsistent with a serious estimate of an enemy's forces or even of a grave strategic or tactical situation, but I hardly need add that a temperament which gives way to weak complainings, which views with apprehension the contact with the enemy, which carps at the individuality of our Allies, and querulously protests at hardships such as all soldiers must expect to endure, marks an unfitness for command of such an officer, and indicates his practical defeat before he goes to battle.

"3. The officer who cannot read hope in the conditions that confront us; who is not inspired and uplifted by the knowledge that under the leadership of our Chief Executive, the heart of our nation is in this war; who shrinks from hardship; who does not exert his own personal influence to encourage his men, and who fails in the lofty attitude which should characterize the General that expects to succeed, should yield his position to others with more of our national courage. The consciousness of such an attitude should in honor dictate an application for relief. Whenever the visible effects of it on the command of such an officer reach me in future, it will constitute grounds for his removal without application.

"JOHN J. PERSHING."

Nothing more was heard of the existence of such sentiments within our army, if, indeed, they had ever found more than a temporary lodgment in the minds of a few naturally timid or critically inclined souls. The mere suggestion that such views might be held only made it all the more imperative to emphasize and develop an aggressive spirit among our troops.

(Diary) Paris, Wednesday, October 24, 1917. General situation on the Western Front not encouraging. The 1st Division entered trenches in quiet sector the night of the 21st. At the start each regiment will be assigned to a French division.

Shipment of troops through England and use of Brest under discussion.

Went to French front Monday, accompanied by Harbord, de Chambrun, Logan and Boyd. Spent the night at Compiègne with Col.

Frank Parker, head of our Mission. Witnessed successful offensive at Chemin des Dames yesterday.

Conferred with a number of officers to-day. Saw Cornelius Bliss and Charles H. Grasty and lunched with Atterbury. German offensive against Italians began this morning.

Chartered transport *Antilles* torpedoed and sunk the 17th.[1]

My general impression of the situation at this time was set forth in a cable to Washington sent on October 21st:

"During the past week the water-soaked ground in Flanders and on the Western Front generally has prevented further development of offensive movements. Summing up wastage of German Army in this year's campaign, a single offensive, such as the Anglo-French in Flanders in progress since July 31st, is insufficient materially to weaken Germany's manpower. Next year must see two offensives, continuously maintained throughout summer, if decisive result is to be obtained. This can only be secured through aid of effective United States Army on this side. * * * The troops on the Western Front have been reënforced by one German division from the Russian front. * * *"

As the training of the 1st Division had now progressed sufficiently, it was put into line in the quiet sector northeast of Lunéville, under the supervision of the French, for actual trench experience. The division was under-officered and short of horses, clothing and many other things, especially rolling kitchens, of which a few had only recently been received from home, and trucks, which were being borrowed from the French.

My repeated cables, beginning in July, for winter clothing had received scant attention and with the coming of colder weather the shortage became critical. The initial stock requested was disallowed, the monthly allotments were totally inadequate and the depots were practically empty. The explanation received from the Quartermaster General's office, that our requests could not be granted on account of the needs at home, showed a total

---

[1] The *Antilles* left Brest as a part of a convoy on October 15th, returning to the United States. On the morning of the 17th she was struck by a torpedo and sank within six minutes. Sixty-seven lives were lost, sixteen being enlisted men of the Army. The survivors were picked up by vessels of the escort and returned to Brest, from which point the message was telephoned to my headquarters. This was the first transport lost in our service.

lack of appreciation of the necessity of properly clothing the fighting man actually at the front in preference to all others.

Notwithstanding all these handicaps, the men were highly enthusiastic over the prospects of contact with the enemy and the rest of us were gratified that at last we were to be represented on the front. Thirty days were allotted for this preliminary training, one battalion of each regiment occupying the line for periods of ten days at a time. The sector had been inactive and uneventful since the stormy days of 1914, when General de Castelnau halted the German advance on the Grande Couronne de Nancy.

A few of the French peasants remained in their homes in advance of our support positions, while on the German side people continued to live near enough to the front lines to be seen going to church on Sundays. This presented to the men an odd contrast to the pictures of war which they had built up in their imaginations.

The offensive by the French on the Chemin des Dames was the second since Nivelle's failure in April. I went to the front upon the invitation of General Pétain, arriving by motor at the headquarters of General d'Espérey, Commander of the Group of Armies of the North, in time for dinner on the evening of the 22d. The plans for the attack were explained to us and, from the extreme care taken in working out the details and from their accurate knowledge of the enemy's force and his position, there seemed to be little doubt of success.

Soon after their victory near Verdun in August, the French began to prepare for this offensive, in which they could not well afford to fail. The advance was made by eight divisions of the Sixth Army on a front of only seven and one-half miles, extending along the Aisne, with the object of gaining a more advantageous position for the winter and also still further building up French morale. General Maistre, the Army Commander, gave the operation his personal attention, prescribing an artillery preparation covering six days, during which the expenditure of ammunition was even greater than in the offensive of August 20th. The long period of artillery fire was considered necessary, as the Germans were strongly fortified along the chalky bluffs of the Aisne, where numerous caverns afforded cover for large garrisons held near the front.

The assaulting lines of infantry, accompanied by numerous tanks, succeeded without difficulty in reaching the limited objectives. Fort Malmaison, the key point, was reduced to a heap of rubbish by the very heavy artillery fire concentrated upon it. The capture of this dominant position by the French caused the immediate withdrawal of the Germans on the right and left, and during the succeeding fortnight they retired behind the Ailette.

As we drove toward the front in the forenoon we met German prisoners being taken to the rear and received reports that progress was very satisfactory. The day was foggy, with rain at intervals, so that aviators were unable to be of much service, and the advance, except at the start, was quite hidden from our view, even from old Fort Condé, a commanding position that had been selected as our observation point.

When the luncheon hour came General d'Espérey asked us into a chamber of the fort, where we sat down and enjoyed a menu that would have done credit to any restaurant in Paris. During the meal the General told us that, several years before, he had crossed America while returning from service in the Orient and his journey through Iowa happened during one of those periods when prohibition was in force in that State. If there is any one thing that a Frenchman cannot understand it is that any people should deliberately enact a law to deprive themselves of the privilege of taking a glass of wine. To have heard him describe how he suffered while in Iowa one would have thought he was telling of a trip across the Sahara Desert.

During the afternoon he took us to visit the headquarters of one of the attacking divisions, the 27th, and after its infantry had penetrated the main German defenses we went by auto to what had been no-man's-land and thence on foot to the enemy's second position. The artillery and machine gun fire were still frequent over that part of the field, which was strewn with the bodies of many gallant Frenchmen whose courage had made the victory possible. Gangs of laborers and truckloads of material which had been held in readiness behind the attacking army had already been brought forward to rebuild the roads across the shell-torn area. From the respect shown General d'Espérey as he passed along, speaking cheerfully to the men, frequently addressing them affectionately as "Mes Enfants," there could be no doubt of his popularity. This was my second contact with one of the most picturesque and delightful personalities in the French Army.

This achievement of the French in capturing positions against which the April offensive by Nivelle dashed itself to pieces had a very stimulating effect upon their morale, but it would have been more lasting had it not been followed so soon by the serious defeat of the Italians at Caporetto. In any event, there was every reason for Generals d'Espérey and Maistre to be proud of the victory, which still further increased their prestige.

After extending thanks to our host, we left for Compiègne, literally covered with mud, stopping there to congratulate General Pétain on the success of the day. While at Compiègne we dropped in at the dispensary where some American women under Miss Elsie de Wolfe maintained a clinic for badly burned gas cases. We also made a brief call at the hospital nearby to see Colonel Bunau-Varilla, of Panama Canal fame, who had lost a leg in the recent French offensive near Verdun. From his cheerful mood he seemed to be rather proud of his wound. It was he who organized and developed the system of water supply and purification for the French armies. In 1927 I took part in the dedication of the Ossuary near Verdun, at which Colonel Bunau-Varilla was present. On the rounds to inspect this fine monument we passed the many bays which contain the bones of men who lost their lives in the great battle. When we came to the bay corresponding to the sector in which he fought, he jovially remarked that he thought his leg must be in there.

Following closely on the heels of this limited French success came a tremendous counterstroke by the Austrians and Germans against the Italians. During preceding months, beginning in May, the Italian armies had made a series of attacks which at first met with considerable success. The Italians made progress in the Julian Alps, causing Austrian losses of some 30,000 prisoners, but the timely arrival of Austrian reënforcements enabled them to prevent serious dislodgment.

Meanwhile, the situation on the Russian front permitted the withdrawal of troops of the Central Powers to an extent that enabled them to assume the offensive against the Italians. Continuous rumors had reached the ears of the Allies that an attack was impending, but they were given little credence, especially by the Italian Commander-in-Chief, who professed every confidence in the strength of his armies.

The Germans had come to realize that operations with limited objectives, involving days of violent preliminary artillery fire, were far too costly when measured by results. They had adopted a new system based on a few hours of heavy bombardment, principally with gas shells, followed by a violent assault on the forward positions by picked battalions supported by an unusually heavy concentration of machine guns and other portable weapons. The defense once broken, fresh troops held close in rear poured through the lines of the leading troops and, increasing the momentum of the attack, rapidly carried the fight beyond the entrenched positions. This plan had already been tested in the battle of Riga, where a complete rupture of the opposing fortified lines was accomplished and the fighting successfully carried on in the open.

The demonstration at Riga by General von Hutier's army was convincing proof of the soundness of the plan and of the correctness of the doctrine of training for open warfare that we were so persistently following in France and so continuously trying to impress upon the War Department at home. It simply proved that nothing in the great war had changed this age-old principle of the art of war. Thenceforth this method was to characterize German attacks, and the capture of Riga was only the precursor of Caporetto and the series of strokes by the Central Powers later on, which were more or less uniformly successful.

The most delicate phase of the system was the secret concentration close to the front of the large force necessary. This was usually accomplished by a series of night marches, the troops being concealed by day in villages and woods. Under German control and reënforced by seven picked German divisions, the Austrian forces, following out this plan, completely surprised the Italian Army on a nineteen-mile front near Caporetto on October 24th during a heavy fog and succeeded in breaking entirely through their lines on the first morning, rapidly forcing the Italians into the open. The advance crossed the Isonzo River and German troops were over the frontier by the 25th.

The feeble resistance of the Italian Second Army, which stood the brunt of the attack, has been attributed to well-organized propaganda on the part of the Austrians, who were said to have fraternized with the Italians on the theory that they were brothers and if they declined to fight each other the war would end. But the inherent weakness of the Italian position was not overlooked by the Germans. It appears, entirely from Italian sources, that there was actually a gap in the Italian lines between their Second and Third Armies at Tolmein, where the Austrian outposts held a commanding position on the high ground in the interval. The Italian reserves were insufficient, few defensive positions had been prepared in the rear, the bridges across the Isonzo were in-

The official portrait of General John J. Pershing. (National Archives photograph)

General Pershing and his staff in Mexico during the Punitive Expedition campaign.(The photograph is a reproduction from the collections of the Library of Congress.)

General Pershing and his staff arrive in Europe in 1917. (The Signal Corps, U.S.A., photograph is a reproduction from the collections of the Library of Congress.)

On November 18, 1917, in Chaumont, France, General Pershing inspects American troops. (National Archives photograph)

General Pershing was very popular with the French people. He is seen here taking a moment to chat with a little French girl. (National Archives photograph)

General Pershing (left) with his aide, Colonel George C. Marshall, Jr., in France in 1917. Pershing met Marshall shortly after his arrival in France and made him his chief staff officer until Pershing retired in 1924. (National Archives photograph)

adequate, and the supply depots, which were in front of the Tagliamento, were too far forward. At any rate, the Third Army was left in a critically exposed position from which it barely escaped by a rapid retreat.

Before the operation ended on November 10th the enemy had advanced some 60-odd miles and was confronting General Cadorna's men on the Piave. More than 300,000 prisoners, 3,000 pieces of artillery and immense quantities of supplies were captured by the enemy. All the Italian gains in the war were wiped out during the first thirty-six hours of this battle. Seemingly in an instant the cause of the Allies had been dealt a master blow and five British and six French divisions were rushed to Italy to save the situation. This victory tremendously strengthened the hands of the German Government.

One gleam of light was revealed in this dilemma. The magnitude of the disaster and its immediate effect on all the Allies forced a realization of the necessity of better understanding and closer coöperation. They soon after made a really determined effort to secure unity of command through the Rapallo Agreement, though a later disaster still more serious was necessary before this ideal could be finally accomplished.

(Diary) Paris, Wednesday, October 31, 1917. Reached St. Nazaire from Paris on Thursday with Harbord, de Chambrun and Nolan and went to artillery camps at Coëtquidan and Meucon. The following day visited St. Nazaire docks, shops and storehouses with Colonels Samuel D. Rockenbach and Louis H. Bash; thence to the new depot at Montoir with Colonel John S. Sewell, and to the hospital at Savenay with Colonel Jos. F. Siler.

On Saturday, with Brigadier Generals R. M. Blatchford, commanding Line of Communications, and Mason M. Patrick, and Colonels Charles R. Krauthoff and David S. Stanley, inspected labor camps at Bordeaux, new docks at Bassens and camp at Souge.

Sunday visited Russian detention camp at Le Courneau, the vilest and most unsanitary place I have ever seen.

Monday inspected hospital at Châteauroux, the aviation center at Issoudun, the great supply depot at Gièvres, and the ordnance depot at Méhun. Took train at Nevers; arrived Paris yesterday.

Received gratifying cable that large consignment of lumber, piles and crossties are en route. Heavy artillery school established at Camp Mailly under Brigadier General Frank W. Coe. Brigadier General Patrick assigned temporarily to command the Line of Communications; Major General Bundy to command the 2d Division.[1] Have requested French Mission to procure authority for entry of Spanish laborers. Had a group of visiting Congressmen [2] to dinner this evening.

This trip of inspection to Coëtquidan and Meucon was made by motor and the route ran through a portion of Brittany, picturesque with the autumn foliage of forests, orchards and hedges. The quiet countryside, the quaint houses with their thatched roofs, the people in old-time costumes, all suggested happiness and contentment regardless of the war.

At Coëtquidan, a French artillery station, we found the artillery of our 26th Division in training under General Lassiter, but the camp was very much crowded, as a regiment of French artillery had been left to assist in the instruction of our men. We then went to Meucon, which was to be another artillery camp, although not yet occupied by any of our troops. En route we passed through the "Landes de la Lanvaux," a sort of lowland covered with scrub pines. We stopped a few minutes at the ancient Château Josselin, where the young Duchess, whose husband, the Duke of Rohan,[3] had been killed in battle a short time before, showed us over the château. The defiant rise of this medieval structure above the cliff, at whose base flows the Oust River, is most striking, while the beautiful façade and the charming interior filled with family paintings and other souvenirs of past glory leave a lasting picture in the mind.

The port of St. Nazaire was found more or less congested, due to several causes. One was that we had not been able to expand the facilities fast enough to keep pace with requirements; an-

---

[1] This division was organized in France and was composed of one brigade of Regular troops and one of Marines.

[2] The following Congressmen constituted the party: C. C. Dill, F. C. Hicks, W. S. Goodwin, R. W. Parker, C. B. Timberlake, D. V. Stephens, J. F. Miller, S. M. Taylor, P. H. Dale and A. Johnson.

[3] This gallant officer, holding the rank of major, was three times severely wounded and sent to the rear, each time returning still convalescent, and was finally killed while leading his unit in battle.

other, that the French insisted on assuming the right to control movements of our transports in and out of the harbor; and, a third, that too many vessels were sent there, owing to the disinclination of our naval authorities in European waters to escort a due proportion of them to Bordeaux. The routing by the Navy of supply ships from home ports and coal boats from England and their disposition at French ports bore no relation whatever at this time to port accommodations available. The Navy pleaded the increased danger from submarines and a shortage of destroyers as the reason, and it was only after earnest and repeated representations and considerable further delay that there was much improvement in this annoying state of affairs.

The stevedore situation was worse even than had been reported and the inability to discharge vessels with rapidity was another cause of their slow turn-around at French ports. In a certain regiment of stevedores, especially recruited for that work, there were only eleven officers with previous experience, out of a total of about thirty, all the rest being absolutely without any knowledge whatever of handling cargo.

The construction of storehouses at Montoir, just out of the city limits, and the necessary rail connections were proceeding very slowly, with the result that valuable property had to be piled up on the docks or be left in the open at the warehouse sites. With adequate railway facilities all supplies could have been forwarded to our main centers, but sufficient rolling stock had not arrived and the French could furnish only a limited number of trains. At that moment the Allies had been called upon to meet the Italian crisis, which required the exclusive use of many trains to transport French and British troops, munitions and supplies to that front. If any further evidence had been needed, the situation thus created proved conclusively that we must develop and control our port accommodations and our own means of land transportation to the fullest extent possible.

The next objective on our trip was Bordeaux, sixty miles up the Gironde River. The city itself has real charm, with its broad proportions, public gardens, quaint old houses along the quays, its modern cathedral and old churches built a thousand years ago. It is the fourth city in France, especially noted for the large quantity and fine quality of its wines, in which it carries on a world-wide commerce.

The larger vessels could not enter the port except at high tide. As the port facilities were sufficient to accommodate only a limited amount of additional medium-draft shipping, we had started the construction of new docks at Bassens, six miles below, where the deep water would permit vessels to come alongside. Although considerable quantities of material had been sent over, this new construction was delayed principally because of lack of long piling which the engineers had planned to have brought from the Pacific Coast.

It became evident that this was impracticable within a reasonable time and that we must obtain as much piling as possible from forests in France. The French authorities were loath to yield to such demands, protesting that they had no standing timber of the necessary dimensions. Having driven through the forest reserves in the Vosges Mountains, I was able from personal observation to assure them that we should have no trouble in finding just what we wanted. Our foresters confirmed my assertion and logging companies were soon turning out quantities of piling. Our forestry service supplied the engineers with a total of 39,000 piles, 15,000 of which were long piles, thereby saving several shiploads, to say nothing of the strain on rolling stock of hauling this amount of material across the continent. Even with piling obtained from French sources, it was necessary to procure an additional quantity from the Pacific Coast.

An incident happened in connection with the shipments of piling from home that would have been amusing if it had not been so serious. One cargo reached Bordeaux that was supposed to consist of especially long piling, but upon inspection the engineers found it much shorter than prescribed. It was learned later that in order to get the piles in between bulkheads the supercargo had sawed the ends off, making them useless for the purpose intended. While speaking of forest products, another example of inefficiency that occurred soon after might be mentioned. One ship from home came over loaded by the Quartermaster Corps with shavings for our cold storage plants, when tons of sawdust and shavings could have been obtained from the logging districts in France.

Continuing the inspection, we went on Sunday to Le Courneau, about forty miles from Bordeaux, thinking it might possibly be available for our use later on. It was then occupied by a brigade of disaffected Russians who, like most of their fellows, had defied their officers and refused to participate further in the war. After being withdrawn from the line, they had given the French so much trouble, even to committing depredations on the people, that they had to be sent out of the Zone of the Armies to this rather remote camp, where they were held practically as prisoners. There was no transportation to carry them back to Russia and as they had been allowed to keep their arms it was difficult to enforce discipline among them. I spoke to two colonels and commented on the lack of sanitation, but it was evident that they were unable to compel the men to work, even to the extent of cleaning out stables, latrines or drains, and the conditions may better be imagined than described. The men were a heavy, stupid-looking lot, who, in their new estate, apparently did not care how bad things were so long as the French continued to feed and clothe them.

We then drove to Arcachon, a well-known watering place on the coast, for luncheon, and returned to Bordeaux through Souge, which later became the site of a hospital and also an artillery camp and remount station. Again boarding the train, the next morning found us at Châteauroux, where we had already begun the construction of a large base hospital, and where we were planning to establish a great depot of supplies similar to the one farther toward the front at Gièvres. At the largest aviation center, Issoudun, our next destination, we found the construction of quarters and the aviation field well under way, with several hundred aviators already receiving instruction, although handicapped by a very limited number of airplanes.

Gièvres, which lies 100 miles directly south of Paris, became the site of our principal supply depot in France. Under Colonel C. J. Symmonds' able and energetic direction, construction to cover an area of twelve square miles was going forward with all possible speed. He was gradually putting order and system into the place. The engineers were building storehouses for rations and a cold storage plant to hold hundreds of tons of fresh meats, and the Transportation Department was rapidly laying the mile upon mile of sidings that would be required. During this period of construction, which had only recently been started, the force at Gièvres was already receiving, classifying and either storing or forwarding supplies in amounts that eventually reached thousands of tons daily.

The ordnance depot at Méhun took but a few minutes, as building was hardly begun. Leaving there about dusk, en route to my train at Nevers, we motored through Bourges and saw the magnificent cathedral as it stood out in all its glory under the full moon. The view of this wonderful example of 12th Century architecture under the circumstances was one of the most impressive sights I have ever seen.

Regardless of the many drawbacks against which the Line of Communications was laboring, there was everywhere a fine spirit among the officers and men, who were generally cheerful and optimistic. After all, considering the lack of men and material, we were making progress on the physical side of the organization that would feed, clothe and furnish munitions for the great army we hoped to have. One of the obstacles was to be found in the number of independent bureaus represented at the ports and the larger centers of activity, not only in our own system, but especially in that of the French, and the consequent difficulty of securing teamwork among them. As a remedy, I sent to each base section a competent general officer with an organized staff to coordinate and systematize the management of affairs, and in a brief time considerable improvement was noticeable in methods of handling troop arrivals and cargo and in the increased progress of construction.

CHAPTER XVI

Conference with Mr. Lloyd George—Allied Ministers Meet at Rapallo—
Supreme War Council Formed—Enemy Raid on 1st Division Trenches
—Political Undercurrents—Aims of Different Allies—Ammunition
Question Acute—Letter from Secretary of War on Preparation, Selec-
tion of Commanders and Morale—Letter to Secretary in Reply

(Diary) Paris, Sunday, November 4, 1917. Went to Chaumont
Friday, returned yesterday. Major Generals Liggett, Parker, O'Ryan,
Clement, and Strong, visiting A.E.F., came to Paris with me. Major
General Morrison left behind ill. Germans made raid on our lines,
killed three, wounded several.

Took breakfast with Mr. Lloyd George this morning. Generals
Sir Henry Wilson, Smuts, and Maurice were in the party. Discussed
the advisability of establishing Supreme War Council. Had luncheon
with Sir Douglas Haig, who does not favor the suggestion. Called
on M. Painlevé. Congratulations from Secretary on splendid total
subscribed by A.E.F. to Second Liberty Loan.

IN our conversation at breakfast, Mr. Lloyd George referred
to the Italian disaster as most serious and pointed out that
sending British and French divisions to Italy had materially
weakened the lines in France. He also spoke at some length on
the lack of concerted action among the Allied armies. I agreed
with him in this and added that in my opinion there never had
been real coöperation on the Western Front between the British
and French, that when one was attacking the other was usually
standing still, and that the Germans were thus left free to concentrate their reserves against the threatened point.

We were facing a grave crisis next year, if not sooner, Mr.
Lloyd George said, and no one knew how it was to be met. The
enemy might attack each one separately, with the same results
as in the case of Italy. He then asked what I thought of creat-

Note: Total strength of the A.E.F. on October 31st, 6,064 officers, 80,969 enlisted
men.

ing a Supreme War Council. Having in mind a council called together in the field to decide upon military operations, I told him that the advice of war councils was not usually of any great value and that the proposition did not appeal to me. I said that authority should be vested somewhere to coördinate the operations on the Western Front and suggested the possibility of having a supreme commander. He replied, in effect, that it was unlikely that the Allies could agree upon any one, as the French would object to any but a Frenchman and the British might not like that.

He expressed the opinion that in any event a permanent council would be useful primarily in bringing the heads of the Allied Governments together at intervals to consider general policies. I admitted that such an organization might serve to unite the Allies in common purpose but that the conduct of operations by the combined armies should be left entirely under military direction. I got the distinct impression that while he was seeking to secure greater unity of action, he also sought some means of controlling the activities of the British Army. During previous months that army had been engaged in an almost continuous offensive practically single-handed, and had suffered very heavy losses without compensating gains.

Mr. Lloyd George went on to say that there was to be a conference of the Prime Ministers at Rapallo, Italy, and that he hoped they might reach some agreement that would result in a council such as he had in mind. He thought that the United States ought to be represented at this meeting and suggested that I should attend. As the purpose of a council seemed to be more for political coördination than for purely military control, I told him that I considered it inadvisable for me to participate without some intimation from my Government to do so.

In the afternoon, I called on M. Painlevé, at his request, and he also told me of the proposal to form a Supreme War Council and wanted me to go to the conference in Italy. I gave him the same reply that I had given Mr. Lloyd George.

The result of the meeting at Rapallo was an agreement among

the Prime Ministers of the Governments participating, as shown by the following:

"Decisions of a Conference of Representatives of the British, French and Italian Governments Assembled at Rapallo on November 7, 1917

"I. The representatives of the British, French, and Italian Governments assembled at Rapallo on the 7th of November, 1917, have agreed on the scheme for the organization of a Supreme War Council with permanent military representation for each power contained in the following paragraph.

"II. (1) With a view to the better coördination of military action on the Western Front, a Supreme War Council is created composed of the Prime Minister and a member of the Government of each of the Great Powers whose armies are fighting on that front. The extension of the scope of the Council to other fronts is reserved for discussion with the other Great Powers.

"(2) The Supreme War Council has for its mission to watch over the general conduct of the war. It prepares recommendations for the decisions of the Governments, and keeps itself informed of their execution, and reports thereon to the respective Governments.

"(3) The General Staffs and Military Commands of the Armies of each power charged with the conduct of military operations remain responsible to their respective Governments.

"(4) The general war plans drawn up by the competent Military Authorities are submitted to the Supreme War Council, which, under the high authority of the Governments, insures their concordance, and submits, if need be, any necessary changes.

"(5) Each power delegates to the Supreme War Council one permanent military representative whose exclusive function is to act as technical adviser to the Council.

"(6) The Military Representatives receive from the Government and the competent military authorities of their country all the proposals, information, and documents relating to the conduct of the war.

"(7) The Military Representatives watch day by day the situation of the forces, and of the means of all kinds of which the Allied Armies and the enemy Armies dispose.

"(8) The Supreme War Council meets normally at Versailles, where the permanent Military Representatives and their staffs are assembled. It may meet at other places as may be agreed upon,

according to circumstances.   The meetings of the Supreme War Coun-
cil will take place at least once a month.
  "III.   The permanent military representatives will be as follows:
  "For France—General Foch
  "For Great Britain—General Wilson
  "For Italy—General Cadorna."

By the inclusion of sub-paragraph (4) it would seem that the
Prime Ministers had it in mind to assume greater control of operations if such action should appear necessary.   While the Commanders-in-Chief of the armies concerned were expected to attend
meetings of the Council, and usually did so and freely expressed
their views, they were not members and had no vote.

The creation of the Supreme War Council did not meet with
universal approval.   The commanders of the British and French
Armies and many high officials in civil circles were opposed to it.
Military commanders were afraid it would result in undue interference with the conduct of operations and it was often referred
to in derision as the "Soviet."   The British Army viewed it with
considerable suspicion, thinking it might substitute politicians for
professional soldiers as directors of the strategy of the war.   A
stronger central control by the French was advocated by influential French papers in the fear that their Government might not
have so much to say in Allied affairs as theretofore.   The formation of this Council indicated, however, a realization that Allied
success in the future would depend upon better coördination of
effort.   The action of the Prime Ministers was a step in the direction of unified command, which was no doubt one reason why
most British as well as French officers, and a considerable number
of those in high civil positions, were lukewarm toward it; yet
not a few who spoke against the Council at the time said later
that they had always been in favor of unified control.   The action
taken at Rapallo was approved by President Wilson on November
17th and that fact appeared in the press a day or so later.   The
President's action strengthened the hands of those who favored
the Council and probably became the influence that saved it.

It is probable that if the French and British army commanders, in a friendly spirit of coöperation, had made a joint study of the military problem on the Western Front as a whole and then had seriously undertaken to pull together, the Supreme War Council might never have been born. And yet, when one analyzed it, coöperation between the armies presented many difficulties with two peoples of such different points of view. For example, as we have seen, the offensive in the spring of 1917, which was under French leadership, received only half-hearted approval of the British. Then later, the British carried on their offensives during most of the summer, but the French conducted only two limited attacks. So they apparently made plans independently, and any advantage gained was purely local, with little material effect upon the final outcome.

The Supreme War Council made a favorable start at its first meeting and gave the impression that a wise and conservative exercise of its really unlimited powers would characterize its actions. It refrained from interfering directly with military commanders and operations and confined itself largely to questions of policy, such as the coördination of Allied resources, and the conservation and distribution of Allied strength. However, as time went on, the Supreme War Council undertook to exercise greater authority over military questions.

As indicated in the diary, our 1st Division had not been long in the quiet sector of the Vosges before the peaceful aspect of things was disturbed by a German raid on an isolated post of the 16th Infantry early in the morning of November 3d. A group was caught in a box barrage and although the men made a courageous resistance against the large raiding party three were killed,[1] five wounded, and twelve captured. These were the first casualties that had occurred in our army to units serving in the trenches. The French took charge of the funeral ceremony and turned out a formal guard in addition to our own. The services

---

[1] Corporal James B. Gresham, Co. F, 16th Infantry.
Private Thomas F. Enright, Co. F, 16th Infantry.
Private Merle D. Hay, Co. F, 16th Infantry.

were conducted by the French General, Bordeaux, who came with his full staff and delivered a beautiful oration over the graves. A large number of French troops also came informally to pay their final tribute. This joint homage to our dead, there under the fire of the guns, seemed to symbolize the common sacrifices our two peoples were to make in the same great cause. It seemed as though their death had sealed a new pact of understanding and comradeship between the two armies.

As to the political situation, the undercurrent at the moment, as nearly as could be learned, showed a continued lack of accord among the different nations, which were not at all in agreement with Mr. Wilson's ideals. Each nation had its own aspirations and each sought to gain some advantage over the others. Some of the divergent war aims had to do with territory distant from France, and troops sent there might have been more usefully employed on the Western Front.

A very reliable agent, an American, who was in close touch with the leading Allied statesmen, brought to me personally a memorandum which voiced the underlying sentiment, and which I at once enclosed in a letter to the Secretary of War:

"November 3, 1917.

"My dear Mr. Secretary:

"I am enclosing you herewith a memorandum, marked 'A,' which I think well worth reading, giving as it does an estimate of the political situation since the Italian disaster.

"Of course, only time will tell just how this Italian defeat is going to affect our allies. I am rather fearful, however, that it may be only the beginning of further successes in that direction by the Central Powers. In this event, there will have to be a more or less complete readjustment of military forces on what may become an extended Western Front.

"I hope to be of some use to Colonel House when he arrives, and shall get in touch with him as to the military outlook at once.

"I am also enclosing a memorandum, marked 'B,' which is a report of a conversation held by a man in my confidence with a British official high up in the councils of Great Britain. The date of this was October 24th. Perhaps it should not be taken too seriously, but is an indication of the British attitude.

"With high esteem and warm personal regards, I am,
"Very sincerely yours,
"JOHN J. PERSHING.

"2 enclosures."

———

"Enclosure 'A'

"THE ITALIAN DISASTER,
ITS DIPLOMATIC CONSEQUENCES; THE 'PACT OF LONDON,'
AND THE UNITED STATES

"It is felt in the soberest political worlds of the Quai d'Orsay and Parliament that the military disaster that has befallen Italy will have among its inevitable consequences at all events one that is peculiarly opportune, and *perhaps indispensable at this hour*. It will have shown the Italians, who love 'waltzing alone,' that the interests of all the allies are identical. It will also have shown the Italians that a religious respect for the *Pact of London* is the sole condition of success in this war. The days of *Nostra Guerra* are numbered. * * * Italian Imperialistic pride has received a rude blow. When the British and French disembark in the Italian ports, Italian hearts will lose a certain cock-sureness; and this change of heart will be all to the good, both for the ultimate peace-negotiations and for the future of the balance of power in the Mediterranean. Italy, in a word, is once again reminded that she has become, in a night, only a humble little Latin Sister.

"On the other hand, this rapid disaster will be a much needed revelation for certain circles in London, Paris, and Washington as to the duplicity of the Austrians. The chief lesson *for statesmen* of this military disaster is that the Central Empires are a block, which only the impact of a more coherent, bigger block can shatter. While the Austro-German Governments were preparing their Italian offensive simple souls in the Parliaments of the world were fancying that their malicious proffers of peace were sincere! Candid victims of Boche blackmail and malice, socialists and radicals everywhere, extolled * * * a policy of seeking to disarm Germany and Austria by resonant declarations in favor of right, repudiating all unholy Imperialistic aims. The very way the Italian disaster has been brought about * * * is a magnificent object lesson."

———

"Enclosure 'B'

"Lord X.

" 'The European Allies and America are not fighting for the same thing. Mr. Wilson thinks a great deal more of his ideas of people governing themselves, of a friendly working arrangement among all the great powers after the war, than he does of territorial or specific things going to this or that country. What he wants is to smash the German military power and have a society of democratic nations afterwards. But to England, France, and Italy these things are phrases, useful perhaps, but of secondary interest. England wants to maintain her colonial possessions, to keep her position on the sea, and her commercial position in the world. We know what France wants —Alsace-Lorraine, as indemnity and security for the future. Italy has definite territorial claims; thus the governments of these countries think a great deal about what they want for themselves and less about ideals, unless these ideals are incidental to success. So there is no clear unity among the Allies in Europe and America.

" 'Suppose the European allies find themselves in a situation where they ought to make the best peace they can, what is the United States going to do? Russia has gone. Is Italy going to be able to stay? We are fresher than any of the other belligerents in Europe, but we cannot win the war alone.'

"A.

" 'The Allies ought certainly to be able to maintain the military equilibrium for another fifteen or eighteen months, until we (the Americans) are prepared to make a great effort.'

"Lord X.

" 'I am glad that you recognize that it will take you that much time. Looked at from this side, you seem to be very deliberate.'

"A.

" 'General Pershing is not going to put his army in the front line until we are ready.'

"Lord X.

" 'General Pershing is quite right, he ought not to go into the front line until he is ready to do something really effective. I wonder if your people are studying the Italian situation.'

"A.

" 'It has seemed, looking at Italy from Paris, that she is going strong, and will be capable of a vigorous campaign next spring.'

"Lord X.

" 'I don't know whether the Italian people will go on; it all depends on whether they have enough to eat this winter, upon whether there

are such great disturbances over food and heating that the government would be greatly weakened in their pressing the war. Well,
if Italy went out we couldn't go on. I think we must give considerable attention to Italy.'"

(Diary) Chaumont, Friday, November 9, 1917. Came back from
Paris by train Tuesday morning; brought along Mr. Charles R. Crane
and Mr. Joseph E. Willard, Ambassador to Spain. General Pétain
and three staff officers stopped for dinner in the evening. His confidential reports indicate Italians lack schools of instruction for staff
and line officers. He thinks the Italian line will hold on the Piave.

Major Generals Kernan, Wm. M. Wright, and George Bell, lunched
with us yesterday.

As French are behind on ordnance deliveries, have again strongly
recommended production at home. Have recommended the use of
Brest for deep draft transports. Directed another urgent cable be
sent for motor transportation. Major Generals Blocksom, Treat,
Greble, Edwards, and Sage took luncheon with us to-day.

Experienced Allied officers in position to know from observation were of the opinion that the Italian Army, especially its artillery, was not so efficient as it ought to have been and that the
training of officers especially had been neglected. It was suspected that the Italian armies had been somewhat affected by the
same doctrines that ruined Russia and that this tended to obscure
the presence and the intentions of the large increase in enemy
forces on that front. At any rate, whether this view was entirely
correct or not, there was sufficient reason for me to give warning
to our War Department by cable that precaution should be taken
in America through the Intelligence Division, General Staff, and
through the Department of Justice, supplemented by counter-
propaganda through pulpit and press, if feasible, in order to
prevent attempts at this sort of propaganda among our people
and in our Army.

The ammunition question again became acute despite our
agreements with the French and their positive assurances that
they would make prompt deliveries, but their explanation was
that we had not furnished the full amount of raw material re-

quired. In previous references to the prospects of procuring artillery of 75- and 155-millimeter calibers and ammunition for its use, it had been expected that nothing should diminish our efforts at home in their manufacture. But when the probability of delay and possible failure of the French to furnish ammunition for these guns was reported to Washington my cable met with the complacent reply, much to my surprise, that "the French Government must furnish it, for there is no other way of getting it. At the present time there is not in this country any actual output of ammunition of the types mentioned. None has been expected."

As the French contracts covered only a part of the amount deemed necessary, it was not understood why the Ordnance Department had done nothing. In view of the Italian disaster and the certainty of serious German offensives in France in the spring, the possibility of shortage in ammunition caused some apprehension. We were already behind in steel deliveries to the French by over 20,000 tons; the supply of powder and explosives was still uncertain; and the prospect of placing further contracts or even of obtaining regular deliveries on those already placed seemed doubtful. The establishment of our own sources of supply at home appeared vital, and setting forth the above situation by cable I added, "I cannot too strongly urge the greatest expedition in the production of artillery matériel and ammunition in America."

The difficulty of providing the French with raw material was largely due to the lack of shipping and, of course, to the unscientific use of what we had. The fact is that the ports at home were overcrowded with all sorts of material and supplies awaiting vessels. The French had over 600,000 tons of supplies at our seaboard which they were unable to move and they were clamoring for 150,000 additional tons of steel rails. The War Department had purchased over 100,000 tons of rails for us but had been able so far to ship only 30,000 tons. The optimistic view of the Department of a month previous that there would be plenty of shipping now began to look visionary.

As the situation in which we found ourselves regarding artillery ammunition was approaching a crisis, it became necessary to lay the whole question before the Inter-Allied Munitions Board. After a full investigation of their resources, both the French and British concluded that they could undertake to meet our requirements, with the distinct understanding that their plants must be greatly increased in capacity and that we should furnish raw materials promptly. General Bliss, Chief of the War Department General Staff, who arrived about this time, brought the latest data from home and his knowledge enabled him to give valuable assistance to General Williams, my Chief of Ordnance, before the Allied conference in our efforts to find a solution to the difficult munitions problem. He urged the manufacture at home of heavy guns and ammunition and also strongly reënforced my appeals for motor transportation.

The following letter from the Secretary of War had only recently been received and gave me an idea of some of his problems:

"September 10, 1917.

"MY DEAR GENERAL PERSHING:

"Your confidential letters of July 9th and 27th reached me safely, the latter through Mr. Frankfurter, whose observations and comments have most helpfully supplemented my information about the conditions in France and particularly about some aspects of your problem about which it would be difficult to get information in any other way.

"At present it seems questionable whether I should come to France. If it were possible for me to go incognito and go over the situation with you on the ground without the interruptions which would be necessary were it known that I was in the country, * * * while if I undertook to visit both London and Paris, my trip would be deemed to have a diplomatic character, which would be inopportune if not embarrassing. Moreover, it seems important for me not to relax my personal supervision of the preparation of supplies and men to be forwarded just at this time. But I am hopeful that I can come a little later and, when our camps are thoroughly established and our preparation going forward as smoothly as I trust it soon will, an absence would be less difficult here and perhaps more helpful to you.

"Meanwhile I am sure you will understand my frankness when I tell you that your course from the moment you landed in England has given both the President and me the greatest satisfaction and pleasure. As you know, you started with our full confidence, but we feel happy to have our judgment justified as it has been at every point by your discretion, tact, and effective activity.

"The work of preparing the Army here has gone forward with remarkable smoothness and in a day or two the National Guard will be in its camps. Already a substantial part of it is in camp and has begun its preparatory work. Meantime, the sixteen National Army cantonments are substantially completed and the first contingent of drafted men are being received apparently without confusion or excitement. Early in October the entire number will be assembled and the arrangements promise speedy training for them, as their officers have already been assembled at the cantonments, a course of instruction prepared and the usual preliminary preparations for active work either begun or well under way.

"On this side we hear rather frequently of the work your men are doing. Such French officers as have come to us and have seen your troops in France are enthusiastic in praise of their alertness and spirit and, as the larger forces begin to arrive, no doubt even more impressive exhibitions will be given of what our people can do.

"There are three points about which I am especially concerned and about which I would be glad to have your confidential observations whenever a convenient means of communicating with me presents itself.

"1. I am especially concerned that our troops should not be engaged in actual fighting in France until they are there in such numbers and have made such thorough preparation that their first appearance will be encouraging both to their own morale and to the spirit of our people here. I think it goes without saying that the Germans will make a very special effort to strike swiftly and strongly against any part of the line which we undertake to defend, in order to be able to report to their people encouragingly about our participation and also with the object of discouraging our soldiers and our people as much as possible. I have no doubt this has all been present to your mind and I refer to it only because I want you to know that we will exercise all the patience necessary on this side and will not ask you to put your troops into action until in your own judgment both the time is opportune and the preparations thoroughly adequate.

"2. In the matter of selecting corps and division commanders, I constantly feel that I ought to have your advice and judgment. You realize of course the difficulty of selecting division commanders out of our army, made up as it is of very zealous and fine men but necessarily men who have had no experience with the sort of warfare now being waged and few if any of them having even had the experience of actually commanding a division of troops in maneuvers. From all that you have said, supplemented by all I have learned elsewhere, the need for young and physically strong men is apparent and I am perfectly willing to go any limit in meeting this requirement. It will, of course, necessitate passing over a substantial number of our older general officers who are very eager to go to France and who in their own ideas and that of the country have certain right to be preferred; but their occupation here in the training of troops is, of course, a valuable contribution to the cause and, whenever I can feel sure in the selection of the younger man that he actually has the capacity to develop to a sufficient extent to justify his being preferred to a man of greater experience, I shall not hesitate. But most of these younger officers present problems of judgment and foresight, and your advice on the subject would be most helpful. At present I am planning to send practically all of the general officers to France for a visit to the front, so that they will come back to their training camps with actual knowledge of the conditions of present methods of warfare. After they have been to France, they are to call on me individually to report and I hope in that way to have opportunity to make personal estimate of their vigor and alertness both of mind and body. In the meantime, you of course will see them all while they are in France and I would be grateful if you would let me have an estimate of the impressions they make on you while they are actually at the scene of war and studying the conditions at the front.

"3. In this country, we have been able to surround our camps with an environment far better than any soldiers in this country have ever had. The problem of drink is certainly under control and the problem of prostitution is in a better condition than we have ever had it. When our troops get to France, however, both of these problems present new and difficult aspects. The local police situation is, of course, difficult, and I have no notion what steps can be taken to minimize these two evils. I think, before very long, I shall ask Mr. Raymond Fosdick, chairman of our recreational committee, to visit France and see whether any helpful solution of these problems can be afforded by an extension of the recreational system which we are devising here to our camps in France. * * *

"There is a fourth subject upon which I want to say a confidential word. General Scott will retire on the 22d of this month. He will, of course, be called back into active service and put in charge of one of our training camps where his fine character and soldierly experience will be an inspiring example to the young men under him. General Bliss, who has three times acted as Chief of Staff, will succeed General Scott for the few months which intervene until his own retirement. But when General Bliss retires in November (December), it will be necessary to select a Chief of Staff and my strong desire is to have a young man who has had some months of experience in France. My mind has rather run in the direction of General March who, by the middle of November, will have had an excellent opportunity to become familiar with the whole situation abroad and whose experience in the War Department has been such that there would be no loss of time on his part in understanding the intricacies of bureau operation here. In addition to that, he is a man of positive and decided character. I realize, of course, that bringing General March away might be a serious loss to you and I have by no means decided upon him for the place, but I would like to have your judgment on this question. It seems to me that coöperation in Washington is of an importance impossible to overestimate and that we can assure it best by having a young, aggressive man who will realize from actual observation and participation your difficulties and be able to understand from the least hint just what is necessary for us to do to be of the maximum support to you.

"With cordial regards, believe me,
"Sincerely yours,
"NEWTON D. BAKER,
"Secretary of War."

In view of the emergency that was so clearly set forth by the Joffre (Viviani) and Balfour Missions when they visited the United States, and which was confirmed after my arrival in France and reported with all emphasis, I have never been able to understand the unnecessary delay due to waiting six months for the construction of large cantonments before calling out men and assembling them for training. Of course it was particularly urgent that the specialists and laborers needed in France to build up our facilities should have been provided as fast as they could be profitably employed, but nothing should have postponed the immediate mobilization of the combat units of the Regular Army and the National Guard. Each of these categories could have been brought to war strength with a proportion of its trained officers and men as a nucleus, reserving the rest for duty in training camps and for assignment to new units. In this way we could have put a greater number of trained units into battle much easier than we did, and without delaying the training of the new army. As it was, the services of most of these already partially trained organizations, especially those of the Regular Army, were not available abroad until it was all but too late.

The following was my reply to the Secretary:

"France, November 13, 1917.

"Dear Mr. Secretary:

"Your letter of September 10th was handed to me by General Treat. First of all, I wish to thank you most sincerely for your cordial expressions of approval for what has been done. It has not been easy at all times to determine the best course to pursue. The British and the French, as you know, are each watching out that the other does not receive too much attention from us. So far we have succeeded in steering fairly clear of breakers, as I have persistently tried to impress both allies that our whole purpose here is to assist in every possible way in beating our common enemy, without any thought of leaning toward one ally more than the other.

"With reference to our entering the trenches for active service, I have emphasized the necessity of thorough preparation, and have been following a logical program leading up to the important final training of artillery and infantry in coöperation. This has been accepted as sound by the military authorities, both French and English, so that unless something very threatening should occur, we should not go in until we are ready. Of course, even then there will be much to learn from actual experience.

"In all my conferences with General Pétain on this subject we have fully agreed that, when our troops go into their sector, they would be fully supported by the French artillery and be in close touch with their infantry. It is also our joint idea that every effort should be made to have the first clash, if possible, a victory for the Americans. Such a result would of course raise the morale of our allies and correspondingly depress the enemy. General Pétain is in full accord with this view, and I am sure that when the time comes he will coöperate to the fullest extent to bring about such a result.

"The venereal and the liquor problems are both extremely difficult. The greatest danger points seem to be our ports of entry. I have recommended to the Minister of War that he declare a 'state of siege' at both Bordeaux and Saint Nazaire, and he has promised to do it. Such a state practically exists in Saint Nazaire already. This corresponds to our martial law and the control of these questions would then be in the hands of the local French military commanders, who, in coöperation with our local commanders, under stringent orders, should be able to keep the ports comparatively clean. There is another serious question there, too, and that is the large number of spies that continuously infest these ports. Martial law should give us a much better control of that danger.

"In the training areas men are kept busy and as this region is entirely under army control the above problems are less difficult, although not easy there. I have established a series of medical aid stations in these areas for the sole benefit of the French people, in coöperation with the leading local French women. This effort is very much appreciated by the inhabitants who, for the most part, have been left almost without medical attention. It is also hoped that venereal cases among the women may eventually visit these dispensaries for treatment. The organization of these stations has been placed under Major Hugh H. Young, who is one of Johns Hopkins' most famous doctors, and who has made a specialty of this class of disease.

"By publishing in orders the ravages of venereal disease in Europe, and the constant dangers of uncontrolled sexual relations, and by encouraging Y.M.C.A. work, and demanding the interest of officers in the welfare of their men, an excellent foundation has been laid. I feel much pleased with the attitude of the army toward this question and am gratified at what is being accomplished toward morality. I shall be very glad to have Dr. Fosdick make a visit here to study the situation and give us the benefit of his experience and advice. We cannot do too much to protect our young men from immorality and consequent disease, to say nothing of its effect upon our fighting strength.

"With relation to the general officers, I wrote you in my letter of October 4th my views in general, and my opinion of several of these officers in particular. * * * I would emphasize my remarks with reference to the others mentioned in my former letter, and am adding some further comment in the enclosure herewith.

"Generally speaking, the young and active officers of a command look upon their division commander as their leader, and if he is inactive they lack the confidence in him necessary to his success. Such a man becomes more or less a figurehead instead of a soldier in whom they believe. The position of division commanders is so important that it may be very truly said the success of this war depends upon them. If a division commander does not know his work and is not up to the high standard found in the Allied armies, he has no place in our army here.

"The matter of recommending a Chief of Staff, and I may say of selecting men in general for important assignments, is the most difficult thing that has so far confronted me, and I can readily understand how puzzling it must be for you. * * * I am very favorably inclined toward General Biddle, and I think perhaps you will find him a broad-minded, energetic man who may measure up to your ideal. * * *

"Next to him, I have an idea that General March would make a good executive. I have always had a high opinion of March and had often thought of him as timber for Chief of Staff, even before I received your letter. I think March is a strong man and that he would be of great assistance to you, especially in the possible reorganization of the War Department, which I think you are going to find necessary. I should miss him here but consider your need the greater.

"I shall have General March come to my headquarters at an early date in order that he may make a study of the general staff organization that I have established here. All of the visiting general officers have been impressed with the plan and especially with the very complete coördination of all staff and supply departments under one control. It might be advisable to have a study made of it for application in the War Department.

"There may be other officers who would do better, but it would be a chance, so therefore I recommend to you the consideration of General Biddle as your Chief of Staff and General March as his assistant. You will then have two good men, and if General Biddle [1] should not turn out to be the man I think he is you would have General March there to take his place or to retain as assistant in case you should not be satisfied as to his qualifications for chief, and conclude to select some one else.

"Just a word as to the supply departments. The general officers sent over complain that their divisions are not being provided with equipment, especially transportation, and say they are told that their transportation and other things that are lacking will be furnished upon arrival in France. Of course there is no transportation here and little else that does not come from home, so that our organizations are now arriving without adequate transportation and generally with none.[2]

"It seems to me quite necessary that each division should be as-

[1] I had a high opinion of General John Biddle and thought that having been in France and England he would measure up to the position of Chief of Staff. Before leaving, however, he said to me that he did not consider himself fitted for the place.
[2] This was unquestionable proof of the inefficiency of the supply department responsible.

sembled at some point near the port of embarkation, where it can
be fully equipped and the division commander be given an opportunity to see that he has everything in readiness. This would insure
his being prepared to take care of himself upon arrival here, and
would avoid confusion in issuing initial equipment at this end and
possibly the more serious inconvenience of not having it at all. I
send you this as I get it, as it may not have reached you in just this
light.

"The War Department now has our complete project for troops
and supplies, estimated on a basis of 1,200,000 men. It also has the
priority schedule for both personnel and matériel. So there should
be less difficulty in handling both when the personnel is organized,
and if the supplies are available. In making these comments I do not
fail, Mr. Secretary, to appreciate the enormity of your problems,
but make them with a view to aiding you in their solution.

"General Bliss and the other members of the Allied conference are
in London. I hope to have an opportunity to go over in detail many
things with General Bliss before he returns. I am writing you in a
separate letter a discussion of the general military situation.

"In conclusion, Mr. Secretary, permit me to congratulate you and
the country in that we have you as a Secretary. You are doing a
great work and doing it well. May I ask you, at your convenience,
to extend to the President my most loyal greetings.

"Believe me, with sincere personal and official regard,
               "Your humble servant,
                              "JOHN J. PERSHING."

Enclosure.

"COMMENTS ON GENERAL OFFICERS

"Confidential for the Secretary of War.

    *   *   *   *   *   *   *

"As to other officers mentioned in my former memorandum * * *
I am more thoroughly convinced than ever that none of them is alert
or physically up to the requirements, and most of them are too old
anyway to begin to learn the important duties that would be required of them. * * *

"With regard to sending officers over as observers to return to their
divisions, I would suggest that only those known to be entirely fit
should be sent, unless you want them especially to train troops at
home later.

"Allow me to suggest, Mr. Secretary, that all division and brigade
commanders be very closely observed at home, and their attitude,

their activity and prowess in training these units be fully taken into consideration and reported upon before it is finally decided to send them over with their commands.

"J. J. P."

Soon after the receipt of the Secretary's letter of September 10th, which was handed to me early in November, it became necessary to report adversely on the fitness of a number of the Major Generals who had been sent over for a visit to the various armies as observers. My message read in part as follows:

> "Earnestly request that only division commanders who have strong mental and physical vigor be sent here as observers. Division commanders who are in any way unable to stand continuous work actually in the trenches under conditions found on the Western Front are useless here. Consider it imposition on Allies to send officers not fit in every particular."

To this cable came the prompt reply:

> "With reference to your * * * every effort will be made to send you suitable division commanders. * * * You will be thoroughly supported in the relief of any officers you care to relieve. * * *"

CHAPTER XVII

Tank Construction—Visit to 26th Division—Military Situation—Letter to Secretary of War—Painlevé Ministry Overthrown—Clemenceau Premier—Motor Transport Corps—Control of Shipping by British— American Tonnage—Cambrai Offensive

(Diary) Chaumont, Wednesday, November 14, 1917. Held conference Saturday on tank question and authorized agreement with British for manufacture of the heavy type.

On Sunday visited 26th Division in billets near Neufchâteau.

Senator Kendrick, an old friend from Wyoming, and Senator Kenyon, of Iowa, came to lunch to-day.

British insist on steel billets and lumber in return for steel products, coal and huts.

UP to this time our efforts to arrange with the Allies for the tanks we should need had resulted only in half promises for a limited number, with considerable doubt whether in the end we should get any at all from either the French or British. With no previous plans for their manufacture, the prospects of obtaining tanks from home by the time they should be required for operations seemed so remote that it appeared best to arrange, if possible, for their manufacture overseas. Meanwhile, an Inter-Allied Tank Commission was formed and Major James G. Drain was appointed the American member. As the French decided to take no active part, the British proposed that we undertake the manufacture of heavy tanks jointly with them, so, upon the conclusion of my conference with Major Drain and Captain Sanderson, of the British Army, approval was given to the plan. It was understood that the British would build the hulls and we would furnish the motors and chassis, the assembling to be done in France.

The units of the 26th Division, Major General Clarence Edwards commanding, began to arrive during the latter part of

September, continued during October, and were now assembled in the billeting area near Neufchâteau. Meanwhile it was necessary to use a part of the division on the Line of Communications because of lack of labor troops. At my inspection, the various organizations presented a very creditable appearance, the officers seemed alert and military, and the personnel looked strong and vigorous. Their instruction had been carried out under the direction of Brigadier General Peter E. Traub, one of the brigade commanders, and was reported to be well advanced. As this division was composed of National Guard units from the New England States, whose troops had borne a fine reputation in all our wars, its preparation for active service was watched with great interest.

The Allies were much concerned over their probable situation in the spring with respect to manpower. The Germans had captured Riga in September. Kerensky's power was at an end and the Bolsheviki government was established, with Lenin and Trotsky in control, and there was no longer any doubt that Russia had become entirely negligible as far as assistance to the Allies was concerned.

An analysis of the probable relative strength of the contestants by early spring showed that Germany would be able to spare a considerable number of divisions from the Russian front. Careful study by my staff, in coöperation with the Allied staffs, had led to the conclusion that the total number of German divisions in the West might be as many as 217, not counting the rather remote possibility of the added strength of 48 divisions from Austria. The greatest number the Allies could muster, according to estimates, would be 169 divisions, or considering two American divisions as four because of their double strength, the number would be 171. Italy could not be counted on for some time to do more than barely hold her own, even with the help of the eleven Allied divisions then on the Italian front. Other American divisions might possibly be in Europe by May 1st, if they should arrive according to schedule, which was doubtful, but the later divisions would be too late to participate in the expected spring operations. At the slow rate of arrival, we should not have more than half of the twenty-one divisions promised by the War Department ready for service by June.

With these possibilities before me I wrote the Secretary of War, setting forth our estimate of the situation and urging that the utmost efforts be exerted to hasten the arrival of American forces. The main points of my letter are quoted as showing the situation as it appeared at the time:

"November 15, 1917.

"Dear Mr. Secretary:

"It seems advisable at this time to send you in this personal way a résumé of the situation here as it appears to me. I am sending a similar letter to General Biddle.[1]

"With reference to memorandum prepared by the Allied Council in August and forwarded to the War Department, recent events on the Russian and Italian fronts now require us to give careful consideration to the problem outlined in that memorandum. * * *

"At the outset it should be remembered that the Central Powers, while relying mainly upon their armies to secure favorable terms of peace, are using every possible means to stir up strife among the people of each of the Allied nations and to create dissension among the powers themselves. As viewed by the world at large, the success of the Central Powers by whatever means would be attributed solely to military prowess. It will therefore be necessary to break their military resistance if the Allies are to dictate the terms of peace. If possible, this ought to be done before the French and British are too weak to stand against the extreme efforts Germany will make to win before the United States seriously enters the war.

"As a result of the several British and French offensives, the German strength on the Western Front has been very much weakened during the past summer. Of the 150 divisions she now has on the Western Front, only 60 are able to take the offensive. Her regiments have suffered serious losses that will have to be made up from the 1920 class—the 18-year-old boys. It is estimated that she will have only about 500,000 of these to put in the lines for the spring campaign, and on the average these will not be of high fighting value. Her annual losses since the beginning have been about 800,000 estimated, so that her manpower will begin to run down about May or June. * * * Conceding this estimate of manpower as correct, we have another reason to believe that the supreme effort of the Central Powers will be exerted between now and midsummer of 1918.

[1] General Biddle was Acting Chief of Staff at Washington at that time.

"* * * The Allied forces cannot be materially increased on any front until America brings her strength into the war. To carry out an Allied offensive on any other than the Western Front with the forces now available would compel a defensive attitude in that theater. * * * The psychological effect on the French and Italian people and probably upon the British and our own people as well of such a defensive rôle would be as depressing to them as it would be encouraging to our enemies.

"Under probable conditions, an Allied offensive on the Western Front could not be carried on by the French or Italians without the British; and the strength of these three powers will probably be so low that the Americans will also be needed. It seems clear to me that the war must be won on the Western Front, and that the efforts of the Allies should continue as now in progress. * * *

"* * * Only a few German divisions have been brought from there (Russia) to the Western Front. * * * As long as Russia does not actually conclude a separate peace, Germany will have to keep a certain number of divisions there.

"Distribution of German Divisions

"It is estimated that there are 150 German divisions on the Western Front; 78 on the Eastern Front; 2 on the Macedonian Front; and 9 on the Italian Front. Of the 78 divisions on the Eastern Front, it is believed that only 36 are fit to take active place against the Allies in the West. Some 22 are capable only of defensive action, and 20 are new levies of Landwehr troops. * * * The 9 divisions in Italy are fit for the offensive anywhere, but the 2 divisions in Macedonia are not likely to be removed.

"* * * Three months would suffice to transfer these divisions to the West. Of 90 divisions on the Western Front not now considered fit to take the offensive, it is estimated that by February 1st 60 will be sufficiently rested to take their places in the line. These, plus the 45 good divisions from the East [1] and the 60 intact in the West, make 165. If we add the 22 Eastern defensive divisions and the remaining 30 in the West, we should have 217.

"Austro-Hungarian Divisions

"It is estimated that 25 Austrian divisions are on the Eastern Front, 2 divisions on the Albanian Front, and 49 divisions on the Italian Front. On the Eastern Front (cavalry excluded) 16 divisions are estimated as 1st class, and 9 as 2d class divisions.

[1] 36 from the Eastern Front and 9 from the Italian Front.

"In Italy, 34 divisions are 1st class and 15 divisions are 2d class. The two in Albania could not well be withdrawn. Of the total, 50 Austrian divisions are sufficiently good to be employed on the Western Front, and the rest would do for the defensive there or elsewhere.

"Seventy-four divisions would then be available if a separate peace were made with both Russia and Italy. If a separate peace were made with Russia only, the number of troops to be held in Italy would only depend upon the line. Assuming the line to be the Adige, and that it were held against Italian troops, 20 divisions on the line and 6 in reserve would probably make it sufficiently secure, so that with these 48 Austrian divisions, Germany might then bring her total number of disposal divisions on the Western Front from 217 to 265.

    *   *   *   *   *   *   *

"The situation in Italy remains uncertain, but it would appear that she has awakened to the point of putting forth her entire strength, which should enable her to hold her defensive positions. * * *

"Relative Strength

"The number of British divisions on the Western Front is now 58; French, 102; American, 2; Portuguese, 1; and of Belgian, 6; making a total of 169 organized and suitable for offensive action, except the Americans.

    *   *   *   *   *   *   *

"With their superiority of about 30 per cent, the Allies have been able to do nothing more on the offensive than to wear down German strength little by little. In turn, an approximate superiority by the Germans, while it would justify them in an offensive, would not necessarily mean a break of the Allies on the Western Front. * * *

"In artillery, still more in munition supply, and in aircraft, the Allies have a superiority with the power of increasing that superiority very greatly. In reserves of manpower the Allies, including America, of course, will soon have a still greater superiority.

"As to France, she cannot be counted on to increase the number or strength of her divisions, and the British will probably be able only to hold theirs at present strength. * * *

"Taking what appears now to be the most unfavorable view (always conceding that France herself will not give way), and considering Russia out of the war, and Italy holding on behind the Adige, it would be possible for the Central Powers to bring 265 divisions (German 217, and Austrian, 48) against 169 Allied divisions on the Western Front. Even under these adverse conditions, it is possible that the Allies would be able to hold their defensive, but it points clearly to the necessity for the utmost effort on our part.

"Other Powers

"The entry of Switzerland into the war has not been considered, but such action is a possibility, and every means should be exerted to bring her in on the side of the Allies, or keep her out altogether. * * *

"As to Spain, if she could be induced to enter on the side of the Allies, it would add considerable force for the defense of the Western Front, and would secure valuable sources of supply. It would guarantee the flow of metals to the Allies, as well as close the Spanish coast as a base for U-boat activities. * * *

"Japan's possible active participation has not been mentioned. Her shipping, at least, should be made available for us, and her arsenals as a source of ordnance supply ought to be given serious thought, not to mention her armies. My remarks on these three countries are presented as having urgent bearing on the general situation.

"General

"It may be accepted that German propaganda is always at work and should be met by counter-propaganda regardless of its cost. This especially applies to Russia, where no stone should be left unturned to counteract Germany's influence there and if possible place Russia again actively in the war.

"The utmost coöperation among the Allies must be secured. The recent endeavor to get the Allies to take a broad general view of the war as a whole shows an awakening. Hitherto, each nation has largely considered only its own interests, thus enabling Germany to beat her enemies in detail.

"It may not have been possible to avoid the Russian collapse or to have saved Roumania, but as has been pointed out, it does seem that with a unified control the Italian failure might have been avoided.

"Conclusions

"Viewed at its best, the situation is, of course, grave, and (this) should be fully realized. America must stand firmly behind the Allies, as any sign of weakness may cause the collapse of Allied resistance. The contingency must also be faced of Great Britain and ourselves being left to carry on the war without material aid from any other power. I have pointed out the dark side of the picture, but in war we must prepare to meet the worst.

"The conclusions, from the purely military standpoint, are evident, and are no doubt fully appreciated, but they cannot be over-emphasized in view of the German advantage that might confront us. It is therefore urged that—

"1. The most intense energy should be put into developing America's fighting forces for active service during the coming summer. Winning the war is vital to our future, and if humanly possible it ought to be done in 1918. There is no telling what might happen if we defer our utmost exertion until 1919.

"2. All available sources of supply of artillery and ammunition should be investigated and developed, having in mind Japan's resources in this regard. France may not be able to meet even our early requirements.

"3. Finally, every possible ton of shipping should be secured by purchase, construction, or otherwise, in the Orient or elsewhere, with the least delay for use in carrying our armies to France.

"It should be no longer a question of how much tonnage can be spared for military purposes, but only the most imperative necessity should permit its use for any other purpose. To secure this result the whole of our shipping ought to be under War Department control, and as much more obtained as possible from neutral or Allied sources.

"Please pardon the length of this note, and accept my high esteem and very sincere regards.

"Yours faithfully,

"JOHN J. PERSHING."

In this war, where the battle lines extended across entire countries, and in which the qualities of the opponents, man for man, were about equal, the outcome was largely a question as to the number and location of divisions on either side; hence the detailed discussion in my letter to the Secretary. In the end success would lie with the side which could provide the necessary superiority of force. In other words, it would depend upon the number of troops that America could send over.

All eyes were on the Eastern Front. To Allied statesmen the collapse of Russia meant possible grave political consequences; to the Allied commanders it forecast the release of approximately 100 divisions and the increase in the enemy's ranks in Belgium and northern France to a preponderance that would be difficult to resist. To us it indicated a race between America's best effort to pour our fighting men into France, and Germany's determination to crush the Allies before our soldiers could arrive in sufficient numbers to dominate the battlefield.

(Diary) Paris, Sunday, November 18, 1917. On Friday inspected trenches of 1st Division, still in sector northeast of Lunéville. Saw several men who were with me in Mexico. Went to headquarters French 18th Division, Major General Bordeaux. Visited graves of three American soldiers recently killed in trench raid.

Major General Morrison dined with us last night.

The Painlevé Ministry has fallen and M. Clemenceau succeeded in forming a new Ministry on Friday.

Reports from all quarters complain of shortage of trucks. Sent cable regarding British control of neutral shipping.

Motored from Chaumont and dined this evening at de Chambrun's with Tardieu.

During my visit to the 1st Division the officers of the French units serving with our regiments spoke with deep feeling of the first Americans to lose their lives at the front. They praised the bravery and courage of the detachment as though the men had been their own. The spirit of comradeship that prompted such sentiment naturally served to draw us closer together and stimulated coöperation as to material things.

A change in the ministry in France had been expected for some time and when M. Painlevé's Government fell on November 15th it occasioned no surprise. Among the reasons given for its unpopularity were the general disapproval of the Supreme War Council, the timidity of the Prime Minister in not pressing charges of disloyalty against high French officials, the cumulative opposition to the Government by many people looking for some one to blame for their misfortune, including Nivelle's failure, and the existence of pessimism in general. The main political fight against M. Painlevé was made by M. Clemenceau, who, as President of the Legislative War Committee, had attained an immense popularity because of his condemnation of the alleged pacifistic tendencies of some of the members of the Ministry. It was, therefore, logical from the French point of view, that he should be selected to form the new Ministry.

Once he became Prime Minister, M. Clemenceau lost no time

in attempting to clear the administrative offices of red tape. He took up energetically the whole question of scandals and vigorously attacked socialistic tendencies. He proclaimed that there were to be "no more pacifistic campaigns, no more German intrigues, and neither treason nor half treason." He tried to get into communication with Kerensky having in view the mobilization of what remained of disciplined forces in southern Russia, but his efforts were fruitless. All these steps demonstrated his activity and his aggressiveness.

By further reference to the diary, a shortage of trucks is noted, and my thoughts revert to our only experience in this field prior to the World War, when the expeditionary forces which I commanded in Mexico were supplied by truck trains managed from Columbus, New Mexico. Although the roads in northern Chihuahua were little more than cross-country trails used by mule teams in supplying the sparsely settled districts, our trucks operated at one time to a distance of more than two hundred miles from the border. The country was dry and the roads rarely muddy, but, with exceptional stretches where the surface was hard-pan or caliche, the soil was generally sandy and the roads required an excessive amount of repair by the engineers. As the distance from the border increased, the need for trucks became greater until altogether twenty-two companies of twenty-five trucks each were in operation, with complete repair shops and a large depot of spare parts at Columbus. Officers and men trained in the management of truck transportation under these adverse conditions became the nucleus of our motor truck organization in France.

The use of motor transport had become an absolute necessity, not only in the supply of troops but in transporting them from one field of activity to another, often in the emergency of battle. An army without such facility for ordinary purposes and without a reserve to meet the exigencies of operations could not be considered as prepared to engage successfully an adversary who was so equipped. It was estimated that our requirements, calculated from our own data and that of our Allies, would be some 50,000 motor vehicles, with an unlimited reserve of spare parts. Our priority schedules contemplated an increasing allowance of motor transportation to correspond to the growth of our forces, but despite my most urgent appeals and the resulting promises from Washington we had to borrow, even at this time, large numbers of trucks from the French.

It was evident almost from the first that the importance of this service demanded that it should have a separate organization. For the time being it was left under the Quartermaster Corps, but eventually it came under the Commanding General, Line of Communications.[1] In anticipation of a full equipment of motor vehicles for our armies, a skeleton organization was created, with extensive depots, repair shops, and the necessary schools for mechanics and chauffeurs.

With our country by far the greatest producer in the world of automobiles and trucks, it was surprising that we were so poorly equipped with them. Advices at one time indicated that the War Department was waiting for our allowance to be manufactured before sending any to France. This, of course, was quite out of the question, and I suggested that the cantonments at home might use horse-drawn vehicles and that their motor transportation be sent to us. It was also suspected that the transport bureau of the Quartermaster Corps at home, not realizing the extent to which motor vehicles were needed, thought our requests excessive.

As to ocean transportation, practically all neutral tonnage then considered available on time charter, was under the Norwegian flag. In attempting to obtain some of this shipping we learned that it was controlled by the Inter-Allied Chartering Executive, orginally organized with representatives of Great Britain, France and Italy, but reported to be dominated by the British Admiralty. The latter dictated the chartering of such tonnage by withholding bunker facilities if any charters were granted without its specific approval. Notification that bunker facilities would be thus with-

---

[1] Motor Transportation was placed under Lt. Col. F. H. Pope, of the Quartermaster Corps, in August, 1917. Col. Pope was succeeded by Brig. Gen. Meriwether Walker, July 9, 1918, when Motor Transportation was made an independent service.

held served on the Norwegian Association of Shipowners by the Chartering Executive was said to have brought about a law in Norway prohibiting charter without the consent of the Association, which practically resulted in placing control in the hands of the British. Even the French Government itself was unable to obtain vessels badly needed, despite the fact that it offered special premiums for direct charters.

In our own case, after signing a charter for eleven steamers, subject to approval of the Norwegian Association, our application was rejected. Knowledge of available shipping always reached London first and the British were at that time not seriously restrained by any sentiment for the Allies or generally speaking by considerations other than those which affected their immediate interests. This attitude in regard to granting the use of shipping to others was apparently little affected by their requirements, as the spirit of coöperation did not then prevail in any liberal sense either among Allied governments, or among their armies.

Our estimate of tonnage required to transport and supply the twenty-four combat divisions and S.O.S. troops which it was considered essential to have in France by the end of June showed that the amount then allotted to us would have to be increased up to May by 2,000,000 tons. No one seemed to know where we were to obtain this additional shipping. It appeared certain then that should disaster befall the Allied armies under these conditions we would be left in an almost hopeless situation.

Taken as a whole, the apparently slow progress of our preparation in Europe caused considerable adverse comment, if not dismay, among the Allies. Inquiries were made directly by the military and civil officials as to why we did not move more rapidly, to which the reply was always, "lack of shipping." It might have been added also that it was due partly to the backward state of our preparations. I always felt confident, however, that tonnage could be found for our purposes if the necessary pressure were exerted to force it into use. Appeals were made continuously and persistently in an effort to get action at home on this vital question, but several months elapsed and a crisis came before relief appeared.

About this time there were difficulties at our end of the line. The sea transport service, then under the Quartermaster Corps, claimed that the congestion of freight at St. Nazaire, and to a lesser degree at Bordeaux, was due to the failure of the railways to remove it promptly. The railway management contended that the Quartermaster Corps was interested only in clearing the ships and would do little to expedite the loading of cars directly therefrom. In order to remove this source of friction, the discharge of vessels was placed under the Transportation Department. As a result, there was much improvement both in the clearing of vessels and in the movement of freight. Another cause of delay in the turn-around of ships was the lack of ballast for returning transports, which had often to wait several days before the necessary quantity of sand, which was ordinarily used, could be obtained.

Regardless of the cause, these delays without doubt served to encourage Allied hopes that we might finally be forced to allow our men to be used as drafts, and made it more difficult to carry out in France the details of arrangements for equipping and organizing an independent army.

(Diary) Paris, Wednesday, November 21, 1917. By invitation, I arrived at British G.H.Q. Monday evening to observe Cambrai offensive. Went over plans with Chief of Staff, Lieutenant General Sir L. E. Kiggell, and the Operations Officer. Attack made yesterday. Returned to Paris. Called on M. Clemenceau this morning. He is well along in years, not strong physically, but vigorous of mind. He spoke in favor of an energetic war policy. Saw Atterbury and discussed continued shortage of freight cars. Am urging haste in sending over car erecting forces and cars.

Immobilized by the mud of Flanders, where British attacks had continued intermittently from the end of July to the middle of November, with rather excessive losses,[1] the British Commander-in-Chief turned to a more southerly portion of his line for the

[1]The casualties in the battle of Ypres, July 31-Nov. 10, were more than 270,000.

final offensive of the year. Choosing the Cambrai front on which to launch the effort, careful preparations, including the concentration of an unusual number of tanks, were made to insure success in overcoming the German defense. The tanks and the infantry were to break through the lines, after which the cavalry was to follow and assault the flanks of the enemy. The French troops held in readiness in the vicinity were to enter and assist. The command of these combined forces when both should become engaged was to be left to the senior general officer in the vicinity, who might be either French or British. In going over the plans, it seemed to me that their idea of securing coöperation after the French should go in was rather vague.

On the first day of the attack, I went to visit General Byng, commanding the British Third Army, who explained further details of the plans and the progress already made. He and his Chief of Staff were busy receiving news from the front and were confident that all was going well. General Byng is a large, fine-looking man and a high type of British soldier, vigorous, forceful, and efficient.

While awaiting the development of the attack, I expressed a wish to visit a field hospital in operation, to which General Byng readily assented, sending Major Watson, a medical officer, along as a guide. We motored towards the front, meeting many groups of prisoners, and shortly reached the hospital. Considerable numbers of the wounded were being brought in and many were there already awaiting their turn. I followed the handling of the patients from the time they arrived until they were tagged for further disposition. Most of the men seemed cheerful and were pleased over what was believed to be a victory. I spoke to several of the poor fellows, among them being a mere boy with the rank of captain, who told me that he received his wound as he was crawling through the wire entanglement. He was especially keen to learn how the battle was going, quite unconcerned that he would probably lose a leg. Noticing several men on cots at one end of the room not receiving attention, and inquiring the reason, I was told in whispers that they were moved aside as being quite beyond hope. I was impressed with the efficiency with which this hospital was managed.

The attack was made on a six-mile front and the British had the advantage from the outset. The sudden debouchment of the long line of tanks, closely followed by the infantry, all without the usual warning of a long preliminary artillery bombardment, completely surprised the Germans. The tanks broke wide gaps in the wire and subdued the machine gun nests, aiding the infantry through the defenses with a minimum of loss.

The front was rather narrow, considering the depth of the objectives. A maximum gain of some four and a half miles was secured the first day and a greater result was prevented, it was said, by a serious check to the tanks at Flesquières. I remained at cavalry headquarters most of the afternoon, hoping to see something of how they handled this arm, in which I had spent many happy years in our own service. It was reported later that a bridge over the Scheldt Canal at Masnières was blown up, so the cavalry was not sent forward. The French were not called into action, presumably because the British cavalry, which was to precede them, could not go forward as planned. The offensive continued for two or three days longer with varying success. It was, however, a decided victory and while not so great as the British expected, it gave encouragement to the Allies on the Western Front and no doubt helped to offset temporarily the depressing effect of the serious defeat recently sustained by the Italian Army.

CHAPTER XVIII

Allied Conference—General Situation—Talk with House—Urge Increased Program—Twenty-four Divisions by June—Robertson and Foch Approve—Determined Attitude—Meeting Supreme War Council—Lloyd George's Note to Mr. House on Use of American Troops—Recommend Regular Divisions—Training—Criticism of Italians

(Diary) Paris, Sunday, November 25, 1917. Delegates are gathering for an Inter-Allied conference.[1] Talked with Winston Churchill Thursday and think we may get some tonnage to bring over steel.

On Friday took General Bliss to call on M. Clemenceau. Had House and Bliss to luncheon.

Attended luncheon given yesterday by President Poincaré to conference delegates.

Mrs. Whitelaw Reid has transferred to A.E.F. her hospital complete with beds for fifty officers.

THE Inter-Allied conference had been planned before the meeting of Prime Ministers at Rapallo which had brought the Supreme War Council into existence. It was one of the periodical assemblies of Allied representatives held for the discussion of problems of common interest concerning the conduct of the war. Its purpose in the present instance was to consider the most effective means by which the resources in men and matériel of Allied countries, including the United States, could be utilized. In an early, informal discussion with Mr. House and General Bliss I gave them an outline of our situation, our relations with the Allies, and the progress of our plans, and explained to them the urgency of our requirements.

At the time the representatives of the different nationalities

[1] The Americans were: Mr. Edward M. House, Head of Mission; Ambassador William G. Sharp; Admiral William S. Benson, U. S. Navy, Chief of Operations; General Tasker H. Bliss, U. S. Army, Chief of Staff; Oscar T. Crosby, for U. S. Treasury; Vance McCormick, Chairman War Trade Board; Bainbridge Colby, Shipping Board; Alonzo E. Taylor, for Mr. Hoover; Thomas N. Perkins, War Industries; and Paul D. Cravath.

gathered in Paris, the current reports of decreasing losses of ocean tonnage and greater destruction of German submarines, with still better prospects in the future had given more of hopefulness to the general situation and had somewhat revived the spirits of the Allies.

The British had won at Cambrai and were making satisfactory progress in their advance on Jerusalem, which, it was said, would be facilitated by the use of their new base at Jaffa. The Italians seemed to have recovered their morale to a limited extent with the stiffening of their lines by British and French divisions, and had successfully held their own against the Austrian attack on the Piave. Although the enemy had made some advances in the Trentino, he had not been able to force an entrance to the Venetian plains. In Switzerland the economic concessions by the United States as to cotton and credits were hailed with satisfaction, which, coupled with the exports by the French, made it practically certain that Switzerland would remain neutral, although there had been a noticeable increase in pro-German sentiment there following the Italian disaster, with talk of a possible German invasion of eastern France through Switzerland.

On the other hand, some rumors were heard of a German-Bulgarian offensive against Salonika, while the armistice on the Eastern Front confirmed the worst fears regarding Russia. The successes of the Germans in Italy had given rise to peace hopes in Germany which proved embarrassing to the new Chancellor, von Hertling, but he had apparently established an accord among the leaders of Prussia, South Germany, and Austro-Hungary.

Not the least hopeful event for the Allies was the step just taken toward unity of command by the creation of the Supreme War Council. The decisive factor in the whole situation, however, if it could be utilized in time, was the tremendous economic and physical power of the United States. To make that power available before it was too late was the problem upon the solution of which depended the success of the Allied cause. Would the Allies see the solution and would they work together to apply it? That was the question.

(Diary) Paris, Thursday, November 29, 1917. Had Major General H. L. Scott, observer, as guest on Tuesday; brought him to Paris last night. Have named Major General F. J. Kernan Commander of Line of Communications, relieving Brigadier General Patrick, who will direct all construction. Brigadier General B. D. Foulois appointed Chief of the Air Service, vice Kenly.

This morning, accompanied by Harbord, attended Inter-Allied conference held at the French Ministry of Foreign Affairs. Afterwards conferred with Foch, Robertson, Bliss, and Vance McCormick.

Took Thanksgiving-day lunch at Hotel Palais d'Orsay with American Club. Heard good speeches by Viviani, Lawrence Benét, Bainbridge Colby and Tardieu. Called at our Embassy and afterward on General Robertson.

Have cabled Washington that heavy guns, howitzers, and mortars absolutely essential in successful offensive.

Before the assembly for the conference,[1] the American delegates, known as the "House party," Harbord and I, met informally in order to have a general understanding regarding our part in the proceedings. Mr. House gave us his ideas on the subject, and we then proceeded to the Ministry of Foreign Affairs where the meeting was to be held.

When all were seated around the table in the assembly room at the Ministry, M. Clemenceau, who presided, spoke briefly, setting forth the importance of the gathering, and the necessity of translating the noble spirit of the alliance into action. No attempts at oratory were in evidence, nor was there prolonged discourse on any subject. Naturally, questions concerning available manpower, shipping, munitions and supplies were mentioned in a general way, but the conference did little more than to agree that the study of the various subjects should be left to committees composed of Inter-Allied representatives.

It was very clear that everybody was looking to America to provide the additional manpower needed to give the Allies su-

[1] The delegates to this conference consisted of the Prime Ministers, Ministers of Foreign Affairs, Commanders-in-Chief, Chiefs of Staff, and other special representatives of the more important Allied nations, and those of various ranks and titles representing the smaller nations, delegates from sixteen nations, in all, being present as follows: France, Great Britain, United States, Italy, Japan, Belgium, Serbia, Roumania, Greece, Portugal, Montenegro, Brazil, Cuba, Russia, Siam, and China.

periority, and none of them were more eager to increase our forces than ourselves. For some time past our reliance upon the Allies for any considerable amount of tonnage had seemed almost in vain, and it looked as though we should have to depend upon our own limited resources for most of it.[1]

At the end of the session I asked Generals Foch, Robertson, and Bliss to meet with me for an exchange of views regarding a definite program to be recommended concerning the number of American troops that should be sent over by spring. I thought that the larger the program that could be agreed upon as necessary and possible the more likely we should be to obtain tonnage concessions from our own and British authorities. After some discussion with the officers mentioned, we found ourselves in agreement upon the proposal I had submitted, which is set forth substantially in the following cablegram:

"December 2, 1917.
"For Secretary of War and Chief of Staff.
"Par. 1.

"With the apparent total collapse of Russia and the recent success of the Central Powers in Italy, German morale is undoubtedly much improved and the probability of a serious offensive against the Western Front is greatly increased. In fact, information indicates German concentration in the Vosges opposite Nancy and also near the Swiss frontier. It seems probable that such an offensive may begin this winter. French military authorities are of this opinion and are actually moving troops to meet further developments at both above points. While it is not probable that the Central Powers can concentrate their full strength on the Western Front for some months, yet their resumption of the offensive clearly points out their purpose to push the war here before the Americans can bring over a large force.
"Par. 2.

"With Russia out of the war it is possible for the Central Powers to concentrate 250 to 260 divisions on the Western Front and still have a certain number on the Eastern Front and 26 divisions to hold the Italians. They could do this without interfering

[1] The British were giving some assistance in the transportation of men, but not nearly enough. American ships had carried up to November 1st, 67,218 men and the British 54,751.

with the *status quo* at Salonika, and these estimates do not take into account the possibilities of using Bulgarian or Turkish troops on the Western Front. Against these German and Austrian divisions the Allies have 169 divisions, some of which are under orders for Italy. This relative strength would give the Central Powers about 60 per cent advantage and make it difficult to hold them. The Allies have had about 30 per cent advantage all summer. Details set forth in letter to Secretary of War now en route.

"Par. 3.

"In view of these conditions it is of the utmost importance to the Allied cause that we move swiftly. The minimum number of troops that we should plan to have in France by the end of June is four army corps, or twenty-four divisions, in addition to the troops for service of the rear. Have impressed the present emergency upon General Bliss and other members of the conference. Generals Robertson, Foch, and Bliss agree with me that this is the minimum that should be aimed at. This figure is given as the lowest we should think of, and is no higher because the limit of available transportation would not seem to warrant it.

"Par. 4.

"A study of transportation facilities shows sufficient American tonnage to bring over this number of troops, but to do so there must be a reduction in the amount allotted to other than army needs. It is estimated that the shipping needed will have to be rapidly increased up to two million tons by May, in addition to the amount already allotted. The use of shipping for commercial purposes must be curtailed as much as possible. The Allies are very weak and we must come to their relief this year (1918). The year after may be too late. It is very doubtful if they can hold on until 1919 unless we give them a lot of support this year. It is therefore strongly recommended that a complete readjustment of transportation be made and that the needs of the War Department as set forth above be regarded as immediate. Further details of these requirements will be sent later.

"Par. 5.

"As to heavy artillery and ammunition it is now probable, after full consideration and investigation, that the British and French will be able to make up our deficiencies.

"Par. 6.

"The questions of sea transportation and artillery are under further discussion by the Allies and full report and recommendations will be made in few days.

"PERSHING."

Grave doubt existed generally as to the ability of the Allies to hold on until we should be able to afford assistance that would turn the balance in their favor. Nevertheless, there was no diminution of the fighting spirit among the leaders, as indicated particularly by the recent inauguration of a very vigorous war policy by M. Clemenceau. However, it was well known that in England outside of Government circles there was a sentiment in certain quarters in favor of ending the war by negotiation. One did not hear so very much of it in France, but those who held this view presented the argument that the Germans, having put Russia and Roumania, and possibly Italy, out of the war, would now have to fight only on the Western Front. They feared that the large numbers of German and Austrian troops that could be relieved from the Eastern Front, together with released prisoners, would give the Central Powers a formidable if not an overwhelming advantage in effective strength before the Americans could be brought over.

The ideas of a "reasonable man's peace" and "no desire to crush Germany," although characterized by the British Government as "pro-German" and "pacifistic," were, nevertheless, supported by not a few influential men, and openly so by Lord Lansdowne. This sort of a peace was also favored by several British newspapers, as reported to me at the time, notably by the *Manchester Guardian,* the *Daily News,* the *Westminster Gazette,* and *The Nation.* The existence of such sentiments without doubt had a more or less depressing effect, for the time being, upon British morale, and it certainly set the rest of us thinking, although, being in close personal touch with all the civil and military leaders, I was not at all of the opinion that it was generally taken seriously.

(Diary) Paris, Wednesday, December 5, 1917. Gave a small dinner on Friday to the Houses, the Sharps, Admirals Benson and Sims, and others.

Supreme War Council met on Saturday. The reverses of the British at Cambrai surprised everybody.

On Monday the second and final session of the Inter-Allied conference was held. President and Madame Poincaré gave formal dinner for all delegates that evening.

A large party, including the American delegates, the Ambassador and his family, and Lord Northcliffe, went yesterday by special train at my invitation to our training area.

Saw M. Clemenceau to-day regarding certain criticisms. Talked with Atterbury on dock construction. After conference with Foulois, made agreement with British for training 15,000 Air Service enlisted personnel in England. Dawes has secured some locomotives from Belgium. Encouraging cables promise shipments some heavy artillery, machine guns, horses, automobile mechanics, car erection forces, and cars.

The results of the British success at Cambrai were not to be permanent, as the Germans quickly retaliated. General von der Marwitz [1] hastily assembled a force of some fifteen divisions and on the 30th suddenly launched a violent counterattack. The British were short of reserves and before von der Marwitz was stopped his troops had regained most of the ground lost during the British attack. This surprising reverse of the British, close on the heels of the success of ten days before, came as a sort of warning of what the Allies might expect when their opponents should seriously assume the offensive in the spring. The turn of the tables against the British served to emphasize the actual pessimism that existed, of which there was considerable evidence at the meeting of the Supreme War Council a day or two later.

It was in this operation that a detachment of our 11th Regiment of Engineers serving with the British became engaged. The men, to the number of 280, were at work in the Gouzeaucourt railway yards when the Germans attacked. There were six killed, one officer and twelve men wounded, eleven men taken prisoners. Various units of the regiment fought with the British until their lines were reëstablished.

[1] General von der Marwitz afterward commanded the German armies on our front in the Meuse-Argonne.

NOTE: Total strength of the A.E.F. on November 30th, 7,696 officers, 118,254 enlisted men.

Divisional units arriving in November included nearly all elements of the 42d Division (National Guard, from twenty-six States and the District of Columbia), Major General W. A. Mann.

The session of December 1st at Versailles was the second con-ference of the Supreme War Council, the first having been held at Rapallo when the Council was created. Our representatives, political and military, at this meeting were Mr. House and General Bliss, respectively. At the opening session, M. Clemenceau drew attention to the general situation, referring especially to the collapse of Russia, the probable release of enemy troops from the Russian front, the adverse situation in Italy, the depletion of Allied manpower, and the reliance of the Allies on American assistance. He enjoined the military representatives [1] "to bear in mind that their function is to advise the Supreme War Council as a body and not merely as representatives of their respective nations on the Council, and that they should view the problems confronting them not from a national standpoint but from that of the Allies as a whole." The military representatives at this conference were instructed to examine the military situation and report their recommendations as to the future plan of operations, to study the condition in Italy from the offensive as well as from the defensive point of view; and to report on the utilization of the Belgian Army.

It was evident that the Supreme War Council was to become a kind of super-parliament not only for the discussion of re-sources, aims, and purposes, but for the determination of policies looking to concert of action in support of military efforts. The spirit in which the problems were approached at this meeting indicated that the Supreme War Council would sensibly promote coöperation among the powers.

When the second meeting of the Inter-Allied conference closed its sessions on December 3d, none of the questions brought before the first session could be settled, but they were taken up by the more permanent body, the Supreme War Council, which, as time went on, undertook to coördinate the work of the various com-mittees which had been formed to handle the problems involved.

---

[1] The military representatives were: For France, General Weygand, who had relieved General Foch; for Italy, General Cadorna; for Great Britain, General Sir Henry Wilson; for the United States, General T. H. Bliss.

During the war, dinners and luncheons, formal and otherwise, were indispensable official features of these Inter-Allied gatherings, and, although infrequent, they no doubt aided in promoting good will and understanding. The dinner given at the Élysée Palace, with Madame Poincaré so graciously presiding, was quite in keeping with the reputation of the French for hospitality. It was interesting and picturesque, with the display of the gold lace of the foreign statesmen's dress, and the polished boots, belts, and spurs of the field uniforms of the army officers.

The special visit to our troops gave our delegates and friends a breath of optimistic ozone which must have been a relief from the supercharged atmosphere of depression and apprehension of the French capital. They were taken to the corps schools at Gondrecourt where they saw the different exercises of the various courses of instruction for officers and men. The glimpse of our G.H.Q. suggested some idea of our organization and of how the problems connected with building up and directing a modern army are worked out.

I had an interesting talk on the train with Lord Northcliffe regarding the formation of an American army and the possibility of sea transportation to bring it across. He thought his Government should do more to help with shipping, but like most Englishmen he believed it best for us to send our men for service with the British. He argued in favor of the proposal that Mr. Lloyd George had recently made to Mr. House that we should incorporate in their units any infantry that we might not be able to organize immediately into complete divisions of our own. I said, "It is all very well to make such an appeal to us but it is impossible to ignore our national viewpoint. The people themselves would not approve, even though the President should lean that way. I am strongly opposed to it. We cannot permit our men to serve under another flag except in an extreme emergency and then only temporarily." I also insisted that we could contribute more largely to Allied success by the use of the American Army as a unit.

Continuing, I said that there was nothing vainglorious in our

MY EXPERIENCES IN THE WORLD WAR   255

attitude, but no people with a grain of national pride would consent to furnish men to build up the army of another nation. I pointed out to him that misunderstandings and recriminations would inevitably follow any reverse by such a mixed force, and that his Government had used none of their Colonials in any such way. It is quite certain that Northcliffe had not considered the subject from our point of view, for, at the conclusion of the conversation, he very frankly said that we were perfectly right. After that, so far as I am aware, he became a consistent advocate of the formation of an American army.

In another conversation, Mr. House asked my views of the proposal which had been sent to him by Mr. Lloyd George. The memorandum in question had been forwarded to Lord Reading for delivery to Mr. House, with a note by Mr. Lloyd George scribbled in his own hand as follows:

"2nd December, 1917.
"My dear R.

* * * * * * *

"The C.I.G.S. [Chief of the Imperial General Staff] is very anxious you should place the enclosed [memorandum] before Colonel House. I entirely concur and urge its acceptance. We shall be hard pressed to hold our own and keep Italy standing during 1918. Our manpower is pretty well exhausted. We can only call up men of 45-50, and boys of 17. France is done. The American soldiers will not be ready to fight as an army until late in 1918. Our experience proves that meanwhile we must keep the fight going. Even half-trained American companies or battalions would fight well if mixed with 2 or 3 years' veterans.

"Beg H. to consider this favorably.
"Yours,
"D.L.G."

Enclosure

* * * * * * *

"Would America therefore be ready to help in another way, as a temporary measure? When she first came into the war we hoped she might send some men for inclusion in the British Armies, as being clearly the quickest way of helping, but for reasons we quite understand she preferred to retain her national identity. No doubt she still desires to do so, but over and above the preparation of her divisions, and without interfering with it, would it be possible for her to provide a company of infantry to replace a British company in such a number of British battalions as America could bring over men? Even 100 such companies would be of the greatest value. Every consideration would of course be given to the companies, and *if they desired they could later on be recalled and posted to the American divisions.* It is thought that this mingling of American and British troops would establish a close and cordial feeling between the two armies, and would also give the American troops useful training. If this system is not possible would America find a battalion to replace a British battalion in as many brigades as possible. There would be no insuperable difficulty in meeting American wishes in any such matters as discipline, rations, and general maintenance. The only difficulty is American national sentiment which we quite understand. On the other hand the system suggested is clearly one which would the most rapidly afford much needed help during, perhaps, the most critical period of the war."

I told Mr. House that Mr. Lloyd George's plan would not do at all and gave him reasons for my belief, and my opinion as to what the result would be. This was, in fact, a revival of the plan put forward by the Balfour Mission. It never received support from any Americans except a few individuals, including some officers who were disposed to criticize generally the management of our interests in France, and who, for their own ulterior purposes, sought to gain the favorable opinion and receive the acclaim of the Allies. But Mr. House and all other upstanding, loyal Americans were from the start strongly in favor of building up our own army.

About this time, Mr. House told me that Pétain had criticized the American ideas of training and also that M. Loucheur, Minister of Munitions, had spoken about the rise in prices caused by American purchases. Mr. House had wisely suggested to these gentlemen, he said, that matters of this kind were for me to settle. I called without delay on M. Clemenceau and told him of the reports and explained my understanding about training agreements with Pétain and also the steps that had previously been taken by our Purchasing Board, in coöperation with his own bureaus, to prevent the rise in prices. I also told him that French dealers were largely to blame if prices had risen, as we had eliminated competition among ourselves, and that our purchases were and had been for some time actually handled through French officials.

I objected to these back-door methods of lodging complaints and emphasized the necessity of frankness and directness in all our dealings. I asked M. Clemenceau to give instructions that if there was any fault to find with our methods it should be brought to my personal attention. He entirely agreed with me and expressed chagrin and surprise that any other course had been followed.

I took occasion a few days later to let Pétain know very politely what I thought of the impropriety of this sort of thing and also criticized him then and there for telling anybody, even Mr. House, as he had done, about our purpose to attack the St. Mihiel salient as the first offensive by the American Army. I was pleased with Pétain's apology and his statement that there would be no further action of this kind on his part.

On the face of it, there was no other conclusion, however, than that both complaints were made for the purpose of finding out just the extent of my independent authority. The French probably regarded Mr. House as a sort of special ambassador and thought that they might be able to lay the foundation for an approach through him to the question of amalgamation.

Just before his return to the States, Mr. House told me that he was convinced that the President and the Secretary of War would leave the whole question of the disposition of our troops to my judgment. Assurance on this point was scarcely necessary, as I had full confidence that this was the case. During his stay in France Mr. House and I formed a friendship which enabled us to discuss all matters most freely and frankly. Before he left for home we arranged for confidential communication by cable should it become necessary to reach either Mr. Baker or Mr. Wilson direct.

(Diary) Chaumont, Tuesday, December 11, 1917. Returned here the 7th; am glad to have horseback rides again.

Chief Surgeon Bradley reported yesterday that he is getting more buildings for hospitals. Talked with Atterbury regarding Army Transport Service and find discharge of transports going better. British under Allenby captured Jerusalem the 9th.

To-day gave French correspondents general outline of progress which may be reassuring. Our training at home not going well. Serious shortage of winter clothing notwithstanding repeated urgent cables.

The difficulties of transatlantic transportation in general made it necessary to limit our demands to those things that could not possibly be obtained abroad within a reasonable time, and every effort was being made toward procurement in Europe. France was responding generously, but her supplies were not inexhaustible. Attention was now turned to the neutral countries of Switzerland and Spain, and also to Portugal. Through negotiations directed by the General Purchasing Agent, it was found that these countries were willing to open up their markets provided the United States would make concessions as to financial accommodations in some cases and remove the embargo in others. The prospects for a time seemed encouraging for obtaining horses, mules, railway ties, and other needed supplies, but the numbers and amounts proved to be limited, and the quality, especially of the animals, unsatisfactory.

The instruction of our troops at home at this time was far from being satisfactory, tests of newly-arrived units having shown that their work was not up to our standards. It was evident that my recommendations were being disregarded. This threw the extra burden upon us of training officers and men after their arrival. I had urged that we should follow our own conception of preparation, emphasizing the rifle and bayonet as the supreme weapons of the infantry soldier, and insisting upon training in all the details of open warfare. It will be pertinent to quote my cable criticizing the policy of the War Department as set forth in one of the training pamphlets sent to me:

"December 7, 1917.

"In my opinion this pamphlet is not in harmony with the recommendations contained in my cablegram in regard to the training of divisions in the United States. The first paragraph of War Department document announces that 'in all the military training of a division, under existing conditions training for trench warfare is of paramount importance.' The program for training contained in the document is prepared accordingly and subordinates all instruction to training for trench warfare. * * * I invite attention to my cablegram and repeat my recommendations contained therein that intensive training in all phases of open warfare be accepted as the principal mission of divisions before embarkation, trench warfare and the use of special arms being taught in connection with the assumption of an offensive from an entrenched position. It is urged that future programs of training for divisions in the United States be prepared accordingly."

The training of officers for the General Staff, which also necessarily had to be undertaken in France, was well under way at the General Staff School, established at Langres, forty miles south of Chaumont, under the able direction of Brigadier General J. W. McAndrew. The three-month course of instruction was based upon our staff organization and was conducted by our own instructors, with two or three French, and an equal number of British officers to assist as lecturers. The difficulty was the scarcity of officers available for detail as students. We were confronted with the task of building up an army of millions that would require as many trained staff officers as we had officers in the whole Regular Army at the beginning of the war. To meet this urgent demand, Washington was asked to send over in advance a small percentage of officers from each division for instruction, but only a few ever came.

The first class at the General Staff School was composed of about seventy-five officers, most of whom were taken from our meager forces then in France. Unfortunately, all the schools were short of student personnel and it was not until the eleventh hour, when new divisions began to come over under pressure late in the spring, that any considerable number of officers could be obtained from our forces for special staff instruction.

(Diary) Chaumont, Sunday, December 16, 1917. Several members of Food Administration [1] lunched with us on Friday and gave an impressive account of restrictions at home.

General Gourko, Russian Army, came yesterday to urge acceptance of their officers in our army, but was told that it is impracticable.

As surest means of having trained troops in the spring, have cabled request for Regular divisions. General Pétain came this evening for dinner, also Colonel de Chambrun, General Ragueneau and Colonel Cornélis DeW. Willcox. Late reports from Italy far from reassuring. Our Remount Service reports shortage of over 15,000 horses and mules.

In considering the composition of our expeditionary forces the question of how to utilize the Regular Army to the best advantage became important. Instead of breaking up its units entirely and allotting the officers and noncommissioned officers to National Guard and National Army units, it was deemed wiser to keep up the Regular units and detach from them such officers and noncommissioned officers as might be needed to leaven the other contingents.

At this moment the training of the first draft had begun, assignments from the Regular units had already been made, and the vacancies filled by new personnel, both officers and men. The basic organization of these Regular units still remained and this with their traditions of service made them the most valuable contingent of our army. It was my opinion, with which both Bliss and Harbord agreed, that the quickest way to provide sorely needed assistance to the Allies would be to hasten the training of the Regular divisions and send them to France as soon as possible.

I recommended that Regular regiments at Honolulu and elsewhere be relieved for this purpose by National Guard regiments. These Regular troops would more nearly approximate the standards of our Allies at the start, and, more important still, their use would diminish the chances of reverses during our first encounters with the enemy. The Acting Chief of Staff at home,

[1] The members present were: Roscoe R. Mitchell, Buffalo, N. Y.; Everett Colby, West Orange, N. J.; J. Bright Lord, New York; Edward F. Trefz, Chicago; Dr. Julius Lincoln, Jamestown, N. Y.; Daniel A. Reed, Flint, Mich.

Major General John Biddle, agreed with my suggestion, but thought that the widely separated locations of these regiments made their replacement impracticable, and only the 3d, 4th, and 5th Divisions came in time for service early in 1918, the 6th and 7th arriving to take part in the fall campaign.

Although the Italians had recently yielded ground west of the Brenta River their lines were then holding on the Piave. However, there was an undercurrent of misgiving among the Allies concerning them, the prevalent belief being that there had been a serious lack of training in their armies originally, and that too little had been done after Italy entered the war. The experience of the other Allies had shown that in order to achieve and maintain a high standard, thorough and continuous instruction was necessary. Especially was this true of staff officers, upon whom so much of the success of an army depends.

It was said that the Italian artillery was not abreast of modern methods and conducted its firing largely without definite data, which was a vital defect, if true, as artillery unable to fire with precision becomes really a menace. When in immediate support of infantry, the barrage must be laid down with such accuracy, just ahead of the advancing troops, as to inspire them with confidence. Liaison between these two arms and with aviation became more and more essential as the war progressed and it could only be perfected by training the three arms together. Officers especially must have specific knowledge of the importance and the technique of coöperation. Yet instruction and preparation in general are of little avail unless positions on the front are wisely selected and protected by well coördinated plans for defense, and unless the armies are trained for open warfare. The other Allies criticized the Italians in all these respects.

The opinion was expressed in certain French circles that the French should take charge of the Italian Army and reorganize it if there was to be anything effective expected on that front. Another suggestion was that a French chief of staff be appointed for the Italians, and that the President of the United States, as a distinguished friend, should put the proposition forward with the necessary pressure to accomplish it.   But, of course, no such changes were necessary or even remotely possible.

Incidentally, it was noticeable that the Allies were quick to criticize each other and allege inefficiency in case of reverses.   In due time the British and French also suffered disastrous defeats and their armies were also open to criticism.   Before the end of the war the records of reverses of the respective armies in the West were about a stand-off.   Hasty criticisms are likely to be unjust. Moreover, the injustice is often perpetuated by ill-advised or malicious repetition.

CHAPTER XIX

District of Paris—Phases of Training—Supply Question—Haig's Proposition—Visit Belgian Army—Allies Pressing for Amalgamation—Pétain Proposes New Method of Training Our Troops—Clemenceau Interferes—Situation December 31st

(Diary) Chaumont, Wednesday, December 19, 1917. Attended commemorative services Monday at Church of St. John, Chaumont. Conferred with the Inspector General, Brewster, and several other staff officers. General Zankevitch called to offer services of Russian officers. Went to Paris in the evening, taking Ragueneau, de Chambrun and Dawes.

Had discussion with M. Clemenceau yesterday on supply and other questions. Arthur Frazier, our observer on Supreme War Council, thinks with me that some outstanding civilian should represent us. Called on Brigadier General E. M. Lewis, commanding Paris District. Visited Atterbury's office and was impressed with businesslike system.

Returned to Chaumont this morning, bringing Tardieu and Ganne. Ordnance motor trucks promised after February.

OUR activities in Paris required that numbers of officers and men be stationed there and many members of the A.E.F. frequently passed through the city in traveling officially, or went there on short leaves of absence, making it necessary to establish some authority to whom they could go for orders or information. Paris was, therefore, made a military district in November, 1917, and upon the removal of the Headquarters Line of Communications, to Tours, in January, 1918, became a separate command. The District Commander, Brigadier General E. M. Lewis, was given jurisdiction over troops stationed in the city and over all casuals. The orders published by General Lewis in December prescribed rules of conduct for members of the A.E.F. while in the city. These regulations generally remained in force under his successors through difficult periods when Paris was full of men seeking recuperation and recreation, and for whose good behavior the district commander was responsible.

When Mr. House and General Bliss, who sat in at the second meeting of the Supreme War Council, returned to the United States, Mr. Arthur H. Frazier, First Secretary of our Embassy, was designated to attend the meetings, but merely as an observer and without any voice in the proceedings. Mr. Frazier felt that he was more or less handicapped from lack of knowledge of military affairs, and thought that we should be actively represented. I agreed with him, although it would have been impracticable for the President to designate any one and clothe him with authority comparable to that of the Prime Ministers. I recommended the appointment of Major General Hunter Liggett as the military representative on the Council, but shortly afterward General Bliss was named for the position, and his selection was very agreeable to me. In addition to his other duties, he performed the functions that might have fallen to a civilian, in that he kept the President advised of the actions of the Council and received instructions from him.

(Diary) Chaumont, Tuesday, December 25, 1917. The Archbishops of Langres and of Chaumont paid a formal call on Thursday.

Visited the 42d Division at Lafauche on Friday and saw a well-conducted simulated attack by its training companion, Major General Monroe's French 69th Division. General de Castelnau and Generals Bullard, Bundy, Edwards, and Traub were present.

Left for Paris Saturday and on Sunday drove to Compiègne, lunching with Pétain.

Lord Milner called yesterday to sound me out on the question of amalgamation. Colonel de Chambrun and I dined with M. Jules Cambon, recently designated to handle certain matters of procurement as head of the "Comité Central des Affaires de Guerre."

Returned to Chaumont to-day and had Christmas dinner at quarters with official family.

Our program of training in France had become fairly well established under the immediate direction and observation of the Training Section of the General Staff. Most of our officers were firm believers in the soundness of our doctrines, although a few continued to defer to the opinions of French instructors, who were generally committed to the theory that only trench training was necessary. Our schedule of instruction consisted of three periods. The first included practice in the use of the various weapons, with tactical exercises for units up to the division over such terrain as might be available. The second embraced a month's tour in the trenches by smaller units with French regiments, supported by French artillery. The third concluded the course with combined work of infantry, artillery, and aviation conducted in the training area, after which the division went again into the trenches under its own officers and as a unit in a French corps.

The plan adopted of training with a veteran division was fairly successful, considering the circumstances, and would have been ideal if the model division could have been American. The objection was that the French were inclined to be too paternal and as a rule they went little further in their instruction than trench fighting.

The fact that many of our own officers were not well grounded in first principles made instruction more difficult. Recent inspections had revealed many deficiencies on the part of our officers, and further confirmed reports regarding the inefficacy of the training at home. In my own experience of many years in training troops it was not uncommon to find field officers with little conception of the practical application of the lessons taught in our elementary text books on minor tactics, and it was not surprising to find such a situation in our new army. It was not sufficient merely to issue instructions or schedules, as some officers in the higher grades seemed to think, but it was necessary that they, themselves, should be competent to teach details of execution, especially in the matter of correct tactical method. The most exacting tests were instituted to bring to all concerned a full realization of its importance.

The following cable sent at this time will explain my point of view:

"December 22, 1917.

"Reference training of troops in States, deficiencies noted here indicate, first, great laxity on the part of division and brigade commanders in requiring officers to learn their duties or perform them efficiently; second, almost total failure to give any instruction in principles of minor tactics and their application to war conditions. Officers from colonels down and including some general officers are found ignorant of the handling of units in open warfare, including principles of reconnaissance, outposts, advance guards, solution of practical problems, and formation of attack; third, no training whatever has been given in musketry efficiency as distinguished from individual target practice on the range. Many officers of high rank are hopelessly ignorant of what this training consists."

I had suggested the establishment of a training branch of the War Department under Major General J. F. Morrison, with Brigadier General R. M. Blatchford as his assistant, two of the best equipped officers in our army for such work. The spirit of the recommendation was not carried out, however, as Morrison was not given the necessary independence and authority that a director should have, and as a result the training continued defective, being usually limited to trench warfare.

After all is said, however, the success of a military commander depends largely upon his practical turn of mind, whether it be in planning and directing military operations in the field or managing the business of transportation and supply. Military science is based on principles that have been deduced from the application of common sense in the conduct of military affairs. While high sounding terms and learned discussions of principles and maxims often enshroud campaigns and operations in mystery, military genius is really only the capacity to understand and apply simple principles founded on experience and sound reasoning.

Of course, theoretical training is invaluable, as in any profession, but, as in most others, it forms merely the groundwork, as no two military situations are ever exactly alike. The necessity of professional education should not be minimized in the slightest degree; it is too highly important; but the best informed theoretical soldier without practical comprehension will often find his plans go wrong. To complete the qualifications essential to the successful soldier, there must be added persistence, force, initiative, and personal leadership.

In so far as supplies were available in France, the system of procurement was working fairly well. There was some improvement in the relations between our different supply departments and those of the French. The procurement of many things pertaining to the special and technical services, such as airplanes and all sorts of artillery and ammunition; matters relating to railways and ports and their management; construction; and the quest of buildings for hospitals, were handled personally by the chiefs of the departments responsible, dealing either directly with the ministry concerned or through another agency recently established called the "Comité Central des Affaires de Guerre." It was in the procurement of more general supplies by the purchasing agency that the French Mission at my headquarters could more advantageously present our requirements to the proper authorities and arrange details of purchases.

The appointment of M. Jules Cambon as chairman of this committee placed him in position to represent us before the Council of Ministers. He invited me to dine with him to discuss the relation that his new office would bear to our officials and agencies on the one side and the French Government on the other. The plan for coördination did not look to be very feasible in the hands of such an elderly and rather inactive official, but later M. Maurice Ganne became Director and later still M. Tardieu, and under these men the committee became very important in coöperation with our purchasing agency and other departments in handling our requests before the Ministry.

(Diary) Chaumont, Wednesday, Jan. 2, 1918. Both French and British pressing us for amalgamation.

Went to Marshal Haig's headquarters Friday by rail, accompanied by Colonel Wagstaff, and spent the night. Motored through heavy snow drifts out from Étaples; gangs of "conscientious objectors" opening up roads. Discussed with Sir Douglas possible shipment by and training of American troops with British.

Visited King and Queen of Belgium and their army at Adinkerke on Saturday. Returned to Paris Sunday, visited Major General J. Franklin Bell in hospital, and later called on M. Clemenceau.

Came to Chaumont Monday. Dispensed with New Year's calls on account of work. Dawes came from Paris and spent the night. Generals Wirbel and Ragueneau called.

Our general situation as to arrival of troops and material far from encouraging.

As we have seen, there had been some talk of the British providing shipping to bring over American troops for training behind their lines. During the evening I spent with Sir Douglas Haig, he presented his plans for training our troops. His idea was to place the battalions as they arrived, one to the brigade, in selected British divisions, preferably those serving on the southern part of their front, and then gradually to increase the number of battalions until the divisions should become wholly American. He was willing to place each of these divisions under an American general as soon as the division should become partly Americanized; or do so from the outset if more desirable, retaining the British divisional staffs, and brigade commanders and staffs, until the divisions should be at least half American, after which our staff officers and brigadiers would gradually replace theirs. He thought the sentiment against our men serving under another army might be thus overcome.

His battalions, when released by Americans, would be broken up to fill depleted ranks elsewhere. In this way such units as they were unable to maintain could be replaced by ours and an American army built up to take its place alongside the British.

NOTE: Total strength of the A.E.F. on December 31st, 9,804 officers, 165,080 enlisted men.

Divisional units arriving in December included elements of the 41st Division (National Guard, Washington, Oregon, Montana, Idaho, Wyoming, North and South Dakota, Colorado, New Mexico, and the District of Columbia), Major General Hunter Liggett.

The 369th Infantry of the 93d Division (National Army, colored) arrived January 1st. The 93d Division was never fully organized and its infantry regiments served with the French.

His plan contemplated that the British and American armies would both be based on the northwest coast of France. His Chief of Rail Transportation, General Nash, thought he would be able to receive our troops at Le Havre and send them up country without disturbing his own arrangements. However, I thought that Nash was not very enthusiastic over his Commander-in-Chief's idea.

Sir Douglas used arguments such as common language and the fact that American hospital units were already with the British, as well as the simplicity and expedition with which the plan could be carried out. Any objections the French might offer he thought would be met by building up the American Army between the two. Besides, he said, this would provide for the extension of the British front and meet the demands of the French, who claimed that the French armies were holding too much of the line in proportion to their forces.

The appeal of this proposition was that we should be able to hasten our shipping program and bring to France a much larger number of men than would be possible with the tonnage then in operation. Hoping to commit the British definitely on the question of tonnage, which up to that time we had not succeeded in doing, I did not offer serious objection to the plan and even approved some of the features, especially those pertaining to the earlier part of the proposed training, and for the moment the question was left open for further conference. In all these discussions, the British were bargaining for men to fill their ranks and we were trying to get shipping to carry over our armies.

I left British headquarters the next morning en route to the Belgian front to pay my respects to the King and Queen of Belgium. As Sir Douglas was off to London, my car was attached to his train and we traveled together to Boulogne, where he boarded the Channel boat and I took a special consisting of my car and one other and proceeded on my way.

We were due at Adinkerke, my destination, at a fixed hour, but to my surprise the train pulled in ten minutes ahead of time. I was changing into my best uniform, in fact was just pulling on the right boot when my aide, Colonel Boyd, stuck his head in at the door of my compartment and breathlessly said, "General, we have arrived." I knew it only too well, as the train had stopped and the royal band outside was playing the *Star Spangled Banner* in the usual mournful cadence common to foreign bands. It was an embarrassing thought that I should be late. In another minute, when the orderly and I were struggling, this time with the left boot, Boyd again appeared and said in a stage whisper that was no doubt heard by the entire escort outside, "Sir, the King is out there standing at the salute."

That was too much, the humor of the situation overcame me, and for an instant all of us, including the orderly, who rarely smiled, were convulsed with laughter. That did not help matters, of course, and meanwhile the band outside, which had already played the national air through three times, was dolefully beginning on the fourth, when I hurriedly descended the steps of my car opposite His Majesty, buttoning my overcoat with one hand and saluting with the other. At my appearance the band started afresh and, as though they had just begun, ran through our national anthem rather more vigorously, cheered up no doubt at last to see me in evidence. A few months later I had the courage to relate the incident in all its details to Their Majesties and they both seemed to enjoy it immensely.

After inspecting the escort in company with the King, he and I drove to their residence, where the Queen, in her most gracious manner, received us at the entrance. We had a very enjoyable luncheon, which Boyd thought was quite gay, especially when I became bold enough to air my dreadful French. After luncheon, King Albert, much to my surprise, said he wished to bestow upon me the Order of the Grand Cordon of Leopold. Although not unappreciative, I hesitated, saying that we were not permitted to receive foreign decorations, but he insisted that I should accept it conditionally, which, of course, was the only thing to do. Boyd was decorated also.

In the afternoon, the King, with his Chief of Staff, took me to his G.H.Q. and then to the front-line trenches, explaining the disposition of the limited force with which their positions were held. It consisted of only the six divisions which had stubbornly retired in 1914 in the face of overwhelming odds. It was then being recruited by Belgians who had escaped from within the German lines at the risk of their lives. During my visit I got a much clearer notion of the spirit of the Belgian Army and of its tenacious resistance, which had been of such importance to the Allies by delaying the German advance.

While driving with King Albert he related with much amusement some incidents of a recent visit by a party of our Congressmen, and inquired whether it was customary in our country for them to be on familiar terms with the President. He said that some of them had called him Albert, and one had slapped him on the back, saying, "King, you're the right sort of a fellow and everybody in America admires you." I explained to him that our Congressmen were more or less privileged characters at home and that they only meant to be friendly. As a matter of fact, I do not think the King was in the least offended at their familiarity.

During my brief visit, I was particularly impressed by the extreme simplicity of the home life of the King and Queen, living there, as they were, in a very modest country place within sound of the enemy's guns and almost within range. The Queen often went into the trenches to cheer the troops, and the fine bearing of Their Majesties through it all made them outstanding heroic figures of the World War.

In view of the suggestions that had come to my headquarters regarding various plans for training our troops with the French and British, it was in no sense a surprise to receive the following cable from the Secretary of War, delivered on Christmas Day:

"Pershing, Amexforce,
"Both English and French are pressing upon the President their desires to have your forces amalgamated with theirs by regiments and companies, and both express the belief in impending heavy drive by Germans somewhere along the lines of the Western Front. We do not desire loss of identity of our forces *but regard that as secondary*

to the meeting of any critical situation by the most helpful use possible of the troops at your command. The difficulty of course is to determine where the drive or drives of the enemy will take place; and in advance of some knowledge on that question, any redistribution of your forces would be difficult. The President, however, desires you to have full authority to use the forces at your command as you deem wise in consultation with the French and British Commanders-in-Chief. It is suggested for your consideration that possibly places might be selected for your forces nearer the junction of the British and French lines which would enable you to throw strength in whichever direction seemed most necessary. This suggestion is not, however, pressed beyond whatever merit it has in your judgment, the President's sole purpose being to acquaint you with the representations made here and to authorize you to act with entire freedom to accomplish the main purposes in mind. It is hoped that complete unity and coördination of action can be secured in this matter by any conferences you may have with French and British commanders and line of action that may be agreed upon.

"BAKER."

During my visit with General Pétain at his headquarters a few days before this we had taken up anew the question of training for our divisions then in France and also for those yet to come. On account of the imminence of a powerful offensive by the Germans on the Western Front, he said we must be prepared to utilize all possible resources, including the Americans, a statement to which I readily agreed as a matter of course. Instead of following the plan then in operation as to training step by step, beginning with the smaller units, he wanted to take a quicker method and have each of the four infantry regiments of each of our divisions, together with the proper proportion of the artillery, engineers and other troops, assigned to a French division at once. After two or three months of service these troops would be reassembled, he said, under their own divisional officers and take their places in line. It was not simply for instruction in quiet sectors that these units were to be used, but for whatever service might fall to the lot of the French divisions to which they were assigned.

This, of course, virtually meant the building up of French

divisions by American regiments and carried with it the probability that we should not be able to get them back without actually reducing the French divisions to a point where they would be much crippled for further line service. Again, the training of our higher officers and their staffs was entirely ignored under this plan. I spoke of that as an objection and also mentioned the difference in language as being an insuperable barrier to any idea of active service under an assignment that might become permanent.

It was evident that the adoption of such a plan would interrupt our steady progress toward the preparation of our divisions, and thus interfere with the formation of our army. I told the French that it seemed to me better, if such a course became necessary, that we should amalgamate with the British, who were still making overtures for our troops. The French did not then offer any objection to this counter-suggestion and it looked as though there was an understanding between them.

In my formal reply to a communication from Pétain embracing his proposal, I declined to agree to the assignment of our regiments as he had suggested, but said that I should be glad to attach them to French divisions solely for training for a period of one month in a quiet sector provided that opportunity should also be given our officers to learn how to handle larger units by actually exercising their proper functions. The Secretary's cable indicated complete coöperation between the French Government and the Army Commander in their endeavor to carry their point. The same could be said of the British.

In the meantime, the following cable was received, showing the means to which Clemenceau resorted to force the issue:

"Washington, January 3, 1918.
"The French Ambassador called on the Secretary of War to-day and read him a dispatch from M. Clemenceau to the effect that General Pershing and General Pétain had conferred as to the wisdom of seasoning American troops by attaching their regimental units to French divisions before committing a part of the line to an American division made up of troops not (sic) accustomed to actual front conditions.

"M. Clemenceau's cablegram stated that General Pershing had reported himself and General Pétain in substantial agreement after conference on the subject but General Pétain conveyed to M. Clemenceau the opposite opinion. Apparently some misunderstanding has arisen which the Secretary of War will be glad to have General Pershing endeavor to clear up by placing himself in communication with M. Clemenceau and reporting the result of the interview.

"The French urge action as outlined above as being safer for American troops than it would be to give them at once an independent place in the line, and urge very strongly that the Secretary of War here accept their view and commend it to you. This the Secretary of War is not willing to do, desiring to leave the matter wholly within your discretion after full consideration of the important elements of the matter.

"The French Ambassador has been told that the Secretary of War would lay the matter before you and would communicate to him your conclusions when they are arrived at."

The following extract of my cable of January 8th conveys the main points of my reply:

" * * * The French have not been entirely frank, as unofficial information indicates they really want to incorporate our regiments into their divisions for such service in the trenches as they desire. As to our instruction, a certain amount of work with French troops is beneficial and this we are having and expect to have. * * * Have expressed a willingness to aid in any way in an emergency but do not think good reason yet exists for us to break up our divisions and scatter regiments for service among French and British, especially under the guise of instruction. * * * The integrity of our own forces should be preserved as far as possible. Shall see M. Clemenceau * * * and expect to hold joint conference with Field Marshal Haig and General Pétain within a few days. Shall have frank discussion of the whole subject. * * * "

It thus appeared quite clear that the French were so intent on their plan that M. Clemenceau presumed to cable Washington as to how our units were to be handled. Upon the receipt of the cable from Washington about the disagreement between Pétain and myself, I wrote at once to M. Clemenceau quoting the cable and adding:

"May I not suggest to you, Mr. President,[1] the inexpediency of communicating such matters to Washington by cable? These questions must all be settled here, eventually, on their merits, through friendly conferences between General Pétain and myself, and cables of this sort are very likely, I fear, to convey the impression of serious disagreement between us when such is not the case. * * * ' "

His reply, translated into English, was as follows:

"My dear General:
"I hasten, without losing a moment, to reply to your letter dated January 5, 1918. I found myself under the necessity of cabling to the Ambassador of France at Washington because the two contradictory responses which I had received from General Pétain and from yourself, when you did me the honor of calling on me, obliged me, in the interest of the common cause, to seek an arbitration between the two Commanders-in-Chief.

"I need not conceal the fact that I placed full confidence in this regard in the American Government. However, it was not to the American Government that I addressed myself. I cabled to the Ambassador of France, as was my right and duty, in order to give him directions for the conversations which might take place either with the Secretary of War or with the President of the United States.

"It might very well have happened that later on I should have addressed the American Government, but I insist on the point, that I have done nothing of the sort. I had not authorized the Ambassador of France to read all or part of my dispatch to the Secretary of War. I regret that he did so, but I do not disavow anything that I wrote.

"So I am giving you here the explanation which I owe you and I shall exercise all the patience of which I am capable in awaiting the good news that the American Commander and the French Commander have finally agreed on a question which may be vital to the outcome of the war.

"With the assurance of my feelings of high esteem and of respect for you personally, I beg you, my dear General, to believe me,

"Sincerely yours,

"CLEMENCEAU."

As the French were dead set on getting our troops under their control, it is very clear that the Prime Minister, feeling that their plans were not working out, sought to create some question in

---

[1] "Président du Conseil" corresponds to "Prime Minister."

the minds of our Administration at Washington regarding the wisdom of my management of things. He no doubt thought that my opposition to amalgamation could thus be overcome. However, at later meetings with Clemenceau and Pétain the alleged differences were seemingly settled amicably, as indicated in my cable which follows:

"January 14, 1918.

"Confidential, for Chief of Staff.

"Par. 1.

"With reference to your 558 and 588, and my cablegram 467, have had entirely frank conference with Prime Minister Clemenceau and General Pétain. Have now definite understanding with French satisfactory to them and to me that our divisions now in France shall complete their training as already begun. In the future, divisions arriving in Zone of French Armies are to have period of training with French, each regiment in a French division. When sufficiently experienced by training in a quiet sector with French, our divisions are to be united under their own commander and will be placed in the line in our own sector.

*   *   *   *   *   *   *

"Par. 3.

"Discussion with Prime Minister Clemenceau and General Pétain was characterized by utmost frankness on both sides and it is believed that we now have complete understanding.

*   *   *   *   *   *   *

"Pershing."

The first few months we were in France were actively employed in working out basic plans and in completing our organization. We had been ready and waiting to assign units to areas and duties as fast as they should arrive and begin or continue their training as might be required. Each of the supply and staff departments had been broadened in scope and new services created and their relation to the whole under the new conditions definitely fixed.

However, our situation as to numbers of troops and as to supplies and construction at the close of the year was not what we had every reason to expect after having been at war nine months. We had not obtained full service from the limited amount of tonnage thus far made available for military use. The supply departments in Washington had failed to provide sufficient material for the construction at ports, which was still very much behind. Only a part of the railroad rolling stock needed had been sent. As we have seen, the Navy, until recently, instead of routing vessels to different ports had brought most of them to St. Nazaire for discharge, at times causing considerable congestion there. Only about 350,000 tons of freight had been received.

We had less than 175,000 men in France, including about 100,000 in four divisions in various stages of organization and training, while there should have been at least ten divisions of combat troops and other forces in proportion. It was a very unsatisfactory state of affairs that confronted us, with little promise of improvement. At home we had forty-five divisions organized, and part of their personnel had been assembled and started in training, but it would take time to assign and instruct the additional drafts and put these into shape.

Apropos of the delay in the shipment of troops and supplies, the following cable, sent December 20th, will show the situation and my appeal:

"Understood here that a shipping program based on tonnage in sight prepared in War College Division in September contemplated that entire First Corps with its corps troops and some 32,000 auxiliaries were to have been shipped by end of November, and that an additional program for December, January, and February contemplates that the shipment of the Second Corps with its corps troops and other auxiliaries should be practically completed by the end of February. (Twelve divisions in all.) Should such a program be carried out as per schedule and should shipments continue at corresponding rate, it would not succeed in placing even three complete corps, with proper proportion of Army troops and auxiliaries, in France by end of May. The actual facts are that shipments are not even keeping up to that schedule. It is now the middle of December and the First Corps (six divisions) is still incomplete by over two entire divisions and many corps troops. It cannot be too emphatically declared that we should be prepared to take the field with at least four corps (twenty-four divisions) by June 30. In view of past performances with tonnage heretofore available such a project is impossible of fulfillment, but only by most strenuous attempts to attain such a result will we be in a position to take a proper part in operations in 1918. In view of fact that as the number of our troops here increases, a correspondingly greater amount of tonnage must be provided for their supply, and also in view of the slow rate of shipment with tonnage now available, it is of the most urgent importance that more tonnage should be obtained at once as already recommended in my cables and by General Bliss."

It hardly need be recorded that we were occasioned much embarrassment in facing the Allies with such a poor showing of accomplishment. Up to this time, we had been handicapped in our efforts by lack of aggressive direction of affairs at home. Whether this was due to inefficiency or failure to appreciate the urgency of the situation, the War Department General Staff, as the superior coördinating agency, must take the greater part of the blame. This situation was an unwelcome confirmation of the opinion formed by me on my first visit to the War Department the previous May. Notwithstanding the lack of plans and experience, it has always been difficult for me to understand why our General Staff clung so long to the antiquated systems and faulty precedents which had guided its activities previous to our entry into the war. It should be observed that the present War Department General Staff as reorganized is and will continue to be efficient so long as it follows the principles developed in the American Expeditionary Forces, upon which its reorganization was based.

Messages of mutual good-will and best wishes for the new year were exchanged between the Commanders-in-Chief of the Allied armies and myself in the name of our respective commands. The following was also received from Washington:

"The President and the Secretary of War send to you and to the American Army in France the most cordial greetings and good wishes for this Christmas Season from the people of the United States. Your comrades in arms of every camp and cantonment send you greetings. From every home to-day goes a prayer for the welfare and success of our troops in France and personally for every man of them. The nation reposes in you and them its full confidence that in God's good time and with God's blessing its troops in France, side by side with their gallant Allies, will bring victory and an abiding peace to the world."

This beautiful message expressed the fine spirit of the American people as exemplified by our war President. Coming at a time when Allied morale was low and the outcome of the war in doubt, the courage, the faith and the prayers of our people at home gave a new impetus to our determination to win.

CHAPTER XX

The West Point Spirit—Liquor Question—Increase of Chaplains—Aviation—Recommendations for Improvement Port Situation—Robertson Offers Sea Transport Conditionally—In Agreement with Pétain—Forage Supply—Letter to Secretary of War, General Conditions Reported

(Diary) Chaumont, Saturday, January 5, 1918. Gave Edwin Marshall, the correspondent, an interview on Thursday and saw Grayson Murphy, who is giving up Red Cross for service with troops.

Accredited correspondents came yesterday to study our organization and had luncheon with us. Generals Headlam and Wagstaff, British Army, dined with us.

Had message to-day from General Robertson requesting conference at Paris the 9th. Considerable discussion in late home papers concerning my orders against drinking.

MAJOR Grayson M. P. Murphy, who had been in charge of the Red Cross work in France, was a graduate of West Point, and before resigning his commission to enter the banking business had seen service in the Regular Army Infantry in the Philippines and elsewhere. When we entered the war he was selected by Mr. Davison to take charge of the Red Cross work in France, but after spending about six months abroad he sought active service with the Army. Major Murphy showed the universal spirit of the men of West Point. Almost without exception those who had gone into civil life returned to the Army during the war and both in the United States and abroad did their part along with other graduates in upholding the high traditions of their Alma Mater.

The necessity for controlling the use of strong drink among our troops had been brought forcibly to my attention through the ease with which alcoholic beverages could be obtained. The use of light wines as a part of the French ration was simply the continuance in the army of the universal custom of the people of having wine with their meals. The wines and beer were not so objectionable, but strong alcoholic spirits were regarded by the French themselves as dangerous and were prohibited to their troops. The prohibition was not well enforced, however, outside the Zone of the Armies.

The problem of controlling the sale to our troops by the French of the stronger liquors was difficult, especially at the ports of entry. Efforts to obtain enforcement through conferences with local authorities and through agreements with the port and district officials were made from time to time, but with little result. I finally appealed to M. Clemenceau for support, but he would only counsel local officials, as he did not wish to declare a "state of siege." In the end it was necessary to take the matter into our own hands and declare every bar and restaurant where the heavy liquor was sold as "off limits" for our troops. Our officers were directed to give their personal attention to the enforcement of this order, which is quoted in part as follows:

"Commanding officers at all places where our troops may be located will confer with the local French authorities and use every endeavor to limit to the lowest possible number the places where intoxicants are sold. It is desired that these authorities be assisted in locating non-licensed resorts, which should be reported immediately to the proper authority for necessary action.

"Soldiers are forbidden either to buy or accept as gifts from inhabitants whiskey, brandy, champagne, liquors or other alcoholic beverages other than light wines or beer. The gift or retail of these (stronger beverages) by inhabitants in the zone of the army is forbidden by French law. Commanding officers will see that all drinking places where alcoholic liquors named above are sold are designated 'Off Limits' (for American troops) and the necessary means adopted to prevent soldiers visiting them."

My most earnest thought and attention were given to this subject early in our experience and throughout the war. The habit of drinking was not only detrimental to efficiency but it often led to other indiscretions. It is a question whether under

ordinary circumstances in times of peace a healthy moral sentiment cannot be created as a safeguard against excesses, yet during
the war when men were not surrounded by the restraining
influences of home life limited prohibition was necessary. Even
though it had been possible of enforcement, I should not have
issued orders to our armies prohibiting the use of light wines
or beer. Armies are simply a cross-section of the people whom
they represent and their psychology is the same, and any attempt
to enforce such an order would have led to difficulties. Furthermore, coöperation by the French to that extent would have been
out of the question. There was in fact comparatively little drinking in our armies and what there was decreased noticeably after
the prohibition of strong drink.

About this time a cable was received from Washington saying
that some publication at home had made a sweeping charge of
both immorality and drunkenness against our men. No such
statement could be based on fact or could serve any purpose except to cause unnecessary anxiety to parents and relatives, and
perhaps satisfy on the part of some one an unworthy desire for
sensation. My reply, which showed the character of our army and
the kind of lives the men were leading, was as follows:

"January 21, 1918.
"Reference your cablegram 643, paragraph 8, there has never been
a similar body of men to lead as clean lives as our American soldiers
in France. They have entered this war with the highest devotion
to duty and with no other idea than to perform these duties in the
most efficient manner possible. They fully realize their obligations
to their own people, their friends, and the country. A rigid program of instruction is carried out daily with traditional American
enthusiasm. Engaged in healthy, interesting exercises in the open
air, with simple diet, officers and men like trained athletes are ready
for their task. Forbidden the use of strong drink and protected by
stringent regulations against sexual evils and supported by their own
moral courage, their good behavior is the subject of most favorable
comment, especially by our Allies. American mothers may rest assured that their sons are a credit to them and the nation, and they
may well look forward to the proud day when on the battlefield these
splendid men will shed a new luster on American manhood."

(Diary) Paris, Thursday, January 10, 1918. Have appointed Major Robert Bacon to be Colonel and A.D.C. on my staff. Bishop L. H. Gwynne, Deputy Chaplain General, British Army, and Bishop Charles H. Brent were my guests at Chaumont on Monday. Went over aviation matters with Foulois, Bolling, and Dodd.

On Tuesday Brent and I discussed increase in number of chaplains, which we both favor. Left for Paris same evening.

Began discussion with Robertson and Maclay[1] yesterday morning about shipment of troops. Robertson and I went with Atterbury, Nash, and Maclay for conference with Claveille in afternoon on use of certain ports for large liners. Had talk with M. Clemenceau, again urging concessions as to berths and port control. Cabled request for rapid shipment of railway cars, 30,000 short.

Resumed discussion with Robertson to-day. Talked with M. Maurice Ganne about his work with the Committee on Franco-American Relations.

Bishop Brent had been selected by me for appointment as Chaplain with a view to his being the Chief of the Chaplain Corps which it was planned to organize. The Bishop did not approve of this idea and in deference to his opinion, and upon his suggestion, a permanent executive committee of chaplains was appointed to study the problems involved and to make recommendations direct to me from time to time. To assist us in organizing the work of our chaplains, Bishop Gwynne, Deputy Chaplain General of the British forces, kindly visited us and explained their methods of control and direction of the chaplains' work, and from their system we adopted such features as were applicable to our service.

Custom in our army, arising from lack of proper appreciation of the important duties of chaplains, had often relegated them to the status of handy men who were detailed to write up boards of survey or operate libraries. It can be said, however, that most chaplains, even in the face of such discouragement, continued in their efforts to fulfill their religious functions. I recall a visit of inspection to one of the regimental camps on the Mexican border before the war, where a most worthy chaplain who had been with me in Mindanao was stationed. Remaining over Sunday, I went

[1] Sir Joseph Maclay was a British expert on shipping.

to the large tent where he was to hold services, expecting to find an audience such as formerly assembled to hear him. As he had been very popular in the Philippine Islands and was noted for his attentions to the sick and wounded during our campaigns, I was greatly surprised to find that my aide and I constituted his congregation. But this attitude changed during the World War and chaplains were generally highly respected, many of them winning the esteem and affection of their units.

In recommending an increase in the number of chaplains, my reason was that I regarded recognition of the value of religious influence among our troops during the war as of special importance. Many temptations confronted our soldiers abroad and it seemed to me that the presence, the example, and the counsel of chaplains of the right sort would exert an excellent moral effect, especially among men without experience away from home. In recommending the increase of chaplains, I sent the Secretary of War the following cablegram:

"January 17, 1918.

"In the fulfillment of its duty to the nation much is expected of our army and nothing should be left undone that will help in keeping it in the highest state of efficiency. I believe the personnel of the army has never been equalled and the conduct has been excellent, but to overcome entirely the conditions found here requires fortitude born of great moral courage and lofty spiritual ideals. Counting myself responsible for the welfare of our men in every respect, it is my desire to surround them with the best influences possible. In the fulfillment of this solemn trust, it seems wise to request the aid of churchmen from home. To this end it is recommended that the number of chaplains in the army be increased for the war to an average of three per regiment. * * * Men selected should be of the highest character with reputations well established as sensible, practical, active ministers or workers, accustomed to dealing with young men. * * * "

This recommendation was approved by the Secretary of War and later enacted into law.

Aviation questions demanded unremitting attention, for in no other service was unpreparedness so evident and so difficult to overcome. Apparently there was earnest effort at home, but it was too often misdirected. The manufacture of airplanes was very uncertain, partly because of indecision as to types, and largely through inexperience in construction. In the A.E.F., differences of opinion and the consequent lack of coöperation among aviation officers upon whom rested the task of organization and training caused confusion and loss of time. The Allies, especially the French, had received a setback in their production program due to the lack of mechanics and the delay in procuring motors and other material, notably spruce. On account of these conditions and their own increased programs, the French and the Italians would not take more than a small proportion of our 1,500 flying cadets who were on the ground, and who, under agreement, were to be instructed by them.

The French Government claimed to be unable to meet its obligations to us owing to the delay in receiving machine tools and raw materials, besides mechanics, motors and spruce. The contract made with us in August was therefore formally abrogated, a possibility which had been forecast in my cables to the War Department. In its stead we later made an agreement whereby the French would provide us with airplanes according to the number of divisions we might have in France.

It developed a few days later that General Pétain had something to do with the decision of the Minister of Munitions regarding airplanes for us. The French program was then being greatly enlarged due to the increased air activity on the part of the enemy. It also appeared that after three years and a half of war the combined aircraft production capacity of the Allies was behind that of the Germans. Pétain was afraid that his armies might run short of planes and had intervened.

He realized our situation, but said that it was necessary to consider the needs of his aviation, which was actually employed, before making provision for us. He thought that by the time we should be ready to put our troops in line the rate of production could be increased so that we might have our due proportion. I suggested that if the French manufacturers were allowed to fulfill their contract with us our aviation would then be ready for service with the French armies, if necessary. But Pétain thought the manufacturers had undertaken more than they could do and that the output should be held as available where most needed. He said that the destruction of French planes had been very great and that it would be a considerable strain on the production capacity of their factories to furnish replacements of losses during the coming year. As I recall it, the replacements were something like 25 per cent per month.

Thus it was impossible to obtain assurance of any fixed number of planes until later when the necessity for the assistance of our aviation became urgent.

Early in December I signed an agreement with Lord Northcliffe, of the British Air Board, that we should send 15,000 enlisted men to England and maintain that number in training in their aircraft factories and air service stations. This plan proved beneficial to both sides, so far as carried out, but especially to ourselves, in providing us with trained men, and saving us the necessity of establishing extra schools. Due to the non-arrival of air personnel from home we were unable to furnish the full number as planned. We still lacked 4,500 men when the need for line troops arose and prevented the completion of our part of the agreement.

The urgency of radical steps to improve the port situation impelled me to lay the whole matter in detail before M. Clemenceau. He promised to do everything possible to correct those things that depended upon his action and asked me for a memorandum of suggestions and recommendations. I sent him a letter including the following summary of remedial action needed, stating that the conditions had been presented to the Ministry of Public Works by myself and by my representatives on several occasions, and that the results so far were unsatisfactory:

"1. That the French Government turn over docks and warehouses at St. Nazaire to A.E.F.

"2. That every berth that can be spared at all ports be placed under control of A.E.F.

"3. That facilities be increased for the quick handling of cargo from transports.

"4. That all available storage space be set apart for our use.

"5. That the most competent and reliable French officers be selected for command of ports.

"6. That certain ports be placed under 'martial law' in order to enforce regulations that will expedite our work."

While no formal reply was received, the number of berths was increased, additional storage was provided, and several changes were made in the French officers on duty at the ports.

When General Robertson came for a conference regarding the shipment of troops for training with the British, he brought along General Nash and Sir Joseph Maclay. As a preliminary, we discussed the general subject of expediting shipments by the use of additional French ports of entry as a means of shortening the time for the round trip. The suggestion that we might send some of the deep-draft vessels to Southampton had been made by Sir Douglas Haig when I saw him at Montreuil, the idea being that ships had to go there for coal, anyway. If used as a port of debarkation our troops could be taken from there across the Channel by the British to ports they were using, and be billeted behind their lines. It was proposed that some shipping other than deep draft might also be sent to Southampton instead of Bordeaux and Brest. Cherbourg and Lorient were also considered as possible ports of debarkation.

Generals Robertson and Nash thought it would be safer to discharge our ships at French ports, and that such a plan would avoid transporting baggage as well as men across the Channel if extra ports, especially Brest, could be made available. So the three of us and General Atterbury called upon M. Claveille, the Minister of Public Works, and made the suggestion, only to find that in the opinion of the French the naval docks at Brest were not suitable for large liners, but that Cherbourg might be available. Later on, when shipments became heavy, necessity compelled the use of both Brest and Cherbourg.

When we began to discuss the details of the disposition to be made of American troops which might be brought over in British shipping, it was found that General Robertson's proposal was practically the same as the one submitted to Mr. House through Mr. Lloyd George. He wanted to bring our infantry and machine gun units by battalions only and pointed out how much more expeditiously this would meet the shortage of men in the British Army than to ship whole divisions with all their equipment and stores. He said he did not wish to interfere with our program of building up an independent army, but thought that if we would agree to let them have as many as 100,000 or 150,000 men in addition to the complete divisions necessary for our army they could find the shipping to carry them. He believed that the British Government would take the risk of releasing temporarily some shipping engaged in carrying food and raw materials if America could see her way to provide the men, although, he said, it could not well undertake the transportation of complete divisions, as not enough men would be brought over in this manner to justify the great risks involved.

The question of drafting our men as individuals was mentioned, but the difficulties of discipline and the total loss of their identity were insuperable objections. The British really proposed two plans: one, suggested by General Robertson, which contemplated that our battalions should be assigned to their divisions and be absorbed; and the other, by Field Marshal Haig, under which they should successively enter selected British units which would eventually become American. General Robertson said that unless we could furnish manpower to build up their divisions there was the possibility of the British reaching such an exhausted condition by the severe fighting in prospect that the Allies would have a very heavy task in winning the war.

The arguments General Robertson advanced clearly indicated that the British were playing for advantage to themselves in offering to transport our troops. In other words, they had the shipping to transport American battalions on condition that they would serve in the British armies. Their purpose was to build up their own units instead of aiding the cause in general by augmenting the number of complete combat divisions on the Western Front.

The question that naturally arose in my mind was that if tonnage was available for this purpose, why had it not been offered to us some time before, or, indeed, why not at that very moment. If the broad view had prevailed that our forces would add just that much to the strength of the Allies, they could have provided additional shipping quite as well before as after the crisis in March. We could then have brought several more divisions to France and had them prepared to go into the line much earlier than was otherwise possible. And it is conceivable that they might have been able to prevent the disasters that came to the British in March and to the French in May. But, of course, the British were not thinking in terms of an American army at all.

However, as General Robertson's proposal would enable us to increase our strength more rapidly, my preliminary cable to Washington reporting the conference recommended that it be given consideration and that if approved the plan should be regarded as a temporary measure to meet an emergency; that as soon as possible the remaining troops of our divisions should be brought over and the units reassembled; that division, brigade, and regimental commanders and their staffs be sent with their infantry for training with the corresponding British units, and that the infantry be taken from those divisions that would not otherwise be transported until after June.

The arrangement proposed by Robertson, if adopted, was not to interfere in any way with our program for bringing our troops in our own tonnage as already planned. My cable suggested we should insist that the British Government continue to provide as many men for their armies as possible, and that it would be pertinent for our Government to inquire just what the British proposed to do to keep up their own forces. I feared that should we make this concession the tendency would be for them to relax and let the burden of keeping up their strength fall on us, to the detriment of preparations for building up our own army later on.

In a telegram to General Robertson, I set forth the report of our conversation which I had cabled the War Department, and further stated that it was of the utmost importance that the British Government should exert every energy to keep up its own manpower. I requested a full statement from him as to British resources, including the men then available and to become so during the year, in order that we might have all the facts before making a final decision on his proposition. In reply, General Robertson sent me the following data in a letter dated January 17th:

"The British Government has given the most anxious consideration to the question of the maintenance of the armies in the field during 1918 and, by making every effort, there will become available for service at the front 449,000 men now under training, plus 100,000 to be called up. In addition there will be called up 100,000 men of lower category who are not fit for the first line, plus 120,000 lads of 18 years of age, who will not be available for service at the front till 1919. Please keep these figures strictly secret."

Nothing further was done toward an agreement until a week or so later, when conversations were resumed.

(Diary) Chaumont, Tuesday, January 15, 1918. Visited Pétain on Friday to discuss further the details of putting divisions in line.

Went to Versailles Saturday and reviewed military situation with Generals Sir Henry Wilson, Cadorna, and Weygand, and Mr. Frazier.

Returned here Sunday, bringing Dawes, Harjes, and M. Van de Vyvere, the Belgian Minister of Finance. Belgians have agreed, upon Dawes' representations, to turn over 300 idle locomotives for the French and ourselves. Sent cable regarding the President's speech before Congress.

Shortage of forage causing serious loss of animals. Lord Derby, British War Minister, proposes conference on land transportation on Western Front. Liaison officers reorganized under Major H. H. Harjes. Had visiting Generals J. Franklin Bell and T. H. Barry to dinner this evening; also M. Charles de Chambrun, who goes to Washington for duty at French Embassy.

Have organized I Corps Headquarters under Major General Liggett, with Colonel Craig as Chief of Staff.

This meeting with Pétain was gratifying in its results, in view of the rather radical differences in our views during the verbal and written discussions of training, which have already been mentioned in a previous chapter. The assignment of our divisions for training with the French was settled as to time and place and it was agreed that our general officers and their staffs should have every opportunity for experience. It was also understood that toward April or May we should take over a portion of the front and occupy it as the American sector. When advised of the conversation with Robertson regarding the amalgamation of American troops with the British, he saw no objection, but regretted that it could not be done with the French also.

To meet the need for replacements in their units, I consented to send temporarily to the French four colored Infantry regiments of the 93d Division. Some of the units had arrived, and others were expected soon to be en route, but they did not have in France even the beginning of a brigade or divisional organization. One regiment was to go to each of four divisions, with the provision that they were to be returned for the formation of the 93d Division when called for. Unfortunately, they soon became identified with the French and there was no opportunity to assemble them as an American division. Very much to my regret these regiments never served with us, but it was gratifying later to hear of their being highly commended by the French.

Our forage supply at this time was entirely inadequate, even for the small number of animals, amounting to about 21,000, then in service. Over a month had passed since the Quartermaster General's office at Washington had promised that the shipment of ninety days' supply would commence at once and be completed within thirty days. The actual situation is set forth in the following extract from my cable:

"January 12, 1918.
"35 per cent of the animals have been on less than half rations of oats for 10 days and also on short rations of hay and some have died from starvation. This, combined with the severe winter weather * * * with the temperature frequently below zero, has caused con-

siderable suffering and decreased vitality among our animals, while, due to the extreme shortage, * * * all transportation has to be worked to its full capacity. French * * * say that their forage crop is short so that we are unable to purchase any forage from them and all that is borrowed must be replaced as rapidly as possible. Advise what shipments are now actually en route and whether the flow of forage can be depended upon."

The problem of Allied rail transportation on the Western Front was brought up in a letter from Lord Derby, who said that the British War Cabinet considered it advisable to review the question with special reference to probable future operations as affected by the mobility of the Allied armies in the field. The rail facilities in France constituted a vital factor in the military situation. The recent movement of French and British troops to Italy had interfered with the railroad service in France by temporarily using a considerable amount of rolling stock, and the possibilities of heavy demands in the spring were causing much concern. At the time no organization existed to which the Inter-Allied Military Staff at Versailles could refer for an opinion as to the feasibility of large movements of Allied troops. So a committee was formed to study the question, General Nash, representing the British, and General Atterbury the Americans.

It was a pleasure to meet both Generals Bell and Barry again and to find them so deeply interested in all they had seen. It was well known that General Bell was and had been for some years in poor health, in fact he spent some time in the hospital while in France. The Chief Surgeon reported him to be wholly unfit physically for active service, and later General Barry was found physically disqualified also. I regretted to lose their services, as both of them would have taken high positions in the A.E.F.

The speech of the President before Congress on January 8th created a profound impression in Europe and was the subject of discussion in all Allied circles. It was eagerly read and its commitment of the American people to the principles of justice was evidently its high inspiration. I tried to convey the sentiment of the A.E.F. in the following cablegram to the Secretary:

"Speaking for our armies in Europe, may I extend to the President our extreme satisfaction upon his masterly declaration of the great fundamental principles of justice in international relations for which our people stand and for which our army and the armies of the Allies must fight to the end. This clear presentation of those principles will be the army's inspiration and its guide. To battle for them is the highest privilege that could be accorded to men. We pledge him everything that is in us that we may see these ideals prevail. May Divine Providence give us direction and determination that our country may be proud of the sacrifices we are more than ever willing to make."

To keep the Secretary advised on conditions and possibly clear up certain questions, I sent him the following letter:

"January 17, 1918.
"Dear Mr. Secretary:

"There are several matters that have been the subject of cables that can be made clearer by writing. One of them is differences we have had with the French on the subject of training.

"When the 1st Division arrived in its training area, the French kindly placed a division nearby to aid in instruction. Through association, the French officers and soldiers and our own became cordial and the spirit of fraternity has been passed on to succeeding divisions. This training alongside the French was limited mainly to the specialties of trench warfare and, under the then division commander, it was left almost wholly to the direction of the French. Their method was mainly to give demonstrations: that is, they went over and over their trench exercises while our platoons, companies and battalions were usually only observers. They failed to realize that for us at least it was necessary that officers commanding their own units should work out problems for themselves instead of remaining mere imitators.

"Another point of difference was as to tactical value of open warfare. We have held that our young officers lacked experience in handling their units in the open, and that a knowledge of the methods of trench warfare was not enough to prepare them for the important duties of commanding units where there was a possibility of open warfare. I have spent much time myself explaining that our company officers must have training in handling units in open attack and defense, and that they must be thoroughly schooled in the principles of what we call 'minor tactics.' The French have taken the opposite view and have held that our officers did not need that training now. Notwithstanding that many instances in both British and French experience prove the contrary, the French are very firm in their view. They are just a little bit inclined to hold themselves superior in the art of war to both the British and ourselves, and that does not always set very well.

"So finally they criticized us, not only to their war office, but General Pétain commented on our methods rather hastily to Mr. House and also to General Bliss. I explained our position to both these gentlemen, adding that I myself had studied, and had required as thorough study as possible by our officers of both French and British methods and experience and had endeavored to select and adopt the best. Naturally it would be quite impossible for us to adopt French tactics throughout. That we must retain our basic principles is agreed to by all officers experienced in training our troops. As we have used the French example less, following more our own ideas of requiring men to think for themselves, and learn practically the principles applicable both to open and trench warfare, the French hastily concluded that we were not progressing.

"This was the main cause of the feeling. As M. Clemenceau was very anxious for harmony, he rather exaggerated the thing in his own mind. I later explained my view to him, as I did also to General Pétain, who saw the force of my position and frankly said so. However, in the course of these discussions and correspondence, it developed that the French were really hoping to have our units amalgamated for service with theirs, with the special object in mind of their not being compelled to reduce the number of their divisions. This was hidden away under the insistence upon taking over our training. Of course we realize that the French are short of men, but, except in a temporary emergency, differences in language and methods would make the combination for actual fighting quite out of the question. In my recent discussions with them, I have made that point clear, and they seemed to have accepted it, so we had but to settle the question of training.

"In the end, my conferences with M. Clemenceau and General Pétain have resulted in what now seems to be a very satisfactory understanding. It has been agreed, then, that we should go on as in the past, aided by French instructors and a more limited number of French units, following such courses of training as we should prescribe, and that later, our regiments should go into French divisions, posted in a quiet sector, for experience in the trenches, the generals and staff officers to have service with corresponding grades and commands in French units. This duty with the French divisions is to be for training only and when finished the elements of our divisions are to be reunited under our own officers. I think the plan is the very best that we could adopt and the French seem equally satisfied. A few days ago I had a very cordial telegram from M. Clemenceau expressing his gratification that an agreement had been reached.

"The question of getting our men over as rapidly as possible is being emphasized by both our allies in France. The British have, as you know, made an offer to transport a number of battalions for service with their divisions. This has already been made the subject of considerable cable correspondence with which you are familiar. Although in serving with the British we should not have differences in language to contend with, the sticking point of the thing is service under another flag. If human beings were pawns it would be different, but they are our own men and we should therefore study carefully our national sentiment and the attitude of our army and the people toward the proposition. Generally speaking the army would be opposed to it, officers and all, but really the question presented is, can we afford not to send over extra men to help our allies in what may be an emergency when the necessary extra sea transportation is offered and we have the spare men. As already cabled, there is less difficulty in sending over men than material, and men will probably be needed before the material can be obtained and men trained to use it. If we agree to this, we must insist upon our men being returned when called for, or at least when we get over the remainder of the organizations from which they may be taken, and, besides, we must insist that the British and French both do their utmost until we can come in with a well organized and well trained force large enough to count. We must look forward to bearing a very heavy part in this conflict before it ends, and our forces should not be dissipated except for a temporary emergency. Moreover, it is unnecessary to say, when the war ends, our position will be stronger if our army acting as such shall have played a distinct and definite part. I have set this out in more or less detail in the dispatches, so shall leave it.

"Just a word as to the railroad situation. As our forces increase, the shortage of freight cars becomes more serious. The French management of railroads is very badly demoralized. They lack men in responsible positions and are very short of operators and laborers. For these reasons we have had trouble in getting men and supplies forward, but these conditions are now improving. With the Belgian locomotives now being put into shape, and an increase in the number of men to repair cars we shall be able to keep ahead of transportation requirements. There are thousands of cars in France that are out of repair, and to repair these and put them in operation will not only expedite matters, but will save much tonnage that can be devoted to something else.

"As stated in my cables, port conditions are much confused, accommodations are limited, material for construction arrives slowly and the procurement of ballast has been difficult. The lack of rail facilities has added to the difficulties, as has the inability of the Navy to convoy vessels to ports where they could find accommodations. All this has caused very great delay in getting transports back. The Navy now agrees to send vessels where we want them, and we have solved the ballast question for the time being. The French still hold control of the ports, notwithstanding their agreement (made by a former ministry) to give us increased, if not absolute control. This was once promised as to St. Nazaire, but has not been carried out. There are so many petty French officers, * * * and we find ourselves often interfered with and delayed by them. I have recently again represented the situation plainly in a strong appeal to M. Clemenceau, and I believe we are in a fair way to get it straightened out. So the situation is improving and promises to improve still further.

"According to cables, there has been some move made in Washington by the Engineer Corps to put the engineers back in control of our railroads here. This would be the greatest kind of a mistake. We now have experienced railroad men in charge of the Railway Transportation Department, and to my mind it would be next to fatal to give it over to engineers to run. None of them has ever had experience in railroading, and all would have to learn the business from the bottom up. As this ordinarily takes a lifetime, I should not think of changing back to their management.

"Coming back to Allied relations, I have succeeded in bringing about a meeting between Sir Douglas Haig, General Pétain and myself. We shall be at Compiègne, French General Headquarters, on Saturday night of the 19th instant. It would be unfair to say that there has been any lack of cordiality between us, or any disinclination to meet together, but it has rather been because each has had his hands full, which all have understood. But the fact remains that we have never met together and observers among the Allies have been inclined to think there might be some other reason for it than the actual one.

"Prompted by my suggestion, no doubt, a meeting of the three commanders-in-chief, together with Generals Robertson and Foch, is planned for next week. In conversation with both M. Clemenceau and General Robertson I dwelt strongly upon the urgency of a complete and harmonious military understanding among the Allied armies on the Western Front, especially as to plans of operation for the spring and summer, and am gratified to record the above as an indication of full accord with this view. I have asked General Foch to hold this meeting here at my headquarters, and think this will be done.

"It is to be noted that General Bliss is to be continued on the active list. I presume you have found his visit here made him very valuable. Moreover, I am not so sure that it would be safe to change now anyway. If you should decide to keep him there, as I think possible, then may I again mention General Liggett as a possibility for the Supreme War Council, if he should be available when the time comes? He once had the War College and I think would be able to give a good account of himself and render valuable assistance to us. I shall be glad if General March can be allowed to remain here to handle the army artillery.

"The Supreme War Council seems to be busy at work on various studies, although its status as yet is not very clearly defined. The opinion generally prevails that its function is only that of an advisory body, although it is credited with having a certain political aspect. There seems little probability of a Supreme War Commander being selected, nor, as I am informed, is it generally favored, especially by members of the Council. All the Allies want concerted action, of course, but for the present thorough understanding and close liaison between the high commands appear to be the only solution.

"May I again, Mr. Secretary, suggest to you the advisability of making a visit to France. Beside being profitable to see the procedure from this point of view, it would give a new inspiration to the Allies and would especially encourage our own forces.

"Begging your pardon for the length of this letter, and extending to you renewed expressions of high esteem and sincere regard, I remain

"Very faithfully yours,

"JOHN J. PERSHING."

With the growth of our armies and the consequent greater need for port and rail accommodations, our situation threatened an early crisis not entirely indicated in my letter to the Secretary.

CHAPTER XXI

Difficulties with Railways—Poor French Management—Conference Commanders-in-Chief and Chiefs of Staff—Defensive Attitude Decided—Joffre against Amalgamation—British Accept my Plan—Meeting Supreme War Council—Outlook and Conclusions—Supreme War Council Decides on Reserve—Letter to Secretary of War—Winter in France

(Diary) Paris, Monday, January 21, 1918. Discussed the whole subject of schools and training on Friday with Training Section. Left Chaumont that night for Paris.

Went to Compiègne Saturday to meet General Pétain and Field Marshal Haig. We dined with Pétain; discussion general.

Reports of conference with Sims' office yesterday indicate more rapid provision of escort for returning transports.

Went with Atterbury again to-day to see M. Claveille about rail transportation. Called with Foulois on Minister of Munitions. As the French fear shortage in artillery ammunition, have given authority for them to draw on our stock.

THE control of French rail transportation was so thoroughly centered in M. Claveille, that he had become autocratic in his methods and in his attitude toward all with whom he had to deal. He was unwilling to permit us any freedom in the operation of trains or turn over to us any fixed amount of rolling stock, or promise that any given amount would be placed at our disposal, even under French management. The British had met with the same difficulty, although by persistent effort they had eventually received satisfactory concessions as to operation.

Up to this time only a limited number of trains had been allotted to our use and these at such irregular intervals that our service was more or less haphazard. We were confronted with an increasing demand for rail transportation which the French did not seem to appreciate. In their own way they appeared to be making an effort to aid us, but Claveille undertook to keep track of every detail of operation, even to the allotment of each piece of transportation to this or that use, and we were left in a continuous state of uncertainty. He would not believe that there could be any method better than that of the French, which we regarded as antiquated. As there were nearly enough damaged or lost cars and engines here and there throughout France to supply our needs if they could only be located and put in order, I offered to send experts to assist in finding them.

With the object of obtaining control over our own movements of trains, with our own railway organization, General Atterbury and I had already made several visits to M. Claveille's office. On the visit mentioned in the diary, I asked that authority at ports, in so far as rail transportation and port management were concerned, be concentrated in one official, to which he agreed, although it was not done for some time. He also promised, as he had done before, better coöperation in furnishing cars. We proposed that the French should turn over to us a fixed number of engines and cars, and let us run them ourselves, but Claveille was obdurate and would not make this concession. It finally became necessary to take the matter up with M. Clemenceau himself before we got any consideration of this suggestion, but some time elapsed before our men were running trains, except a daily train between Chaumont and Tours.

(Diary) Paris, Thursday, January 24, 1918. Went to Chaumont on Tuesday. Made arrangements yesterday for 26th Division to go into quiet sector with the French near Soissons on February 5th.

Returned to Paris this morning. Conference looking to better understanding and closer coöperation held at Compiègne to-day. Field Marshal Haig, Generals Pétain, Foch, Robertson, Pershing, and Chiefs of Staff in the field, Generals Lawrence and Anthoine, and Colonel Boyd were present. Had dinner with General Bliss, who has returned from Washington to be our military representative on the Supreme War Council.

Every one in authority realized that all resources the Allies could muster would be required to meet successfully the great offensive of the Central Powers expected in the spring, but to use them effectively close coöperation among commanders would be imperative. It was with this in mind that I proposed to M. Clemenceau that the Commanders-in-Chief and Chiefs of Staff should get together to examine the situation and if possible determine a general program of combined action. He thought that would be a good thing to do and at once approved the suggestion. It was also favorably received by General Foch, who, it will be recalled, was Chief of the French General Staff. I proposed that the meeting be held at my headquarters, but the French selected Compiègne, Pétain's G.H.Q.

At the meeting, Robertson spoke first and suggested that we ought to have a general statement on the following points: (1) Mutual support between Allied armies; (2) Situation as to reserves; (3) Question of troops in Italy; (4) Situation as to the transportation of the American Army and facilities given it in France.

Pétain thought that for the present the Allies would be forced to remain on the defensive on account of lack of men. He said that the French Army had ninety-seven divisions with an infantry strength of from 5,000 to 6,000 men each, some thirty-odd of these divisions being in reserve and the rest in the trenches; besides eight cavalry divisions, two of which were dismounted and six mounted. All divisions, he thought, could be kept up until April if there should be no fighting, but later on, even without a battle, he would have to break up five divisions in order to maintain the others. The six mounted cavalry divisions would have to be reduced to four, and before the end of the year the total force would have to be reduced by twenty divisions.

Assuming that the Allies must remain on the defensive, he was prepared, he said, to retire to successive lines. He explained that the French had organized counteroffensive operations on four army fronts, to be utilized according to circumstances, with a force of about fifteen divisions in each one, and that he would be ready to transport available reserves by rail either to relieve tired troops or assist in the defense of any threatened front. The French reserves would be at the disposition of Sir Douglas Haig and he expected a similar arrangement to be made by the British.

The reserves, he said, were so located that they could be started in any direction within twelve hours.

Sir Douglas said the British had adopted the same policy as the French, one-third of their divisions being in reserve and the rest in line; that he had three lines of resistance; and that he had prepared three different localities for offensive actions of about five divisions each, one in the direction of Gonnelieu, the second toward Lens, and the third in the vicinity of Gheluvelt-Becelaere.

Foch declared that the best means of halting a strong and persistent offensive was a powerful counteroffensive and he thought that we should draw some lessons from the experience of 1916. At that time, he said, an offensive had been prepared by the Allies on the Somme, which was delayed by the unexpected German attack on Verdun. He added, "The German offensive at Verdun was stopped not by our resistance there but by our offensive on the Somme. Such an operation is possible only when foreseen and prepared beforehand. * * * In planning for the counteroffensive, I think," he continued, "that the entire front must be considered as a whole and not the French as one part and the British as another. The plan must envisage them together preparing for offensive action on a common battlefield with all the forces at their disposal."

Pétain said the situation was different from what it was at the time of the battle of Verdun and that there "the Germans attacked only at one point, with only 125 divisions at their disposal; now they will have 170, 180, or possibly 200 divisions, and they can attack at three points at once or successively, and at each point the attack can be more violent than at Verdun. * * * When they attack at one point," he asked, "should we then launch a counterattack?" Answering his own question, he said, "We cannot prepare such a counterattack because we shall not know where the enemy is going to strike and we must be ready with some reserves to meet it. We must be very prudent."

Foch remarked that one could not fix the moment of attack beforehand and declared that the counteroffensive launched on the Somme, to which he had referred, had been prepared long before, otherwise it could not have taken place. He did not favor these small counterattacks but thought we should look forward to a grand offensive action with all possible force,—French, British, and American. Pétain stated that he agreed in principle, but added that the suppression of twenty divisions would leave them without available troops for an offensive.

Robertson declared that it was not certain that the enemy would attack in so many places at once and that it did not seem possible to do more than prepare to support the army that might be attacked, and be ready to counterattack. "Anyway," he said, "one could not win the war by remaining on the defensive," and he then inquired of Foch how and where one ought to prepare for this counteroffensive.

Foch said he had not been charged with studying a combined counteroffensive and could not tell where the principle would be applicable, but it would be necessary for us to prepare for a great offensive together. Robertson expressed accord with Foch, but he did not see where or with what means such an offensive could be executed, and again stated that the war could not be won by remaining on the defensive.

Haig said, "Give us back the troops from Salonika and we will commence offensives." Foch replied, "We were not speaking of offensives but of counteroffensives." Robertson remarked that of course the French and British could reënforce each other and make counterattacks, and then asked, "Could they do more than that?" Pétain spoke up and said, "Not without the Americans." Robertson then said, "I think our only hope lies in American reserves," and he wanted to hear from me.

I stated that but few of the Allied authorities seemed to realize that our participation would depend upon the amount of shipping available for the transportation of our troops, and that the time when Americans would be needed was near at hand. As there had been some reference to amalgamation, I also took occasion to emphasize the point that we expected as a matter of course that the American Army would have its own front as an independent force and would not be used merely as a reserve to be sent here and there. One insuperable reason, I said, why we could not amalgamate with the French was the difference in language, and added that we would not use our troops in that way at all unless it became absolutely necessary.

I then discussed our problems, calling attention to the delays at the French ports and our shortage of rail transportation, and touched on the backward state of procurement of equipment, munitions, and airplanes. They all appeared surprised to learn of our difficulties, especially General Foch, although, even as Chief of the General Staff, he apparently could not interfere in matters handled directly by the Ministry. It was astonishing to find how little comprehension any of them had of the enormous task that confronted us.

Foch said, "None of these questions has been referred to me," whereupon Pétain retorted that, "One should not wait until such things are brought to his attention but should look around and find them." Pétain added at once that he would send an official to study our situation. Haig later sent one of his officers, who offered many suggestions out of the British experience.

It was the sense of the conference that every assistance should be given us in getting our troops across, and all seemed fully to realize that no successful offensive could be undertaken without us.

The declarations of the French and British Commanders-in-Chief that the reserves of each were available for the use of the other could mean much or it could mean nothing, depending upon the conception of the situation that might confront each of them and also upon the relations that might exist between them at the time. In the light of their previous experience, it should have been apparent that the difficulties of securing the necessary close coöperation between these two Allied armies might lead to disaster. While the meeting was perhaps worth while, if only for an exchange of views and the conclusion that the Allies must remain on the defensive, yet no definite understanding was reached as to real unity of action and the conference had little more effect than the one held in the preceding August.

(Diary) Paris, Saturday, January 26, 1918. Prince Arthur of Connaught called on Friday and referred to our having met in 1906 in Tokyo, where he took part in the Fourth of July celebration at the American Legation. Conversations with Robertson continued, with Bliss present.

This afternoon Harbord, Boyd, and I called on Marshal Joffre. Have requested 2,400 men to repair cars and same number to repair locomotives. Tank Corps created with Colonel S. D. Rockenbach as Chief. Additional motor mechanics, stevedores, and material for port construction promised by War Department.

This meeting with Robertson took place in the evening at the Crillon Hotel. The same arguments were repeated in favor of incorporating American units into British divisions. My immediate interest lay mainly in getting additional tonnage for the transportation of our men to form our own army and it was not my intention at any time to agree to amalgamation in any permanent sense with either of the Allies. So far we were not committed to any such plan, but Bliss, who came into the conference under instructions from the Secretary of War, was much impressed with the British point of view and almost out of a clear sky frankly expressed himself in favor of the Robertson plan.

Of course, American troops behind the British Army, even temporarily, would be an encouragement to its morale, and if the emergency should arise they could actually be put into the fighting line, but to agree to the transfer of American battalions to build up British divisions could not be thought of. When Bliss spoke in favor of it, I was forced to declare myself then and there. My stand was not quite what Robertson had expected and the meeting was adjourned with the position of all concerned no longer in doubt.

General Bliss and I met later by appointment to talk the matter over between ourselves and if possible come to an understanding. After some discussion, he suggested that each of us cable his views to Washington and ask for a decision. It was not my policy then or at any other time to put anything up to Washington that I could possibly decide myself. This would have been the last thing to do in this case, especially as the Secretary had left in my hands the determination as to how our troops should be employed. For two men in our positions to have appealed in this way would have indicated a clash, and Washington had enough trouble; besides, the Secretary could not possibly have been in touch with the undercurrent of these negotiations. So I said, "Well, Bliss, do you know what would happen if we should do that? We would both be relieved from further duty in France and that is exactly what we should deserve." We then spent some time examining the question from all angles, until finally he came around to my view and said, "I think you are right and I shall back you up in the position you have taken."

During an informal visit to Marshal Joffre, on the 26th, I was gratified to hear him confirm my objections to amalgamation. He observed that with all the conferences that were being held I must be quite well occupied. In due course, the conversation drifted to military matters and, speaking of the French Army, he said the class of 1918 recruits was available and the class of 1919 would soon be called. He said the French were combing the country for what he called "Embusques," or slackers, all of which taken together he thought would obviate the necessity of reducing the French Army by more than three or four divisions, and then not until late in the year.

The view of Marshal Joffre was that the British were not in such good shape, and, as we knew, they were under the necessity of reducing the number of battalions in each division from twelve to nine. He said: "The British plan to bring over 150 battalions of Americans is no doubt for the purpose of building up their weakened divisions."

Launching into the question of amalgamation, and speaking as a friend of mine and also in the interests of the Allies, Marshal Joffre said, "It would be a mistake to incorporate American battalions in British divisions, as it would adversely affect the divisions," and that "orders might be given by a British general or his staff that would be resented by Americans, but the same orders would be accepted without question if given by an

American commander. In case of a reverse, there would be the tendency to place the blame on the Americans.

"Furthermore," he went on to say, "in case of an attack, your infantry would have to be supported by British artillery, and here again there might be differences." He did not believe it possible that there could exist between them that perfect confidence and liaison that was absolutely necessary between the infantry and artillery. As an indication that it was not a policy suggested by good practice and experience, he pointed out that during the whole course of the war the British had never found it advisable to incorporate Canadians, Australians, New Zealanders, Indians, Portuguese, or even Scotch, in the same divisions with English. "Then," he said, "you must consider the American people at home and their interest in and their support of the war, which would be adversely affected by amalgamation." He said that of course his views were given to me confidentially as an act of friendship. Here, then, was a distinguished French soldier who could see these questions in their true perspective without prejudice or bias.

In speaking of the threatened German offensive against the Western Front, Marshal Joffre said there were those who thought that the defection of Russia would enable the Germans to bring as many as 230 divisions against approximately 170 Allied divisions, but he did not agree with them. Such talk, he said, was causing much uneasiness among the French people not under arms, and he felt that it was a mistake to allow such statements to appear in the press. Some people thought that the Allies were going to be overwhelmed, but he was morally certain that such a thing could not happen.

As between 230 and 170 divisions, of course the discrepancy was great, but he thought that the Allies could hold, and anyway he did not believe such a discrepancy would exist. He expressed the view that the enemy would have not more than 190 divisions on the Western Front at the outside, and allowing the Allies 168 instead of 170 the difference was not enough to cause any doubt in our ability to hold them. He said that in 1914 the Germans had an excess of 300,000 men over the Allied 700,000 and a great preponderance of artillery, and they did not break the line, and he thought their chances less favorable now. He was discussing, he said, the probabilities as they existed at the moment, and although he mentioned the prospective arrival of two American divisions per month and evidently had them in mind, he did not include them in his estimate as to relative numbers on both sides.[1] In all this he said he did not want to appear as criticizing his Government, but he deprecated its attitude in permitting the people to be frightened by the stories of a heavy German offensive.

It was about this time that I met a distinguished Englishman, who took occasion to discuss the same subject, saying practically just what Marshal Joffre had said, and advising strongly against mixing nationalities. Not that there was a shadow of doubt in my mind as to the soundness of my attitude, yet coming as did these independent views just at the moment of apparently greatest pressure by nearly all of official France and Great Britain to force our hand on this question, they had considerable significance.

There were Allied officers very closely in touch with my headquarters who, although very careful in our presence, secretly advised their superiors to make every concession in order to get control of American units, with the idea that they would then be in position to use them in any manner they saw fit. Among these there was one British officer who suggested to his superiors that they should aid us ostentatiously in building up a corps, which he thought would quiet the American people, especially if we were permitted to wave the flag hard enough. Of course any such idea of domination as this, the existence of which we were well aware, only served to stiffen our attitude. It is probable that many of those who were in favor of amalgamation believed it best purely from the standpoint of haste in preparation. But there were also many who no doubt advocated the principle

---

[1] We then had five divisions in France, numerically equal to ten Allied divisions, but they were not all sufficiently trained for offensive action.

in order to prevent the ultimate formation of an independent American army.

(Diary) Paris, Wednesday, January 30, 1918. Accidental explosion of trench mortar the 27th at demonstration near French front injured Major General Leonard Wood and Lieutenant Colonel Charles E. Kilbourne slightly, Major Kenyon A. Joyce severely, and killed several French officers and soldiers.

Had a pleasant call by Captain Amundsen, the Arctic explorer, who is visiting our army. Saw Atterbury; urged him to insist on better railway service from French.

Talked over with Kernan on Monday reorganization of Line of Communications and pressed him to hasten construction of port facilities. Cabled request of French for forage, which is running low.

Bliss and I held conference at Versailles yesterday with Mr. Lloyd George, Lord Milner, Field Marshal Haig, General Robertson, and General Wilson on transportation and use of American troops.

Went to Versailles again to-day in fog extremely dense; lunched with Lloyd George, who accepted my proposal of yesterday.

Supreme War Council began its third session to-day.

Once General Bliss and I had reached an understanding as to what our attitude should be toward amalgamation, he gave me his support in later conferences. When we met the British representatives as indicated in the diary, they presented their case, reiterating previous arguments. Mr. Lloyd George then asked Bliss for his views, to which he replied, "Pershing will speak for us and whatever he says with regard to the disposition of the American forces will have my approval." I submitted a compromise program which Bliss had already seen and the British concluded to take it under advisement.

The following day, while we were en route to Versailles together, Bliss expressed some doubt whether they would accept. At the meeting, Mr. Lloyd George acknowledged that my objections to amalgamation were sound and told me that he had said so to his confrères the day before. An agreement was then signed by Mr. Lloyd George, General Maurice, and myself as set forth in the following copy of the memorandum submitted and later cabled to Washington:

"CONFIDENTIAL. "January 30, 1918.

* * * * * * *

"Following memorandum of our position was presented in conference between ourselves and British and was agreed upon. Memorandum has approval of General Bliss.

"A.—This memorandum refers to the request made by General Sir William Robertson, representing the British War Office, that the American Government send by British shipping to France 150 battalions of infantry for service in British divisions on the Western Front. Replying to this proposal, the following objections appear: 1st.—The national sentiment in the United States against service under a foreign flag; 2d.—The probability that such action by the United States would excite serious political opposition to the Administration in the conduct of the war; 3d.—The certainty of its being used by German propagandists to stir up public opinion (in the U.S.) against the war; 4th.—It would dissipate the direction and effort of the American Army; 5th.—Differences in national characteristics and military training of troops and consequent failure of complete coöperation would undoubtedly lead to friction and eventual misunderstanding between the two countries; 6th.—Additional manpower on the Western Front could be provided as quickly by some plan not involving amalgamation.

"B.—In order to meet the situation as presented by Sir William Robertson and hasten the arrival and training of troops, it is therefore proposed that the British Government use the available sea transportation in question for bringing over the personnel of entire divisions under the following conditions:—

"1. That the infantry and auxiliary troops of these divisions be trained with British divisions by battalions, under such plan as may be agreed upon.

"2. That the artillery be trained under American direction in the use of French matériel as at present.

"3. That the higher commanders and staff officers be assigned for training and experience with corresponding units of the British Army.

"4. That when sufficiently trained, these battalions be reformed into regiments and that when the artillery is fully trained, all the units comprising each division be united under their own officers for service.

"5. That the above plan be carried out without interference with the plans now in operation for bringing over American forces.

"6. That question of supply be arranged by agreement between the British and American Commanders-in-Chief.

"7. That question of arms and equipment be settled in similar manner."

A few days later the Secretary replied stating his views, as follows:

"We have no objections to the program which you suggested by the way of substitute in subparagraph of your 555 but in our judgment it would be wiser for the British to undertake to transport six complete divisions across the sea to be disposed of and trained as you direct, in conference of course with the commanding officers of the other forces."

Of course this was in accord with my views as stated in the proposal I made to the British and to which they agreed, except that the artillery pertaining to the divisions was not to be sent to the British but was to be trained under our own supervision. However, the fortunes of war intervened more than once to prevent adherence to plans and agreements.

(Diary) Paris, Saturday, February 2, 1918. The Supreme War Council in session the past three days.

Sir John Asser called on Thursday, sent by Haig; his experience on British lines of communication will enable him to give us valuable suggestions.

Called yesterday evening on Ambassador Sharp.

Have sent Colonel Logan, General Staff, G.H.Q., on special inspection of the Line of Communications to get better coöperation.

At the opening of the session of the Supreme War Council, Mr. Lloyd George spoke in some detail of the situation on the Allied fronts. He mentioned the large number of casualties the Allies had suffered during 1917 and in a very pointed manner declared that the costly offensives had produced no tangible results. Moreover, he said, the Allies now found themselves short of manpower at a crucial period of the war. His sharp criticism was evidently directed at Sir Douglas Haig and General Robertson, but neither was given an opportunity to reply.

NOTE: Total strength of the A.E.F. on January 31st, 12,785 officers, 203,003 enlisted men.

The Military Representatives presented a joint note with reference to military policy, as directed at the December meeting, and the opinion given was practically the same as that of the conference at Compiègne, on January 24th, and of the meeting in Paris in August. The note held the view that the campaign under General Allenby then in progress in Palestine should be continued. It will be recalled that these two informal conferences of Commanders-in-Chief had concluded that the Allies should remain on the defensive on all fronts until the Americans should arrive in sufficient force to warrant the offensive. The joint note was approved as the decision of the Council, with the understanding, as suggested by the French, that no white troops should be sent from France to Palestine. It was decidedly the opinion of M. Clemenceau, and of all others present who expressed themselves, that the war could not be ended until 1919, when the American Army, it was thought, would reach its maximum power.

Of our five divisions then in France, none would be ready for active service for two or three months. However, the prospect was that in addition to these we should have a few others ready by June, and by September possibly seventeen, or the equivalent of thirty-four French divisions. The danger on the Western Front lay in the continuous increase of the German armies and in their ability to concentrate in turn against the French and British, and as neither had sufficient reserves of their own, it was clear that some arrangement must be made for better coördination and support.

The Military Representatives submitted another joint note which proposed the organization of a General Allied Reserve. The plan provided that the British, French, and Italian armies should each set apart a certain number of divisions to constitute this reserve, which would be called into action only in a great emergency. The discussion of this question became rather acrimonious. Haig and Pétain, also Robertson, were against such a reserve. They pointed out how they would be short of divisions very soon in case of severe fighting and presented figures on the subject that were very disturbing.

But the Council's scheme was cut and dried. The recommendations set forth in the note were adopted then and there. A General Reserve was prescribed and its control was placed under an Executive War Board to consist of Generals Foch, representing the French, Chairman; Bliss, the Americans; Cadorna, the Italians; and a British general officer to be named. At this same meeting of the Council, Mr. Lloyd George designated General Sir Henry Wilson as the British representative, to the very evident disappointment of General Robertson, who was present at the session. The selection of Wilson was regarded by the British High Command and the War Office as an open disapproval of their conduct of the war.

In accordance with the decision, the Executive War Board, as the administrative authority of the Supreme War Council, sent out instructions directing the French and British Commanders-in-Chief each to select a certain number of divisions to form a part of the General Reserve. The number was finally fixed at thirty in all; ten British, thirteen French, and seven Italian.

The use of these reserves appeared somewhat indefinite, but the idea as brought out in the discussion seemed to be that the divisions designated as constituting the General Reserve would be so situated that they could be moved expeditiously to the support of the army seriously attacked. Their use was to be determined after consultation between the Executive War Board and the Commander-in-Chief of the army affected. This plan of the Supreme War Council did not meet with the approval of the armies, especially the British, who apparently regarded it merely as an indirect means of assuming supreme command.

One other matter somewhat linked up with this question of a general reserve was the proportion of line that should be held by the French and British armies. The French occupied about 340 miles of front, with their right on the Swiss border, while the British had only about 110 miles, extending from the French left near St. Quentin to the right of the Belgian army. The French argued that they were holding a greater proportion of line than the British, but the latter contended that a large part of the French front was inactive and did not require many troops, while the British front was active. After considerable discussion, the question was referred to the Military Representatives on the Council for an opinion. Their recommendation was not acceptable to the French, so the matter was finally decided by agreement between General Pétain and Field Marshal Haig, under which the British were to extend their front some twenty-eight miles, to a point near Barisis. This concession was used later by Sir Douglas Haig as one reason why he could not spare divisions for the General Reserve.

The following letter to the Secretary of War covers matters of interest as viewed at that time.

"France, February 4, 1918.
"Dear Mr. Secretary:

"I am sending this letter by General March, giving a brief report of the negotiations concerning the troops to be brought over by the British and trained with their divisions.

"After fully considering the matter, I am quite convinced that it would be unwise for us to break up divisions by turning over infantry battalions, as such, for extended service with the British. The main reasons are set forth in my memorandum cabled to the Department, copy of which is enclosed herewith.

"As to the question of obtaining extra shipping from the British, it does not look favorable from this end of the line, but I hope we may increase our tonnage by every possible means.

"I am also enclosing two other memoranda, one a conversation with Marshal Joffre, which I would request be held in the strictest confidence, and another giving a synopsis of a conference held between ourselves and the British on the subject of their request for men. From the former it will be seen that the Marshal takes the same view that I do regarding service with the British. He further does not look upon the situation on the Western Front with quite so much alarm as is indicated in statements by Marshal Haig and General Pétain.

"One more word regarding this discussion. General Bliss, upon his arrival, was inclined to accede to the British request, basing his action upon the cable he received from the Chief of Staff, which stated that the proposition had my approval, although I had not intended to convey that impression. So, after further conference with him, in which I set forth the views of Marshal Joffre and similar views of a British officer of high rank, given me in confidence, General Bliss agreed with me, and we [later] appeared before Mr. Lloyd George in full accord. My views were then fully set forth and were afterward declared by Mr. Lloyd George to be entirely sound.

"The Supreme War Council has been in session since last Wednesday, during which time the whole subject of the conduct of the war has been discussed in its different phases. The establishment of a general reserve was determined upon and its control was placed in the hands of an executive committee consisting of General Foch and the following-named military advisers on the Supreme Council:— General Sir Henry Wilson, British; General Cadorna, Italian; and General Bliss, American. I think the arrangement for unity of command all that could be desired without one supreme commander, which ideal is apparently considered by all concerned as impossible.

"Generally speaking, the meeting of the Supreme Council was a success, and the utmost harmony finally prevailed. Personally, I am pleased with the outlook for military coöperation. We are at some disadvantage on the diplomatic side in the Council. I stated to Mr. House when he was here that I thought he should be our representative. He undoubtedly has the confidence of the Allied governments and would add great strength to the Supreme Council. I see by the dispatches that Mr. Lane [1] has also been suggested.

"Among the enclosures, I am sending you a copy of a compilation made for the Supreme War Council, showing the strength of both the Allies and the Central Powers on the date mentioned. It puts the matter in condensed form and will enable you to get a better idea of the manpower on both sides than any other statement yet sent you.

"Conditions at our ports are improving, and I am pushing the turn-around of transports with all possible speed. The Navy is giving us better service of late in convoying transports as requested. The shortage of railway cars is easing up, and will grow better as the number of repaired cars to be obtained from the Belgians increases.

"General March is returning to America as you requested. He will be difficult to replace, but I feel that you need the best man we can find, so I cheerfully let him go. He is in touch with plans, organization, and progress here and understands the situation very well.

[1] Mr. Franklin K. Lane, then Secretary of the Interior in Mr. Wilson's Cabinet.

"I shall not take up more of your time. Please accept my very sincere regards, and renewed congratulations upon your success.
"Yours faithfully,
"JOHN J. PERSHING."

The winter of 1917-18 was the most severe of the war. The cold was at times so intense as to make the generally unheated houses, barns and lofts used as billets nearly uninhabitable. The gloom of short days and long nights in the isolated and largely depopulated French villages can hardly be described. The snow was unusually heavy in eastern France, and periodical thaws, with consequent mud and slush in the trenches and dugouts, greatly added to the hardships of the men of all armies. Training in the open was often impossible for days, and under the conditions even the regular supply of necessary food for men in the trenches became a formidable task. Restricted areas in village streets were kept cleared for daily exercises only by the constant work of troops. The northeastern part of France, while beautiful in summer, is certainly somber and unattractive in winter.

The natural tendency of all troops, but especially Americans, under such conditions was to use an excessive amount of fuel. Nothing delights our soldiers more than to gather around a rousing fire either in or out of doors. But the allowance of fire-wood was limited and there was no such thing in France as stealing the top rail from fences, as our troops did in the Civil War. Many units had to go into the forests and cut their own wood, and the winter was well along before our forestry troops got to the point of keeping up the supply.

Then, the shortage of heavy winter clothing from home had not been met. The demands were no doubt greater than the Quartermaster Corps could supply. Much of the clothing that we received for our troops was reported to be shoddy. I saw numbers of men wearing uniforms which were light and thin and which, of course, offered insufficient protection. The lack of clothing had been met in part by purchases from the British. Our troops did not take kindly to the idea of wearing the uniform of another nation, and it was with considerable protest and chagrin that they did so.

I recall an incident that occurred in one of the regiments which was composed largely of Irish-Americans. This organization had received British uniforms on which the buttons had not been changed to our own. When the uniforms were issued a wave of opposition swept through the outfit against wearing buttons with the British coat of arms. In order to pacify the objectors, an automobile was sent post haste with American buttons, the changes were made, and the regiment then turned out looking both smart and serene.

The necessity for haste in preparation and for the maintenance of morale required that our program of training be carried out almost regardless of the weather, and even though it entailed some discomfort the constant outdoor life kept the troops in good health and hardened them for the work ahead. To the credit of our officers and men, be it said that they generally ignored adverse conditions and, barring some irritation at French methods and occasionally at our own, they kept at their tasks with commendable determination. Looking back over the different phases of the war, I regard that winter, with its difficulties, anxieties, and apprehension for the future, as the most trying period of them all.

CHAPTER XXII

Stars and Stripes—Tuscania Torpedoed—Labor Procurement—Shipping Improvement—2d Division—Reorganization Line of Communications —G.H.Q. General Staff—Visit from Foch—Aircraft Needs—Port Situation—Letter to Secretary,

(Diary) Chaumont, Friday, February 8, 1918. Dawes called Sunday in Paris with Captain Dean Jay, his assistant; Captain Cutcheon, who will head board on Contracts and Adjustments; and Major Jackson, Labor Procurement.[1]

Called Monday on M. Clemenceau and General Foch taking with me General March, who will be Chief of Staff in Washington.

Returned from Paris on Tuesday. Conforming to efforts at home, have issued strict orders on conservation of food. British fear invasion and their request that any of our troops in England should stand ready to aid approved by the Secretary of War. Arrangements made for coöperation between General Trenchard, British Air Service, and General Foulois, our Chief of Aviation.

Visited Intelligence Section to-day, under Colonel Nolan; find it well organized. Military Mission[2] being sent to Italian G.H.Q. First number of *Stars and Stripes* issued to-day. *Tuscania,* carrying American troops, reported torpedoed off Irish Coast, 166 missing. Went to Langres with Harbord and Boyd and found schools making excellent progress. January reports show increased rate of arrival of men and material.

W E were always concerned that the morale of our troops should be kept up to a high pitch. As an aid in this direction, it seemed to me that a publication of some sort that would be available to all the troops would be useful. By my direction, the question was taken up by Colonel Nolan and

[1] Major J. P. Jackson had been formerly Labor Commissioner of the State of Pennsylvania; Captain F. W. M. Cutcheon was a prominent lawyer in New York; and Captain Dean Jay had been Vice President of the Guaranty Trust Company of New York.

[2] The Mission consisted of Maj. Gen. Eben Swift, Col. John McA. Palmer, General Staff, Lt. Col. R. U. Patterson, Medical Corps, and later Capt. F. H. LaGuardia, Air Service.

the result was the *Stars and Stripes*—the official newspaper of the A.E.F. This publication was under the management of Lieutenant G. T. Viskniskki, who assembled as editors of the various departments a remarkable group taken entirely from the enlisted personnel of the Army. From the start, no official control was ever exercised over the matter which went into the paper —it was entirely for and by the soldier. The first number was issued on February 8, 1918, and its success was immediate. Before the Armistice its circulation grew to more than 500,000. I do not believe that any one factor could have done more to sustain the morale of the A.E.F. than the *Stars and Stripes*.

At dusk on the evening of February 5th, off the Irish Coast, a torpedo launched from an enemy submarine struck the British convoyed liner *Tuscania,* having on board American troops, causing a loss later reported to be 113 men. The fine discipline of the men and the efficient handling of a difficult situation by those in command, together with the splendid work of the British Navy, contributed to account for relatively light casualties. We were filled with profound appreciation of the devoted conduct of the British destroyers, which, notwithstanding the fact that hostile submarines were lurking in the vicinity, rendered every assistance and remained on the scene until all survivors were brought safely ashore. At the small ports of Ireland and Scotland where our men were landed they met with a warmhearted reception on the part of the people, who gave them every possible comfort and care.

In seeking to obtain additional labor abroad, a request was made for Italians from among those employed by the French, but it was found that none could be spared from the important work of constructing new lines of defense behind the French front. As we needed some 50,000 laborers, I started an inquiry as to the possibility of obtaining part of them direct from Italy. But as the American Ambassador at Rome had reported that the Italian Government was opposed to sending any more men out of the country, on the ground that they were needed at home, this plan did not appear very promising. Our need for laborers was pressing and a bureau for labor procurement was therefore created under the Purchasing Board, and the question was taken up with M. Ganne, of the Cambon Mission, to see what could be done.

At the ports the amount of freight received in January was somewhat encouraging, being about two-fifths as much as during the preceding seven months. The rate of discharge was accelerated to some extent through a better distribution of our transports by the Navy to the different ports. More construction material, including piles, was being delivered where it was most needed, and the future was somewhat clarified in this respect by the arrival of additional logging machinery.

During the month there was also an increase in troop arrivals, including divisional troops and 20,000 men for the Line of Communications. By the end of January approximately 120,000 combat troops, 34,000 engineer troops, and 61,000 for other services were in France. Although promising, that was, of course, only a beginning, as we were still far behind our schedule, and the shipments of men and material from home remained haphazard and not in the proportions needed. We were rapidly approaching the time when we were expected to be of some help to the Allied cause and it was necessary that our forces should be balanced to make them as independent as possible. Coöperation by the General Staff at home was needed.

In the absence of any preparation for war beforehand, the principle can hardly be questioned that the commander at the front and not the staff departments in Washington should decide what he needs. The employment of our armies in Europe had been fully covered by general instructions and there were no problems of strategy or questions concerning operations that devolved upon the War Department staff. These were matters for the Commander-in-Chief of the A.E.F. to determine. It remained, then, for the War Department simply and without cavil to support our efforts to the fullest extent by promptly forwarding men and supplies as requested. The Secretary of War was completely in accord with this conception, but it was evident that the staff departments had not grasped it or else the disorganization and confusion were such that it could not be carried out.

The increase in our tonnage appeared very small in the face of the demands from both the French and British for raw material, most of which we had promised for their manufacturing programs and upon which we must largely depend for munitions. Briefly, the French needed 120,000 tons of steel, 30,000 tons of copper and brass, 6,000 tons of tin, lead, and antimony, 9,000 tons of spelter, 31,000 tons of cast iron, and 30,000 tons of powder and explosives. The British required 165,000 tons of steel, 23,000 tons of copper and brass, 1,200 tons of tin, lead, and antimony, and 36,000 tons of explosives and powder, making a total of over 400,000 tons of material due the Allies from America. The manner of meeting these requirements now presented a most difficult problem, both of tonnage and priority.

Due, no doubt, to their anxiety, there was a tendency among our Allies, especially the French, to exaggerate the urgency of their requests for material. Oftentimes after investigation it turned out that their estimates could be substantially reduced and in some instances ignored altogether. So faulty was the organization and management of the Government's business that at times the French lost track of considerable amounts of raw materials they had actually received from abroad. Confusion was not entirely limited to America.

(Diary) Chaumont, Wednesday, February 13, 1918. Inspected 2d Division last Sunday in Bourmont area.

Met committee on staff reorganization to-day and decided important points for better administration. Saw Murphy, Perkins, and Eliot Wadsworth on Red Cross matters. Had E. H. Sothern and Mr. and Mrs. Winthrop Ames to luncheon.

Have received assurance of increased shipments of subsistence, forage, and clothing, to be followed by locomotives and cars. Weekly reports by Medical Department of health conditions continue favorable.

The 2d Division, commanded by Major General Bundy, which had been organized in France in October, was composed of an infantry brigade, with artillery and auxiliary troops of the Regu-

MY EXPERIENCES IN THE WORLD WAR 321

lar Army, and one brigade of Marines. The 9th and 23d Regiments, forming the brigade of Regulars, were of the old army and their experience and the traditions behind them, even with the large accession of recruits in their ranks, gave ample assurance of what they would do. The 5th and 6th Regiments of Marines had become a part of our forces at the suggestion of Major General George Barnett, then Commandant of the Marine Corps, and with my approval. These troops united with the brigade of infantry, formed a division of relatively well-trained troops; and with such an advantage at the start, this division was destined soon to take its place among the best on the Western Front.

In the process of development abroad of our great military machine, certain changes in the original organization were indicated. The probable early increase in our combatant strength made it necessary to plan for the rapid expansion in all activities, the development of which had been delayed for causes which have already been mentioned. As a great commercial concern, the Services of Supply [1] was charged with the reception, transportation, storage and distribution of everything the army had to have, and also with hospitalization of the sick and wounded. Without sound business administration it could not be successful. Its commander must have broad discretionary powers and the territorial or section commanders under him must also have certain independence of action. Wise and efficient management of an organization embracing so many interests and spread over such an extent of territory demanded decentralization in all matters on which a policy could be fixed.

In the new organization the chiefs of the supply departments of the A.E.F., respectively, acting under their titles and authority as members of the staff of the Commander-in-Chief, were to exercise all their functions of procurement, supply, transportation, and construction under the direction of the Commanding General, Services of Supply. The Judge Advocate General, the Adjutant General, and the Inspector General, whose duties did not pertain to supply but to general administration, remained at G.H.Q. The

[1] Heretofore referred to as the Line of Communications.

Transportation Department, the Motor Transport, and the Forestry Service, were placed under a Chief of Utilities, through whom their activities were coördinated under the Services of Supply. Although these technical staff and supply services were subject to the orders of the Commanding General, Services of Supply, a representative or group of each was attached to the General Staff at G.H.Q. to maintain the close liaison necessary for prompt service in the Zone of Operations.

In the successful command of an army such as ours eventually became, it was necessary to bring the supervision of all elements of the administrative and technical departments under the control of the Headquarters General Staff. None of the departments entered upon their duties with any experience in war, nor had they in any real sense been trained even theoretically to solve the problems that urgently demanded solution. During times of peace each department had grown relatively independent of the others, and each chief had directed the affairs of his department with little control, except of a very general character.

With reference to the General Staff, the same thing may be said as to experience in war or real preparation for it. In fact, so faulty had been the training of the General Staff as members of a great directive group that both the individuals and the group lacked initiative and purpose for want of a clear conception of their tasks. It was to overcome this inertia that I vested in the General Staff well-defined powers to give such direction, by my authority, as might become necessary to coördinate the different parts of the organization. This assumption of directive control did not reduce or affect the efficiency of the administrative or technical department chiefs or their assistants, because they too, under supervision, were given independent rôles, encouraged and moderated at the same time by the one requirement—success. Such was the broad conception of the organization built up as the G.H.Q., A.E.F.

(Diary) Chaumont, Monday, February 18, 1918. General Foch and General Weygand visited headquarters on Thursday, had luncheon with us, and examined the general staff organization. Captain

Todd, Director of Naval Construction, came to confer regarding wire-less station at Bordeaux. Colonel Henry L. Stimson, former Secretary of War, now an efficient Colonel of Artillery, called and asked to be left with troops. Cable says Major General March appointed Chief of Staff at Washington, relieving Major General Biddle, ordered to England.

Left Friday, spent Saturday and Sunday with 1st Division in An-sauville sector; inspected infantry in front line trenches and the ar-tillery. Saw General Debeney, commanding French First Army, under whom 1st Division is serving.

Returned to Chaumont to-day, stopping at aviation park, Colombey-les-Belles. Camouflage work exceptionally well done. Passed through Mirecourt to see General de Castelnau, who speaks highly of our troops. Went to Vittel and Contrexéville where newly arrived hos-pitals were found in poor condition; thence to Bourbonne-les-Bains and Montigny-le-Roi to inspect 3d Cavalry and engineer detachments and found discipline lax.

As General Foch had shown some surprise when, at the meeting at Compiègne in January, I told of the delays and dif-ficulties we were having at the ports and in the operation of railways, I invited him to make a visit to my headquarters, hoping to put him in touch with our activities. We had already reached a state of development that confirmed the soundness of our organ-ization and could forecast its ability to meet all requirements. I went with him to the various sections of the General Staff and while he expressed no opinion about what he saw, his aide and spokesman, General Weygand,[1] a staff officer of experience, was very complimentary. Foch never seemed interested when I talked with him of our problems and I doubt whether at the time he ever thought, knew, or cared much about our organization, or our questions of transportation and supply. He was essentially a student and teacher of history and strategy.

The very extensive and intricate organization necessary to handle a modern army engaged in war beyond the seas was not

[1] On one occasion during his visit to the United States Marshal Foch and I were speaking of our respective war-time staffs, and he referred particularly to Major General Weygand and Colonel Desticker, who, he said, were very close to him and who always thought as he did on any military subject. According to the Marshal, what either of these officers said was as though he, himself, had said it.

easy to grasp. Indeed, the details were not entirely understood in our own army except by a limited number of officers charged with the functions of direction and coördination.

One way to get an idea of the difficulties that had to be met would be to imagine that the 500,000 people residing in the city of Washington, D.C., were all capable of bearing arms and were sent to France and provided with clothing, food, arms, equipment, medical attention, and there trained for war. Then imagine that about the time they had been located in various towns and villages in France, the entire population, 1,500,000 people, of the city of Detroit, were also sent over, at the rate of 250,000 per month, to be handled under the same conditions and with the same object in view. This would be only a part of the problem, as the greater proportion of this multitude would then have to be moved to the battle front, or to its vicinity, and eventually engage the enemy in battle, in a coördinated effort involving infantry, supported by artillery, aviation, tanks, and all other auxiliary forces, controlled and moving toward a designated enemy position against all the opposition and violence the enemy could bring to bear. As to numbers and general description this is exactly what eventually happened. This comparison may assist the lay reader to obtain a better notion of our problem.

As to wireless communications, the possibility of interference by the enemy with our cables had caused some concern and the projected radio station at Bordeaux was a precautionary measure to meet such a contingency. Very properly, it was a naval proposal and plan, as the navy system had charge of the transmission of our confidential messages and was especially interested in those relating to the movements of transports. Although the Navy undertook the construction of this station at once, it was not completed until after the Armistice, and has since been turned over to the French as a link in their radio system.

In aviation development a crisis had been reached in raw materials, especially spruce and fir. Owing to the delay in furnishing these things, our aviation program abroad, which depended largely upon Allied production, was very much retarded. According to the Inter-Allied Aviation Commission, of which General Foulois was the American member, there was not enough spruce and fir in France to keep the French factories going more than a month longer, when they would require something like a million feet. The British and Italian factories were in about the same predicament. Our aviation control at home had made an allocation by which they had retained from 30 to 40 per cent of the production of these woods, although it was apparent that no such quantity could be utilized in the manufacture of American airplanes in time to be of use to the Allied cause. Questions of details of construction were still under discussion between our aircraft board at home and that abroad. The fact is that with us the industry had to be built from the ground up, and it had to be done with no experience to guide us.

A recommendation was cabled requesting that the three other countries involved be given a larger share of materials which they needed in building airplanes for themselves, and for us also, until our output could meet our own requirements. It has never been clear to me just why we should not have given full assistance and preference to factories[1] abroad that were already turning out planes of approved pattern, instead of clinging to the exaggerated claim of our airplane manufacturers that they could supply our armies within a reasonable time. That such a delusion still clouded the issue is shown by the promise made by Washington about the middle of February that by March 31st there would be something over 300 planes ready for shipment, and by May 1st a total of 1,600 would be completed, the numbers increasing monthly to a grand total of nearly 12,000 by the 1st of November. The first thousand planes were to reach the army in France by July 15th. We shall see in later chapters how much these promises lacked of being fulfilled.

At this moment there were several hundred of our men await-

[1] Orders were placed with the Italian Government for 700 planes and 2,400 engines, but our failure to deliver sufficient raw material, and the Italian reverses in the fall of 1917 prevented their fulfillment.

My contract with the French in August, 1917, for 5,000 planes and 8,500 engines was abrogated mainly on account of our non-delivery of raw material.

ing training, the French and Italian schools were full, and we had an insufficient number of planes to train them ourselves. Only nine squadrons [1] out of the sixty that we should require by June 30th for front line service could be considered at this time as anywhere near ready, and the prospects were that even this small number would have to use inferior types of planes purchased from the French, unless the receipt of raw material from the States and consequently the production in France could be materially hastened. In the face of our failure to produce planes at home or to fulfill our engagements to furnish raw material for their manufacture in France, it was small wonder that the French found themselves in a situation that would only warrant a promise of planes as our divisions arrived.

I had recently inspected several stations like Vittel and Bourbonne-les-Bains, which were commanded by Regular officers, of whom, naturally, much was expected, and had found the personnel there careless in dress and none too strict in discipline. The conditions of service in France demanded serious attention to these essentials, not only as a matter of pride but because of the general effect upon morale and efficiency. Good discipline is the first requisite to successful military effort and the degree of its enforcement in a command is an almost certain index of the character of performance in battle. Likewise, an officer or soldier who takes no pride in his personal appearance is usually found careless in other respects, and to that extent less reliable in time of stress. It need hardly be added that those of this class who came under my observation and who did not immediately respond to suggestion were very soon replaced by others of different attitude.

(Diary) Chaumont, Saturday, February 23, 1918. Saw Maurice Ganne, M. Cambon's successor, who is earnestly helping in procurement.

Had conference yesterday with Atterbury, Taylor, Harbord, and

[1] Each monoplane pursuit squadron consisted of 31 officers, 181 enlisted men, and 25 planes. The number of officers for biplane squadrons was 34, and for observation squadrons 43. We were to have 120 squadrons at the front by December, 1918.

Connor on port and rail situation. Prepared detailed report for
Secretary of War. Have cabled Washington important report by
Inter-Allied Metals Committee.[1] Just learned that there has been
some criticism in Congress of French management of ports.

Since last entry Generals Swift, Bell, Crozier, and Wood have been
guests at various times.

Although there had been some improvement in the rapidity
of discharge of freight, we were still handicapped by lack of
modern mechanical appliances, the receipt and installation of
which had been considerably delayed. This applied particularly
to gantry cranes. A difference of opinion had arisen between
engineers of the construction corps and those in the rail transportation as to the advisability of using them on the new docks.
After several attempts to bring about an understanding between
the agencies concerned, I ordered these cranes brought over for
employment. Their use was made possible by strengthening the
docks in question.

The continued shortage of railway cars to move freight from
the docks aggravated the situation. It was true that some 30,000
damaged cars still lay on side-tracks here and there, but little
or no attempt was made by the French to repair them. Repair
personnel from home could not be obtained and we were able
only partially to carry out our proposals to undertake the task.
At this time 8,000 tons were discharged daily at all ports, but
only 3,000 tons were being removed, although we should have
reached a point by this time where it would have been possible
to handle three or four times that much. Additional storage
might answer temporarily, but it was easy to see that congestion
could become serious.

Washington was naturally solicitous and even expressed hesitation about making further shipments, instead of complying with
our requests and rushing over the personnel and matériel that
would have permitted us to overcome the difficulties. In order

---

[1] The Inter-Allied Metals Committee undertook to adjust the requirements of various
Allied Governments in products peculiarly necessary in the manufacture of metals for
munitions and other purposes. These products were tungsten, chrome, zinc, spelter,
tin, retort carbon, cryolite and emery.

to put before the Secretary of War a complete statement of conditions and causes, an analysis of immediate requirements was cabled in detail and also sent to him by letter. It was estimated that we must have sufficient tonnage, with accommodations and personnel, to have in France 287,000 men by April, and 771,000 by September. To correspond to this inflow, 8,700 tons of cargo must arrive daily in April, rising to 21,000 in September.

We had at this time ten berths at St. Nazaire, four at Nantes, three at La Pallice, four at Rochefort, six at Bassens, and four in prospect at Brest. The construction of berths at Bassens, ten in number, was well under way, and some were already in use. However, all berths could not be kept occupied, as ships, very properly, were still brought over in groups under convoy. Therefore, it was necessary to have an increased number of berths to accommodate several ships at once. With this provision at various ports and the completion of cargo-handling facilities, Atterbury and his associates in the Transportation Department, and W. D. Connor, of the general staff section, in charge, felt every assurance that the tonnage estimates could be promptly handled.

Concerning this question, it was explicitly stated in my cables as imperative that we must increase our storage space by rapid construction, and our rail facilities by a large accession of engines and cars, new and repaired. In addition, we had to have material to carry on the progressive laying of main-line tracks and 125 miles per month of sidings. It was equally pressing that we should have more rail and stevedore personnel without delay. With the fulfillment of these requirements, I insisted that there should be no hesitation in sending over troops, emphasizing the point that the exigencies of the military situation in France should govern, and that no obstacle, imaginary or otherwise, should prevent the full use of every available ton of shipping.

There continued to be considerable cause to find fault with the attitude and methods of French bureau officials. They had been repeatedly urged to turn over certain docks and facilities for our exclusive use, and while some concessions had been made, it was always grudgingly and by piecemeal, and we were never certain of more than temporary occupancy. Under the circumstances, I did not hesitate to call M. Clemenceau's attention to the remarks made in our House of Representatives criticizing the French attitude toward affording us port accommodations. While this resulted in a somewhat more liberal policy, it did not remove the necessity for constant pressure on our part.

In the S.O.S. a true spirit of coöperation was often absent among subordinate French officials, who seemed to make little attempt to understand our problems. Among the higher officials the desire was usually there, but only by dint of constant urging could we obtain the meager and insufficient facilities that we had to put up with. In all our relations with them throughout the Services of Supply, at the ports and in railway traffic, it was an ever recurring matter of surprise to me how our officers in direct daily contact with the many obstacles remained hopeful instead of becoming pessimistic. It must be said, however, that the French officers of the liaison group as individuals attached to various organizations were always found anxious to make things go smoothly, though in many instances they clung to the notion that we should adopt French ideas and methods. It can also be said that the services of our American liaison officers with the French at various offices and organizations in the Services of Supply were almost without exception praised by the French.

Apropos of the experience of many of our officers, I recall that one of the most efficient officers on duty at a very important port once said to me, "General, the trouble is that these subordinate French officials in immediate charge are either so hide-bound or else so conceited that it would be as easy to convince a Greek statue as to make one of them understand. How in the world it happens, Sir, that we do so well I do not see. Here we have come 3,000 miles to help them and yet we are treated like mendicants on the street corner holding a tin cup for passing pennies. I know, Sir, that coöperation is necessary if we hope to win the war, but it requires an excessive effort on our part, with more failures than successes to our credit." This was harsh comment, but there were times in the experience of most officers when it seemed to fit the case fairly well.

The following letter was sent to the Secretary of War in the hope of reaching him before he should sail on his contemplated visit to the armies:

"February 24, 1918.

"Dear Mr. Secretary:

"I hope this letter will reach you before you start for Europe, as I am sending a brief outline of the work that has been accomplished here by the various departments, in order to give you a view of the situation as a whole. Enclosure 'A' will give you a sketch of the projects, and the chart marked 'B' will show the progress that has been made in each. The other enclosures are a copy of my new general staff organization just adopted, and a small map showing the location of our troops in the line.

"I am having a résumé made up of our immediate needs as to material and labor, which I shall cable in a day or two and which should receive attention at once. The prospective early increase in the number of vessels available for transport and the consequent large increase in cargo and personnel will require increased accommodations without delay. As you know, * * * material and labor for these purposes are very much behind or we should have been in better shape. We must now push port work to the utmost. In this connection, the next most vital improvement necessary are the railroads, and I am sending in a condensed cable to-day covering that also. Both ports and railways, however, should go along together.

"I presume General Bliss has reported the results of the last meeting of the Supreme Council at Versailles, so I shall not go into that further than to say that the plan of operations on the Western Front meets with my entire approval and I think that the lines can be held in case the Germans carry out their much heralded offensive. But we must lose no time in getting ready for our part as the necessity for our aid may come very soon.

"Since my last letter on the subject of training and service of our units with the French and British armies, there has been much discussion, with the final result as cabled you. I think both the British and French now fully understand that we must look forward to the upbuilding of a distinctly American force instead of feeding our units into their organizations. Your decision on that point has settled all thought of our doing anything else.[1]

[1] This did not prove to be correct.

"I want to say that General Bliss is a most excellent choice for the post he now holds, and that our relations are most harmonious and I feel sure must remain so. He is an able man, as square as a die, and loyal to the core. I do not think you could have found any one to fill the place with greater credit to us all. He is very much occupied and has not been to my headquarters as yet, but I expect him shortly.

"In accordance with a tentative agreement made by General Pétain and myself, we shall in time have a sector of our own as soon as our divisions are able to act independently. It will probably begin where the 1st Division is now finishing its training, between St. Mihiel and Pont-a-Mousson, from which base we shall likely extend both to the west and east. I hope that the work they will be called upon to do may not at first be too severe, but one cannot always tell what is going to happen in war.

"It takes a long time to get troops in shape because the officers require so much practice and experience. This applies particularly to higher officers and officers of the staff. The multitude of detail that they have to grasp and prepare for can only be learned finally and thoroughly by application in the front lines.

"The particular sector selected, being one side of a German salient, is least likely to be the point of great German pressure, and it will afford, on the other hand, a better opportunity for offensive action than most other places within reach of our front. Of course, it should be understood that our divisions, when ready, even though in the line, should be considered available to go anywhere in an emergency.

"With reference to the enclosed memorandum on general officers, I think we must follow the experience of our Allies in that as in other lessons the war has taught. The ineptitude of the older officers so far tried completely bears out the experience of both British and French. It will not be profitable to spend any time trying to teach such men. In time we are going to develop a capable lot of younger men for higher commands.

"As to the General Staff, the work of all sections has been excellent under the former organization and designations, but in the new draft I have been able to correct defects that became apparent. The new designations for sections is an improvement. I must mention the work of G-4 (Coördination), as I think it very essential to have some such body who shall have a large view of the problem as a whole and be able to give directions that relieve me and the Chief of Staff of many details. I would suggest the application of this principle in the General

Staff at Washington if you have not already inaugurated it. * * *

"May I extend to you, Mr. Secretary, my sincerest good wishes for your success, and add that I have no sympathy with all this political fault-finding, which is serving no good purpose but which only tends to shake the confidence of our own people and give our enemy encouragement.

"With very warm personal regard, I remain, as always,

"Yours very faithfully,

"John J. Pershing."

CHAPTER XXIII

Air Service Difficulties—Extravagant Claims of Press at Home—Procurement Abroad—A.E.F. Gardens—Tonnage Situation Improving—M. Clemenceau Visits 1st Division—French Praise—Make Inspection of Troops—Cooking in Our Army—Casualty Lists—Decorations Authorized—Secretary Baker Arrives—Usual Calls—Visits Principal Activities

(Diary) Chaumont, Thursday, February 28, 1918. Held conference Monday with senior aviation officers, Foulois and W. B. Burtt, and later Mitchell. Newspaper clippings from home proclaim thousands of American airplanes in France. Have cabled protest.

Had call Tuesday from Mr. J. J. Davis and ex-Congressman Lentz, here in interests of Order of the Moose. Conferred with Brewster; troops making progress. Appealed for more Regular officers as instructors staff college and schools.

Bishops Brent and J. N. McCormick called yesterday and dined with us. Held conference with our members of Allied Maritime Transport Council, who lunched with us to-day. War Department has appointed representatives on various Committees of Supreme War Council.[1]

IT will be recalled that aviation was separated from the Signal Corps early in the history of the A.E.F. The difficulties of its organization were naturally inherent to those of any newly formed unit. The lack of a well-considered scheme worked out in time of peace was sorely felt. Differences in the views of the senior officers of the corps were not easily reconciled. Jealousies existed among them, no one had the confidence of all the others, and it was not easy to select from among the officers of the corps any outstanding executive. However, the questions of training and supply were fairly well worked out, but the handicap of shortage in both personnel and matériel was not readily overcome. A number of excellent officers had been transferred from both

[1] Brig. Gen. B. D. Foulois, Aviation; Col. A. D. Andrews, Transportation; and Col. S. D. Rockenbach, Tanks.

line and staff to aviation, but their lack of technical knowledge reduced their usefulness in helping to build up this service. The whole subject gave me serious concern. However, the latest conference, mentioned in the diary, was somewhat more encouraging.

Meanwhile, some of the more sensational newspapers at home were making extravagant claims about the large number of American planes then actively engaged in France when in fact up to this moment there was not a single plane of American make on the Western Front. Of course unfounded reports of this sort were very harmful and their appearance led me to make a strong protest against its being permitted, as will be shown by the following cablegram:

"February 28, 1918.

"Newspaper clipping from United States received here to effect that United States has thousands of fliers in France and that thousands of American airplanes are flying above the American forces in Europe to-day. As a matter of fact there is not to-day a single American-made plane in Europe. In my opinion the result of such bombastic claims in the American press has had the effect of materially stiffening German production. Some sane statement might be given the press at home to counteract these exaggerations. These statements are grossly exaggerated and are extremely detrimental to the future efficiency and expectations of the Air Service, American Expeditionary Forces. Emphatically protest against newspaper publicity of this nature and urgently recommend drastic steps be taken to stop publication of such articles. One clipping in question is being returned by mail to-day. Suggest this matter be brought to the attention of Mr. Howard Coffin."

The frequent German raids and renewed activity all along the front indicated that the great German offensive might start at any time. The French General Staff thought the Allies would be able to hold without serious difficulty until we could help, but it was doubtful enough to cause considerable apprehension. It was depressing to think that ten months had elapsed since our entry into the war and we were just barely ready with one division of 25,000 men. With all our wealth, our manpower and our ability, this was the net result of our efforts up to the moment; all because our people had been deceived by a false and fatuous theory that it was unnecessary in time of peace to make even preliminary preparations for war. Here we were likely to be confronted by the mightiest military offensive that the world had ever known and it looked as though we should be compelled to stand by almost helpless and see the Allies again suffer losses of hundreds of thousands of men in their struggle against defeat. In spite of these reflections, there was the hope that with the utmost effort we should yet be able to develop our latent power in time to save our friends. At least, now that we were about to face the crisis, it was vital that America should exert herself to the utmost to complete what she had so leisurely begun.

It was evident to all that every available ton of shipping would have to be used to insure the fulfillment of our program. Hence, the saving in tonnage was becoming more and more important. The Allies were more alive than ever to the necessity of our obtaining as many things abroad as possible. The French had held out the promise to do their best to help us with horses and there was some hope that negotiations then in progress for 20,000 mules from Spain would be successful. With these prospects in view for obtaining animals, it was recommended that shipments from home could be postponed four or five months.

Our Forestry Department was in better shape than ever and gave every assurance that most of the timber and lumber for docks, wharves, and other construction would be obtained in France. Efforts were being made to improve the rail situation by securing more complete coöperation among the Allies in the matter of use of rolling stock, by urging the French to repair the thousands of damaged freight cars, and, in general, by keeping cars moving instead of allowing both loaded and empty cars to stand on sidetracks for days and even weeks at a time.[1] There was no doubt that the French railroads were very much run down and it was our task to help relieve this condition as soon

[1] This question of idle and damaged cars was taken up by letter addressed to the Chief of the French Mission, and in reply General Ragueneau explained, in substance, that all the 35,000 cars provided by the British were in use by their armies, and that 26,000 cars had to be employed by France in service for Italy, besides those required

as possible. Urgent cables were again sent asking that the shipment of rolling stock be hastened. Our agencies were vigorously at work trying to obtain labor from Italy, Spain, England and Norway for use on the railways and elsewhere. And as to procurement, no source, however limited, was overlooked.

As a means of relieving the burden on tonnage, it will be recalled that the suggestion had been made to bring farmers to France from the States to help increase agricultural production. Although that did not seem practicable, approval was given to the suggestion that suitable land left unproductive by the French who had gone to the front might be cultivated by and under supervision of our troops. To this end the Quartermaster Corps started a central garden at Versailles under a general superintendent of gardens who was to provide tools and distribute seeds to various units. Each division was instructed to begin a garden wherever practicable in its area and if transferred elsewhere to pass it on to the unit that followed. If successful, fresh vegetables that could not be obtained in any other way except in small quantities might thus become available. However, changes of units from place to place came in such rapid succession during the following months that the scheme did not reach expectations. But during the spring and summer, wherever they had an opportunity, our men aided the French on the farms near their billeting areas, with results that often accrued to our benefit.

As we have seen, a committee was appointed at the Inter-Allied conference in November to consider the question of Allied shipping, out of which developed the Allied Maritime Transport Council. At my request, several of our members [1] of the Maritime Council came to my headquarters to study the subject of our requirements and to continue their investigations regarding tonnage, both Allied and neutral, available for the use of our armies.

for the Americans, who had so far furnished only a limited number themselves; also, that their needs had been met by a great reduction in civilian traffic, but the tremendous wear and tear on rolling stock had made it difficult to keep it repaired with the limited amount of labor available.

[1] Dwight W. Morrow, R. B. Stevens, L. H. Dow, and George Rublee.

So far, there had been no definite or dependable allotment for our purposes, and commercial demands had been all too often given precedence over those of the army. The prospects of early relief by construction at home were not promising as only one vessel had been turned out in almost a year. Our members of the Council had given considerable study to the question of shipping and the information they had obtained enabled me to make a very strong appeal to the War Department for a greater allotment. The result was a reasonable increase in the number of vessels under our own flag to be assigned as transports and also the accession of some captured tonnage, which, together with that obtained by charter from the British, gave some promise that we should be able to carry out the estimates set forth in a preceding chapter. We were still much concerned, however, over the large requirements in tonnage necessary to meet our commitments in raw materials and supplies to the Allies and the considerable amounts of wheat, oats, and flour promised to the Swiss.

The heartening news of these additions to our passenger and cargo fleet stimulated activity in the various supply and equipment agencies both at home and abroad. It looked as though confusion and delay might give way to promptness and co-operation, or in any event this was the hope of those of us who had impatiently waited for such a turn of affairs.

(Diary) Chaumont, Wednesday, March 6, 1918. Heavy German raid repulsed by 1st Division on Friday morning. The enemy also raided the 26th Division lines and were driven off.

Had meeting Saturday with Colonels Johnson Hagood and Andrews on S.O.S. organization. Lord Brooke and Frazier house guests. Some American women journalists visited me that afternoon.

Went to Ligny-en-Barrois Sunday to meet M. Clemenceau, who came to congratulate the 1st Division on success repulsing raid. Met General Debeney, who was enthusiastic over conduct of our men. Spent the night at 1st Division Headquarters.

Motored to Langres with Harbord Monday to speak at opening of second session of General Staff College. Germans made raid on 42d Division that morning.

Yesterday, with de Chambrun and Boyd, went to Baccarat to see 42d Division.

Visited hospital this morning and found men wounded during raid in fine spirits. Also visited the 165th, 167th, and 168th Regiments; all making progress. Conferred with Generals C. T. Menoher, M. J. Lenihan and R. A. Brown. Experienced an air raid during dinner at Nancy and drove to Chaumont afterwards.

Upon conclusion of this inspection of the 1st Division I considered it ready to take the offensive at any time. It had been in France eight months, with varied experiences in training, had occupied an independent position in the St. Mihiel sector, and had made several successful trench raids. Duncan and Buck had their infantry brigades in efficient shape and Summerall had carried the training of the artillery brigade to a high degree. As to the 42d, 26th and 2d Divisions, the first two being then with the French in quiet sectors, and the 2d about to enter, each had yet to serve in line as an independent division to complete its training. In view of the certainty of determined German action at an early date, the quality and condition of our units were studied with solicitude by the French no less than by ourselves.

It was M. Clemenceau's custom while Prime Minister to spend Sundays visiting different portions of the front. As mentioned in my diary, he came especially to congratulate the 1st Division on its success in repulsing the raid and was enthusiastic over the conduct of the troops on that occasion. The vigor and the aggressive spirit he displayed, notwithstanding his age, were contagious. On these visits, he wanted to talk with the men right up at the front, and while it was not always convenient to humor him, one had to admire his attitude.

I wished especially to be present at the opening of the General Staff School in order to emphasize the importance of staff training. My speaking during the war was entirely extemporaneous, but it seemed more effective than if read from manuscript. In

NOTE: Total strength of the A.E.F. on February 28th, 16,547 officers, 235,342 enlisted men.

Divisional units arriving during February included elements of the 32d Division (National Guard, Michigan and Wisconsin), Major General William G. Haan.

this talk I stressed the necessity of preparation for duties that were expected of staff officers and dwelt on their obligations and their relation to the line. The new class for the second three-month session consisted, as usual, of officers selected from the various units of staff and line. The course of instruction had been carefully laid out by Brigadier General McAndrew and his assistants, all graduates of our Fort Leavenworth school, and consisted of an intensive study of lectures, specially prepared texts, and practical problems.

On the visit to the 42d Division we spent the night at Baccarat as guests of M. and Mme. Michaut. At dinner, with all the children and grandchildren present, the family formed a most charming group. The town had been partially destroyed early in the war and now that the Germans were again active because of the presence of Americans it looked as though they might make the destruction complete. I recall that when the possibility of putting an end to war was mentioned during the conversation at dinner, the grandmother of the household said, "No, that is not likely. We have had war here in this part of Europe every fifty years during the last thousand." That is the view of nine out of ten people and still they go about the work of reconstruction as though such a thing as war could never happen again.

The front occupied by the 42d Division, near Badonviller, had been under a severe artillery attack on the 4th and a trench mortar platoon had been almost completely destroyed. The French Army Commander congratulated General Menoher on the way in which our troops repulsed this raid. After an inspection of the different regiments of the division and a visit to the scene of this action, I went to the hospital to see the wounded. They were all very cheerful, especially a young officer, Lieutenant A. W. Terrell, 151st Field Artillery, who had lost one of his legs. He said that he wanted to stay through to the end of the war and hoped he could find something to do as a clerk. All these first contacts with the enemy were relatively small affairs, of course, but they furnished many examples of what we could expect of the American soldier.

(Diary) Paris, Sunday, March 10, 1918. Spent Thursday morning with Kernan, W. C. Langfitt and Atterbury and made adjustments in port and railway construction and management. Visited Camp de Mailly, where seacoast artillery is having splendid training under Brigadier General Frank W. Coe. Put up that night at a quaint little tavern in Montmirail.

On Friday visited Edwards' 26th Division, serving on Chemin des Dames under General de Maud'huy, the French Corps Commander. Lunched at headquarters with General Edwards and visited brigades under Traub and C. H. Cole. Arrived in Paris late at night during airplane attack. Branch of Judge Advocate General's Office established at my headquarters.

Upon Colonel Bradley's report of only thirty-day medical supplies on hand, sent urgent cable requesting immediate shipments. Cabled disapproval of suggestion by Mr. Paderewski for organization of division of men with Polish antecedents. Secretary of War landed at Brest to-day.

Major General de Maud'huy spoke with considerable enthusiasm of the men and of the officers of the 26th Division below regimental commanders, and especially praised their conduct of trench raids. He complimented Traub, one of the brigade commanders, but was of the opinion that the higher officers, generally, needed more experience to make them efficient. American troops that served with Maud'huy held him in high esteem. He was scrupulous regarding their instruction, to which he gave special attention.

He was very solicitous of the welfare of our troops, even going so far as to interest himself in the preparation of their food by detailing French cooks to teach ours the art. When I expressed my appreciation of his action, he said, "You know we are a nation of cooks and we delight in preparing good things to eat." After their instruction, the cooks in these units did better, thanks to the initiative of this fine old French general.

The cooks in our new units lacked experience in preparing the field ration, and in the beginning the men did not fare so well as our troops of the Regular Army on the frontier, where many cooks became experts. Personal supervision by officers and the establishment of cooking schools in the A.E.F brought improvement in due course of time. However, there is little doubt that much of the intestinal trouble among our men during the first months of their service abroad was caused by poorly cooked food.

As soon as our troops began serving in the front line in quiet sectors, we were faced with the problem of handling casualty lists. The solution reached was to defer cabling the lists until some time after the engagement and then to send them in groups, to be given out by the War Department, so that the particular battle in which the casualty occurred could not be identified. If we had given the names to the press at home immediately, it would have been equivalent to telling the enemy the engagement in which they occurred. The French published no lists, but the information was sent to the local mayor, who in turn notified the family of the soldier, at the same time extending them his condolences. Contrasted with this quiet, sympathetic way of giving such news to relatives, the method of publishing column after column of killed and wounded in the papers which people would eagerly scan day after day seemed inconsiderate and cruel.

The problem of decorations in our army had long been a knotty one, and except for the Medal of Honor and Certificate of Merit we had only campaign badges and those given for marksmanship. The Allies desired to confer their decorations on our men who served with distinction under them, but we were not permitted to accept foreign decorations without permission from Congress. There is no doubt that some sort of visible evidence of exceptional military service arouses pride and stimulates effort. The generous bestowal of decorations in each Allied army by its Commander-in-Chief was unquestionably an important factor in maintaining the morale of their troops. Our own Medal of Honor had inspired many an heroic act.

As it was a matter of importance to our officers and men, the whole question of decorations was taken up by the War Department on my suggestion with the result that Congressional action established certain medals of our own and authorized our soldiers to receive those of foreign governments. The medals created by Congress at this time were the Distinguished Service Cross for extraordinary heroism in connection with military operations against an armed enemy, and the Distinguished Service Medal for exceptionally meritorious service in a position of great responsibility. These were in addition to the Medal of Honor, our highest decoration, established in 1862, for gallantry and intrepidity at the risk of life above and beyond the call of duty. The award of the Certificate of Merit was discontinued.

Authority was also eventually given the War Department to confer our decorations on Allied officers and men who had rendered deserving service with our armies. The different grades of medals in the various countries were not entirely the same as ours. We had none that corresponded to the French or Belgian Croix de Guerre. There ought to have been one for gallantry in action somewhat less conspicuous than that covered by the Medal of Honor or the Distinguished Service Cross. I made a recommendation to this effect, but nothing came of it. There were thousands of instances in our armies where a medal of this class should have been bestowed. We were as liberal in decorating Allied officers and men as the provisions of our law would permit, and there is no doubt that the exchange of decorations helped materially to promote friendly relations.

(Diary) Chaumont, Sunday, March 17, 1918. This has been a busy week. Early Monday morning I met the Secretary of War upon his arrival in Paris and escorted him to Hotel Crillon. Later he and I called on Ambassador Sharp, M. Clemenceau and Marshal Joffre. The party,[1] together with the Ambassador and Secretaries Bliss and Frazier, lunched with me. There was a severe air raid that night, several bombs dropping near my quarters.

The Ambassador gave a dinner for the Secretary on Tuesday evening, after which we left by rail to visit the Services of Supply.

Returned to-day, having inspected our most important ports, depots, hospitals, regulating stations, aviation centers, motor parks and schools.

Word received of selection for shipment of six divisions for training

---

[1] The Secretary's party consisted of Maj. Gen. W. M. Black, Chief of Engineers; Lt. Col. M. L. Brett; Comdr. R. D. White, of the Navy; and Mr. Ralph Hayes, his secretary.

with British—28th, 30th, 77th, 78th, 80th and 82d.   Successful trench raids by our troops continue.

It was essential that the Secretary of War be given every opportunity to inspect our whole system, from the Services of Supply to the trenches, in order that he might become familiar with our plans, observe the progress toward their completion, and obtain first-hand information of our requirements, all of which he was especially anxious to do.

Leaving Paris on the 12th, our first stop was Bordeaux. Spending a few minutes for an informal welcome at the station by the French commander, and the representative of the Base Section Commander, Brigadier General W. S. Scott, who was ill, we went at once to inspect the permanent port works. The next thing was a visit to Bassens, six miles down the Gironde, where we were using six berths turned over to us by the French. Since my last visit, much progress had been made on our own project of ten new berths. Then came the St. Sulpice storage area, just out of Bordeaux, where a network of railway sidings led to row after row of new storehouses being filled with property that required cover, while other classes were being accumulated in the open storage space. We concluded the morning with a walk through the base hospital, which had accommodations for 1,000 patients, and then went to one of the leading restaurants, the Chapeau Rouge, for luncheon.

The inspection of other activities a few miles out occupied the afternoon, and included the artillery camp of instruction at Souge, under Brigadier General Ernest Hinds, where several regiments at a time could be trained; the large hospital at Beau Desert, all ready for convalescents; and the principal remount depot, with a few hundred horses and mules.

On the following morning we reached St. Nazaire, omitting the smaller ports such as La Rochelle and La Pallice mainly used for special purposes. We were met by the section commander, Brigadier General R. D. Walsh, accompanied by the French Admiral de Marguery and by the Sous-Préfect, who, with unfailing adherence to the hospitable custom, was there to read his couplet of welcome, doing so with quaking voice and trembling knees.

After the formalities we inspected docks at which ten berths were to be assigned to us and found several ships discharging cargo while others were awaiting their turn. At all ports, according to reports we received, thirteen vessels were being unloaded that day, which was somewhat encouraging, as it set a new record. The dock facilities at St. Nazaire were to be augmented by construction of piers on the Loire, at Montoir, but lack of material had delayed the beginning of that work. An engine erecting plant was established at this port in February and a car erecting plant was located at La Rochelle. The motor parks, which came next, contained relatively few of the thousands of cars and trucks needed.

After luncheon we motored to Montoir, in the suburbs, where we boarded a flat car arranged with seats and were taken by rail over miles of sidetracks through the immense storage yard covering acres. We passed rows of warehouses, finished and unfinished, being filled with perishable supplies, while out in the open were quantities of various classes of material for which cover was not necessary. We then inspected the well-ordered base hospital located in the central school building at Savenay. It had accommodations for several hundred patients and was already filled. Mr. Baker had a cheerful word for each man as we walked through the wards. The nurses looked especially neat and military. We also saw the large dam at Savenay and the reservoirs at St. Nazaire which had been constructed by our engineers to augment the meager water supply for the various camps and other installations in the vicinity.

As we were making something of a flying trip, the same evening found us under way for Saumur, where we arrived the following morning, to visit our artillery school for officers. It occupied the accommodations of the famous French cavalry school and had capacity for handling 600 students. The commanding officer, accompanied by the French artillery instructors, escorted us through the classrooms and gave us a practical exhibition on the drill ground, all of which left in our minds a good impression of efficiency. During an examination of one of the 75-millimeter field guns, a French officer described its mechanism but omitted the details of the recoil system. When asked to explain it to the Secretary, the officer, faithful to his early instructions, replied that it was a military secret. Although the same guns were being made at factories in the States and every artillery officer of our Army was familiar with the principle, the young Frenchman admirably stood his ground and declined to take the chance of betraying his trust.

Our next destination was Tours, the headquarters of the S.O.S., Major General Kernan commanding. We glanced through the offices and the Secretary spoke briefly to the assembled officers and complimented them on their evident efficiency. We then saw the large salvage plant, under Captain F. D'Olier of the Quartermaster Corps, which was receiving, renovating and repairing uniforms, shoes and equipment of every kind and description from all parts of the A.E.F.

When a unit was relieved from the trenches every man was required to cast off his entire outfit of clothing and his equipment also, if badly worn, take a bath, go through the delousing process, and then draw a fresh outfit complete. All this was prescribed in orders for sanitary reasons and to save time. The clothing and unserviceable articles of equipment left behind were gathered up by the Salvage Service, Quartermaster Corps, and shipped to salvage depots by trains that would otherwise have returned empty. The system, by making most of these things available for reissue to the troops, saved many millions of dollars' worth of property during the war, to say nothing of the corresponding economy in tonnage.

Midday found us making a three-hour run to the small town of Gièvres, about 125 miles directly south of Paris, on our main line of supply running to the front. Here 20,000 men were employed in managing our largest interior depot. It conveys only a vague impression of the magnitude of this plant to say that it eventually covered twelve square miles, had 165 storehouses, with nearly 4,000,000 square feet of storage space, connected by 143 miles of sidetracks. It had storage for 2,000,000 gallons of gasoline, refrigerator capacity for 6,500 tons of fresh meat, and warehouse space for clothing and food for 30 days' supply of 2,000,000 men, not to mention the thousands of tons of medical, signal, engineering, and ordnance supplies, excepting ammunition.

To illustrate the celerity with which the system operated, we need take but one example, which later occurred when everything in the depot was in full swing. At 8:15 one morning in August a telegram was received ordering exactly 4,596 tons of supplies, including 1,250,000 cans of tomatoes, 1,000,000 pounds of sugar, 600,000 cans of corned beef, 750,000 pounds of tinned hash, and 150,000 pounds of dry beans. At 6:15 o'clock in the evening, or just ten hours later, this colossal requisition, which required 457 cars for transport, was loaded and on its way to the advance depot.

No other place gave such an impression of the tremendous task of supplying our armies and of the perfection of organization necessary to do it efficiently. We spent almost two hours going about on a flat car following the labyrinth of tracks and sidings in looking over this plant.

It was necessary for the Secretary, because of lack of time, to omit a number of stations, depots, repair shops, and aviation centers, including the large ordnance shops at Méhun for rebuilding heavy artillery, the ammunition depot at Jonchery, and the hospitals along the line of communications representing a total of beds and equipment for 50,000 sick and wounded.

The main Air Service School, at Issoudun, Lieutenant Colonel W. G. Kilner commanding, which we visited the following day, was a hive of activity, being one of the fifteen schools where early instruction in flying was given. General Foulois went with us through the school, the shops and the Red Cross and Y.M.C.A. buildings. I was pleased that the Secretary should see the really expert flying considered necessary to prepare aviators for their hazardous life at the front. I was able to draw a comparison between the British and French aviators on the one hand and ours on the other, and found that ours, even at that time, were fully up to the highest standards of either.

It was said that opposing aviators during the early days of the war often saluted each other as they passed on flights of observation. But they soon took another attitude and enemy planes became immediate objects of attack. By the time we entered the war aviation was an important auxiliary arm. Airplanes were built and classified for different missions and training was based upon certain principles of attack and defense. Our aviators had these things to learn, but they were remarkably quick in doing so. The aerial photography of the air service became the main source of information regarding the enemy's trenches, his movements and his positions, upon which firing data for the artillery was largely based.

From Issoudun our party went to Nevers, Colonel A. Johnson commanding, in the vicinity of which were extensive hospitals, the main railroad shops, where most of the relatively small French engines and cars were repaired, and the principal motor, machine and construction shops, virtually a large automobile factory. Several of our new hospital trains were also held at Nevers in readiness for service.

The most interesting point we visited, probably because of its intimate relation to the battle front, was the regulating station at Is-sur-Tille, southeast of Chaumont, under Colonel Milosh R. Hilgard. Supplies were received in bulk from the main storage plants in the rear, segregated, and sent forward to the railheads by the trainload, each division usually receiving one trainload a day. All the details were explained to the Secretary, who took pains to understand the mechanism of the system.

We next motored to Langres, where the great central group of schools was located, with hundreds of officers and men undergoing instruction. The Secretary and I had luncheon with Brigadier General W. R. Sample, commanding the Advance Section, S.O.S. Then, beginning with the General Staff School, we looked over the schools for infantry officers, and those for machine gun and tank instruction and several others. It was gratifying to see the interest shown by the students. A more earnest lot was never assembled together and they exemplified fully the fine spirit that prevailed throughout the A.E.F.

We completed the rounds of the Services of Supply on March 17th, reaching the headquarters at Chaumont that evening by motor. The Secretary had been given a bird's-eye view of the general plan of handling supplies for an army of 2,000,000 men which, with additional construction, would enable us to meet the demands of an army twice that size. Yet he had seen only the main features or types of activities. The entire system extended over almost the whole of that part of France contiguous to the ports and to our main lines of communication. It was estimated that construction, generally speaking, was nearly half completed at that time, although all activities were going concerns and practically fulfilling the demands made upon them notwithstanding the constant shortage of labor and transport facilities.

The vast institution, the Services of Supply, which we had inspected, functioned according to the system shown on the accompanying diagram. This system assured to the troops a con-

stant and adequate flow of supplies, while, at the same time, as a measure of safety against submarine and other losses, there was maintained in France a sufficient reserve.

Shipments from the United States, augmented by such supplies as were purchased in Europe, were placed in the warehouses within the Base Sections. From these base depots there was a constant flow of shipments to the storage depots in the Intermediate Section, so controlled as to maintain therein a large, fixed reserve of all supplies needed by the troops. These storage depots themselves served as a reservoir from which the depots of the Advance Section were stocked and in which a reserve adequate for fifteen days' needs of the troops was held. Emergency shortages were filled direct from base depots. The function of these advance depots was to fill the bulk requisitions of the regulating stations in the forward areas, sending the shipments in trainloads to the proper stations. At these, the supplies for each division were made up into trains and sent forward to the railheads, where they were received by the units to which they were consigned. Each combat division required the equivalent of twenty-five carloads of supplies daily, and these supplies had to be delivered promptly and regularly to points within short truck-haul of the location of the troops.

(Diary) Chaumont, Wednesday, March 20, 1918. On Monday handled several matters observed during inspection. Cabled request that locomotives and cars be sent complete to save trouble of erecting them here. Have asked for light-draft vessels that enter shallow ports. Sent cable about shortage of nitrate in France. Mr. Baker was shown through headquarters and later spoke to General Staff officers in complimentary terms. We went to Langres in the afternoon to witness a tactical demonstration, after which the Secretary left with Harbord for the front.

To-day Henry P. Davison, Perkins and Wadsworth took luncheon with us and Davison explained the world-wide activities of the Red Cross. This afternoon went to Tréveray, where Mr. Baker reviewed John L. Hines' brigade of the 1st Division. Returned by way of the birthplace of Joan of Arc. To-night we leave by special train for French G.H.Q.

When the Secretary of War visited the headquarters and spoke to the assembled officers of the General Staff, he said that his conception of the tremendous task was very different since his coming to France. He appreciated, he said, the complexities of the problem and affirmed the determination of the administration at home to support the A.E.F. in its great work. He was agreeably pleased with the organization and thanked the General Staff officers for their loyalty and devotion to the sacred cause.

I brought to the attention of the Secretary our serious handicap due to an insufficient number of general staff officers and urged that more should be sent over in view of the approaching German offensive. We discussed the exchange between general staff officers at home and abroad, which had been suggested by the Chief of Staff in order that he might have more officers at home familiar with our difficulties in France. The idea would have been carried out later, but events of such importance followed one after another that our officers could not be spared and the principle never found regular application.

Secretary Baker and I talked over the subject of promotions, which had already been the occasion of considerable cabled correspondence. The point was that many officers had received advancement in the States ahead of others in France whose experience and abilities had shown them especially qualified for promotion. In order to do justice to all, I proposed that rank should attach to the position and not necessarily to the individual. With the Secretary's approval and his expressed desire that it should receive consideration by Congress at an early date, a cable was sent to the Department embracing the idea, as follows:

"An officer assigned to the command of troops or to a staff position in the American Expeditionary Forces by orders from competent authority shall, during such assignment, have rank and be entitled to the pay and allowances appropriate to the command so exercised or the staff position so occupied as shown in approved organization tables. An officer so assigned to command shall take rank over all officers in the command to which he is assigned."

The recommendation was never enacted into law, but such a provision would have been entirely fair and would have made it less embarrassing to replace officers who did not prove efficient. If the tenure of office in time of war were made to depend upon the character of performance, an officer could be continued if satisfactory or if not he could be relieved and could not claim consideration simply on account of his rank. There were many instances both in France and at home where officers of high rank had to be replaced and there was no appropriate duty commensurate with their permanent rank to which they could be assigned. Permanent rank should be made to depend upon the efficiency shown while holding the temporary rank.

CHAPTER XXIV

German Offensive Begins—British Driven Thirty-seven Miles—Confer with Pétain—British Proposals to the Secretary of War—Italians Appeal for American Troops—Supreme War Council Requests Accelerated Shipment of Infantry and Machine Gun Units—Foch Selected to Coordinate Allied Action—Visit to Clermont to Offer Foch American Troops—German and Allied Tactics in March Offensive

(Diary) Chaumont, Monday, March 25, 1918. Arrived Compiègne on Thursday with Secretary Baker, took luncheon with General Pétain, who afterward explained the military situation. We could hear heavy artillery firing which proved the beginning of the German attack, although no definite news had then been received. The Secretary, with Colonel Palmer and Major Collins, left to call on Field Marshal Haig on their way to London and I returned with Boyd to Paris.

Drove to Versailles on Friday to see Bliss, and later saw Atterbury on shortage of rolling stock caused by large number of trains now moving troops.

Returned by auto to Chaumont Saturday. Received reports on Sunday of long-range German gun [1] firing on Paris the day before.

Went to Compiègne this afternoon to offer Pétain all our available divisions as needed. Am urging Washington that State and Treasury insist on our getting 15,000 laborers from Italy in return for loan of $30,000,000. Think we must replace 9,000 tons of foodstuff and forage we have purchased from French.

IT will be recalled that the plan of the Supreme War Council, adopted in February, was to form a general reserve to be composed of thirteen French, ten British, and seven Italian divisions. The British Commander-in-Chief claimed, however, that in taking over from the French Army the additional front

---

[1] This gun was afterwards known as "Big Bertha." It was 120 feet long, caliber 8¼ inches, and used a shell weighing 264 pounds. It was fired from different positions, at ranges varying from 56 to 75 miles, and at intervals from March 23d to August 9th, using 367 shells, killing 250 people and wounding 640. Seven of these guns were manufactured. The life of each gun was but 50 rounds, when it had to be rebored to a somewhat larger caliber. *The Paris Gun*, by Col. Henry W. Miller.

from opposite St. Quentin to Barisis in January he had to put in divisions that might otherwise have been available, and that he had none left for the general reserve. The directions regarding the reserves were not carried out, and an agreement between Haig and Pétain as to mutual support was substituted in its stead.

When these facts were made known to the Supreme War Council by the British Commander-in-Chief they occasioned much surprise. But the lack of divisions on the part of the British was explained to the Supreme War Council on March 14th at its meeting in London, and the Haig-Pétain arrangement was accepted by the Council as satisfactory. The agreement was in substance the confirmation of the understanding between Haig and Pétain as explained at the military conference held in Compiègne in January. The time had now come for the fulfillment of this agreement.[1]

On March 21st the great German offensive began against the British armies between the Oise and the Scarpe, near the junction of the French and British lines, on a front about fifty miles in length, extending from near La Fère to Arras. Near the center of the attack was General Gough's Fifth Army, with the Third Army under General Byng on its left. The artillery bombardment preceding the infantry advance was of short duration but of great intensity, with an unusually high proportion of gas shells. Following a heavy barrage, the German infantry, using the same tactical methods that had been so successful at Riga and Caporetto, delivered its blow. The weather favored the enemy, as a heavy fog continued intermittently for three days, much to the disadvantage of the defense. The overwhelming force of sixty-four specially trained German divisions out of their 192 then on the Western Front[2] compelled the British lines to yield. Although at the end of the first day the Fifth Army had not entirely given away, its losses had reached several thousands

---

[1] Discussed in Chapter XXI.

[2] The relative strength of the two sides on the Western Front on April 1st was estimated by my own and Allied Intelligence Sections: German rifles 1,569,000 and Allied rifles 1,245,000, giving the Germans a superiority of 324,000 rifles.

and there was no question that the Germans were making a serious attempt to separate the British and French armies.

While there seemed to be every confidence before the attack that the lines could hold, full consideration had not been given to the certain use of open warfare tactics by the Germans, in which neither the British nor the French had been sufficiently trained. Adherence by the Allies on the Western Front to trench

Ground gained by German Offensive
March 21–April 5, 1918

warfare methods proved advantageous to the Germans. Except for the Verdun affair of 1916, Germany had been on the defensive in the West while completing the conquest of Russia and the Near East. As expected, the collapse of Russia and the total defeat of Roumania released a large number of German divisions for the 1918 offensive in the West, where the Germans gained numerical superiority for the first time since 1914. With this advantage, they promptly began training for open warfare with the object of forcing their adversaries out of the trenches and beating them in the open.[1] In this sort of warfare the British

[1] During the winter 1917-18, German divisions were given intensive instruction and training in mobile warfare with unceasing drill from morning until night. By February 10th, 58 divisions had completed a four weeks' course.

were seriously handicapped on account of their long adherence to stabilized warfare. Their officers said that when the men had to leave the trenches they acted as though something were radically wrong in that there was not another trench somewhere for them to get into.

On the second day of the battle the last of Gough's reserves were put in, yet he received no support to stop the widening gap in the British front until the following day, when one French infantry division and one French dismounted cavalry division arrived. On the 24th four other French divisions got into position. These divisions and others that came in the next two or three days were put into battle by General Fayolle without regard to the integrity of units or the order of their entry, some of them being very short of ammunition.

The British Fifth Army was evidently sorely pressed from the start, yet no British reënforcements were sent to Gough until the 24th, and then only one division, no others arriving during the first week. By the end of the fifth day the German forces had driven a salient into the British front some thirty-seven miles deep and were threatening the important railway center of Amiens, the capture of which would probably have made a complete breach between the French and British armies.

A small American unit participated in the defense against the German attack. Several companies of the 6th Engineers, which were on duty behind the British Fifth Army on railway repair work, were furnished arms and engaged in the operation until after the lines were established.

In view of the agreement for mutual support, it is not clear why the British and French should not have had a greater number of reserve divisions within easy reach of the point of juncture. Certainly it seemed logical that the enemy would endeavor to separate the two armies by attacking at that point. In fact, our information for some time previous indicated that he intended to do so. In the extension of the British front, the French had gained several divisions for their reserves, but when the blow came few of them were near enough to be of immediate service.

The French staff seemed to fear that their front might be the German objective, and this might account for the lack of French reserves near the junction of the two armies. Whether the general reserve would have been adequate or not, there is no doubt that the substitute agreement for mutual support did not fully meet the situation.

In the moment of greatest stress, when it seemed very doubtful whether the German advance could be stopped, General Pétain sent the following order to his armies:

"The enemy has hurled himself upon us in a supreme effort.

"He hopes to separate us from the English so as to open the way to Paris. Cost what it may he must be stopped.

"Hold your ground! Stand firm! Our (American) comrades are arriving. All together you will throw yourselves upon the invader.

"The battle is on. Soldiers of the Marne, of the Yser and of Verdun, I call upon you. The fate of France hangs in the balance."

British losses were reported to have been not less than 150,000. Lord Northcliffe, whom I recall meeting on the 24th, was almost unable to speak of it, so many of his friends had lost relatives. The depression among their people was probably worse than at any other period of the war. Among the French there was much anxiety as to the safety of Paris, and there was talk of moving the Government to Bordeaux again, as was done in 1914.

The reports from the front gave an extremely dark picture of disaster and I felt that we should do everything possible to render assistance. It was to offer General Pétain such of our troops as could be used that I went to Compiègne on the 25th. I arrived about 10:00 P.M., to find him and his Chief of Staff, General Anthoine, waiting for me, but ready to leave for Chantilly, which had been selected as their G.H.Q. when the German advance had endangered Compiègne.

The General's customary confident and nonchalant attitude was entirely gone and he wore a very worried expression. Our conference was necessarily limited to a hurried discussion of the situation. We went over the maps of the latest positions, which he thought could be held, but he had few reserves left. I told

him that for the moment I should waive the idea of forming our
I Corps and that any of our divisions that could be of service
were at his disposal, but with the qualifying remark that of course
we should look forward eventually to their assembly under their
own commander.

Pétain thought that certain of our units might be placed in
the battle line but he hesitated to give us at once a portion of the
front that might become active, preferring to have them sent into
quiet sectors to release French divisions, which amounted to the
same thing so far as it affected numbers in the battle line. He
suggested that if the action continued it might be necessary to
straighten out his line either at Verdun or in the vicinity of Nancy
and Toul in order to obtain extra French divisions for service
elsewhere. In that event he would have to execute a maneuver
which could be entrusted only to experienced staffs.

We discussed briefly the general subject of handling new units
as they should arrive, and finally I left with the understanding
that American units would be used as circumstances might demand. As the reënforcement of the British was a vital necessity,
I was willing to accept any arrangement that would release
French divisions for that purpose, or put our divisions into the
battle if thought best. I gave orders at once that our units should
be held in readiness for any eventuality.

(Diary) Paris, Wednesday, March 27, 1918. Telegram from Mr.
Baker in London renews Mr. Lloyd George's plea for infantry.

Talked yesterday with General Rawlinson and General Giardino,
who replaces Cadorna at Versailles, and both urge American troops
for their armies. In evening met Secretary and party, just back from
London. Gare du Nord was packed with French refugees from the
front.

American mechanics reported en route to repair French locomotives and cars. Saw Mr. Oscar T. Crosby and Mr. Paul D. Cravath
this morning and discussed the possibility of getting laborers from
Italy. Mr. Winston Churchill in letter suggests formation of an Inter-
Allied Commission for Chemical Warfare Supply. Chief Surgeon
reports non-effective rate for the week at 4.41 per hundred, the lowest
this year.

Mr. Baker went to London to discuss with the British authorities the prospects for additional shipping and also the general subject of munitions. While there he sent me the following telegram embodying suggestions from the Prime Minister which showed the deep anxiety of the British:

"London, March 25th.

"I have just had a long talk with the Prime Minister. He urges three proposals for your consideration: First, that our divisions in France be placed immediately in line to relieve French divisions for service elsewhere, quiet sectors being chosen for troops with least training. Second, that all available engineer troops be taken from Lines of Communication work and sent to aid of British engineers preparing positions back of present lines. It is urged that suspension of our work would be but temporary and that the work suggested is imperative. Third, that infantry be sent first of the entire six divisions to be transported by British in view of present acute needs of that Army. No answer to the foregoing is necessary until I see you to-morrow when we can discuss the suggestions fully. If railroads in France are too fully occupied to make the Italian trip possible I should abandon it. At any rate we should not permit diversion of engines and cars if they can be used in present emergency. We leave here to-morrow, Tuesday, at 7:30, for Paris.

"BAKER."

Meanwhile, Sir Douglas Haig had asked for engineers and heavy artillery, of which three regiments of the former were placed at his disposal at once and the personnel of two regiments of the latter about to arrive were offered.

During my visit to Versailles on March 26th, General Giardino made an appeal for an allotment of our troops. He argued that their presence would be tangible proof of the intense feeling of coöperation that inspired the American nation, that it would encourage those Italian working people who had been in America, that it would increase their confidence in the successful outcome of the war, and that, above all, they needed help. No doubt much of this was true, but it would have opened the way for similar concessions to the other Allies and in the end our forces would have been frittered away probably to little or no purpose. These appeals by the Allies, presented anew from time to time, only served to fix in our minds the idea that each was thinking in terms of its own army rather than of benefit to the Allies as a whole.

The railroad station at Paris on the evening I met the Secretary presented a scene that was most pathetic. The terror-stricken crowds from threatened villages and farms were fleeing they knew not whither, many of them for the second time during this war, from an enemy whose invasion of their country in days gone by had perhaps driven out their fathers and mothers before them. War in its effects upon the armies themselves is frightful enough, but the terror and the suffering that it causes women and children are incomparably worse. These thousands were leaving everything behind them, going to some distant part of their country to become, many of them, dependent upon their friends, others, perchance friendless and penniless, to live by charity as a burden to the community or to beg from door to door. There was even then hope that they might return later and through the help of the Government rebuild their homes. But will the shadow of this dreadful experience ever pass, or will war come again to cause like suffering to their posterity? No one can answer, but all can strive to the end that such ill fortune, which is the heritage of lands where the embers of hatred and jealousy are kept alive at the fireside, may come no more.

(Diary) Chaumont, Friday, March 29, 1918. Held conference with the Secretary of War and General Bliss yesterday morning on joint recommendation of Military Representatives of the War Council, after which the Secretary left for Chaumont by motor. I then went to Clermont-sur-Oise to offer Foch our troops. Roads very congested as we approached the front.

Left Paris this morning by way of Fontainebleau and reached Chaumont in four hours and twelve minutes, distance 155 miles. At Pétain's request, the 1st Division ordered to battle line, which Mr. Baker said people at home would enthusiastically approve. Mr. Cravath dined with us this evening, and, speaking of unity, favored placing control in the hands of a committee composed of Marshal Haig, General Pétain, and myself.

The situation was considered so serious that the Military Representatives seemed to think it necessary to recommend that all previous plans for the shipment of American troops be disregarded and that nothing but infantry and machine gun units be shipped until otherwise directed by the Supreme War Council. This they did in the form of a joint (or unanimous) note, which was, of course, approved by the Supreme War Council. I was very much surprised at the attitude of General Bliss, our military representative with the Council, as without his consent the joint note could not have been submitted to the Council.

The presence of the Secretary of War fortunately afforded me the opportunity to discuss with him not only the demands of the particular situation existing at that time but the general attitude of our Allies regarding the manner in which Americans should be employed. When the joint note was presented to Secretary Baker, I pointed out to him and General Bliss that the proposal, if approved by the President, would place the disposition of American units entirely in the hands of the Supreme War Council and take them quite out of our control, even for training, and would without doubt destroy all possibility of our forming an American army. The Secretary was as strongly opposed to any such outcome as I was and after some discussion he dictated his views in a cable to the President, explicitly recommending that the control of our forces should be retained by our Commander-in-Chief and that the joint note be approved only in that sense, as follows:

"March 28, 1918.

"Paragraph 1. The Secretary of War this morning directed this telegram be sent direct to the President with copy for Secretary of State and Secretary of War and Chief of Staff. Following Joint Note 18 of the Permanent Military Representatives with the Supreme War Council is transmitted for the action of the President. Following the text of the Joint Note are the recommendations of the Secretary of War dictated by him this morning.

"Paragraph 2. The following Joint Note 18 was adopted by the Permanent Military Representatives March 28, 1918, quote:

"(1) In paragraph four of Joint Note No. 12, dated 12th of January, 1918, the Military Representatives agreed as follows:
"After the most careful and searching inquiry they were agreed on the point that the security of France could also be assured. But in view of the strength of the attack which the enemy is able to develop on this front, an attack which, in the opinion of the Military Representatives, could reach a strength of 96 divisions (excluding reënforcements by roulement), they feel compelled to add that France will be safe during 1918 only under certain conditions, namely:

"(a) That the strength of the British and French troops in France are continuously kept up to their present total strength, and that they receive the expected reënforcements of not less than two American divisions per month.

"(2) The battle which is developing at the present moment in France and which can extend to the other theaters of operations may very quickly place the Allied armies in a serious situation from the point of view of effectives, and the Military Representatives are from this moment of opinion that the above detailed condition (a) can no longer be maintained and they consider as a general proposition that the new situation requires new decisions.

"The Military Representatives are of opinion that it is highly desirable that the American Government should assist the Allied armies as soon as possible by permitting, in principle, the temporary service of American units in Allied army corps and divisions, such reënforcements must however be obtained from other units than those American divisions which are now operating with the French, and the units so temporarily employed must eventually be returned to the American Army.

"(3) The Military Representatives are of opinion that, for the present time, in execution of the foregoing, and until otherwise directed by the Supreme War Council, only American infantry and machine gun units, organized as that Government may decide, be brought to France, and that all agreements or conventions hitherto made in conflict with this decision be modified accordingly.

"Paragraph 3. The following is the action recommended by the Secretary of War:

"To the President:

"The foregoing resolutions were considered by General Bliss, General Pershing, and me. Paragraph (3) proposes a change in the order of shipment of American troops to France and necessarily postpones the organization and training of complete American divisions as parts of an independent American army. This ought to be conceded only in view of the present critical situation and continued only so long as that situation necessarily demands it. The question of replacements will continue to embarrass the British and French Governments, and efforts to satisfy that need by retaining American units assigned to them must be anticipated, but we must keep in mind the formation of an American army, while, at the same time, we must not seem to sacrifice joint efficiency at a critical moment to that object. Therefore, I recommend that you express your approval of the Joint Note in the following sense:

"The purpose of the American Government is to render the fullest coöperation and aid, and therefore the recommendation of the Military Representatives with regard to the preferential transportation of American infantry and machine gun units in the present emergency is approved. Such units when transported will be under the direction of the Commander-in-Chief of the American Expeditionary Forces and will be assigned for training and use by him in his discretion. He will use these and all other military forces of the United States under his command in such manner as to render the greatest military assistance, keeping in mind always the determination of this Government to have its various military forces collected, as speedily as their training and the military situation will permit, into an independent American army, acting in concert with the armies of Great Britain and France, and all arrangements made by him for their temporary training and service will be made with that end in view.

"BAKER."

This action by the Military Representatives just at this crisis was intended to put the weight of the Supreme War Council behind the idea of maintaining the strength of Allied units by American replacements as a policy. The text of the joint note made it entirely plain that this was their purpose.

Returning to the battle then going on, it had developed on March 24th that the French divisions on the left of their line had received instructions that if the enemy continued his drive in the direction of Amiens they were to fall back so as to cover Paris. Marshal Haig, apprehensive that such action would result in separating the two armies, at once communicated his fears to his Government. This brought about the important conference at Doullens on the 26th between members of the British and French

Governments to consider the question of better coöperation between the two armies.

President Poincaré presided at the conference, which was attended by M. Clemenceau, M. Loucheur, Lord Milner, Marshal Haig, General Sir Henry Wilson, and General Foch. According to information received by General Bliss, and transmitted to the Secretary and me, there was much difference of opinion concerning what should be done. One suggestion made prior to the formal meeting was that M. Clemenceau be selected as the Allied Commander-in-Chief, with General Foch as his Chief of Staff. Finally it was decided that General Foch, as the senior military member of the Executive War Board, should be charged with coordinating the action of the Allied armies on the Western Front. General Foch immediately took command of the situation and under his direction the French lines were extended to the left as far as the Luce River.

As soon as I learned of the action of the Doullens Conference I decided that General Foch himself should know of our desire to do whatever we could to strengthen the Allies. Although I had offered our troops to Pétain on the 25th, it seemed to me that it might be better to make it emphatic by letting Foch know that I was prepared to put into the battle every man that we could muster. I had often thought of the possibility of a crisis that would require such a step and I wished Foch to know our attitude.

After my important conference with Mr. Baker and Bliss on the morning of the 28th, I motored in the afternoon to Clermont-sur-Oise to see Foch. As we approached his temporary field headquarters, the continuous columns of motor trucks, slowly working their way forward with troops and supplies, blocked the road here and there and it took much time to make the journey. At the headquarters of the French Third Army, in the town, every one professed ignorance of the General's whereabouts until a staff officer, an old friend of Captain de Marenches, my aide, put a French soldier in the car who directed the chauffeur around the edge of town, thence through a lane of tall poplars to a small, typically French farmhouse well off the road, and hidden among the trees.

We waited outside for a few minutes among the shrubbery and spring flowers and especially admired a beautiful cherry tree in full bloom that stood on the lawn. The place was quaintly picturesque and quiet, entirely undisturbed by the sound or sight of anything suggestive of war. Yet only a few miles to the northeast the French were at that moment making a furious counterattack against the enemy at Montdidier in one of the critical battles of the war. As we entered the house, Clemenceau, Foch, Pétain, and Loucheur were intently studying a map spread on the table. The situation was pointed out to me, showing that already the British had used thirty divisions and the French seventeen against the Germans' seventy-eight. It seemed to be the opinion that the British Fifth Army was getting back on its feet and that the lines would hold for the time being.

Intimating that I had come to see General Foch, the others withdrew into the yard, leaving us alone. I told him that the Americans were ready and anxious to do their part in this crisis, and that I was willing to send him any troops we had. I asked him for suggestions as to how we might help. He was evidently very much touched and in his enthusiasm took me by the arm and without hesitation rushed me out across the lawn to where the others stood and asked me to repeat what I had said to him. They, of course, showed keen interest, especially M. Clemenceau, as I told them what I had said to General Foch. Colonel Boyd, my aide, was kind enough to say that, under the inspiration of the moment, my French was spoken with a fluency that I could not have mustered ten minutes before or after. It appeared in the French papers the next morning, although I feel certain that it was written up in much better French than I actually used.

"Je viens pour vous dire que le peuple américain tiendrait à grand honneur que nos troupes fussent engagées dans la présent bataille.

"Je vous le demande en mon nom et au sien.

"Il n'y a pas en ce moment d'autres questions que de combattre.

"Infanterie, artillerie, aviation, tout ce que nous avons est à vous.

"Disposez-en comme il vous plaira.

"Il en viendra encore d'autres, aussi nombreux qu'il sera nécessaire.

"Je suis venu tout exprès pour vous dire que le peuple américain serait fier d'être engagé dans la plus grande bataille de l'historie." [1]

At the conclusion of my visit, the details of making use of our troops were left to be arranged with Pétain, who remarked that he and I had already discussed their employment. If the responsibility had been mine, I should not have hesitated a moment to put into the battle any or all of our five divisions then in France. The 1st Division was the only one used for the time being, the others being placed in quiet sectors, each to relieve two French divisions. As our divisions were more than twice as large as theirs, it amounted to almost immediate reënforcement of ten divisions.

It was the prevalent British view that General Foch was simply a liaison officer between the two armies, with advisory and coordinating authority only. Although inadequate to meet all circumstances, even this concession was a stride in the right direction, and his position was soon to be more clearly defined. In fact, President Wilson sent General Foch the following message on March 29th:

> "May I not convey to you my sincere congratulations on your new authority. Such unity of command is a most hopeful augury of ultimate success. We are following with profound interest the bold and brilliant action of your forces.
>
> "WOODROW WILSON."

The following telegram, received at my headquarters on April 1st and cabled to Washington, is General Foch's reply to President Wilson's message of congratulations:

[1] "I have come to tell you that the American people would consider it a great honor for our troops to be engaged in the present battle. I ask you for this in their name and my own.

"At this moment there are no other questions but of fighting.

"Infantry, artillery, aviation, all that we have are yours; use them as you wish. More will come, in numbers equal to requirements.

"I have come especially to tell you that the American people will be proud to take part in the greatest battle of history."

"A Monsieur le Président de la
    République des Etats-Unis.

"En pleine confiance grace à la parfaite Union des Alliés et en particulier au noble élan de l'Armée Américaine demandant a entrer immediatement dans la bataille, je vous addresse mes vifs remerciements pour votre télégramme de félicitations.

                                                                "Foch." [1]

Mr. Cravath's idea that command of the Allied forces be vested in a committee was never seriously considered by any one in authority, and it fell short of absolute unity of command, but it would more likely have met the situation than the plan adopted by the Supreme War Council. In theory, the plan for a general reserve appeared to be a reasonable method of avoiding the difficulties inherent in any plan for mutual support between the French and British armies. Upon analysis, however, one could not escape the conclusion that its application would result in the senior officer of the Executive Board assuming supreme control of the joint action of the two armies, at least on the defensive. With thirty reserve divisions at his command, he would be in position to dictate what should be done. The failure of the plan to become operative for lack of divisions to constitute the General Reserve fortunately led to the selection of an Allied Commander-in-Chief, which was probably the object sought by some of its far-sighted advocates.

Mr. Baker's message of March 28th to the President, forwarding the joint note with his recommendation was answered on the 30th as follows:

"The President concurs in the Joint Note of the Permanent Military Representatives of the Supreme War Council in the sense formulated in your number 67, March 28th, and wishes you to regard yourself authorized to decide questions of immediate coöperation or replacement."

It was thought that this statement, coming from the President, would check, at least for the time being, the demands of the Allies

[1] "To the President of the United States.

"In full confidence, thanks to the perfect union of the Allies and especially to the noble spirit of the American Army requesting to enter immediately into the battle, I extend to you my sincere thanks for your telegram of congratulations. Foch."

that we provide units for building up their divisions, but, as we shall see later, their insistence continued.

The President's message was followed on March 30th by a cable from the War Department, which stated: "The recommendations of Secretary of War to President * * * that preferential transportation be given to American infantry and machine gun units in present emergency understood and will be followed." It went on to say that these units pertaining to three divisions, the 3d, 5th, and 77th, would be sent at once and those of three other divisions about May 1st.

Replying on April 3d to the Department's cable, the fact was emphasized that it was "not intended that our units shall replace the losses of British or French organizations and therefore our artillery should be held in readiness to follow when called for," although it was possible that the situation might become "so serious that some of our infantry units will be forced to serve with British temporarily." My intentions were further indicated by saying that "Americans must not lose sight of the purpose to build up divisions and corps of their own," and also that "we must avoid our tendency to incorporate our infantry into British divisions where it will be used up and never relieved." My cable recommended that the infantry of two divisions should be sent by British shipping and two by our own, but that present plans should go no further than this. It was my purpose not to become too deeply involved in an agreement that would make it impossible later to form our own independent force under our own officers.

The German offensive which created such great concern in the ranks of the Allies was the first serious effort the enemy had undertaken since his costly attacks at Verdun in 1916. During the whole of 1917 he was outnumbered on the Western Front but in this recent attack he had a decided advantage both in strength and position. From a selected concentration zone within the great salient that projected into France, the enemy could strike with superior force to the west against the British or to the south against the French. He was doubly favored, for he had the advantages not only of the initiative but also of interior lines of communication, and was thereby enabled to keep the Allies in doubt as to the appropriate points for their concentrations of reserves.

The precise methods employed by the enemy at Riga and Caporetto were definitely known, as already mentioned, and information had been obtained prior to the spring offensive which clearly indicated that his forces in France were being carefully trained in the same system of attack. This "maneuver of rupture," as it was called, contemplated a penetration of six to eight miles the first day and a much more rapid exploitation thereafter. The attack was to penetrate quickly by infiltration and turn the successive positions by striking them in rear. A weak resistance by one group, or its demoralization by artillery fire or by the enemy infantry, would naturally involve adjacent groups and possibly force the whole to give way.

To meet this form of attack the French had, as far as possible, prepared a defensive system of great depth, and the British had adopted somewhat the same idea. In theory such distribution of forces was tactically correct, but when this German offensive began there was a lack of reserves near the line where the principal resistance was to be made. As both of the Allied armies were almost completely wedded to trench fighting and their troops had been given little or no training in open warfare, they were at great disadvantage once they were forced out of the trenches.

Although experience had actually demonstrated that instead of placing too many troops out in the front lines a carefully selected position of resistance, not too far forward, should be strongly held behind a thin outpost zone well in advance, the principle was often neglected. It may be noted in passing that this was exactly the system laid down in our own tactical regulations before the war.

In carrying out our plans for the organization of an American army on the Lorraine front, with the reduction of the St. Mihiel salient planned as the initial operation, the volume of construction necessary along our line of communications had been pushed as fast as conditions permitted. The establishment of advance depots and other installations in Lorraine were well under way. On January 16th the 1st Division (Bullard) had entered the line north of Toul, with the understanding that other divisions would follow as they became sufficiently trained, and that when four divisions were available an American army corps would be formed and the sector would pass definitely under American control. The 26th Division (Edwards) had been withdrawn

LOCATION AMERICAN DIVISIONS
MARCH 20, 1918
Battle line——— International bdy.—·—·—
Numerals indicate Divisions ;
circled numerals those not in line.

from the Chemin des Dames on March 21st, and the 42d Division (Menoher) from east of Lunéville two days later, and both were prepared to take their places beside the 1st. These were to be followed by the 2d Division (Bundy) then in line for preliminary experience at Sommedieue, south of Verdun, while the 32d Division (Haan), which had only recently arrived, would come in later.

The headquarters of the I Corps (Liggett), which had been organized at Neufchâteau in January, was to move up to Toul as soon as there were three divisions in the line. It could be said that an important step in organizing an American army would then be taken. But just as our hopes were about to be realized the storm broke, the situation on the British front created a grave crisis, and the concentration of our troops in an American sector, much to my regret, was voluntarily and indefinitely postponed.

CHAPTER XXV

Conference at Beauvais—Foch Chosen Allied Commander—President Wilson Approves—Limits of Authority—Lack of Training—Inspection of Divisions—Troops for Training with British—Letters to and from Secretary—Mr. Baker Departs for Home

(Diary) Paris, Thursday, April 4, 1918. The Secretary left for Italy on Saturday. Ex-Senator Percy, Y.M.C.A., dropped in on Monday. Conference Tuesday with Colonel Fox Conner, Chief of Operations, regarding disposition new divisions. Reports indicate that they seriously lack instruction, especially the replacements.

Left Chaumont yesterday morning and went to Beauvais for conference. War Council decided on General Foch as Allied Commander-in-Chief.

Advised Elmer Roberts, Associated Press, this morning of action of conference. The Secretary and party returned from Italy to-day and are stopping with us. Visit of the Prince of Wales planned for to-day has been postponed. Two French and one British divisions and four brigades of British field artillery being withdrawn from Italian front. Labor situation improving; 6,000 on hand with 12,000 possible from Italy. Sent cable to help Third Liberty Loan.[1] Brigadier General Williams, my Chief of Ordnance, ordered to Washington to be Chief.

M R. BAKER felt that he should pay a visit to Italy while in Europe and left Paris on the 30th for that purpose, accompanied by Colonel T. Bentley Mott, who was entirely familiar with the Italian situation. Before his departure, he and I took up the question of a supreme commander, which

[1] "For Secretary McAdoo: Every dollar subscribed to the Liberty Loan is a dollar invested in American manhood. Every dollar subscribed as the result of self-denial means partnership in the hardships and risks of our men in the trenches. Every dollar subscribed will confirm the determination of our people at home to stand by the army to a victorious end. An overwhelming subscription to the Third Liberty Loan will be a patriotic expression of confidence in our ability as a nation to maintain all that we hold dear in civilization."

Facilities were provided in the army in France for making subscriptions to this loan but no active campaign was instituted.

371

we had discussed before and were ready to accept in principle when proposed. Apropos of its probability, he sent the President the following cable:

"March 30, 1918.

"I have just been shown a copy of a message from Lloyd George to you with regard to General Foch and American troops. The situation seems to be that Lloyd George is personally in favor of a Supreme Commander but fears British opinion will be the other way because such a Commander could sacrifice the Channel ports to the defense of Paris. The arrangement therefore is that General Foch is to be supreme enough to coördinate but without being called Supreme Commander. General Pershing will, of course, act under General Foch as Pétain and Haig have agreed to do. I venture to suggest that in replying to that part of Lloyd George's message you might go further than he asks and say that we are willing to accept a general Supreme Command whenever the French and British are. Perhaps the relative smallness of our present forces and our having no immediate defensive object in France would make it unwise for us to urge the point though the present events would seem to have demonstrated the need. * * * General Pershing's prompt and fine action with regard to the use of our troops and facilities here in the emergency has won enthusiastic commendation from French and British. Our 1st Division will shortly be withdrawn from trenches and used in battle.

"BAKER."

The main points of Mr. Lloyd George's message to President Wilson are contained in a message, dated March 29th, received by General Bliss and sent by him to the Secretary of War and me, as given below:

"The following has been handed to me by the military representative of Great Britain and is transmitted for the information of the Secretary of War and General Pershing:

"Secret. From the Prime Minister.

"Subparagraph A.

"Please communicate to General Bliss that I have cabled to President Wilson asking him to approve of Foch exercising the same * * * authority over the American Army as he is exercising over the British and French; to send men over to France with the utmost possible speed to make good losses; and to agree to arrangements made by General Pershing to their being brigaded as they become available with French and British divisions for the duration of the crisis.

"Subparagraph B

"The Prime Minister thinks that before this fighting is over, every man may count, and he can see no other way of making splendid American material available in this crisis of the war.

"BLISS."

In response to a notice from M. Clemenceau, I went on April 3d to Beauvais, about forty-five miles north of Paris, to meet with the Supreme War Council. This curious old town, not far from the active front, has much of historical interest. Arriving early, Colonel Boyd and I strolled about and visited the cathedral, a fine specimen of Gothic architecture of the 13th Century, and then had to wait an hour at the Hôtel de Ville before M. Clemenceau and Lloyd George came into the conference room. Marshal Haig and Generals Foch, Pétain, Sir Henry Wilson, Bliss, Weygand, and I were the others participating. Brigadier General Spiers acted as interpreter and Lieutenant Colonel Sir Maurice Hankey, who usually accompanied Mr. Lloyd George, acted as recorder. The meeting was finally called to order by M. Clemenceau, who stated its purpose, saying in substance:

"We have come together to settle a very simple question regarding the functions of General Foch. I think we are all in agreement as to the coördination of Allied action, but there is some difference in the understanding of General Foch's powers as conferred upon him at the Doullens conference of March 26th. General Foch will explain his difficulties."

General Foch then set forth briefly his situation, about as follows:

"The powers conferred by the Doullens conference were limited to the coördination of action between the Allies. They were conferred while the action was on. The power to coördinate has been construed to be limited to the time the Allies were in action. That was March 26th at Doullens. It is now April 3d. Now that the two op-

NOTE: Total strength of the A.E.F. on March 31st, 18,966 officers, 299,655 enlisted men.

Divisional units arriving in March included elements of the 3d Division (Regular Army), Major General Joseph T. Dickman, and 5th Division (Regular Army), Major General John E. McMahon. The major portion of the 5th Division did not arrive until May.

posing armies are no longer in action but have stopped and are facing each other, there is nothing to coördinate. There should be authority to prepare for action and direct it. So that we are right back where we were before, and nothing can be done until an action starts again."

Mr. Lloyd George then entered the discussion, saying substantially:

"We have had more than three years of this war, and we have not had unity of action during that time. During the last year we have had two kinds of strategy, one by Haig and another by Pétain, both different, and nothing has been gained. The only thing that was accomplished was by General Nivelle when he was in supreme command. The Germans have done exactly what General Nivelle tried to do. The Supreme War Council that met in February adopted a plan for handling a general reserve, but through the action of those concerned nothing has come of it. It is a nullity. What has happened recently has stirred the British people very much and must not happen again, as the people will demand why it has happened, and somebody will be called to account. They want some sort of unity of command. General Foch is now empowered to coördinate the action of the Allied armies, but this does not go far enough as he has no authority to control except by conferring with the respective Commanders-in-Chief. He wants authority to prepare for action. I think the resolution made at Doullens should be modified so that we may have a better understanding. I should like to hear what General Bliss and General Pershing have to say."

General Bliss read the Doullens resolution, which was as follows:

"General Foch is charged by the British and French Governments to coördinate the action of the Allied armies on the Western Front. To this end he will come to an understanding with the Commanders-in-Chief, who are to furnish him all the information necessary." [1]

He interpreted it to mean, first, that General Foch was given no authority to act except in conference with the two Commanders-in-Chief; second, that they should furnish him certain information regarding the situation of their respective forces. He went

[1] Le général Foch est chargé par les gouvernements britannique et français de coordonner l'action des armées alliées sur le front ouest. Il s'entendra à cet effet avec les généraux en chef, qui sont à lui fournir tous les renseignements nécéssaires.

into some further analysis of the resolution to the effect that in order to meet all situations the powers conferred upon General Foch should be enlarged.

I then gave my view, which was set forth in a brief memorandum prepared in pencil after the discussion began, as follows:

"The principle of unity of command is undoubtedly the correct one for the Allies to follow. I do not believe that it is possible to have unity of action without a supreme commander. We have already had experience enough in trying to coördinate the operations of the Allied armies without success. There has never been real unity of action. Such coördination between two or three armies is impossible no matter who the commanders-in-chief may be. Each commander-in-chief is interested in his own army, and cannot get the other commander's point of view or grasp the problem as a whole. I am in favor of a supreme commander and believe that the success of the Allied cause depends upon it. I think the necessary action should be taken by this council at once. I am in favor of conferring the supreme command upon General Foch."

When I had finished reading it, Mr. Lloyd George came over to where I sat, took me by the hand, and said:

"I agree fully with General Pershing. This is well put."

Mr. Lloyd George then asked for the views of Marshal Haig, who said:

"We have had practically complete unity of action. I have always coöperated with the French, whom I regard as in control of the strategical questions of the war. I was placed directly under the command of General Nivelle, and General Pétain and I have always worked well together. I agree with General Pershing's general idea that there should be unity of command, but I think we have had it."

The views expressed by General Pétain were practically the same as Marshal Haig's, although I think they both realized the necessity of some definite coördinating control.

As a result, after some further informal discussion, a draft of a resolution was submitted which omitted reference to the American Army. Whereupon I called attention to the oversight, saying:

"I think this resolution should include the American Army. The arrangement is to be in force, as I understand it, from now on, and the American Army will soon be ready to function as such and should be included as an entity like the British and French armies."

General Pétain remarked:

"There is no American army as such, as its units are either in training or are amalgamated with the British and French."

To which I replied:

"There may not be an American army in force functioning now but there soon will be, and I want this resolution to apply to it when it becomes a fact. The American Government is represented here at this conference and in the war, and any action as to the supreme command that includes the British and French armies should also include the American Army."

The foregoing account of the conference may not be an exact record of the language used, but is given as my aide took it down at the time.

The following resolution was then read and adopted:

French	*English*
Beauvais, le 3 Avril 1918.	Beauvais, April 3, 1918.
Le Général Foch est chargé par les Gouvernements Britannique, Français et Américain de coordonner l'action des Armées Alliées sur le front occidental; il lui est conféré à cet effet tous les pouvoirs nécessaires en vue d'une réalisation effective. Dans ce but, les Gouvernements Britannique, Français et Américain confient au Général Foch la direction stratégique des opérations militaires.	General Foch is charged by the British, French and American Governments with the coördination of the action of the Allied Armies on the Western Front; to this end there is conferred on him all the powers necessary for its effective realization. To the same end, the British, French and American Governments confide in General Foch the strategic direction of military operations.
Les Commandants en Chef des Armées Britannique, Française et Américaine exercent dans sa plénitude la conduite tactique de leur Armée. Chaque Commandant en Chef aura le droit d'en appeler à son	The Commanders-in-Chief of the British, French and American Armies will exercise to the fullest extent the tactical direction of their armies. Each Commander-in-Chief will have the right to appeal to his Government, if in his opinion his

Gouvernement, si dans son opinion, son Armée se trouve mise en danger par toute instruction reçue du Général Foch.

Army is placed in danger by the instructions received from General Foch.

G. Clemenceau
Pétain
F. Foch
D. Lloyd George
D. Haig, F.M.
Henry Wilson, General, 3.4.18.
Tasker H. Bliss, General and Chief of Staff.
John J. Pershing, General, U.S.A.

G. Clemenceau
Pétain
F. Foch
D. Lloyd George
D. Haig, F.M.
Henry Wilson, General, 3.4.18.
Tasker H. Bliss, General and Chief of Staff.
John J. Pershing, General, U.S.A.

While the momentous events of the previous two weeks had been in progress, it had become increasingly evident that the lack of coördination between the Allies had prevented the best use to be made of their combined strength. The conclusion was inevitable to any one conversant with the facts that some arrangement for better teamwork must be found. The idea of an Allied commander-in-chief had been suggested and discussed many times unofficially, but for various reasons, political and otherwise, it had never been adopted by the Supreme War Council. With the distrust that existed among the Allies, it was not easy to bring about the decision in favor of a supreme commander and it was only made possible by the extreme emergency of the situation.

It was natural that the position of supreme commander should fall either to a French or a British officer. An American could hardly have been considered for the one reason, if for no other, that we then occupied no front of our own and our force was still relatively small. While the two Allies should have realized the necessity for closer coöperation, yet the sentiment in the armies and among noncombatants of each against selecting any one from the army of the other was difficult to overcome. The British held that the Channel ports must be defended at all costs and feared that this might not be fully appreciated by a French supreme commander. The French were compelled to protect their capital and were uncertain of the attitude in that regard that a British supreme commander might take. These obligations were, of course, important, and each was considered vital by the Government concerned. The common objective of their combined forces, however, was the German Army, though this fact was apparently often obscured by the individual point of view of each of the Allies. Previous to this crisis they did not seem to realize fully that the success of their common cause demanded complete unity of action, both on the offensive and defensive, and that without it they could not win.

Human nature is the same whether it be regarded as affecting the actions of individuals or of nations. The subordination of a national undertaking of any kind to the authority of another nation can hardly be thought of except under the most pressing necessity. In this case national pride entered to an unusual degree. Although we were face to face with the greatest crisis of the war, none of the Governments concerned was willing to place its army under control of a supreme commander chosen from another army. This was shown in the Beauvais resolution by the limitations placed upon the authority of the Allied Commander-in-Chief. He could coördinate the action of the armies and determine the strategy, but each Commander-in-Chief was alone responsible for the tactical direction of his own army. The right was given each one to appeal to his Government in case there should be any interference with this prerogative. It was the safeguard against the identity of any of the armies being disregarded. While the powers of the Allied Commander-in-Chief were thus defined, yet, under the agreement as adopted, unity of action was secured as far as was necessary, and the independence and initiative of the respective armies were protected.

It was proposed by the French that the title of Commander-in-Chief of the Allied Armies in France should be given to General Foch. On April 15th I received a letter from M. Clemenceau advising me that Mr. Lloyd George had approved the suggestion, and asked if I agreed. I replied in a personal note expressing my approval, subject to the confirmation of the President, which came on the 17th.

Once the question of supreme command was settled, the co-ordinated energies of the Allied armies could be directed with maximum effect toward a common end. Although dark days were still ahead, we were spared the chagrin of inefficiency through lack of teamwork. With unity of command and the still more important fact of almost unlimited American reënforcements looming on the horizon, the chances of Allied success were much improved.

Yet, scarcely had the appointment of Foch been announced than considerable outspoken dissatisfaction among the British began to appear. One newspaper, *The Globe,* supposed at that time to represent the views of the British High Command in the field, said:

> "Our objections to a Generalissimo (which we believe to be shared by our readers and by practically all Englishmen outside the war cabinet and its press) remain. They are not so much military as political. Any Generalissimo is the servant of the state that appoints him. Consequently such an office involves (the possibility) that the Allied Army passes under the control of foreign politicians. * * * Indeed the feeling on this side of the Channel is so strong that we may safely assume that the appointment of that honored soldier, General Foch, as Generalissimo is a temporary arrangement for the present operations, and as such it is as welcome in London as it is understood to be at G.H.Q."

Now that the supreme effort must be made on our part, and when units were sorely needed for active service, it was all the more deplorable that the divisions then coming to France contained a large percentage of untrained men. This condition, mainly the result of a very grievous lack of appreciation by the War Department of the urgency of continuous and thorough training of complete units must, as already pointed out, be blamed upon the General Staff. It failed to provide men for special services and relied upon taking them from combat divisions instead of anticipating such requirements and segregating these specialists from the start and training them as such.

This was a most vicious continuance in time of war of a very objectionable habit that had grown up in our Army in time of peace. The practice was carried to such an extent that divisions of 25,000 men, which should have been held intact, and each one perfected as an organized team, were constantly called upon to send large groups of their trained soldiers to other duties. The numbers taken aggregated from 15,000 to 40,000 men for each division. As green men were substituted, the result was that training had to be practically started all over again with each such reduction. Although the War Department eventually established a replacement system, as urgently recommended by me, it was done too late to be of material benefit even to the last divisions that came over in the fall of 1918.

Although the thirty-four National Guard and National Army divisions that eventually came to France were, with two exceptions, organized in August and September, 1917, they did not receive training as complete units from that time on. They were filled gradually and by piecemeal, weeks and even months usually elapsing before they reached full strength, and, as we have seen, the personnel was constantly changing.

Therefore, when the time came for service abroad, a very large proportion of the men in these divisions had little or no experience, and the training of the unit as a whole had been seriously delayed. Moreover, training methods at home had not improved, as preparation for trench warfare still predominated. All this was discouraging to their officers, disastrous to morale, threw upon the A.E.F. an extra burden of training, and resulted in our having a number of divisions only partially trained when the time came to use them.

The indications were that incoming units would soon have to be put in the front lines, with no time to carry out a complete course of training in France for units composed largely of recruits. I therefore sent a vigorous protest against the practice of taking men out of the units in training and emphasized again the necessity of open warfare exercises for all organizations including the division. The urgency of target practice and musketry training of platoons and companies was especially stressed and it was requested that no men be sent over without four months of intensive training.

This condition of things signalized the failure on the part of the General Staff at home to realize that their most important function was to supervise the organization and training of complete divisions for combat and provide them with equipment and supplies. Their obligations to the armies in the field were not fulfilled by merely sending units carelessly prepared and with an undue proportion of green officers and men to fight against trained veterans.

Only 300,000 men had joined the colors in France up to April 1st, and of the latest group a sizable proportion of the men had been in training only a few days. In order to provide the men and give them as much time to train as possible, I laid before the Secretary of War while he was in France the urgency of calling out all the men that we should be likely to need by fall and putting them in training at once. He seemed willing to do so but pointed out that this would probably cause a shortage of labor for planting and harvesting the crops. I thought that this demand ought to be met in some other way and that the military needs, under the circumstances, were of first importance.

(Diary) Paris, Sunday, April 7, 1918. Went to Chaumont on Friday, accompanied by Colonel Boyd and Lieutenant G. E. Adamson, my secretary. Mr. Baker remained in Paris.

Yesterday saw part of 1st Division at Toul entraining for the Somme. Found General Bullard ill in hospital. Visited 26th Division, in quiet sector but anxious for active employment. Saw 2d, in line south of Verdun, equally keen. At Souilly called on Major General Hirschauer, Commanding French Second Army, who spoke in high praise of our soldiers. Conferred with Harbord, Fox Conner, and Fiske in evening about use of our divisions.

Came to Paris this afternoon, where Mr. Baker and I conferred with Generals Whigham and Hutchinson, British War Office, on shipment and use of American troops. Discussed with Generals Ford and Dawney from British G.H.Q. the training of our troops with British. The Secretary left this evening for Brest, en route home.

In view of their possible early employment, I wanted especially to look into the general state of efficiency of our available divisions and give some personal instructions about training. On going the rounds, I met General Hirschauer, who was one of the able French generals, and found him very enthusiastic about the 2d Division, which had been in line at Sommedieue under his command. He said that without doubt it was then as efficient as any of his French divisions, confirming my own opinion formed from observation and reports. The 1st Division was further advanced than any of the others and its morale was high at the prospect of going into the battle line.

Recent developments had brought into immediate consideration the question of the employment of American troops. The President's qualified approval of the recommendation of the Supreme War Council, as embodied in Joint Note No. 18, was seized upon by the Allies and construed as a concession for the unlimited absorption of our troops in their armies. No doubt my offer to Foch lent encouragement to the Allied view. At the conclusion of the Beauvais conference, Mr. Lloyd George told me that a cable had been received from Lord Reading, the British Ambassador at Washington, stating that he had approached President Wilson with the view of obtaining the dispatch to Europe of 120,000 infantry and machine gun units per month, beginning with April, provided the necessary shipping could be obtained.

On the following day a cable came from the War Department, quoting information received through British shipping channels, as follows:

"We have informed War Cabinet that in shipping provided by Great Britain we shall be able to embark in America in April some 60,000 men. Admiral Sims' estimate of carrying power of American troop fleet is 52,000 per month. In addition there is certain Dutch tonnage available for use by America and we are obtaining use of certain Italian tonnage. In total it is considered that 120,000 American troops can be embarked in April and if anything rather more in following months. In view of urgent military needs Lord Reading has approached the President with the view of obtaining dispatch of

120,000 infantry per month to Europe between now and July, infantry and machine gun units only. Men to be brigaded with British and French divisions on the same basis as in case of six-division plan. This means using all troop-carrying ships to carry American infantry without reference to recent controversy. The President agrees that all possible measures must be taken to insure maximum use of troop tonnage."

The receipt of this plan from British sources evidently created something like consternation in the War Department, judging from its cabled comments, in which it was stated that "this program would practically stop all shipments of artillery, technical units, service of rear, army, and corps troops."

On the day of the Secretary's departure Generals Whigham and Hutchinson came over from the British War Office to discuss arrangements for the transportation of American troops, in accordance with the provisions of Joint Note No. 18. The conversation indicated that the British understood that we were to send 60,000 men per month to train with them and that they were to bring over the same number, making a total of 120,000 per month beginning with April. They held that the President's approval of Joint Note No. 18 had superseded agreements previously made, including the six-division plan. General Whigham said:

"The interpretation of the British War Office is that the Versailles agreement (Joint Note No. 18) wipes out all previous agreements and it is now a question of sending infantry and machine gun units to be trained by British, French, and Americans, the proportion to go to each to be decided later."

The whole tenor of the conversation showed that the British then regarded it as certain that our troops were to be used to build up the French and British armies. But neither Mr. Baker nor I had received any intimation that the President had agreed to the British proposal mentioned in the above cable, and his qualified approval of Joint Note No. 18 did not commit us to any such program as the British claimed. Moreover, I was opposed to any commitment that would tie our hands and make it impossible to form an American army. My attitude toward the proposal was made perfectly clear. Mr. Baker knew nothing more than the declaration contained in the joint note, which stated no figures.

The British conferees entirely ignored the specific condition that the final arrangements as to training and disposition of all our units were to be left in my hands. Their error was pointed out and Mr. Baker then said:

> "What is pertinent to the present discussion is that American troops are going to the British for training. I don't want the British public or army, or the French public or army, to get an exaggerated idea that this scheme provides or will provide a means by which their losses will be made up in the future. I want no feeling of disillusionment when General Pershing calls for the troops entrusted to them for training."

The conference ended with the understanding that 60,000 American infantry and machine gun units to be brought over by the British in April should go to them for training. It was also understood that the disposition of other troops would be left for later decision. Certain deficiencies in land transportation, clothing and machine guns were to be provided by the British. While they accepted this at the moment and declared that they thoroughly understood, that was not to be the last of it, as the whole question was taken up again in conference in London later in the month.

Mr. Baker's visit to our armies during this critical period was fortunate as he could thus see the problems that confronted us in their true perspective. He had an opportunity to meet the Allied leaders, both civil and military, and to get in touch with conditions in the different countries. Of still greater importance, he saw with his own eyes the building of our organization. He was a keen observer, with clear understanding and a logical mind, and obtained in a short time an accurate conception of our task and its difficulties. As to our relations, he gave me from the start that strong and sympathetic support which means so much to a military commander in the field, and I undertook to keep him and the President at all times in confidential touch with our armies and the plans for supplying and handling them.

When Mr. Baker left, it was felt that the result of his visit would be that under his direction the War Department would function with a better understanding of our task and therefore with greatly increased efficiency and energy. Before sailing, he sent the following letter, which was published to the command:

"General Orders⎫   "American Expeditionary Forces,
   "No. 57 ⎬   "France, April 15, 1918.
"1. The Commander-in-Chief takes pleasure in publishing the following letter from the Secretary of War:

" 'France, April 7, 1918.
" 'To the Officers and Men of the American Expeditionary Forces in France:

" 'After a thorough inspection of the American Expeditionary Forces, I am returning to the United States with fresh enthusiasm to speed the transportation of the remainder of the great Army of which you are the vanguard. What I have seen here gives the comfortable assurance that plans for the effectiveness of our fighting forces and for the comfort and welfare of the men have been broadly made and vigorously executed. Our schools and systems of instruction are adding to the general soldier training the specialized knowledge which developed among our French and British associates during the four years of heroic action which they have displayed from the beginning of the war.

" 'Fortunately, the relations between our soldiers and those of the British and French are uniformly cordial and happy, and the welcome of the civil population of France has been met by our soldiers with chivalrous appreciation and return.

" 'We are building a great army to vindicate a great cause, and the spirit which you are showing, the courage, the resourcefulness and the zeal for the performance of duty both as soldiers and as men is not only promising of success, but it is worthy of the traditions of America and of the Allied Armies with which we are associated. Press on!

" 'NEWTON D. BAKER,
" 'Secretary of War.'

"In adding his own high appreciation of the splendid spirit of our army, the Commander-in-Chief wishes to impress upon officers and men of all ranks a keen sense of the serious obligations which rest upon them, while at the same time giving fresh assurance of his complete confidence in their loyalty, their courage, and their sincere devotion to duty.

"2. This order will be read to each company and separate detachment at its first assembly after the receipt of the order.

"By command of General Pershing:
"JAMES G. HARBORD,
"Chief of Staff."

Fearing that I would not see Mr. Baker again before he sailed for home, I sent him the letter quoted below, and although we later discussed its contents briefly, it is given as showing the reaction of at least part of the British press at the time:

"April 5, 1918.

"DEAR MR. SECRETARY:

"I noticed the other day that one of the British papers, in referring to the fact that plans had been made to send American troops to the assistance of the Allies, stated that this would relieve the British of the necessity of depleting the strength of the forces kept at home for defensive purposes.

"This suggests to my mind a certain political phase of the British situation which may give us additional explanation as to why Mr. Lloyd George and British representatives are so urgent in their appeals for assistance from America. The train of thought leads me to conceive the existence of a condition that may be fraught with danger to the cause, in that it indicates a serious lack of coöperation between the civil and military authorities of Great Britain, as was also indicated to you in some of the things I repeated to you yesterday. * * *

"Following this further, may I suggest that you give the matter serious thought. There is so very much at stake for us that it seems to me that very frank representations should be made to the British Government as to the urgency of their putting into the army every possible man that can be mustered to meet the immediate emergency. It need not be pointed out that there is a limit to the rapidity with which our troops can be brought over, and there seems to me to be a very real danger of the British political world allowing itself to be lulled into inaction upon the theory that the Americans are in a position to meet all possible contingencies that may arrive.

"It may be that you would think it advisable to go to London, or else to intimate to the President by cable the urgency of Great Britain's putting into the ranks every possible man to withstand the present German onslaught, even if they have to promise to withdraw them in six months, and of their doing so without waiting on us or counting on us in the slightest degree. There will be few enough men even with the best we all can do. It will be time enough for Great Britain to consider the defense of England after she has put forth every possible energy on the continent. Here is the place to beat Germany, and not on British soil. In writing this I have in mind what you told me regarding available men in England.

"I give you the following from General Sir William Robertson in a letter to me dated January 17th:

" ' * * * The British Government has given the most anxious consideration to the question of the maintenance of the armies in the field during 1918 and, by making every effort, there will become available for service at the front 449,000 men now under training, plus 100,000 men to be called up. In addition, there will be called up 100,000 men of lower category who are not fit for the first line, plus 120,000 lads of 18 years of age, who will not be available for service at the front till 1919. Please keep these figures strictly secret.'

"It may be that some of these have already been called out, but I am informed that large numbers of men are held for home defense.

"Believe me, with very sincere regard and high esteem,
                    "Yours faithfully,
                                        "JOHN J. PERSHING."

CHAPTER XXVI

Awakening of Allies—Greater Activity Necessary—Airplane Situation—
Liberty Motor—Water Supply—New Burdens on S.O.S.—1st Division
in Picardy—Talk to its Officers—Visit to Foch—Marshal Haig's Order
of April 11th—Letter to Clemenceau on Unified Supply—President's
Liberty Day Proclamation

(Diary) Chaumont, Friday, April 12, 1918. Washington reports
140,000 increase in cargo tonnage by use of Dutch ships. Infantry
and machine gun personnel of four divisions promised this month.
Brest selected as terminal of *Leviathan,* formerly the German *Vater-
land.* Expansion of all activities necessary.

Conferred on Monday with Generals Kernan, as to ports, Rogers on
quartermaster supplies, Williams about ordnance, and Foulois as to
aviation. Talked yesterday with General Hinds, who will be Chief
of Artillery.

THE Allies were at last thoroughly alive to the urgency of
making an extraordinary effort to provide tonnage for the
transportation of our troops. After months of delay and
discussion, they now realized fully that the superiority of forces
vitally necessary to avert defeat must come from across the
Atlantic. America was their reliance. Early aid was imperative.

Mr. Baker's first-hand knowledge of the situation in France
enabled him to give a fresh impetus to the efforts of the War
Department. With General Peyton C. March as Chief of Staff,
the General Staff and the supply departments began to exert more
energy. The War Industries Board, under the leadership of
Mr. B. M. Baruch, had taken definite steps toward the control of
the Nation's industries for war purposes. During the preceding
year, through lack of authority and organization, there had been
much confusion and little progress.

Acting under the direct authority of the President, the object
of the Board was to mobilize the country's resources and coördi-

nate the demands of the fighting forces with those of the civilian population. It undertook to stimulate production of war materials and limit that of war non-essentials. The Board controlled and harmonized output and determined priority. It made allotments to the different departments of the Government and to the Allies of necessary raw materials and manufactured products. The remarkable success of its efforts points to the wisdom of invoking a similar civilian super-agency in case of any future major war emergency.

In the face of the crisis, our hope for an improvement in methods and a more competent coördination of effort seemed about to be realized. If a similar awakening had taken place in the previous autumn, we should probably have had at least one-half million combat troops in France ready for the spring campaign and they would have been better trained than those who were arriving. Moreover, we would have been in position to answer more effectively the Allied arguments for amalgamation.

The larger program of shipments contemplated that twice the number of troops previously considered possible would be sent to France. Realizing the enormous problem that now confronted us, every element of the A.E.F. concerned attacked it vigorously. Fortunately, the larger ports of Brest and Cherbourg were available for the debarkation of personnel, leaving our regular ports to handle the increase of cargo. Meanwhile, we had secured a a few more berths and had gradually improved our port facilities, even with shortage in labor and material. At the same time, considerable progress had been made in expanding rail transportation. New engines and cars were arriving from the States, the repair of cars was progressing steadily, and the construction of additional storage was under way to meet the new requirements. Consequently when inquiry came from Washington again indicating some apprehensions regarding our ability to take care of the increasing arrivals of troops and cargo there was no hesitancy in replying: "Send over everything you have ready as fast as you can. The responsibility for failure will be ours."

The aviation question began to look more promising at this time. According to recent cables the shipments of airplanes from the States were expected to begin in May and increase to 600 per month by October. The manufacture of planes by the French had slowed down for want of mechanics and spruce, but we had given them considerable assistance and there was a possibility that agreements might be partially fulfilled. The combined programs promised to approximate the numbers that we should need for divisions that were likely soon to be engaged.

During the preceding months the War Department had made every effort to secure quantity production of an improved airplane motor, to be called the "Liberty." The design had been finally determined, and the manufacture was under way. The introduction of a new type of our own seemed the only way out of the bewildering confusion of this problem, even though it somewhat retarded the schedule of airplane manufacture. In the end, this superior motor proved to have been essential to meet an urgent demand, both by the Allies and ourselves.

New training and billeting areas for the increased numbers of divisions and detachments in prospect were none too easy to find within the already crowded space near the front, and it became necessary to open up new territory near the ports to provide temporary accommodations for incoming troops until the pressure could be relieved by readjustment and by the entry of the more advanced units into the lines.

Water supply was comparatively simple as long as our troops occupied areas that had previously been used, but when they were assigned to other localities it was often difficult to procure the necessary quantity and quality. The problem varied depending upon the region and the activity and size of the forces to be supplied. The systems of towns were utilized wherever possible, but frequently new wells had to be dug, pumps installed, and pipe lines laid. Water was often obtained from streams and lakes. Water carts were employed, especially by troops at the front, and chemical treatment was applied wherever necessary. This duty of providing water for our units in various parts of France was performed by the engineers.

The burden upon our staff and supply organizations in France became exceedingly heavy. The rapidly increasing numbers of men and the precipitate rush of supplies would be of no avail unless they could be mustered in orderly fashion. The crisis had found us with less than 320,000 officers and men in France, of which about 100,000 were necessarily engaged in the Services of Supply. There was great danger that the enemy would be able to defeat the French and British armies before substantial aid could be brought from America. If our forces could not be put into the lines in sufficient numbers within the next few months it might be too late. The war was up to America to win or lose.

No army was ever thoroughly trained or fully organized; in fact, there is no such thing except in theory. Governments or commanders who wait for absolute perfection in organization and training, or who expect every detail of equipment and supply to be complete before they act, are likely to lose opportunities and risk possible defeat at the hands of a more daring opponent. Vigorous action is necessary when the hour comes whether everything is entirely ready or not. It is a question of balance between opportunity and preparation.

(Diary) Paris, Tuesday, April 16, 1918. Bradley called at Chaumont Sunday, reporting again slow arrival of field hospitals, personnel and medical supplies. Discussed with Atterbury the rail situation; efficiency improving, but operating personnel needed to replace shortage of French. Left for Paris in afternoon.

Went to Chaumont-en-Vexin yesterday to witness practice maneuver of the 1st Division. Bullard back to duty. Met the Duke of Connaught in Paris and chatted a few minutes.

Visited 1st Division again this morning and spoke to the assembled officers. Went to Sarcus to confer with Foch, who looked tired and careworn. Arranged to send Colonel Mott to his headquarters as liaison officer.

At Pétain's request, the 1st Division was withdrawn from the line near Toul and sent to Chaumont-en-Vexin, northwest of Paris, to go into an active sector. The occasion of my visit was to witness the division's final maneuver in open warfare. Both officers and men were in splendid condition, notwithstanding their long rail journey, and all were ready for the test of actual battle. General Micheler, who commanded the French Fifth Army, to which the 1st Division had been assigned, came also to witness the maneuver. He spoke highly of the condition of the troops and their efficiency. The weather was clear but rather sharp. The countryside was radiant with its green meadows and early flowers and one could not help thinking how different would be those other fields on which this unit was soon to be engaged.

This division, composed as it was of Regular units with a nucleus of trained soldiers, did not present the difficulties to be met in organizing our new units. It is relatively easy to absorb partially trained recruits in veteran organizations, but it is quite another matter to create new organizations entirely of raw material. There were not enough officers in the Regular Army to furnish an adequate number to our new units. Even in the Regular regiments the percentage of Regular officers was low, and this applied to staff organizations as well. The I Corps had only seven per cent of officers from the Regular Army. Less than one per cent of all captains of the line in the A.E.F. at that time had been in the service a year. However, the 1st Division had been under training in France for several months and even with a large proportion of new officers there was no doubt that it would do well.

It was a source of real regret to me not to command the division in person and this coupled with the fact that its entry into the battle was of considerable moment led me to speak a word of confidence and encouragement. When the officers, about 900 in all, were assembled in the grounds of the château occupied as division headquarters, they formed a rare group. These splendid looking men, hardened by the strenuous work of the fall and by two months in winter trenches, fairly radiated the spirit of courage and gave promise that America's effort would prove her sons the equals of their forefathers.

I shall lay aside modesty and record my remarks, spoken under the inspiration of the moment:

"General Bullard and Officers of the 1st Division:

"It has not been convenient for me to meet the assembled officers of the 1st Division before, but I did not want you to enter into real participation in this war without my having said a word to you as a body.

"You have now been on French soil ten months, and you have carried out a progressive system of instruction under varied circumstances. You have lived in billets according to the custom of European armies; you have served in different sections of the trenches as a part of your training and have taken on a military complexion akin to that of our Allies. Officers of the Allies, in passing judgment upon your work, have expressed themselves as completely satisfied. I, myself, having witnessed your maneuvers, and closely followed the progress of your work in the trenches and elsewhere, now express myself as well satisfied. I believe that you are well prepared to take your place along with the seasoned troops of our Allies.

"But let us not for a moment forget that, while study and preparation are necessary, war itself is the real school where the art of war is learned. Whatever your previous instruction may have been, you must learn, in the actual experience of war, the practical application of the tactical principles that you have been taught during your preliminary training. Those principles are as absolute as they are immutable. Whatever may be the changing conditions of this war, those principles remain practically the same, and you should constantly bear them in mind. Now that you are going to take a place in the line of battle, you will be called upon to meet conditions that have never been presented to you before. When confronted with a new situation, do not try to recall examples given in any particular book on the subject; do not try to remember what your instructor has said in discussing some special problem; do not try to carry in your minds patterns of particular exercises or battles, thinking they will fit new cases, because no two sets of circumstances are alike; but bear in mind constantly, revolve in your thoughts frequently, and review at every opportunity, those well-established general principles, so that you may apply them when the time comes.

"While it is necessary to know how to apply the general principles of military tactics to the problems of actual battle, yet the main reliance after all must be upon your own determination, upon the aggressiveness of your men, upon their stamina, upon their character and upon their will to win. It is this will to win, more than anything else, that will carry you over the trying periods that you are soon to meet.

"You should always have the interests of the individual soldier at heart, for he is the principal part of the machine upon which you are to rely to carry you to success. His morale must be kept up to the highest pitch. That morale is affected by his confidence in his officers, by a realizing sense that they are his example. They should really be an example in everything that personifies the true soldier, in dress, in military bearing, in general conduct, and especially an example on the battlefield.

"To get the best out of your men they must feel that you are their real leader and must know that they can depend upon you. They must have confidence in you. Do not hold yourself aloof from your men, but keep in close touch with them. Let them feel that you are doing the very best you can for them under all circumstances, not only in providing their personal wants, in looking forward to a regular supply of food, and clothing, but that, as their leader, you are directing them wisely in the trying conditions of battle. On the other hand, you should always endeavor to make them realize their own responsibility and that you, in turn, rely fully upon them, and that when the occasion demands it they must make the supreme sacrifice.

"I did not come here to make a speech, I am not given to speech-making, so only a word more. I have every confidence in the 1st Division. You are about to enter this great battle of the greatest war in history, and in that battle you will represent the mightiest nation engaged. That thought itself must be to you a very appealing thought and one that should call forth the best and the noblest that is in you. Centuries of military tradition and of military and civil history are now looking toward this first contingent of the American Army as it enters this great battle. You have behind you your own national traditions that should make you the finest soldiers in Europe to-day. We come from a young and aggressive nation. We come from a nation that for one hundred and fifty years has stood before the world as the champion of the sacred principles of human liberty. We now return to Europe, the home of our ancestors, to help defend those same principles upon European soil. Could there be a more stimulating sentiment as you go from here to your commands, and from there to the battlefield?

"Our people to-day are hanging expectant upon your deeds. Our future part in this conflict depends upon your action. You are going forward and your conduct will be an example for succeeding units of our army. I hope the standard you set will be high—I know it will be high. You are taking with you the sincerest good wishes and the highest hopes of the President and all of our people at home. I assure you in their behalf and in my own of our strong belief in your success and of our confidence in your courage and in your loyalty, with a feeling of certainty in our hearts that you are going to make a record of which your country will be proud."

That afternoon I motored to Sarcus to see General Foch and sound him out regarding the prospects of uniting our divisions in a sector of our own. I told him that the Secretary of War, when in France, had expressed an earnest desire to hasten the formation of an American army and that this was also the wish of the President. It was my opinion, I said, that early action would be of great importance in stimulating the morale of our troops and our people. Now that the 1st Division was to go into line, the people at home would expect soon to hear that an American army was engaged on its own front. I suggested the possibility that the I Corps might be assembled near the 1st Division as a beginning.

General Foch agreed in principle to the suggestion, but was uncertain when the other divisions could be spared, which I, of course, fully appreciated. He remarked that the enemy was very aggressive and referred to his severe attack against the British on the Lys between Lens and Ypres which began on the 9th and was still in progress. But looking beyond, I insisted that the 26th and 42d Divisions might be withdrawn at any time from quiet sectors, to be followed by the 2d and the 32d and also the 3d a few days later. I pointed out that this force of six divisions, including the 1st would equal twelve French divisions and gave it as my opinion that it would be better to use this American group for active operations than to detain the units in quiet sectors and send French divisions to the battle front. My understanding after this discussion was very definite that the plan would soon be carried out, leaving the exact time and place to be determined. It was immaterial to me just where it should occur, the point being to get it done.

The German offensive on the Lys was another formidable attempt to break the British lines. The attack was made to the north and south of Armentières on a front of twenty-four miles by twenty-seven German divisions. The exhausted British, though they fought with most commendable courage and skill, were forced again to yield, with heavy losses to themselves and the division of Portuguese that was with them. It was in this ex-

tremity that Marshal Haig's famous order to his armies dated April 11th was issued:

> "Three weeks ago to-day the enemy began his terrific attacks against us on a 50-mile front. His objects are to separate us from the French, to take the Channel ports and destroy the British Army.
> "In spite of throwing already 106 divisions into the battle and enduring the most reckless sacrifice of human life, he has as yet made little progress towards his goals.
> "We owe this to the determined fighting and self-sacrifice of our troops. Words fail me to express the admiration which I feel for the splendid resistance offered by all ranks of our Army under the most trying circumstances.
> "Many amongst us now are tired. To those I would say that victory will belong to the side which holds out the longest. The French Army is moving rapidly and in great force to our support.
> "There is no other course open to us but to fight it out! Every position must be held to the last man; there must be no retirement. With our backs to the wall, and believing in the justice of our cause, each one of us must fight on to the end. The safety of our homes and

the freedom of mankind alike depend upon the conduct of each one of us at this critical moment."

Although several French divisions were hurried to the Lys front, it was a week after the attack began before they were put into the line. They then relieved British divisions at the famous Kemmel Hill, only to be surprised and defeated themselves on April 25th, much to their chagrin. The battle was practically ended by the last of the month with a gain by the Germans of ten or eleven miles, but they failed in their effort to capture the important objective of Hazebrouck.

> (Diary) Paris, Thursday, April 18, 1918. Had a call yesterday from Major General Sackville-West, who is with Supreme War Council.
> Lord Milner, recently appointed British Minister for War, came to-day to suggest conference on shipment of our troops. Went to see M. Clemenceau to discuss Inter-Allied supply control.
> Washington cables Ordnance Department will furnish some 600 guns army and navy heavy artillery, but delivery far off. Another brigade infantry and machine gun units of marines to be sent by naval shipping. Sixth Engineers receive high praise from British for conduct in battle March 21-April 3. Covered space for storage at ports now practically amounts to 2,250,000 square feet.

One effect of unified control of the combatant forces was to emphasize the desirability of applying the same principle to the question of supplies. In practice, the French and ourselves had been slowly moving in that direction for several months. A fairly good working basis had already been established through the efforts of our General Purchasing Board in conjunction with the French Mission attached to my headquarters. The principle was already applied to certain classes of supplies, but there was no assurance of its larger application under stress of circumstances when it might possibly be vital to success.

The expansion of its scope was particularly important to us, as we were short of many supplies, and if they could be procured from the Allies it would save tonnage. Unless coöperation should become more general there might be some doubt of our obtaining needful equipment and munitions to enable our increasing armies fully to do their part. On the other hand, the Allies were seeking in our markets raw material for their factories, and much tonnage might be saved if they could be induced to pool their demands. Such action appeared reasonable and it had often been discussed, yet, like the unity of command, it looked as though only a crisis in the question of procurement, resulting especially from lack of tonnage, could bring the supply agencies of the different governments to give the question serious consideration.

When I visited M. Clemenceau's office and explained the idea to him, he was quick to see the advantages of such a plan and asked me to present my views in writing so that he could have it studied. This was done in the letter quoted below:

"France, April 19, 1918.
"DEAR MR. CLEMENCEAU:
"Referring to our conversation of yesterday, permit me to confirm my suggestion that all supplies and war materials that are used in common by the Allied armies be pooled and that the principle be extended as far as possible to the civil populations of the Allies in Europe.

    *   *   *   *   *   *   *

"The defects of present methods of handling supplies have long been recognized * * * but each of the Allied armies continues to think only in terms of its own requirements independently of the other armies. While it is fully realized that there are many classes of supplies that are used by all the Allies which could be pooled and issued to a particular army as required, a practical solution to the problem has not yet been reached.

" * * * The A.E.F. has recently reduced or postponed its requirements in tonnage to the lowest limit to save sea transportation, and a study of the subject leads to the conclusion that our Allies could do much more than is now being done.

"While some attempt has been made through coördinating Allied committees, including the Supreme War Council, these bodies are only advisory. * * * The authority to order the allotment and distribution of supplies to the different armies does not exist. * * *

" * * * The following classes of supplies, naturally, would be included: Aviation material, munitions as far as practicable, horses, oats, hay, meat, flour, coal, gasoline, wagons, harness, motor transport, depots, warehouses, lumber and timber. Such concentration or control of supplies would probably result in economy of port construction and especially in storage facilities.

"To meet the situation in question, I propose to you the designation of one occupying a position as to supplies and material similar to that of General Foch, as to military operations, who shall have authority to decide just what supplies and material should be brought to France by the Allies and determine their disposition.

"May I urge that this matter be given early attention? Permit me to suggest that Colonel Dawes, Purchasing Agent of the A.E.F., be called into consultation with such officers of the French Army as you may designate to discuss this important subject.

"I remain, with high personal and official esteem,
"Your obedient servant,
"JOHN J. PERSHING."

This subject was also taken up with Washington and with the British, but the question of pooling in general and of having any single individual determine the allotment of supplies to various armies did not meet with entire approval. M. Clemenceau became much interested in the idea involved and met with an Inter-Allied committee charged with its consideration. He approved the plan in principle, which gave us hope that some definite understanding would eventually be reached. Naturally, the success of the plan would have required a joint board of Allied officers to canvass the supply situation and make recommendations to the controlling authority. Later an eminently satisfactory arrangement was perfected whereby the coördination of supplies was placed in the hands of such a board.

The Third Liberty Loan was getting under way, as indicated by the cable conveying the President's Liberty Day Proclamation, which was such a patriotic utterance that it must be quoted in full:

"An enemy who has grossly abused the power of organized government and who seeks to dominate the world by the might of the sword, challenges the right of America and the liberty and life of all the free nations of the earth. Our brave sons are facing the fire of battle in defense of the honor and rank of America and the liberty of nations. To sustain them and to assist our gallant soldiers in the war, a generous and patriotic people have been called upon to subscribe to the

Third Liberty Loan. Now, therefore, I, Woodrow Wilson, President of the United States of America, do appoint Friday, the 26th day of April, 1918, as Liberty Day. On the afternoon of that day, I request the people of the United States to assemble in their respective communities and liberally pledge anew their financial support to sustain the Nation's cause. A patriotic demonstration will be held in every city, town, and hamlet throughout the land under the general direction of the Secretary of the Treasury and the immediate direction of the Liberty Loan committees organized by the Federal Reserve Bank. Let the Nation's response to the Third Liberty Loan express in unmistakable terms the determination of America to fight for peace, the permanent peace of justice. For the purpose of participating in Liberty Day celebrations all employees of the Federal Government throughout the country whose services can be spared may be excused at 12 o'clock noon on Friday, April 26th."

The following instructions were received from the Secretary of War:

"Liberty Day will be observed by the troops in your command to the extent that you deem wise, but wherever patriotic programs are presented, public reading of the President's proclamation will be included."